Accounting
For Canadians

4th Edition

by Cécile Laurin, CPA, CA, and Tage C. Tracy

with John A. Tracy,
coauthor of previous editions

A Wiley Brand

Accounting For Canadians For Dummies®, 4th Edition

Published by: **John Wiley & Sons, Inc.**, 111 River Street, Hoboken, NJ 07030-5774, www.wiley.com

Copyright © 2024 by John Wiley & Sons, Inc., Hoboken, New Jersey

Published simultaneously in Canada

No part of this publication may be reproduced, stored in a retrieval system or transmitted in any form or by any means, electronic, mechanical, photocopying, recording, scanning or otherwise, except as permitted under Sections 107 or 108 of the 1976 United States Copyright Act, without the prior written permission of the Publisher. Requests to the Publisher for permission should be addressed to the Permissions Department, John Wiley & Sons, Inc., 111 River Street, Hoboken, NJ 07030, (201) 748-6011, fax (201) 748-6008, or online at http://www.wiley.com/go/permissions.

Trademarks: Wiley, For Dummies, the Dummies Man logo, Dummies.com, Making Everything Easier, and related trade dress are trademarks or registered trademarks of John Wiley & Sons, Inc. and may not be used without written permission. All other trademarks are the property of their respective owners. John Wiley & Sons, Inc. is not associated with any product or vendor mentioned in this book.

LIMIT OF LIABILITY/DISCLAIMER OF WARRANTY: WHILE THE PUBLISHER AND AUTHORS HAVE USED THEIR BEST EFFORTS IN PREPARING THIS WORK, THEY MAKE NO REPRESENTATIONS OR WARRANTIES WITH RESPECT TO THE ACCURACY OR COMPLETENESS OF THE CONTENTS OF THIS WORK AND SPECIFICALLY DISCLAIM ALL WARRANTIES, INCLUDING WITHOUT LIMITATION ANY IMPLIED WARRANTIES OF MERCHANTABILITY OR FITNESS FOR A PARTICULAR PURPOSE. NO WARRANTY MAY BE CREATED OR EXTENDED BY SALES REPRESENTATIVES, WRITTEN SALES MATERIALS OR PROMOTIONAL STATEMENTS FOR THIS WORK. THE FACT THAT AN ORGANIZATION, WEBSITE, OR PRODUCT IS REFERRED TO IN THIS WORK AS A CITATION AND/OR POTENTIAL SOURCE OF FURTHER INFORMATION DOES NOT MEAN THAT THE PUBLISHER AND AUTHORS ENDORSE THE INFORMATION OR SERVICES THE ORGANIZATION, WEBSITE, OR PRODUCT MAY PROVIDE OR RECOMMENDATIONS IT MAY MAKE. THIS WORK IS SOLD WITH THE UNDERSTANDING THAT THE PUBLISHER IS NOT ENGAGED IN RENDERING PROFESSIONAL SERVICES. THE ADVICE AND STRATEGIES CONTAINED HEREIN MAY NOT BE SUITABLE FOR YOUR SITUATION. YOU SHOULD CONSULT WITH A SPECIALIST WHERE APPROPRIATE. FURTHER, READERS SHOULD BE AWARE THAT WEBSITES LISTED IN THIS WORK MAY HAVE CHANGED OR DISAPPEARED BETWEEN WHEN THIS WORK WAS WRITTEN AND WHEN IT IS READ. NEITHER THE PUBLISHER NOR AUTHORS SHALL BE LIABLE FOR ANY LOSS OF PROFIT OR ANY OTHER COMMERCIAL DAMAGES, INCLUDING BUT NOT LIMITED TO SPECIAL, INCIDENTAL, CONSEQUENTIAL, OR OTHER DAMAGES.

For general information on our other products and services, please contact our Customer Care Department within the U.S. at 877-762-2974, outside the U.S. at 317-572-3993, or fax 317-572-4002. For technical support, please visit https://hub.wiley.com/community/support/dummies.

Wiley publishes in a variety of print and electronic formats and by print-on-demand. Some material included with standard print versions of this book may not be included in e-books or in print-on-demand. If this book refers to media such as a CD or DVD that is not included in the version you purchased, you may download this material at http://booksupport.wiley.com. For more information about Wiley products, visit www.wiley.com.

Library of Congress Control Number: 2023946592

ISBN 978-1-394-21630-7 (pbk); ISBN 978-1-394-21631-4 (ebk); ISBN 978-1-394-21632-1 (ebk)

SKY10056826_100523

Contents at a Glance

Table of Contents

Introduction

You may know individuals who make their living as accountants. You may be thankful that they're the accountants and you're not. You may prefer to leave accounting to the accountants, and think that you don't need to know anything about accounting. This attitude evokes the old Greyhound Bus advertising slogan "Leave the Driving to Us." Well, if you could get around everywhere you wanted to go on the bus, that would be no problem. But if you have to drive most places, you'd better know something about cars. Throughout your life, you do a lot of "financial driving," so you should know something about accounting.

Sure, accounting involves numbers. So does watching your car mileage, knowing your blood pressure, keeping track of your bank balance, negotiating the interest rate on your home mortgage, monitoring your retirement fund, and bragging about your kid's grade point average. You deal with numbers all the time. Accountants provide *financial numbers* and these numbers are important in your financial life. Knowing nothing about financial numbers puts you at a serious disadvantage. In short, financial literacy requires a working knowledge of accounting, which this book provides.

About This Book

Here are some advantages this book offers over other accounting texts:

>> We explain accounting in plain English with a minimum of jargon and technical details.

>> We carefully follow a step-by-step approach in explaining topics.

>> We include only topics that non-accountants should understand; we avoid topics that only practising accountants have to know.

>> We provide candid discussions of certain sensitive topics that go unmentioned in many accounting books.

>> We combine our vast experience of both *theoretical accounting* (that is, how it is taught in the classroom) with actual *practiced accounting* (how accounting is applied in real-world businesses) to provide a deep, robust, and practical approach to understanding accounting.

>> We've set up the book so you can read the chapters in any order you please. You can tailor your reading plan to give priority to the chapters of most interest to you and read other chapters as time permits.

We want to emphasize that this book is *not* an accounting textbook. Introductory accounting textbooks are ponderous, dry as dust, and overly detailed. However, textbooks have one advantage: They include exercises and problems. If you have the time, you can gain additional insights and test your understanding of accounting by working through the exercises in *Accounting Workbook For Dummies* (John Wiley & Sons, Inc., 2006) by John A. Tracy.

Foolish Assumptions

We've written this book with a wide audience in mind. You should find yourself more than once in the following list of potential readers:

>> **Business managers (at all levels):** Trying to manage a business without a good grip on financial statements can lead to disaster. How can you manage the financial performance of your business if you don't even understand the financial statements in the first place?

>> **Business buyers and sellers:** Anyone thinking of buying or selling a business should know how to read its financial statements and how to "true up" the accounting reports that serve as a key point of reference for setting a market value on the business.

>> **Entrepreneurs:** As budding business managers, entrepreneurs need a solid grasp of accounting basics.

>> **Active investors:** Investors in marketable securities, real estate, and other ventures need to know how to read financial statements both to stay informed about their investments and to spot any signs of trouble.

>> **Passive investors:** Many people let the pros manage their money by investing in mutual funds or using investment advisers to handle their money. Even so, they need to understand the investment performance reports they get, which use plenty of accounting terms and measures.

>> **Accountants and bookkeepers:** Strengthening their knowledge of accounting helps these professionals to improve their effectiveness and value to the organization and advance their careers.

>> **People who want to take control of their personal finances:** Many aspects of managing your personal finances involve accounting vocabulary and the accounting-based calculation methods.

- » **Anyone interested in economic, business, and financial news:** Articles in the *Financial Post* and other financial news sources are heavy with accounting terms and measures.

- » **Administrators and managers of government and not-for-profit entities:** Making profit is not the goal of these entities, but they have to stay within its revenue limits and keep on a sound financial footing.

- » **Politicians at municipal, provincial, and federal levels:** These people pass many laws having significant financial consequences, and the better they understand accounting, the better their votes should be (we hope).

- » **Investment bankers, institutional lenders, and loan officers:** We don't have to tell these folks that they need to understand accounting; they already know.

- » **Business and finance professionals:** This group includes lawyers and financial advisers, of course, but even clergy counsel the members of their flock on financial matters occasionally.

Icons Used in This Book

The following icons can help you find information quickly and easily.

REMEMBER

This icon points out important ideas and accounting concepts that are particularly deserving of your attention. These concepts that are the undergirding and building blocks of accounting — concepts that you should be clear about because they will clarify your understanding of accounting principles in general.

TECHNICAL STUFF

We use this icon sparingly; it refers to specialized accounting stuff that is heavy going, which only a Chartered Professional Accountant (CPA) could get really excited about. However, you may find these topics interesting enough to return to when you have the time. Feel free to skip over these points the first time through and stay with the main discussion.

TIP

This icon calls your attention to useful advice on practical financial topics. It saves you the cost of buying a yellow highlighter.

WARNING

Taking special note of this material can steer you around a financial road hazard and keep you from blowing a fiscal tire. In short — watch out!

Beyond the Book

This book is packed with useful information, but if you're looking for a compact overview of the most important points, check out the online Cheat Sheet. Go to www.dummies.com and search for "Accounting For Canadians For Dummies Cheat Sheet". You'll also find a glossary of accounting terms we've produced as an online companion to this book. Check it out here: www.dummies.com/go/accountingfcfd4e.

Where to Go from Here

There's no law against starting on page 1 and reading through to the last page. However, you may first want to scan the book's Contents at a Glance and see which chapters pique your interest.

Perhaps you're an investor who is very interested in finding out more about financial statements and the key financial statement ratios for investors. In that case, you might start with Chapters 6, 7, and 8, which explain the three primary financial statements of businesses, and then head to Chapter 11, on reading a financial report. (And don't overlook Chapter 19.)

Perhaps you're a small business owner or manager with a basic understanding of your financial statements, but you need to improve how you use accounting information for making your key profit decisions, and for planning and controlling your cash flow. You might jump right into Chapters 15 and 17, which explain the analysis of profit behaviour and budgeting cash flows.

Finally, note that sidebars (the shaded boxes of text scattered throughout the chapters) dig into the details of a given topic, but they aren't crucial to understanding it. So feel free to skip them if you're short on time.

1
Opening the Books on Accounting

Discover how accountants are the financial information gatekeepers in the economy and why accounting is so important for for-profit businesses, not-for-profit organizations, and government agencies.

Find out how a business or other entity prepares its financial statements, its tax returns, and the reports to its managers. Know how to make sure these documents conform to established standards.

Get the lowdown on bookkeeping — the recordkeeping part of accounting — to ensure that a business's financial information is complete, accurate, reliable, and timely, especially the numbers reported in financial statements and tax returns.

Understand why safeguarding company assets is an integral part of an accountant's job and how the digital age, the cloud, and technology are transforming the world of accounting.

Delve into the various types of business legal entities, find out how accounting differs for each one, and get helpful hints on when different legal structures are best used.

IN THIS CHAPTER

» **Recognizing how accounting is relevant to you**

» **Grasping how all economic activity requires accounting**

» **Understanding the accounting function's primary role**

» **Following an accounting department in action**

» **Shaking hands with business financial statements**

Chapter **1**

Accounting in Today's Economy

A ccounting is all about financial information — capturing it, recording it, configuring it, analyzing it, and reporting it to persons who use it. We don't say much about how accountants capture, record, and configure financial information in this book. But we talk a lot about how accountants communicate information in financial statements, and we explain the *valuation methods* or *measurement methods* accountants use — ranging from measuring profit and loss to putting values on a business's assets and liabilities.

As you go through life, you come face to face with accounting information more than you would ever imagine. Regrettably, much of this information is not self-explanatory or intuitive, and it does not come with a user's manual. Accounting information is presented with the assumption that you have a basic familiarity with the vocabulary of accounting and the accounting methods used to generate the information. In short, most of the accounting information you encounter is not transparent. The main reason for studying accounting is to understand its vocabulary and its valuation and measurement methods so you can make more intelligent use of the information.

People who use accounting information should know the basic rules of play and how the financial score is kept, much like spectators at a hockey or baseball game. The purpose of this book is to make you a knowledgeable spectator of and sometimes a participant in the accounting game.

REMEMBER

You should know accounting basics for another reason, too — we call it the *defensive* reason. Some people in the financial world might take advantage of you, not necessarily by illegal means but by withholding key information and by diverting your attention from unfavourable aspects of certain financial decisions. The best defence against such tactics is to know some accounting, which can help you ask the right questions and understand the financial points that those who are trying to sway or convince you don't want you to know.

Knowing That Accounting Is Not Just for Accountants

One main source of accounting information is in the form of *financial statements* packaged with other information in a *financial report*. Accountants keep the books and record the financial activities of an entity (such as a business). From these detailed records, the accountant prepares financial statements that summarize the results of the activities.

Financial statements are sent to people who have a stake in the outcomes of the activities. If you own shares in BCE, for example, or you have money in a mutual fund, you receive regular financial reports. If you invest your hard-earned money in a private business or a real estate venture, or you save money in a bank, you receive regular financial reports. If you're a member of a not-for-profit association or organization, you're entitled to receive regular financial reports.

REMEMBER

One important reason for studying accounting is to make sense of the financial statements in the financial reports you get. We guarantee that Warren Buffett knows accounting and how to read financial statements.

Affecting both insiders and outsiders

People who need to know accounting fall into two broad groups: insiders and outsiders. Business managers are insiders; they have the authority and responsibility to run a business. They need a good understanding of accounting terms and the methods used to measure profit and put values on assets and liabilities. Accounting information is indispensable for planning and controlling the business's financial performance and condition. Likewise, administrators of not-for-profit and governmental entities need to understand the accounting terminology and measurement methods in their financial statements.

REMEMBER

The rest of us are outsiders. We are not privy to the day-to-day details of a business or an organization. We have to rely on financial reports from the entity to know what's going on. Therefore, we need to have a good grip on the financial statements included in the financial reports. For all practical purposes, financial reports are the only source of financial information we get directly from a business or other organization.

By the way, the business's employees — even though they obviously have a stake in the business's success — do not necessarily receive its financial reports. Only the investors in the business and its lenders are entitled to receive the financial reports. Of course, a business *could* provide this information to those of its employees who are not shareowners, but generally speaking most businesses do not. The financial reports of public businesses are in the public domain, so their employees can easily view them on the Internet.

In our personal financial lives, a little accounting knowledge is a big help for understanding investing in general and how investment performance is measured, as well as many other important financial topics. With some basic accounting knowledge, you'll sound more sophisticated when speaking with your banker or broker. We can't promise that understanding accounting will save you big bucks on your income taxes, but it can't hurt and will definitely help you know what your tax preparer is talking about.

Keep in mind that this is *not* a book on bookkeeping and recordkeeping systems. We offer a brief explanation of procedures for capturing, processing, and storing accounting information in Chapter 3. Even experienced bookkeepers and accountants should find some nuggets in that chapter. However, this book is directed to users of accounting information. We focus on the end products of accounting, particularly financial statements, and not how information is accumulated. When buying a new car, you're interested in the finished product, not details of the manufacturing process that produced it.

Overcoming the stereotypes of accountants

A cartoon showed the young son of clowns standing in a circus tent dressed as a clown but holding a business briefcase. He is telling his clown parents that he is running away to join a CPA firm. Why is this funny? Because it plays off the stereotype of the CPA (Chartered Professional Accountant) as a "bean counter" who wears a green eyeshade and has the personality of an undertaker (no offence to morticians). Maybe you've heard the joke that an accountant with a personality is one who looks at *your* shoes when they are talking to you, instead of their own shoes.

Like most stereotypes, an element of truth exists in the preconceived image of accountants. We have met and known a large number of accountants, and most are not as gregarious as used-car sales people. Accountants certainly are more detail-oriented than your average person. However, you don't have to be good at mathematics to be a good accountant, because they use very little math (no calculus and only simple algebra). Accountants are very good at one thing: They want to see both sides of financial transactions — the give and take. They know better than anyone that, as economists are fond of saying, there's no such thing as a free lunch.

If you walked down a busy street in Vancouver, Toronto, or Montreal, we doubt that you could pick out the accountants. We have no idea whether accountants have higher or lower divorce rates than others, whether they go to church more frequently, or whether they generally sleep well at night. We do think that accountants are more honest in paying their income taxes than other people, although we have no proof of this.

CHARTERED PROFESSIONAL ACCOUNTANTS (CPA)

What is a *Chartered Professional Accountant* (CPA) and what does it take to obtain the CPA designation?

The CPA designation is a widely recognized and respected badge of a professional accountant. A person must meet ongoing educational and experience requirements and pass a national uniform exam to qualify to practice as a CPA.

Most CPAs are not in public practice; they work for business organizations, government agencies, and not-for-profit organizations, or they teach accounting (a plug for educators here, if you don't mind!). CPAs in public practice are licenced to do audits of financial reports, and they also provide tax, management, and financial consulting services.

Relating accounting to your personal financial life

We're sure you know the value of understanding personal finance and investing fundamentals. Well, a great deal of the information you use in making personal finance and investing decisions is *accounting information*. One knock we have on books in these areas is that they often don't make clear that you need a basic understanding of accounting terminology and valuation methods to make good use of the financial information.

TIP

We recommend reading Eric Tyson and Tony Martin's two books: *Personal Finance For Canadians For Dummies*, 6th Edition (John Wiley & Sons, Inc., 2018), and *Investing For Canadians For Dummies*, 4th Edition (John Wiley & Sons, Inc., 2018).

You have a stake in the financial performance of the business you work for, the government entities you pay taxes to, the churches and charitable organizations you donate money to, the retirement plan you participate in, and the businesses you buy from. The financial performance and viability of these entities has a direct bearing on your personal financial life and well-being.

REMEMBER

We're all affected by the profit performance of businesses, even though we may not be fully aware of just how their profit performance affects our jobs, investments, and taxes. For example, as an employee your job security and your next raise depend on the business making a profit. If the business suffers a loss, you might be laid off or asked to take a reduction in pay or benefits. Business managers get paid to make profits happen. If the business fails to meet its profit objectives or suffers a loss, its managers might be replaced (or at least not get their bonuses). As authors, we hope our publisher continues to make a profit so we can keep receiving royalty cheques.

Your investments in businesses, whether direct or through retirement accounts and mutual funds, suffer if the businesses don't turn a profit. We hope the stores we trade with make profits and continue in business. The federal government and many provinces depend on businesses making profits to collect income taxes from them.

Looking for Accounting in All the Right Places

Accounting extends into virtually every walk of life. You're doing accounting when you make electronic fund transfers and when you fill out your income tax return. When you sign a mortgage on your home, you should understand the accounting method the lender uses to calculate the interest amount charged on your loan each period. Individual investors need to understand accounting basics to figure their return on invested capital. And it goes without saying that every organization, profit-motivated or not, needs to know how it stands financially.

Check out this quick sweep to get an idea of the range of accounting:

>> Accounting for profit-motivated businesses and accounting for not-for-profit organizations (such as hospitals, condominium corporations, churches, universities, and colleges)

>> Income tax accounting while you are living, and planning for estate tax accounting before you die

>> Accounting for farmers who grow their products, accounting for miners who extract their products from the earth, accounting for producers who manufacture products, and accounting for retailers who sell products that others make

>> Accounting for businesses and professional firms that sell services rather than products, such as the legal, entertainment, transportation, and personal care industries

>> Accounting where periodic financial statements are legally mandated (public companies are the primary example) and accounting where such formal accounting reports are not legally required

>> Accounting that adheres to historical cost (mainly businesses), and accounting that records changes in market value (investment property firms, for example)

>> Accounting in the private sector of the economy and accounting in the public (government) sector

>> Accounting for going-concern businesses that will be around for some time and accounting for businesses nearing bankruptcy that might not be around tomorrow

Accounting is necessary in a free-market, capitalist economic system. It's equally necessary in a centralized, government-controlled, socialist economic system. All economic activity requires information. The more developed the economic system, the more the system depends on information. Much of the information comes from the accounting systems used by the businesses, institutions, individuals, and other players in the economic system.

Some of the earliest records of history are the accounts of wealth and trading activity. The need for accounting information was a main incentive in the development of the numbering system we use today. The history of accounting is interesting, but beyond the scope of this book.

Understanding Accounting's Two Primary Roles

REMEMBER

The accounting function in most businesses has two primary purposes:

>> The accounting function and systems must be able to produce complete, accurate, reliable, and timely (that is, CART) financial information on which businesses can base sound decisions. In today's intensely competitive global economy, it has never been more important for accounting systems to produce and deliver vital financial information on a timely basis for review and management action.

>> The accounting function must be developed, implemented, managed, and periodically revised and updated to safeguard company assets. We are not just talking about preventing theft of liquid or hard assets such as cash or inventory. Rather, the accounting function is now one of the critical gatekeepers associated with helping protect company intellectual property, shelter invaluable customer data and databases, preserve the integrity of critical financial information, control and direct the distribution of confidential financial operating results to the appropriate parties, and assist with critical risk management and insurance protection strategies . . . just to name a few.

As you progress through this book, it becomes clear that the accounting function has evolved into something much more than a bunch of bean counters, working with debits and credits, producing financial statements, and trying desperately to meet the annual income tax reporting deadlines. The COVID-19 pandemic showed that the speed at which economic business models are now formulated, launched, disrupted, expanded, contracted, and potentially eliminated from the global market is in warp drive. Massive volumes of raw confidential business data are now considered one of the most valuable assets a company owns and monetizes to generate profits (aided by huge technological advancements). As such, accounting's role in producing CART financial information in coordination with helping protect this data has never been more critical. Throughout this book, we provide examples and make references to accounting in the new, digital age (for example, Chapter 4 dives into the digitization of accounting and a new era of risks).

Taking a Peek Behind the Scenes

Every business, government, and not-for-profit entity needs a reliable bookkeeping system (see Chapter 3). Keep in mind that *accounting* is a much broader term than *bookkeeping*. For one thing, accounting encompasses the problems in measuring the financial effects of economic activity. Furthermore, accounting includes the function of *financial reporting* of values and performance measures to those who need the information. Business managers and investors, and many other people, depend on financial reports for information about the performance and condition of the entity.

Bookkeeping refers to the process of accumulating, organizing, storing, and accessing the financial information base of an entity, which is needed for two basic purposes:

>> Facilitating the day-to-day operations of the entity

>> Preparing financial statements, tax returns, and internal reports to managers

Bookkeeping (also called *recordkeeping*) can be thought of as the financial information infrastructure of an entity. Of course, the financial information base should be CART (complete, accurate, reliable, and timely). Every recordkeeping system needs quality controls built into it, which are called *internal controls* or *internal accounting controls*. When an error creeps into the system, it can be difficult to root out and correct. Data-entry controls are particularly important. The security of online and computer-based accounting systems has become a top priority of both for-profit businesses and not-for-profit entities. Cyber threats are a serious problem and can bring a big business to its knees, which we discuss further in Chapter 4.

REMEMBER

Accountants design the internal controls for the bookkeeping system, which serve to minimize errors in recording the large number of activities that an entity engages in over the period. The internal controls that accountants design are also relied on to detect errors and deter theft, embezzlement, fraud, and dishonest behaviour of all kinds. In accounting, internal controls are the ounce of prevention that is worth a pound of cure.

We explain internal controls in Chapter 3. Here, we want to stress the importance of the bookkeeping system in operating a business or any other entity. These back-office functions are essential for keeping operations running smoothly, efficiently, and without delays and errors. This is a tall order, to say the least.

Most people don't realize the importance of the accounting department in keeping a business operating without hitches and delays. That's probably because accountants oversee many of the back-office functions in a business — as opposed to sales, for example, which is front-line activity, out in the open and in the line of fire. Go into any retail store, and you're in the thick of sales activities. But have you ever seen a company's accounting department in action?

Folks might not think much about these back-office activities, but they would notice if those activities didn't get accomplished. On payday, a business had better not tell its employees, "Sorry, but the accounting department is running a little late this month; your pay will be deposited to your account later." And when a customer insists on up-to-date information about how much they owe to the business, the accounting department can't very well say, "Oh, don't worry. Just wait a week or so and we'll get the information to you then."

Typically, the accounting department is responsible for the following:

» **Payroll:** The total wages and salaries earned by every employee every pay period, which are called *gross wages* or *gross earnings,* have to be calculated. Based on detailed private information in personnel files and earnings-to-date information, the correct amounts for income taxes and several other deductions from gross wages have to be determined.

   Stubs, or *pay statements,* report various information are produced each pay period and given to the employee. The total amounts of withheld income taxes, Canada or Quebec Pension Plans, and Employment Insurance premiums imposed on the employee and employer have to be paid to the federal government (and, in the case of Quebec, the provincial government) on time. Retirement, vacation, sick pay, and other benefits that employees earn have to be updated every pay period.

   In short, payroll is a complex and critical function that the accounting department performs. Many businesses outsource payroll functions to companies or banks that specialize in this area.

» **Cash collections:** All cash received from sales and from all other sources has to be carefully identified and recorded, not only in the cash account but also in the appropriate account for the source of the cash received. The accounting department makes sure that the cash is deposited or received in the appropriate business chequing accounts and that the business keeps an adequate amount of cash to pay employees and suppliers on time. Accountants balance the business's bank account and control who has access to incoming cash receipts. (In larger organizations, the *treasurer* might be responsible for some of these cash flow and cash-handling functions.)

» **Cash disbursements:** In addition to electronic payroll payments, a business writes many other cheques or processes numerous electronic payments during the course of a year to pay for a wide variety of purchases, to pay property taxes, to repay loan principal and interest, and to distribute some of its profits to the business's owners, for example. The accounting department prepares all these cheques and transfers for authorization by business officers. The accounting department keeps all the supporting business documents and files to know when the payments should be made, makes sure that the amount to be paid is correct, and forwards the cheques or payment through electronic transfer for signature.

More and more businesses are switching to electronic methods of payments, which avoid the need for writing and mailing cheques. Electronic access to accounts must be carefully protected not only to guard against hackers but also to make sure that employees make only authorized payments.

>> **Purchasing and inventory:** Accounting departments usually are responsible for keeping track of all purchase orders that have been placed for *inventory* (products to be sold by the business) and all other assets and services that the business buys — from office supplies to forklifts. A typical business makes many purchases during the year, many of them on credit, which means that the business receives items bought today but pays for them later. This area of responsibility includes keeping files on all liabilities that arise from purchases on credit so that cash payments are processed on time. The accounting department also keeps detailed records on all products that the business holds for sale and, when the products are sold, records the cost of the goods sold.

>> **Costing:** Costs are not as obvious as you might think. Tell someone that the cost of a new car is so many dollars, and most people accept the amount without question. Business owners and managers know better. Many decisions have to be made regarding which factors to include in the manufacturing cost of a product or in the purchase costs of products sold by retailers such as Costco and Wal-Mart. Tracking costs is a major function of accounting in all businesses.

>> **Property accounting:** A typical business owns many different substantial long-term assets called *property, plant, and equipment* — including office furniture and equipment, retail display cabinets, computers, machinery and tools, vehicles (autos and trucks), buildings, and land. Except for relatively small-cost items, such as screwdrivers and wrenches, a business maintains detailed records of its property, both for controlling the use of the assets and for determining the appropriate amount of depreciation for accounting and tax calculations. The accounting department keeps these property records.

>> **Tax compliance:** The task of managing multiple tax accounting, reporting, and compliance functions usually falls on the shoulders of the accounting department. This extends well beyond simply completing annual income tax returns, because most businesses must deal with a slew of other tax reporting and compliance matters, including GST/HST (Goods and Services Tax and Harmonized Sales Tax), payroll, and other forms of taxation at the federal and provincial level.

>> **Liabilities accounting:** An entity must keep track of all relevant details about every liability it owes — from short-term purchases on credit to long-term notes payable. No entity can lose track of a liability and not pay it on time (or negotiate an extension) without hurting its credit rating.

REMEMBER

The accounting department serves other functions as well, but this list gives you a clear idea of the back-office functions that the accounting department performs. A business could not operate if the accounting department did not do these functions efficiently and on time. We repeat one point: To do these back-office functions well, the accounting department must design a good bookkeeping system and make sure that it is complete, accurate, reliable, and timely.

Focusing on Transactions

REMEMBER

Accounting focuses on transactions. A good bookkeeping system captures and records every transaction that takes place. *Transactions* are economic exchanges between a business or other entity and the parties with which the entity interacts and makes deals. Transactions are the lifeblood of every business, the heartbeat of activity that keeps it going. Understanding accounting, to a large extent, means understanding how accountants record the financial effects of transactions.

The financial effects of many transactions are clear-cut and immediate. However, figuring out the financial effects of other transactions is puzzling and dependent on future developments that can be difficult to predict. Accounting for transactions is not always a cut-and-dried process.

Separating basic types of transactions

A business is a whirlpool of transactions. Accountants categorize transactions into three broad types:

>> **Profit-making transactions** consist of *revenue* and *expenses* as well as gains and losses outside the normal sales and expense activities of the business. We explain earlier in the chapter that one way to look at profit is as an increase in retained earnings. Another way of defining *profit* is as the amount of total revenue for the period minus all expenses for the period. Both viewpoints are correct.

Included in this group of transactions are those that take place before or after the recording of revenue and expenses. For example, a business buys merchandise that will be held for future sale. The purchase of the merchandise is not yet an expense. The expense is not recorded until the merchandise is sold. The purchase of merchandise for future sale must be recorded when the purchase takes place.

>> **Investing transactions** refer to the acquisition (and eventual disposal) of *long-term operating assets* such as buildings, heavy machinery, trucks, and office furniture. Some businesses also invest in *financial assets* (shares and

bonds, for example). These are not used directly in the operations of the business; the business could get along without these assets. These assets generate investment income for the business. Investments in financial assets are included in this category of transactions.

>> **Financing transactions** refer to raising capital and paying for the use of the capital. Every business needs assets to carry on its operations, such as a working balance of cash, inventory of merchandise held for sale, and long-term operating assets (as described in the preceding bullet point). Broadly speaking, the capital to buy these assets comes from two sources: debt and equity. *Debt* is borrowed money, on which interest is paid. *Equity* is ownership capital. The payment for using equity capital depends on the capability of the business to earn profits and have the cash flow to distribute some or all of the profit to its shareholders.

REMEMBER

Profit-making transactions, also called *operating activities*, are high frequency. During the year, even a small business has thousands of revenue and expense transactions. (How many cups of coffee, for example, does your local coffee store sell each year? Each sale is a transaction.) In contrast, investing and financing transactions are generally low frequency. A business does not have a high volume of these types of transactions, except in unusual circumstances.

Knowing who's on the other side of transactions

Another way to look at transactions is to look at the *counterparties* of the transactions; this term refers to the persons or entities with which the business enters into an economic exchange. A business interacts with a variety of counterparties. A business is the hub of transactions involving the following persons and entities:

>> **Customers,** who buy the products and services that the business sells.

>> **Employees,** who provide services to the business in exchange for wages and salaries. The business provides employees with benefits, such as a retirement plan and dental and vision insurance, and pays for workers' compensation coverage and Employment Insurance premiums.

>> **Suppliers** and **vendors,** who sell a wide range of things to the business such as legal advice, products for resale, electricity and gas, and Internet and telephone services.

>> **Government entities,** which are the federal, provincial, and municipal agencies that collect income taxes, payroll-related taxes, GST/HST, and property taxes from the business.

>> **Debt sources of capital,** who loan money to the business and charge interest on the amount loaned that the business must repay at definite dates in the future.

>> **Equity sources of capital,** the individuals and financial institutions that invest money in the business and expect the business to earn profits on the capital they invest.

Recording events

Even a relatively small business generates a surprisingly large number of transactions, and all transactions have to be recorded. Other events that have a financial effect on the business have to be recorded as well. These are called *events* because they're not based on give-and-take bargaining — unlike the something-given-for-something-received nature of economic exchanges. Events such as the following have an economic effect on a business and are recorded:

>> A business might lose a lawsuit and be ordered to pay damages. The liability to pay the damages is recorded.

>> A business might suffer an uninsured flood loss. The waterlogged assets might have to be *written down,* meaning that the recorded values of the assets are reduced to zero if they no longer have any value or use to the business. For example, products that were being held for sale to customers (until they floated down the river) must be removed from the inventory asset account.

>> A business might decide to abandon a major product line and downsize its workforce, and therefore must pay severance compensation to the laid-off employees.

As we explain in more detail in Chapter 3, at the end of the year the accountant makes a special survey to make sure that all events and developments during the year that should be recorded have been recorded, so that the financial statements and tax returns for the year are complete and correct.

Taking the Pulse of a Business: Financial Statements

We devote a good deal of space in this book to discussing financial statements. In Chapter 2, we explain the fundamental information components of financial statements, and then Part 2 gets into the nitty-gritty details. Here, we simply want to introduce you to the three primary kinds of financial statements so you know from the get-go what they are and why they're so crucial.

REMEMBER

Financial statements are prepared at the end of each accounting period. A period might be one month, one quarter (three calendar months), or one year. Financial statements report *summary amounts*, or *totals*. Accountants seldom prepare a complete listing of the details of all the activities that took place during a period, or the individual items making up a total amount. Business managers occasionally need to search through a detailed list of all the specific transactions that make up a total amount. When they want to drill down into the details, they ask the accountant for the more detailed information. But this sort of detailed listing is *not* a financial statement — although it may be very useful to managers.

Outside investors in a business see only summary-level financial statements. For example, investors see the total amount of sales revenue for the period but not how much was sold to each customer.

Meeting the balance sheet (statement of financial position)

One type of accounting report is a "Where do we stand at the end of the period?" type of report. This report is called the *statement of financial position* or, more commonly, the *balance sheet*. The date of preparation is given in the header, or title, above this financial statement. We present and explain a typical balance sheet in Chapter 2; here we simply present the basic content in a balance sheet.

A balance sheet shows two sides of the business, which you could think of as the financial yin and yang of the business:

>> **Assets:** On one side of the balance sheet the business's *assets* are listed, which are the economic resources owned, controlled, and being used in the business. The asset *values* reported in the balance sheet are the amounts recorded when the assets were originally acquired — although we should mention that an asset is written down below its historical cost when the asset has suffered a loss or an impairment in value. (And to complicate matters, some assets are written up to their current fair values.) Some assets have been on the books only a few weeks or a few months, so their reported historical values are current. The values for other assets are their costs when they were acquired many years ago.

>> **Sources of assets:** On the other side of the balance sheet is a breakdown of where the assets came from, or their *sources*. Assets come from two basically different sources: creditors and owners. First, the *creditors:* Businesses borrow money in the form of interest-bearing loans that have to be paid back at a

later date, and they buy things on credit that are paid for later. So, part of total assets can be traced to creditors, which are the *liabilities* of a business. Second are the *owners:* Businesses require that their owners invest capital (usually money) in the business. Also, businesses retain part or all of the annual profits they make, and profit increases the total business's assets. The total of invested capital and retained earnings is called *owners' equity.*

Suppose a business reports $2.5 million in total assets (without going into the details of which particular assets the business holds). We know that the total of its liabilities, plus the capital invested by its owners, plus its retained profit, adds up to $2.5 million. Otherwise, its books would be out of balance, which indicates bookkeeping errors.

Continuing with this example, suppose that the total amount of the business's liabilities is $1.0 million. This means that the total amount of *owners' equity* in the business is $1.5 million, which equals total assets less total liabilities. Without more information, we don't know how much of total owners' equity is traceable to capital invested by the owners in the business and how much is the result of profits retained in the business. But we do know that the total of these two sources of owners' equity is $1.5 million.

The business's financial condition in this example is summarized in the following *accounting equation* (in millions):

$$\text{\$Assets} = \text{\$Liabilities} + \text{\$Owners' Equity}$$

Looking at the accounting equation, you can see why the statement of financial position is called the *balance sheet;* the equal sign means the two sides balance.

REMEMBER

Double-entry bookkeeping is based on the accounting equation — the fact that the total of assets on the one side is counterbalanced by the total of liabilities, invested capital, and retained profits on the other side. Basically, double-entry bookkeeping simply means that both sides of transactions are recorded. For example, if one asset goes up, another asset goes down — or either a liability or owners' equity goes up. This is the economic nature of transactions. Double-entry means *two-sided,* not that the transactions are recorded twice. We discuss double-entry bookkeeping in Chapter 3.

Reporting profit and loss, and cash flows

REMEMBER

Other financial statements are different from the balance sheet in one important respect: They summarize the *flow* of activities over the period. (An example of a *flow number* is the total attendance at Toronto Blue Jays home games over the entire regular baseball season; the cumulative count of spectators passing through the turnstiles over the season is the *flow.*) Accountants prepare two types of financial flow reports for a business:

>> The **income statement** summarizes the inflow from sales revenue that is offset by the outflows for the expense during the period. Deducting expenses from revenue leads down to the well-known *bottom line,* which is the final net profit or loss for the period and is called *net income* or *net loss* (or some variation of these terms). Alternative titles for this financial statement are the *statement of financial performance, statement of operations,* and the *statement of earnings.* Inside a business, but not in its external financial reports, the income statement is commonly called the *profit and loss statement,* or *P&L* report.

>> The **statement of cash flows** summarizes the business's cash inflows and outflows during the period. The accounting profession has adopted a three-way classification of cash flows for external financial reporting: cash flows from making sales and incurring expenses (commonly referred to as operations); cash flows from investing in long-lived assets and selling these assets; and cash flows from raising capital from debt and equity sources, returning capital to these sources, and making distributions from profit to owners.

Recognizing management's role

We explain more about the three primary financial statements (balance sheet, income statement, and statement of cash flows) in Chapter 2. They constitute the hard core of a financial report to those persons outside a business who need to stay informed about the business's financial affairs. These individuals have invested capital in the business, or the business owes them money; therefore, they have a financial interest in how well the business is doing.

The managers of a business, to keep informed about what's going on and the business's financial position, also use these three key financial statements. They are essential in helping managers control the performance of a business, identify problems as they come up, and plan the future course of a business. Managers also need other information that is not reported in the three basic financial statements. (In Part 4, we explain these additional reports.)

The three primary financial statements constitute a business's financial centre of gravity. The president and chief executive officer of a business (plus other top-level officers) are responsible for seeing that the financial statements are prepared according to applicable financial reporting standards and according to established accounting principles and methods.

WARNING

If a business's financial statements are later discovered to be seriously in error or deliberately misleading, the business and its top executives can be sued for damages suffered by lenders and investors who relied on the financial statements. For this reason, business managers should understand their responsibility for the financial statements and the accounting methods used to prepare the statements. In a court of law, they can't plead ignorance.

We have met more than one business manager who doesn't have a clue about their financial statements. This situation is a little scary; a manager who doesn't understand financial statements is like an airplane pilot who doesn't understand the instrument readouts in the cockpit. Such a manager *could* run the business and "land the plane safely," but knowing how to read the vital signs along the way is more prudent.

Business managers at all levels need to understand financial statements and the accounting methods used to prepare them. Also, lenders to a business, investors in a business, business lawyers, government regulators of business, entrepreneurs, anyone thinking of becoming an entrepreneur and starting a business, and, yes, even economists should know the basics of financial statement accounting. We've noticed that even experienced business journalists, who ought to know better, sometimes refer to the balance sheet when they're talking about profit performance. The bottom line is found in the income statement, not the balance sheet!

Chapter **2**

Introducing Financial Statements

I f you read Chapter 1, you got a brief introduction to the three primary business financial statements: the income statement, the balance sheet, and the statement of cash flows. In this chapter, you get some juicy details. Then, in Part 2, you really get the goods. Think back to when you learned to ride a bicycle. Chapter 1 is like getting on the bike and learning to keep your balance. In this chapter, you put on your training wheels and start riding. Then, when you're ready, the chapters in Part 2 explain all 21 gears of the financial statements bicycle, and then some.

For each financial statement, we introduce its basic information components. The purpose of financial statements is to communicate information that is useful to the readers of the financial statements, to those who are entitled to the information. Financial statement readers include the managers of the business and its lenders and investors. These constitute the primary audience for financial statements. Think of yourself as a shareholder in a business. What sort of information would you want to know about the business? The answer to this question should be the touchstone for the accountant in preparing the financial statements.

The financial effects of making profit are not as simple as you might think. Profit-making activities cause changes in the financial condition of a business — but maybe not the changes you suppose. Many people assume that making a profit increases a business's cash balance by the same amount and that's the end of it. That's simply not true. Making profit leaves many footprints on the financial condition of a business.

Also in this chapter, we briefly discuss financial accounting and reporting standards. Businesses comply with established rules for recording revenue, gains, expenses, and losses; for putting values on assets and liabilities; and for presenting and disclosing information in their financial reports. The basic idea is that all businesses should follow uniform methods for measuring and reporting profit performance, and reporting financial condition and cash flows. Consistency in accounting from business to business is the goal. We explain who makes the rules, and we discuss two important developments: the internationalization of accounting standards, and the increasing divide between financial reporting for public and private companies.

Setting the Stage for Financial Statements

This chapter focuses on the basic *information components* of each financial statement reported by a business. In this first step, we do not address the classification, or grouping, of these information packets within each financial statement. The first step is to get a good idea of the information content reported in financial statements. The second step is to become familiar with the architecture, rules of classification, and other features of financial statements, which we explain in Part 2.

To better illustrate the three primary financial statements, we need a realistic business example. The information content of its financial statements depends on the line of business a company is in — in other words, which types of products and services it sells. The financial statements of a movie theatre chain are different from those of a bank, which are different from those of an airline, which are different from an automobile manufacturer. Here, we use a fairly common type of business example.

We use these particulars of the business for the example:

>> It sells products, mainly to other businesses (not on a retail level).

>> It sells on credit, and its customers take 45 days before they pay.

>> It holds a fairly large stock of products awaiting sale (its inventory).

» It owns a wide variety of long-term operating assets that have useful lives from 3 to 30 years or longer (a building, machines, tools, computers, office furniture, goodwill, intellectual property, and so on).

» It's been in business for many years and has made a profit most years.

» It borrows money for part of the total capital it needs.

» It's organized as a corporation and pays federal and provincial income taxes on its annual taxable income.

» It has never been in bankruptcy and is not facing any immediate financial difficulties.

TIP

Upcoming figures present the company's annual income statement for the year just ended, its balance sheet at the end of the year, and its statement of cash flows for the year. Dollar amounts in the three financials are rounded off to the nearest dollar. Dollar amounts can be reported out to the last dollar, or even the last penny for that matter. But too many digits in a dollar amount are hard to absorb, so many businesses round off the dollar amounts in their financial statements.

REMEMBER

These financial statements are stepping-stone illustrations that are concerned mainly with the basic information components in each statement. Full-blown, classified financial statements are presented in Part 2. (We know you can't wait to get to those chapters.) The financial statements in this chapter do not include all the information you see in actual financial statements. Also, we use descriptive labels for each item rather than the terse and technical titles you see in actual financial statements. And we strip out subtotals that you see in actual financial statements because they are not necessary at this point. So, with all these conventions in mind, let's get going.

First, we should give you quick heads-up on a few characteristics of financial statements. Financial statements are stiff and formal. No slang or street language is allowed, and we've never seen a swear word in one. Financial statements would get a G in the movie rating system. Seldom do you see any graphics or artwork in a financial statement itself, although you do see a fair number of photos and graphics elsewhere in the annual reports of public companies. And virtually no humour appears in financial reports. (However, we do like that in his annual letter to the shareholders of Berkshire Hathaway, Warren Buffett includes some wonderful humour to make his points.)

Understanding the income statement

First on the minds of financial report readers is the profit performance of the business. The *income statement* is the all-important financial statement that summarizes the profit-making activities of a business over a period of time. Its more formal name is the *statement of financial performance*. Figure 2-1 shows the basic information content for an *external* income statement: one released outside the business to its owners and lenders.

REMEMBER

Internal financial statements stay within the business and are used mainly by its management; they aren't circulated outside the business because they contain competitive and confidential information.

Presenting the components of the income statement

Figure 2-1 presents the major ingredients, or information packets, in the income statement for a technology company that sells products and services. As you may expect, the income statement starts with *sales revenue* on the top line. There's no argument about this.

Sales revenue is the total amount that has been or will be received from the company's customers for the sales of products and services to them. Our business example, like most businesses, has adopted a certain set of procedures for the timeline of recording its sales revenue.

Recording expenses involves much more troublesome accounting problems than revenue problems for most businesses. Also, there's the fundamental question regarding which information to disclose about expenses and which information to bury in larger expense categories in the external income statement. We say much more about expenses in later chapters. At this point, direct your attention to the five kinds of expenses in Figure 2-1. Expenses are deducted from sales revenue to determine the final profit for the period, which is referred to as the *bottom line*. Actually, the preferred label is *net income*, as you see in the figure.

TIP

The five expense categories you see in Figure 2-1 should almost always be disclosed in external income statements. These constitute the minimum for adequate disclosure of expenses. The *cost of goods sold* or *cost of sales* (for service companies) is just what it says: the cost of the products sold or services delivered to customers. The cost of the products or services delivered should be matched against the revenue from the sales, of course.

Only one conglomerate operating expense has to be disclosed. In Figure 2-1, it's called *selling, general, and administrative expenses,* which is a popular title in income statements. This is an all-inclusive expense total that mixes together many kinds of expenses, including administrative employee wages and benefit costs, advertising expenses, depreciation of assets, and so on. But it doesn't include interest expenses, income tax expenses, or other expenses; these three expenses are generally reported separately in an income statement.

QW Example Tech., Inc. Income Statement for the Fiscal Year Ending 12/31/2024	
Description	**Amount**
Total amount of revenue from sales of products and services during the year, including discounts and returns	$71,064,000
Total costs of goods sold that are included in sales revenue, including the costs of manufacturing the products, purchasing the products, direct labour costs, and other directly variable costs of sales	($26,891,000)
Gross profit (sometimes referred to as gross margin): Total sales revenue less total costs of goods sold	$44,173,000
Selling, general, and administrative expenses, which is the total amount of operating expenses of the business for the year (excluding other expenses listed separately in the income statement)	($36,678,000)
Income before interest, taxes, and other expenses	$7,495,000
Total interest expense charged to a business for the year on the amount of its interest-bearing debt	($350,000)
Total other expenses (or income) incurred or earned by the business during the year that is not in the normal course of operations	($250,000)
Income taxes related to the activities above	($2,413,000)
Net income earned during the year: Sometimes referred to as net earnings or net profit	$4,482,000

© John Wiley & Sons, Inc.

FIGURE 2-1: Income statement information components for a technology company that sells products and services.

The cost of goods sold or cost of sales expense and the selling, general, and administrative expenses take the biggest bites out of sales revenue. The other three expenses (interest, income tax, and other expenses) are relatively small as a percent of annual sales revenue but are important enough in their own right to be reported separately. And though you may not need this reminder, *bottom-line profit* (net income) is the amount of sales revenue in excess of the business's total expenses. If either sales revenue or any of the expense amounts are wrong, then profit is wrong.

REMEMBER

A service business does not sell products; therefore, it doesn't have the traditional cost of goods sold expense (as it is not selling any tangible goods). In place of cost of goods sold, a service business often simply refers to the direct costs as *costs of sales,* which generally capture labour expenses for wages, payroll taxes, benefits, and other expenses that directly vary with sales revenue. Most service businesses are labour intensive; they have relatively large labour costs as a percent of sales revenue. Service companies differ in how they report their operating expenses. For example, Air Canada breaks out the cost of aircraft fuel. The largest expense of the insurance company TD Insurance is payments on claims. We offer these examples to remind you that accounting should always be adapted to the way the business operates and makes profit. In other words, accounting should follow the business model.

Income statement pointers

TIP

Most businesses break out one or more expenses instead of disclosing just one very broad category for all selling, general, and administrative expenses. For example, Apple, in its 2022 consolidated income statement, discloses research and development expenses separate from its selling, general, and administrative expenses. A business could disclose expenses for advertising and sales promotion, salaries and wages, research and development (as does Apple), and delivery and shipping — though reporting these expenses varies quite a bit from business to business. Businesses do not disclose the compensation of top management in their external financial statements, although this information can be found in other filings of public companies that are filed with Canadian Securities Administrator (CSA). In summary, the extent of details disclosed about operating expenses in externally reported financial reports varies quite a bit from business to business. Financial reporting standards are rather permissive on this point.

Inside most businesses, a profit statement is called a *P&L (profit and loss) report.* These internal profit performance reports to the managers of a business include more detailed information about expenses and about sales revenue — a good deal more! Reporting just five expenses to managers (as shown in Figure 2-1) would not do. Chapter 13 explains P&L reports to managers.

Sales revenue refers to sales of products or services to customers. In some income statements, you also see the term *other revenues and gains,* which generally refers to amounts earned by a business from sources other than sales. For example, a real estate rental business receives rental income from its tenants. (In the example in this chapter, the business has only sales revenue.)

REMEMBER

The income statement gets the most attention from business managers, lenders, and investors (not that they ignore the other two financial statements). The much-abbreviated versions of income statements that you see in the financial press, such as in *The Wall Street Journal,* report the top line (sales revenue and income) and the bottom line (net income) and not much more. Refer to Chapter 6 for more information on income statements.

Figuring out the balance sheet

A more accurate name for a balance sheet is *statement of financial position,* but the term *balance sheet* has caught on, and most people use this term. The most important thing is not the "balance" but rather the information reported in this financial statement.

REMEMBER

In brief, a balance sheet summarizes on the one hand the assets of the business and on the other hand the sources of the assets. However, looking at assets is only half the picture. The other half consists of the liabilities and owner equity of the business. Cash is listed first, and other assets are typically listed in the order of their nearness to cash. Liabilities are typically listed in order of their due dates (the earliest first, and so on), and are listed ahead of owners' equity. We discuss the ordering of the components in a balance sheet in Chapter 7.

Presenting the components of the balance sheet

Figure 2-2 shows the building blocks of a typical balance sheet for a business that sells products and services on credit. As mentioned, one reason the balance sheet is called by this name is that its two sides balance, or are equal in total amounts. In this example, the $27.172 million total assets equals the $27.172 million total liabilities and owners' equity. The balance or equality of total assets on the one side of the scale and the sum of liabilities plus owners' equity on the other side of the scale is expressed in the *accounting equation,* which we discuss in Chapter 1. *Note:* The balance sheet in Figure 2-2 shows the essential elements in this financial statement. In a financial report, the balance sheet includes additional features and frills, which we explain in Chapter 7.

Take a quick walk through the balance sheet. For a technology company that sells products and services on credit, assets are reported in the following order: First is cash, then receivables, then cost of products held for sale, and finally the long-term operating assets of the business. Moving to the other side of the balance sheet, the liabilities section starts with the trade liabilities (from buying on credit) and liabilities for unpaid expenses. Following these operating liabilities is the interest-bearing debt of the business. Owners' equity sources are then reported below liabilities. So, a balance sheet is a composite of assets on one hand and a composite of liabilities and owners' equity sources on the other hand.

REMEMBER

A balance sheet is a reflection of the fundamental two-sided nature of a business (expressed in the *accounting equation,* which we discuss in Chapter 1). In the most basic terms, assets are what the business owns, and liabilities plus owners' equity are the sources of the assets. The sources have claims against the assets.

Liabilities and interest-bearing debt have to be paid, of course, and if the business were to go out of business and liquidate all its assets, the residual after paying all its liabilities would go to the owners.

QW Example Tech., Inc. Balance Sheet 12/31/2024	
Description	**Amount**
Assets:	
Cash	$11,281,000
Accounts receivables: Sales made on credit and expected to be collected	$8,883,000
Inventory: Unsold product stated at purchase cost or manufacturing cost	$1,733,000
Prepaid expenses	$325,000
Long-term assets such as machinery, equipment, buildings, computers, etc., stated at cost less cumulative amount of depreciation expense recorded over the years	$4,350,000
Other long-term assets such as intellectual property, goodwill, investments, notes receivable, and other assets, stated at cost, market value or net realizable value	$600,000
Total Assets	**$27,172,000**
Liabilities and Shareholders' Equity:	
Accounts payable and accrued liabilities: Non-interest-bearing liabilities from purchases made on credit and for unpaid outstanding expenses	$4,213,000
Notes and loans payable: Interest-bearing liabilities or debt owed by the business to third parties, both short-term and long-term	$7,000,000
Total Liabilities	**$11,213,000**
Shareholders' equity: Capital invested in business plus retained profits less amounts paid for distributions or dividends	$15,959,000
Total Liabilities and Shareholders' Equity	**$27,172,000**

© John Wiley & Sons, Inc.

FIGURE 2-2: Balance sheet information components for a technology business that sells products and services on credit.

A company that sells services doesn't have an inventory of products being held for sale. A service company may or may not sell on credit. If a service business doesn't sell on credit, it won't have two of the sizable assets you see in Figure 2-2: receivables from credit sales and inventory of products held for sale. Generally, this means that a service-based business doesn't need as much total assets compared with a products-based business with the same size sales revenue.

The smaller amount of total assets of a service business means that the other side of its balance sheet is correspondingly smaller. In plain terms, this means that a service company doesn't need to borrow as much money or raise as much capital from its equity owners.

As you'd suspect, the particular assets reported in the balance sheet depend on which assets the business owns. We include just six basic assets in Figure 2-2. These are the hardcore assets that a business selling products on credit would have. In this example, the business owns *property, plant, and equipment* (also referred to as *fixed assets*). They are *fixed* because they are held for use in the business's operations and are not for sale, and their usefulness lasts several years or longer.

Balance sheet pointers

So, where does a business get the money to buy its assets? Most businesses borrow money on the basis of interest-bearing bank loans, promissory notes, or other credit instruments for part of the total capital they need for their assets. Also, businesses buy many things on credit and at the balance sheet date owe money to their suppliers, which will be paid in the future. These operating liabilities are never grouped with interest-bearing debt in the balance sheet. The accountant would be tied to the stake for doing such a thing. Note that liabilities are not inter-mingled among assets — this is a definite no-no in financial reporting. You cannot subtract certain liabilities from certain assets and report only the net balance.

Could a business's total liabilities be greater than its total assets? Well, not likely — unless the business has been losing money hand over fist. In the vast majority of cases, a business has more total assets than total liabilities. Why? For two reasons:

>> Its owners have invested money in the business, which is not a liability of the business.

>> The business has earned profit over the years, and some (or all) of the profit has been retained in the business. Making profit increases assets; if not all the profit is distributed to owners, the company's assets increase by the amount of profit retained.

WARNING

In the example (refer to Figure 2-2), owners' equity is about $16 million ($15.959 million to be exact). Sometimes this amount is referred to as *net worth*, because it equals total assets minus total liabilities. However, net worth is not a good term because it implies that the business is worth the amount recorded in its owners' equity accounts. The market value of a business, when it needs to be known, depends on many factors. The amount of owners' equity reported in a balance sheet, which is called its *book value*, is not irrelevant in setting a market value on the business but is usually not the dominant factor. The amount of owners' equity in a balance sheet is based on the history of capital invested in the business by its owners and the history of its profit performance and distributions from profit.

TIP

A balance sheet could be whipped up anytime you want — say, at the end of every day. Typically, preparing a balance sheet at the end of each month is adequate for general management purposes, although a manager might need to take a look at the business's balance sheet in the middle of the month. In external financial reports (those released outside the business to its lenders and investors), a balance sheet is required at the close of business on the last day of the income statement period. Say the annual or quarterly income statement ends September 30; the business would report its balance sheet at the close of business on September 30.

The profit *for the most recent period* is found in the income statement; periodic profit is not reported in the balance sheet. The profit reported in the income statement is before any distributions from profit to owners. The cumulative amount of profit over the years that has not been distributed to its owners is reported in the owners' equity section of the company's balance sheet.

TIP

Notice that the balance sheet in Figure 2-2 is presented in a top-and-bottom format instead of a left-and-right format? Either the vertical (portrait) or horizontal (landscape) mode of display is acceptable. You see both layouts in financial reports. Of course, the two sides of the balance sheet must be kept together, either on one page or on facing pages in the financial report. You can't put assets up front and hide the other side of the balance sheet in the rear of the financial report.

Checking out the statement of cash flows

To survive and thrive, business managers fulfill three financial imperatives:

>> **Make an adequate profit (or at least break even, for a not-for-profit entity).** The income statement reports whether the business made a profit or suffered a loss for the period.

>> **Keep the financial condition in good shape.** The balance sheet reports the financial condition of the business at the end of the period.

>> **Control cash flows.** Management's control over cash flows is reported in the *statement of cash flows,* which presents a summary of the business's sources and uses of cash during the same period as the income statement.

This section introduces you to the statement of cash flows. Financial reporting standards require that the statement of cash flows be reported when a business reports an income statement.

Presenting the components of the statement of cash flows

Successful business managers tell you that they have to manage both profit *and* cash flow; you can't do one and ignore the other. Business managers have to deal with a two-headed dragon in this respect. Ignoring cash flow can pull the rug out from under a successful profit formula.

Figure 2-3 shows the basic information components of the statement of cash flows for the business example we've been using in this chapter. Chapter 8 is fully dedicated to the statement of cash flows. The cash activity of the business during the period is grouped into three sections:

>> The first section reports the company's cash from operating activities. Almost all statements of cash flow start where the income statement left off — that is, by presenting the net profit or loss for the period. You'll notice that the net profit at the bottom of the income statement in Figure 2-1 agrees with the net profit at the top of the statement of cash flows in Figure 2-3 (which it should).

Next, all non-cash expenses such as depreciation and amortization expenses (see Chapter 7 for more information) are called out, which get added back to net profit. This should make sense given that the expenses are "non-cash."

Finally, the next figure in arriving at cash from operating activities reconciles net income for the period with the cash flow from the business's profit-making activities, or *operating activities*, including increases and decreases in current assets (for example, accounts receivables and inventory) and current liabilities (for example, accounts payables and accrued liabilities).

>> The second section summarizes the company's *investing* transactions during the period, or more specifically, what long-term assets the company purchased or invested in.

>> The third section reports the company's *financing* transactions, or more specifically, whether the company raised cash from securing a loan or selling shares or whether the company used cash to repay loans or pay a dividend.

The net increase or decrease in cash from the three types of cash activities during the period is added to or subtracted from the beginning cash balance to get the cash balance at the end of the year.

QW Example Tech., Inc. Statement of Cash Flows for the Fiscal Year Ending 12/31/2024	
Description	**Amount**
Net income (loss): Statement of cash flows starts with the net income or loss generated by the company for the like reporting period	$4,482,000
Non-cash expenses: Addback all non-cash expenses incurred by the business for items such as depreciation expense, amortization expense, and others	$1,739,000
Change in cash from operating activities: Increase or decrease in current assets and current liabilities impacting cash from normal operating activities during the period	$1,372,000
Change in cash from operating activities	$7,593,000
Change in cash from investing activities: Increase or decrease in cash resulting from making investments in or disposals of long-term capital/operating assets (equipment, patents, etc.)	($750,000)
Change in cash from financing activities: Increase or decrease in cash resulting from transactions with lenders and owners including new loans, repayment of loans, new equity, distributions or dividends paid to owners, and others	$3,650,000
Change in cash during the period	$10,493,000
Cash at beginning of period	$788,000
Cash at end of period	$11,281,000

FIGURE 2-3: Information components in the statement of cash flows.

© John Wiley & Sons, Inc.

In the example, the business earned a $4.482 million profit (net income) during the year (see Figure 2-1), which included non-cash expenses of $1.739 million (primarily for depreciation expense) that need to be added back to properly reconcile cash changes during the period. The cash result of its operating activities was to increase its cash by $1.372 million, which you see in the first part of the statement of cash flows (see Figure 2-3). The actual cash inflows from revenues and outflows for expenses run on a different timetable from when the sales revenue and expenses are recorded for determining profit. The result called *cash from operating activities*, in the amount of $7.593 million, has converted net income into cash generated from operations. We give a more comprehensive explanation of the differences between cash flows and sales revenue and expenses in Chapter 8.

The next part of the statement of cash flows sums up the long-term investments the business made during the year, such as constructing a new production plant or replacing machinery and equipment. If the business sold any of its long-term assets, it reports the cash inflows from these divestments in this section of the statement of cash flows. The cash flows of other investment activities (if any) are reported in this part of the statement as well. As you can see in Figure 2-3, the business invested $750,000 in new long-term operating assets (trucks, equipment, tools, and computers).

The final part of the statement sums up the dealings between the business and its sources of capital during the period — borrowing money from lenders and raising capital from its owners. Cash outflows to pay debt are reported in this section, as are cash distributions from profit paid to the owners of the business. The final part of the example statement shows that the result of these transactions was to increase cash by $3.650 million. (By the way, in this example, the business did make a dividend payment to the shareholders from profit. It probably could have been larger, but it wasn't — which is an important point that we discuss in the later section "Why no (or limited) cash distribution from profit?")

As you see in Figure 2-3, the net result of the three types of cash activities was a $10.493 million increase during the year. The increase is added to the cash balance at the start of the year to get the cash balance at the end of the year, which is $11.281 million.

REMEMBER

We should make one point clear: The $10.493 cash increase during the year (in this example) is never referred to as a cash flow *bottom line* or any such thing. The term *bottom line* is reserved for the final line of the income statement, which reports net income — the final amount of profit after all expenses are deducted.

Statement of cash flows pointers

Imagine you have a highlighter in your hand, and the three basic financial statements of a business are in front of you. What are the most important numbers to mark? Financial statements do not come with headlines, like newspapers. You have to find your own headlines. Bottom-line profit (net income) in the income statement is one number you should mark. Another key number is *cash flow from operating activities* in the statement of cash flows. You don't have to understand the technical steps of how the accountant gets this cash flow number, but pay attention to how it compares with the profit number for the period. (We explain this point in more detail in Chapter 7.)

WARNING

Cash flow is almost always different from net income. The sales revenue reported in the income statement does not equal cash collections from customers during the year, and expenses do not equal cash payments during the year. Cash collections from sales minus cash payments for expenses gives cash flow from a company's profit-making activities; sales revenue minus expenses gives the net income earned for the year. Sorry, but that's how the cookie crumbles.

Digging into the statement of changes in shareholders' equity

Many business financial reports include a *fourth* financial statement — or at least it's called a "statement." It's really a summary of the changes in the constituent elements of owners' equity (shareholders' equity of a corporation). The corporation is one basic type of legal structure that businesses use. In Chapter 5, we explain the alternative legal structures available for conducting business operations. We don't show a statement of changes in owners' equity here. We show an example in Chapter 9, in which we explain the preparation of a financial report for release.

REMEMBER

When a business has a complex owner's equity structure, a separate summary of changes in the components of owners' equity during the period is useful for the shareholders, the board of directors, and the top-level managers. On the other hand, in some cases, the only changes in owners' equity during the period were earning profit and distributing part of the cash flow from profit to owners. In this situation, there isn't much need for a summary of changes in owners' equity. The financial statement reader can easily find profit in the income statement and cash distributions from profit (if any) in the statement of cash flows. For details, see the later section "Why no (or limited) cash distribution from profit?"

Gleaning Key Information from Financial Statements

The point of reporting financial statements is to provide important information to people who have a financial interest in the business — mainly its outside investors and lenders. From that information, investors and lenders can answer key questions about the business's financial performance and condition. We discuss some of these key questions in this section. In Chapters 11, 12, and 20, we discuss a longer list of questions and explain financial statement analysis including using ratios to evaluate financial results.

How's profit performance?

Investors use two important measures to judge a company's annual profit performance. Here, we use the data from Figures 2-1 and 2-2 for the company.

>> **Return on sales** = profit as a percentage of annual sales revenue:

$4.482 million bottom-line annual profit (net income) ÷ $71.064 million annual sales revenue = 6.3%

>> **Return on equity** = profit as a percentage of owners' equity:

$4.482 million bottom-line annual profit (net income) ÷ $15.959 million owners' equity = 28.1%

Profit looks pretty thin compared with annual sales revenue. The company earns only 6.3 percent return on sales. In other words, 93.7 cents out of every sales dollar goes for expenses, and the company keeps only 6.3 cents for profit. (Many businesses earn 10 percent or higher return on sales.) However, when profit is compared with owners' equity, things look a lot better. The business earns more than 28 percent profit on its owners' equity. We'd bet you don't have many investments earning 28 percent per year.

Is there enough cash?

Cash is the lubricant of business activity. Realistically, a business can't operate for long with a zero cash balance. It can't wait to open the morning mail or look at the bank account online to see how much cash it will have for the day's needs (although some businesses try to operate on a shoestring cash balance). A business should keep enough cash on hand to keep things running smoothly even when interruptions occur in the normal inflows of cash. A business has to meet its payroll on time, for example. Keeping an adequate balance in the chequing account serves as a buffer against unforeseen disruptions in normal cash inflows.

At the end of the year, the business in our example has $11.281 million cash on hand (refer to Figure 2-2). This cash balance is available for general business purposes. (If there are restrictions on how it can use its cash balance, the business is obligated to disclose those restrictions.) Is $11.281 million enough? Interestingly, businesses do not have to comment on their cash balance. We've never seen such a comment in a financial report.

The business has $4.213 in operating liabilities that will come due for payment over the one- to three-month period (refer to Figure 2-2). So, it has enough cash to pay these liabilities. But it doesn't have enough cash on hand to pay its operating liabilities and its $7.0 million interest-bearing debt. Lenders don't expect a business to keep a cash balance more than the amount of debt; this condition would defeat the purpose of lending money to the business, which is to have the business put the money to good use and be able to pay interest on the debt.

Lenders are more interested in the business's capability to control its cash flows so that when the time comes to pay off loans it will be able to do so. They know that the business's other, non-cash assets will be converted into cash flow. Receivables will be collected, and products held in inventory will be sold and the sales will generate cash flow. So, you shouldn't focus just on cash; throw the net wider and look at the other assets as well.

Taking this broader approach, the business has $11.281 million cash, $8.883 million in trade receivables, and $1.733 million inventory, which adds up to $21.897 million of cash and cash potential. Relative to its $11.213 million in total liabilities ($4.213 million in operating liabilities plus $7.0 million of debt), the business looks in pretty good shape. On the other hand, if it turns out that the business is not able to collect its receivables and is not able to sell its products, it would end up in deep trouble.

TIP

One other way to look at a business's cash balance is to express its cash balance in terms of how many days of sales the amount represents. In the example, the business has an ending cash balance equal to 58 days of sales, calculated as follows:

$71.064 million annual sales revenue ÷ 365 days = $194,696 sales per day

$11.281 million cash balance ÷ $194,696 sales per day = 58 days

The business's cash balance equals almost two months of sales activity, which most lenders and investors would consider adequate.

Can you trust the financial statement numbers?

Whether the financial statements are correct or not depends on the answers to two basic questions:

>> Does the business have a reliable accounting system in place and employ competent accountants?

>> Has top management manipulated the business's accounting methods or deliberately falsified the numbers?

We'd love to tell you that the answer to the first question is always yes, and the answer to the second question is always no. But you know better, don't you? A survey of 400 chief financial officers and financial executives revealed that they think that about 20 percent of corporations distort their earnings reports (income statements) — even though the companies stay within the boundaries of accepted accounting standards. We estimate that for most businesses, you should take their financial statements with a grain of salt and keep in mind that the numbers could be manipulated in the range of 10 to 20 percent higher or lower. Even though most people think accounting is an exact science, it isn't. There's a fair amount of play in the numbers, as we discuss later in this book (see Chapter 14).

In our experience, many businesses don't put much effort into keeping their accounting systems up to speed, and they skimp on hiring competent accountants. In short, a risk exists that the financial statements of a business could be incorrect and seriously misleading.

To increase the credibility of their financial statements, many businesses hire independent auditors to examine their accounting systems and records and to express opinions on whether the financial statements conform to established accounting standards. In fact, some business lenders insist on an annual audit by an independent public accounting firm as a condition of making the loan. The outside, non-management investors in a privately owned business could vote to have annual audits of the financial statements. Public companies have no choice; a public company is required to have annual audits by an independent public accounting firm. We discuss audits in Chapter 11.

WARNING

Two points: Audits are not cheap, and these audits are not always effective in rooting out financial reporting fraud by high-level managers. Chartered Professional Accounts (CPAs) that are hired as auditors are supposed to apply *professional skepticism* in doing their audits, but this doesn't always lead to discovery of fraud.

Why no (or limited) cash distribution from profit?

In this chapter's example, the business did not distribute any of its profit for the year to its owners. Distributions from profit by a business corporation are called *dividends*. (The total amount distributed is divided up among the shareholders, hence the term *dividends*.) Cash distributions from profit to owners are included in the third section of the statement of cash flows (refer to Figure 2-3). In our example, the business made a cash distribution in the form of a dividend from profit of $400,000 — even though it earned $4.482 million of net income (see Figure 2-1), or just 8.9 percent of profits ($400,000 ÷ $4.482 million). The $400,000 is included in the change in cash from financing activities of $10.493 million. Why is the amount of the dividend so low?

It's clear that the company has plenty of cash available to issue a dividend, as not only did it generate $4.482 million in net profit, but it also generated another $3.111 million in cash from non-cash expenses and operating activities ($1.739 million plus

$1.372 million; see Figure 2-3). Should the business have distributed, say, at least half of its cash flow from profit, or roughly $3.8 million, to its owners? If you owned 20 percent of the ownership shares of the business, you would have received 20 percent, or roughly $760,000, of the dividend. But you got almost no cash return on your investment in the business. Your shares should be worth more because the profit for the year increased the company's owners' equity. But you did not see any of this increase in your wallet.

REMEMBER

Deciding whether to make cash distributions from profit to shareholders is in the hands of the directors of a business corporation. Its shareowners elect the directors, and in theory the directors act in the best interests of the shareholders. Evidently the directors thought the business had better uses for the $7.593 million cash flow from operating activities than distributing some of it to shareholders. In our example, the company does indeed have something big planned for the use of its cash hoard of $11.281 million, as it has earmarked funds to support buying a complimentary business in future years. Generally, the main reason for not making cash distributions from profit is to finance the business's growth — to use all the cash flow from profit for expanding the assets needed by the business at the higher sales level (which is the case here). Ideally, the business's directors would explain their decision not to distribute any money from profit to the shareholders. But, generally, no such comments are made in financial reports.

Complying with Accounting and Financial Reporting Standards

When an independent CPA audits the financial report of a business, there's no doubt regarding which accounting and financial reporting standards the business uses to prepare its financial statements and other disclosures. The CPA explicitly states which standards are being used in the auditor's report. What about unaudited financial reports that are used for internal purposes? Well, the business could clarify which accounting and financial reporting standards it uses, but you don't see such disclosure in all cases.

REMEMBER

When the financial report of a business is not audited and does not make clear which standards are being used to prepare its financial report, the reader is entitled to assume that appropriate standards are being used. However, a business may be way out in left field (or out of the ballpark) in the "guideposts" it uses for recording profit and in the preparation of its financial statements. A business may make up its own "rules" for measuring profit and preparing financial statements. Audits give a third independent party's opinion on the financial statements. They also confirm whether the appropriate financial reporting standards have used in the preparation of the financial statements. Unaudited financial statements may be unreliable. In this book, we concentrate on authoritative standards, of course.

Imagine the confusion that would result if every business were permitted to invent its own accounting methods for measuring profit and for putting values on assets and liabilities. What if every business adopted its own individual accounting terminology and followed its own style for presenting financial statements? Such a state of affairs would be a Tower of Babel.

Recognizing Canadian and international standards

The authoritative standards and rules that govern financial accounting and reporting by businesses based in Canada are called *generally accepted accounting principles* (GAAP). When you read the financial statements of a business, you're entitled to assume that the business has fully complied with GAAP in reporting its cash flows, profit-making activities, and financial condition — unless the business makes clear that it has prepared its financial statements using some other basis of accounting or has deviated from GAAP in one or more significant respects.

WARNING

If GAAP are not the basis for preparing its financial statements, a business should make clear which other basis of accounting is being used and should avoid using financial statement titles that are associated with GAAP. For example, if a business such as a farm uses a simple cash receipts and cash disbursements basis of accounting — which falls way short of GAAP — it should not use the terms *income statement* and *balance sheet*. These terms are part and parcel of GAAP, and their use as titles for financial statements implies that the business is using GAAP.

We won't bore you with a lengthy historical discourse on the development of accounting and financial reporting standards in Canada. The general consensus (backed up by law) is that businesses should use consistent accounting methods and terminology. Bombardier and BCE should use the same accounting methods; so should Shopify and Canadian Tire. Of course, businesses in different industries have different types of transactions, but the same types of transactions should be accounted for in the same way. That is the goal.

Around 4,000 publicly owned corporations have their shares traded on the Toronto Stock Exchange (TSX). Now, are we telling you that all these businesses should use the same accounting methods, terminology, and presentation styles for their financial statements? Putting it in such a stark manner makes us suck in our breath a little. The correct answer is that all businesses *should* use the same rulebook of GAAP. However, the rulebook permits alternative accounting methods for some transactions. Furthermore, accountants have to interpret the rules as they apply GAAP in actual situations. The devil is in the details.

In Canada, as in the majority of countries around the globe, GAAP, which include international standards, constitute the gold standard for preparing financial statements of business entities (although the gold is somewhat tarnished, as we discuss in later chapters). The presumption is that any deviations from GAAP would cause misleading financial statements. If a business honestly thinks it should deviate from GAAP — to better reflect the economic reality of its transactions or situation — it should make clear that it has not complied with GAAP in one or more respects. If the business does not disclose the deviations from GAAP, the business may have legal exposure to those who relied on the information in its financial report and suffered a loss attributable to the misleading nature of the information.

Getting to know the Canadian, U.S., and international standard setters

Okay, so everyone reading a financial report is entitled to assume that GAAP have been followed — unless the business clearly discloses that it is using another basis of accounting.

REMEMBER

The basic idea behind the development of GAAP is to measure profit and to value assets and liabilities *consistently* from business to business — to establish broad-scale uniformity in accounting methods for all businesses. The idea is to make sure that all accountants are singing the same tune from the same hymnal. The purpose is also to establish realistic and objective methods for measuring profit and putting values on assets and liabilities. The authoritative bodies write the tunes that accountants have to sing.

Who are these authoritative bodies? In Canada, we have two bodies setting standards for businesses:

>> **The main authoritative accounting standards setter is the International Accounting Standards Board (IASB), which is based in London, U.K.** The standards set by this body are called International Financial Reporting Standards (IFRS) and they have been adopted by Canada for all publicly traded companies. These standards can be found in Part 1 of the *CPA Canada Handbook*.

>> **The second body making pronouncements on Canadian GAAP for private enterprises and for keeping these accounting standards up-to-date is the Accounting Standards Board (AcSB) of CPA Canada.** The standards set by this body are called Accounting Standards for Private Enterprises (ASPE) and can be found in Part 2 of the *CPA Canada Handbook*.

The body in the United States is the Financial Accounting Standards Board (FASB). Unlike in Canada, the U.S. federal Securities and Exchange Commission (SEC) has broad powers over accounting and financial reporting standards for publicly traded companies.

All GAAP (Canadian, U.S., and international) also include minimum requirements for *disclosure,* which refers to how information is classified and presented in financial statements and to the types of information that have to be included with the financial statements, mainly as notes. Chapter 10 explains the disclosures that are required in addition to the three primary financial statements of a business (income statement, balance sheet, and statement of cash flows).

Some people think the rules have become too complicated and far too technical. If you search through the many parts of the *CPA Handbook,* you'll see why people come to this conclusion. The *Handbook* (a.k.a. *CPA Canada Standards and Guidance Collection*) is a complete electronic source of guidance on accounting, audit, and more, which is continuously updated by the CPA Canada. However, if the rules are not specific and detailed enough, different accountants will make different interpretations that will cause inconsistency from one business to the next regarding how profit is measured and how assets and liabilities are reported in the balance sheet. The AcSB was between a rock and a hard place. Consequently, two sets of GAAP were put into place — one for public companies (IFRS) and one for private companies (ASPE). For the most part the AcSB issues rules that are detailed and technical but take care of the major concerns of most businesses.

Going worldwide

Although it's a bit of an overstatement, today the investment of capital knows no borders. Canadian capital is invested in European and other countries, and capital from other countries is invested in Canadian businesses. In short, the flow of capital has become international. Recognizing the need, the AcSB joined the IASB and adopted IFRS for public companies.

The need to make GAAP uniform globally (at least for public companies) also applies to the United States. Of course, political issues and national pride come into play in trying to achieve this goal. The term *harmonization* is favoured, which sidesteps difficult issues regarding the future roles of the FASB and IASB in the issuance of international accounting standards.

One major obstacle deterring the goal of worldwide accounting standards concerns which sort of standards should be issued:

>> The FASB follows a *rules-based* approach. Its pronouncements have been detailed and technical. The idea is to leave little room for differences of interpretation.

>> The IASB favours a *principles-based* method. Under this approach, accounting standards are stated in fairly broad general language and the detailed interpretation of the standards is left to accountants in the field.

The two authoritative bodies have disagreed on some key accounting issues, and the road to convergence of accounting standards will be rocky, in our view.

In Canada and internationally, the guidelines are more flexible. Accountants use their professional judgment and experience to decide which method is best in situations where different options for how to account for transactions are available. Accountants use additional sources of GAAP outside the *Handbook* to decide which accounting practice to follow.

No country's economy is an island to itself. The stability, development, and growth of an economy depend on securing capital from both inside and outside the country. The flow of capital across borders by investors and lenders gives enormous impetus for the development of uniform international accounting standards. Stay tuned; in the coming years, we think we will see more and more convergence of accounting standards in the remaining countries that have not yet adopted IFRS.

Noting a divide between public and private companies

Up until the adoption of IFRS for public companies, GAAP and financial reporting standards were viewed as equally applicable to public companies (generally large corporations) and private (generally smaller) companies. We witnessed a growing distinction between accounting and financial reporting standards for public versus private companies. Although most accountants don't like to admit it, there has always been a de facto divergence in financial reporting practices by private companies compared with the more rigorously enforced standards for public companies.

REMEMBER

It's probably safe to say that the financial reports of most private businesses measure up to GAAP standards in all significant respects. At the same time, however, little doubt exists that the financial reports of some private companies fall short. Private companies do not have many of the accounting problems of large, public companies. For example, many public companies deal in complex derivative instruments, issue stock options to managers, provide highly developed defined-benefit retirement and health benefit plans for their employees, enter into complicated inter-company investment and joint venture operations, have complex organizational structures, and so on. Most private companies do not have to deal with these issues.

Finally, we should mention that smaller private businesses do not have as much money to spend on their accountants and auditors. Big companies can spend big bucks and hire highly qualified accountants. Furthermore, public companies are legally required to have annual audits by independent public accountants. The annual audit keeps a big business up-to-date on accounting and financial reporting standards. Frankly, smaller private companies are somewhat at a disadvantage in keeping up with accounting and financial reporting standards.

Following (and bending) the rules

An often-repeated accounting story concerns three people interviewing for an important accounting position. They are asked one key question: "What's 2 plus 2?" The first candidate answers, "It's 4," and is told, "Don't call us, we'll call you." The second candidate answers, "Well, most of the time the answer is 4, but sometimes it's 3 and sometimes it's 5." The third candidate answers: "What do you want the answer to be?" Guess who gets the job. This story exaggerates, of course, but it does have an element of truth.

The point is that interpreting GAAP is not cut and dried. Many accounting standards leave a lot of wiggle room for interpretation. *Guidelines* would be a better word to describe many accounting rules. Deciding how to account for certain transactions and situations requires seasoned judgment and careful analysis of the rules. Furthermore, many estimates have to be made. Deciding on accounting methods requires, above all else, *good faith.*

WARNING

A business might resort to creative accounting to make profit for the period look better, or to make its year-to-year profit less erratic than it really is (which is called *income smoothing*). Like lawyers who know where to find loopholes, accountants can come up with inventive interpretations that stay within the boundaries of GAAP. We warn you about these creative accounting techniques — also called massaging the numbers — at various points in this book. Massaging the numbers can get out of hand and become accounting fraud, also called *cooking the books.* Massaging the numbers has some basis in honest differences for interpreting the facts. Cooking the books goes way beyond interpreting facts; this fraud consists of inventing facts and good old-fashioned chicanery.

IN THIS CHAPTER

» **Distinguishing between bookkeeping and accounting**

» **Getting to know the bookkeeping cycle**

» **Making sure your bookkeeping and accounting systems are rock solid**

» **Doing a double-take on double-entry accounting**

» **Deterring and detecting errors and outright fraud**

Chapter **3**

Bookkeeping and Accounting Systems

We think it's safe to say that most folks are not enthusiastic bookkeepers. You may balance your chequebook against your bank statement or your online bank activity report every month or so and somehow manage to pull together all information you need for your annual income tax return. But if you're like us, you use the paperless feature with most of the businesses you deal with, use the automatic debit feature offered by your bank, pay most bills with your credit card, and stuff your other bills in a drawer and just drag them out once or twice a month to pay them. You may have been caught not paying a bill on time because of all the automated payment options at your disposal.

And when was the last time you prepared a detailed listing of all your assets and liabilities (even though a listing of assets is a good idea for fire insurance purposes)? Personal computer programs and phone apps are available to make bookkeeping for individuals more organized, but you still have to enter a lot of data into the program, and most people decide not to put forth the effort.

We don't prepare a summary statement of our earnings and income for the year. And we don't prepare a breakdown of what we spent our money on and how much we saved. Why not? Because we don't need to! Individuals can get along quite well without much bookkeeping — but the opposite is true for a business. A business needs a good bookkeeping system simply to operate day to day.

REMEMBER

One key difference exists between individuals and businesses. Every business must prepare periodic financial statements, tax returns, reports to managers, and so on. The completeness, accuracy, reliability, and timeliness (the acronym CART that you see referenced time and again throughout this book) of these reports is critical to the business's survival. If its accounting records are incomplete or inaccurate, its financial statements, tax returns, and management reports are incomplete or inaccurate. And inaccuracy simply won't do. In fact, inaccurate and incomplete bookkeeping records could be construed as evidence of deliberate fraud (or at least of incompetence). Suppose, for instance, that the Canada Revenue Agency decides to audit a business. The business won't get very far with the excuse that it doesn't have records to back up the deductions in its tax returns.

Business managers have to be sure that the company's bookkeeping and accounting system is dependable and up to snuff. This chapter shows you what bookkeepers and accountants do, mainly so you have a clear idea of what it takes to be sure that the information coming out of your accounting system is complete, accurate, reliable, and timely. Strong internal accounting controls are absolutely necessary.

Separating the Duties of Bookkeepers and Accountants

REMEMBER

Bookkeeping refers mainly to the recordkeeping aspects of accounting and is heavily weighted toward processing transactions (for example, billing a customer, paying a vendor, and so on); it's essentially the process (some would say the drudgery) of preparing documents or managing computer-based digital data entries for recording all the detailed information regarding the transactions and other activities of a business (or other organization, venture, or project). Bookkeeping is an indispensable subset of accounting. The term *accounting* is much broader, going into the realm of designing the bookkeeping system, establishing controls to make sure the system is working well, and analyzing and verifying the recorded information. Accountants give orders; bookkeepers follow them.

Bookkeepers spend most of their work time keeping the recordkeeping process running smoothly according to the system established by the business — and they also spend a fair amount of time dealing with problems that inevitably arise in recording so much information. Accountants, on the other hand, have a different focus.

TIP

Think of accounting as what goes on before and after bookkeeping. Accountants prepare reports based on the information accumulated by the bookkeeping process: financial statements, tax returns, and various confidential reports to managers.

Measuring profit is a critical task that accountants perform — a task that depends on the accuracy and completeness of the information that the bookkeeper records. The accountant decides how to measure sales revenue and expenses (as well as any special gains and losses) to determine the profit or loss for the period. The tough questions about profit — how to measure it in our complex and advanced economic environment, and what profit consists of — can't be answered through bookkeeping alone. We discuss accounting problems in Chapter 9.

Bookkeeping builds up the financial database of the entity. This is a perpetual, nonstop process for a business of any size. A business does bookkeeping every day. Bookkeeping has two main jobs:

>> Recording the financial effects and other relevant details of the wide variety of transactions and other activities of the entity

>> Generating a *constant* stream of reports and outputs to keep the business operating every day

Accounting, on the other hand, focuses on the *periodic* preparation of three main types of output: reports to managers, tax returns (income tax, GST/HST, payroll tax, and so on), and financial statements. These outputs are done according to established timetables. For example, external financial reports are prepared every *quarter* (3 months) and at the end of the *year* (12 months). Tax returns have their own timetables, as dictated by the tax laws and regulations. Accountants have much more choice in deciding how often to prepare financial reports to managers. The managers of some businesses require daily or even hourly financial reports; in other businesses, quarterly reports are adequate to keep on top of things.

REMEMBER

In this book, we explain the fundamentals of financial reporting to the "outside," or non-management creditors and investors of a business. The main focus is on the financial statements sent to them (check out Chapters 6 through 10). This field of accounting is referred to as *financial accounting* (although it might be better called *external financial accounting*). The externally reported financial statements are useful to managers as well, but managers need considerably more detailed information than is reported in the external financial statements of a business. Much of this management information is confidential and not for circulation outside the business. We offer some discussion of accounting to managers in Part 4.

Pedalling Through the Bookkeeping Cycle

Bookkeeping is a very repetitive process. Certain basic steps are done in virtually every bookkeeping system. These steps are done in a certain order, although the specific methods and procedures of each step vary from business to business. For example, entering the data for a sale could be done by scanning barcodes in a grocery store, or it could require an in-depth legal interpretation for a complex order from a customer for an expensive piece of equipment. We briefly explain the basic steps in this section. (See also the later section "Double-Entry Accounting," which explains how the books are kept in balance by using debits and credits for recording transactions.)

Getting to the end of the period

REMEMBER

Although the means and specific procedures regarding how the bookkeeping process is carried out vary from business to business, all businesses walk through the following steps during the accounting period. These basic four steps take up most of the time spent on recordkeeping:

1. **Prepare original source documents or electronic references for all transactions, operations, and other business events.**

   When buying products, a business gets a *purchase invoice* from the supplier. When borrowing money from the bank, a business signs a promissory *note payable* or a *formal loan agreement,* a copy of which the business keeps. When a customer uses a credit card to buy the business's product, the business gets the credit card receipt (or an electronic alternative) as evidence of the transaction. When preparing payroll electronic payments, a business depends on *salary rosters* and *time cards.* All of these key business forms and electronic source documents serve as sources of information into the bookkeeping system — in other words, information the bookkeeper uses in recording the financial effects of the business's activities.

2. **Determine the financial effects of the transactions and other business events.**

   Transactions have financial effects that must be recorded — the business is better off, worse off, or at least "different off" as the result of its transactions. Examples of typical business transactions include paying employees, making sales to customers, borrowing money from the bank, and buying products to sell to customers. The bookkeeping process begins by determining the relevant information about each transaction. The business's chief accountant establishes the rules and methods for measuring the financial effects of transactions. Of course, the bookkeeper should comply with these rules and methods.

3. **Make original entries of financial effects into journals and accounts, with appropriate references to source documents.**

   Using the source document(s) or electronic files, the bookkeeper makes the first, or original, entry into a journal; this information is later recorded in accounts (see the next step).

   A *journal* is a chronological record of transactions in the order in which they occur — like a detailed personal diary. Each piece is recorded in the two or more accounts that are affected by the transaction.

   A simple example illustrates recording a transaction in a journal: a retail bookstore, expecting a big demand from its customers, purchases on credit 100 copies of *Accounting For Canadians For Dummies* from the publisher, Wiley. The books are received and placed on the shelves. (One hundred copies is a lot to put on the shelves, but our relatives promised to rush down and buy several copies each.) The bookstore now owns the books and also owes Wiley $1,500, which is the cost of the 100 copies. Here we look only at recording the purchase of the books, not recording subsequent sales of the books and paying the bill to Wiley.

   The bookstore has established a specific inventory account called "Inventory — Trade Paperbacks" for books like this one. And the purchase liability to the publisher should be entered in the account "Accounts Payable–Publishers." Therefore, the original journal entry for this purchase records an increase in the inventory asset account of $1,500 and an increase in the liability accounts payable of $1,500. Notice the balance in the two sides of the transaction: An asset increases $1,500 on the one side, and a liability increases $1,500 on the other side. All is well (assuming there are no mistakes).

   Summing up, a journal entry records the whole transaction in one place at one time. All changes caused by the transaction are chronicled in one entry. However, making journal entries does not provide a running balance for the individual assets, liabilities, and other financial components of a business (or other entity) — which leads to the next step in the bookkeeping process.

4. **Post the financial effects of transactions in the accounts changed by the transactions.**

   Journal entries are the sources for recording changes caused by transactions in the accounts of the entity. An *account* is a separate record or file for each asset, each liability, and so on. The pluses and minuses of the transaction are recorded in the accounts changed by the transaction. In this way, a running balance is kept for each. Recording the effects of transactions from journal entries to accounts is called *posting*.

   Think of each account as an address. The changes recorded in the original journal entries are "delivered," or posted to the accounts. A business (or other entity) establishes an official *chart,* or list of accounts, that is used for posting transactions. The original journal entry records the whole transaction in one place; in the second step (posting), each change is recorded in the separate accounts affected by the transaction.

TIP

We can't exaggerate the importance of entering transaction data correctly and in a timely manner — both in original journal entries and in the posting step. The prevalence of data-entry errors is one important reason that most retailers use cash registers that read barcoded information on products; this approach more accurately captures the necessary information and speeds up the entry of the information. One way of stressing this point is the well-known data-processing expression "garbage in, garbage out."

Finishing up for the period

After doing the four bookkeeping procedures explained in the preceding section, the business is ready to finish the process. At the end of the period, certain steps are necessary to make the business's accounts ready for the preparation of its financial statements (and other accounting reports such as tax returns). We continue the numbering from the preceding section, starting with Step 5:

5. **Perform end-of-period procedures — the critical steps for getting the accounting records up to date and ready for the preparation of management accounting reports, tax returns, and financial statements.**

   A *period* is a stretch of time — from one day to one month to one quarter (three months) to one year — determined by the business's needs. A year is the longest period of time that a business would wait to prepare its financial statements. Most businesses need accounting reports and financial statements at the end of each quarter, and many need monthly financial statements.

TECHNICAL STUFF

Before the accounting reports can be prepared at the end of the period, the bookkeeper must bring the business's accounts up-to-date and complete the bookkeeping process. Generally these end-of-period procedures consist mainly of making *adjusting entries* in the accounts of the business. One such end-of-period adjusting entry, for example, is recording the depreciation expense for the period (see Chapters 6 and 7 for more on depreciation). Another step is getting an actual count and making a critical inspection of the business's inventory so that the inventory records can be adjusted to account for shoplifting, employee theft, and other inventory shrinkage.

The accountant needs to be heavily involved in end-of-period procedures and checking for errors in the business's accounts. Data entry clerks and bookkeepers may not fully understand the unusual nature of some business transactions and may have entered transactions incorrectly. One reason for establishing internal controls (discussed in the later section "Enforce strong internal controls") is to keep errors to a minimum. Ideally, accounts should contain very few errors at the end of the period, but the accountant can't make any assumptions and should do a final check for errors that might have fallen through the cracks.

6. **Compile the adjusted trial balance for the accountant, which is the basis for preparing management reports, tax returns, and financial statements.**

    After all end-of-period procedures have been completed, the bookkeeper compiles a complete listing of all accounts called the *adjusted trial balance,* which is typically computer generated. Modest-sized businesses maintain hundreds of accounts for their various assets, liabilities, owners' equity, revenue, and expenses. Larger businesses keep thousands of accounts, and very large businesses might keep more than 10,000 accounts. In contrast, external financial statements, tax returns, and internal accounting reports to managers contain a relatively small number of accounts. For example, a typical external balance sheet or an income tax return report only 25 to 30 line items (maybe even fewer).

    The accountant takes the adjusted trial balance and groups similar accounts into one summary amount that is reported in a financial report or tax return. For example, a business might keep hundreds of separate inventory accounts, every one of which is listed in the adjusted trial balance. The accountant collapses all these accounts into one summary inventory account that is presented in the business's external balance sheet. In grouping the accounts, the accountant should comply with established financial reporting standards and income tax requirements.

7. *Close the books* **— bring the bookkeeping for the fiscal year just ended to a close and get things ready to begin the bookkeeping process for the coming fiscal year.**

    Books is the common term for a business's complete set of accounts. A business's transactions are a constant stream of activities that don't end tidily on the last day of the year, which can make preparing financial statements and tax returns challenging. The business has to draw a clear line of demarcation between activities for the year (the 12-month accounting period) ended and the year yet to come by closing the books for one year and starting with fresh books for the next year.

TIP

Most medium-size and larger businesses have an *accounting manual* that spells out in great detail the specific accounts and procedures for recording transactions. A business should regularly review its chart of accounts and accounting rules and policies and make revisions. Companies do not take this task lightly; discontinuities in the accounting system can be major shocks and have to be carefully thought out. Nevertheless, bookkeeping and accounting systems can't remain static for very long. If these systems were never changed, bookkeepers would still be sitting on high stools making entries with quill pens and bottled ink in leather-bound ledgers.

Managing the Bookkeeping and Accounting System

In our experience, too many business managers and owners ignore their bookkeeping and accounting systems or take them for granted — unless something goes wrong. They assume that if the books are in balance, everything is okay, and that you can simply hit a "print report" button to produce quality financial information. The later section "Double-Entry Accounting" covers exactly what it means to have "books in balance" — it does *not* necessarily mean that everything is okay.

To determine whether your bookkeeping system is up to snuff, check out the following sections, which provide a checklist of the most important elements of a good system.

Categorize your financial information: The chart of accounts

Suppose you're the accountant for a corporation and you're faced with the daunting task of preparing the annual income tax return for the business. This demands that you report the following kinds of expenses:

>> Advertising and promotion

>> Bad debts

>> Compensation of officers

>> Cost of goods sold

>> Depreciation and amortization

- » Employee benefit costs
- » Interest
- » Internet and telephone
- » Pensions and profit-sharing plans
- » Rent
- » Repairs and maintenance
- » Salaries and wages
- » Taxes and licences

You must provide additional information for some of these expenses. For example, the cost of goods sold expense is determined in a schedule that also requires inventory cost at the beginning of the year, purchases during the year, cost of labour during the year (for manufacturers), other costs, and inventory cost at year-end.

Where do you start? Well, if it's December 1 and the tax return deadline is December 31, you start by panicking — unless you were smart enough to think ahead about the kinds of information your business would need to report. In fact, when your accountant first designs your business's accounting system, they should dissect every report to managers, the external financial statements, and the tax returns, breaking down all the information into categories such as those we just listed.

REMEMBER

For each category of information that you need to include in an accounting report, you need an *account*, a record of the activities in that category. An account is basically a focused history of a particular dimension of a business. Individuals can have accounts, too — for example, your chequebook (physical or digital) is an account of the cash inflows and outflows and the balance of your chequing account (assuming that you remember to record all activities and reconcile your chequebook against your bank account balance). We doubt that you keep a written account of the coin and currency in your wallet, pockets, glove compartment, and sofa cushions, but a business needs to. An account serves as the source of information for preparing financial statements, tax returns, and reports to managers. *Note:* We use the term *chequebook* to include not only cheques but other forms of payment such as electronic funds transfers, which are far more common than cheques.

The term *general ledger* refers to the complete set of accounts established and maintained by a business. The *chart of accounts* is the formal index of these accounts — the complete listing and classification of the accounts used by the business to record its transactions. *General ledger* usually refers to the accounts and often to the balances in these accounts at some particular time. The chart of accounts, even for a relatively small business, normally contains 100 or more accounts. Larger business organizations need thousands of accounts. The larger the number, the more likely that the accounts are given number codes according to some scheme — for example, all assets might be in the 100 to 300 range, all liabilities in the 400 to 500 range, and so on.

TIP

As a business manager, you should make sure that the controller (chief accountant), or perhaps an outside professional accountant, reviews the chart of accounts periodically to determine whether the accounts are up-to-date and adequate for the business's needs. Over time, income tax rules change, business economic models evolve, the company goes into new lines of business, the company adopts new employee benefit plans, or managers want the accounting information prepared in more detail. Most businesses are in constant flux, and the chart of accounts has to keep up with these changes.

Standardize source document forms and data-entry procedures

Just like you need a constant circulation of blood to live, businesses need a constant flow of documents and electronic activity! Even in this age of the Internet, the cloud, electronic communication, and computers, a business generates and depends on lots of documentation (either hard paperwork or digitized documents). And much of this documentation is used in the accounting process. Placing an order to buy products, selling a product to a customer, determining the earnings of an employee for the month — virtually every business transaction needs some documentation, generally called *source documents.* When you pay a bill, for example, don't you want a "hard copy" to examine before you write the cheque?

TECHNICAL
STUFF

Source documents serve as legal evidence of the terms and conditions agreed upon by the business and the other person or organization that it's dealing with. Both parties receive some kind of source document. For example, for a sale at a cash register, the customer gets a sales receipt, and the business keeps a running record of all the transactions in the register, which can be printed out later if need be.

Clearly, an accounting system needs to standardize the forms and procedures for processing and recording all normal, repetitive transactions and control the generation and handling of these source documents. From the bookkeeping point of view, these business forms and documents are important because they provide the input information needed for recording transactions in the business's accounts. Sloppy documents leads to sloppy accounting records, and sloppy accounting records just won't do when the time comes to prepare tax returns and financial statements.

TIP

If you're the owner of a small business, you probably want to check out an office supply store or, better yet, online documentation websites to see the kinds of forms that you can buy right off the shelf or download with the stroke of a key. You can find many of the basic forms and documents that you need for executing and recording business transactions. Also, modern computer accounting software systems include templates for most business forms and source documents needed by a business.

Hire competent, trained personnel

A business shouldn't be penny-wise and pound-foolish: What good is meticulously collecting source documents if the information on those documents isn't entered into your system correctly? You shouldn't try to save a few bucks by hiring the lowest-paid people you can find. Bookkeepers and accountants, like all other employees in a business, should have the skills and knowledge needed to perform their functions. Here are some guidelines for choosing the right people to enter and control the flow of your business's data and for making sure that those people *remain* the right people:

>> **University or college degree:** Many accountants in business organizations have a university or college degree with a major in accounting. However, as you move down the accounting department, you find that more and more employees do not have a degree and perhaps don't even have any courses in accounting — they learned bookkeeping methods and skills through on-the-job training. Although these employees may have good skills and instincts, our experience is that they tend to do things by the book; they often lack the broader perspective necessary for detecting errors, improvising, and being innovative. So you want to at least look twice at a potential employee who has no university- or college-based accounting background.

TIP

>> **CPA:** When hiring higher-level accountants in a business organization, determine whether they should hold a professional accounting designation. Most larger businesses insist on this credential, along with a specific number of years' experience in public accounting or in the private sector.

In our opinion, a business is prudent to require a professional designation for its chief accountant (who usually holds the title of *controller*). Or a business should consult regularly with a public accountant for advice on its accounting system — especially regarding how to treat particularly unusual transactions and accounting problems that come up.

Depending on the complexity of the issues that might come up during regular operations, the requirement or need to have someone on staff who holds a professional designation will vary. Having experience in the industry likely is the most valuable asset a candidate brings to the business.

>> **Continuing education:** Bookkeepers and accountants need continuing education to keep up with changes in the income tax law and financial reporting requirements, as well as changes in how the business operates. Ideally, bookkeepers and accountants are able to spot needed improvements and implement these changes — to make accounting reports to managers more useful, for example. Fortunately, many short-term courses, home-study programs, and the like are available at reasonable costs for keeping up on the latest accounting developments. Many continuing education courses are available on the Internet, but be sure to check out the standards of an Internet course.

CPA Canada requires members to stay up to date on professional development to keep their memberships in good standing. Structured activities such as advanced post-secondary education courses or unstructured learning such as on-the-job training or technical research would qualify for this requirement. What is essential is that the activity be relevant and appropriate to the accountant's work and professional responsibilities, and that it contains significant intellectual or practical content.

For example, the CPA Ontario's requirements for CPAs include the completion of *continuing professional development* (CPD) activities. The minimum requirement is 120 hours for a three-year period with 50 percent that is verifiable. Licensed accounting practitioners are subject to an additional level of scrutiny of their professional work. Mandatory practice inspection ensures that their work is done in accordance with the professional standards. All licensed accounting practitioners must also purchase liability insurance. These rules are in place to protect the public's interest.

WARNING

>> **Integrity:** What's possibly the most important quality to look for is also the hardest to judge. Bookkeepers and accountants need to be honest people because of the control they have over your business's financial records. Conduct a careful background check when hiring new accounting personnel. After you hire them, periodically (and discreetly) check whether their lifestyles match their salaries, but be careful not to invade their privacy. Small-business owners and managers have closer day-in and day-out contact with their accountants and bookkeepers, which can be an advantage — they get to know their accountants and bookkeepers on a personal level. Even so, we could tell you many true stories about long-time, "trusted" bookkeepers who made off with some of the family fortune.

Complete the process with end-of-period procedures

Suppose that all transactions during the year have been recorded correctly. Therefore, the business's accounts are ready for preparing its financial statements, aren't they? Not so fast! As we explain earlier in "Finishing up for the period," certain additional procedures are necessary at the end of the period to make sure that the accounts are correct and complete for preparing financial statements for the year. Two main things have to be done at the end of the period:

» **Record normal, routine *adjusting entries*:** For example, depreciation expense isn't a transaction as such and therefore isn't included in the flow of transactions recorded in the day-to-day bookkeeping process. (Chapter 6 explains depreciation expense.) Similarly, certain other expenses and income may not have been associated with a specific transaction and, therefore, have not been recorded. In many businesses, there's a normal lag in recording certain transactions, such as billing customers for services already provided. These *catch-up entries* should be recorded. Year-end adjusting entries are necessary to have correct balances for determining profit for the period, and to make the revenue, gain, expense, and loss accounts up-to-date and correct for the year.

» **Make a careful sweep of all matters to check for other developments that may affect the accuracy of the accounts:** For example, the company may have discontinued a product line. The remaining inventory of these products may have to be removed from the asset account, with a corresponding loss recorded in the period. Or the company may have settled a long-standing lawsuit, and the amount of damages needs to be recorded. Layoffs and severance packages are another example of what the chief accountant needs to look for before preparing reports.

TIP

Lest you still think of accounting as dry and dull, we will tell you that end-of-period accounting procedures can stir up controversy of the heated-debate variety. These procedures require that the accountant make decisions and judgment calls that upper management might not agree with. For example, the accountant might suggest recording major losses that would put a big dent in profit for the year or cause the business to report an overall loss. The outside auditor (assuming that the business has an independent audit of its financial statements) often gets in the middle of the argument. These kinds of debates are precisely why business managers need to know some accounting: to hold up their end of the argument.

This also touches on a concept that you may hear from time to time — that accounting is just as much of an art form as a science. What we mean by this is that while accounting is a technical profession that has a large amount of authoritative content to work with and provides guidance, the actual application of accounting concepts, rules, and regulations (in the real world where internal management pressures can be significant) is often fairly subjective.

Leave good audit trails

Good bookkeeping systems leave good audit trails. An *audit trail* is a clear-cut path of the sequence of events leading up to an entry in the accounts. An accountant starts with the source documents and follows through the bookkeeping steps in recording transactions to reconstruct this path. Even if a business doesn't have an outside public accountant do an annual audit, the accountant has frequent occasion to go back to the source documents and either verify certain information in the accounts or reconstruct the information in a different manner. Suppose that a salesperson claims some suspicious-looking travel expenses; the accountant would probably want to go through all this person's travel and entertainment reimbursements for the past year.

WARNING

If the Canada Revenue Agency (CRA) comes in for a field audit of your business, you'd better have good audit trails to substantiate all your expense deductions and sales revenue for the year. The CRA has rules about saving source documents for a reasonable period of time and having a well-defined process for making bookkeeping entries and keeping accounts. Think twice before throwing away source documents too soon. Also, ask your accountant to demonstrate and lay out for your inspection the audit trails for key transactions, such as cash collections, sales, cash disbursements, and inventory purchases. Even computer-based accounting systems recognize the importance of audit trails. Well-designed computer programs provide the capability to backtrack through the sequence of steps in the recording of specific transactions.

Look out for unusual events and developments

WARNING

Business managers should encourage their accountants to be alert to anything out of the ordinary that might require attention. Suppose the accounts receivable balance for a customer is rapidly increasing — that is, the customer is buying more and more from your company on credit but isn't paying for these purchases on time. Maybe the customer has switched more of their company's purchases to your business and is buying more from you only because they are buying less from other businesses. But maybe the customer is planning to stiff your business and take off without paying their debts. Or maybe the customer is planning to go into bankruptcy soon and is stockpiling products before the company's credit rating heads south.

Don't forget internal time bombs: A bookkeeper's reluctance to take a vacation could mean that they don't want anyone else looking at the books.

To some extent, accountants have to act as the business's eyes and ears. Of course, that's one of the main functions of a business manager as well, but the accounting staff can play an important role.

Design truly useful reports for managers

We've seen too many off-the-mark accounting reports to managers — reports that are difficult to decipher and not very useful or relevant to the manager's decision-making needs and control functions. These bad reports waste the manager's time . . . one of the most serious offenses in management accounting.

Part of the problem lies with the managers themselves. As a business manager, have you told your accounting staff what you need to know, when you need it, and how to present it in the most efficient manner? When you stepped into your position, you probably didn't hesitate to rearrange your office, and maybe you even insisted on hiring your own support staff. Yet you most likely lay down like a lapdog regarding your accounting reports. Maybe you assume that the reports have to be done a certain way and that arguing for change is no use.

REMEMBER

On the other hand, accountants bear a good share of the blame for poor management reports. Accountants should proactively study the manager's decision-making responsibilities and provide the information that is most useful, presented in the most easily digestible manner. To a certain extent, this is what we mean when we say "reliable" (in the acronym CART). While financial information may be accurate, reliability speaks to the concept of producing and reporting financial information in a way that truly benefits a business manager and assists them in making informed business decisions. Don't assume that accuracy automatically equates to reliability.

In designing the chart of accounts, the accountant should keep in mind the type of information needed for management reports. To exercise control, managers need much more detail than what's reported on tax returns and external financial statements. And as Chapter 15 explains, expenses should be regrouped into different categories for management decision-making analysis. A good chart of accounts looks to both the external and the internal (management) needs for information.

TIP

So what's the answer for a manager who receives poorly formatted reports? Demand a report format that suits your needs! See Chapter 15 for a useful profit report model, and show it to your accountant as well.

Enforce strong internal controls

REMEMBER

Any accounting system worth its salt should establish and vigorously enforce effective *internal controls* — basically, additional forms and procedures over and above what's needed strictly to move operations along. These additional procedures serve to deter and detect errors (honest mistakes) and all forms of dishonesty by employees, customers, suppliers, and even managers themselves. Unfortunately, many businesses pay only lip service to internal controls; they don't put into place good internal controls, or they don't seriously enforce their internal controls (they just go through the motions).

Internal controls are like highway truck weigh stations, which make sure that a truck's load doesn't exceed the limits and that the truck has a valid plate. You're just checking that your staff is playing by the rules. For example, to prevent or minimize shoplifting, most retailers now have video surveillance, as well as tags that set off alarms if the customer leaves the store with the tag still on the product. Likewise, a business should implement certain procedures and forms to prevent (as much as possible) theft, embezzlement, kickbacks, fraud, and simple mistakes by its own employees and managers.

WARNING

Do the names Enron and Nortel ring a bell? Regulatory changes have been put in place to try to prevent accounting scandals. In the United States, passage of the federal Sarbanes-Oxley Act (SOX) of 2002 put even more demands on organizations' internal controls. SOX imposes new responsibilities on top-level executives to make sure the controls are in place and working well. SOX regulations apply not only to businesses operating in the United States but also to businesses owned by U.S. companies that operate in other countries, including Canada.

In Canada, many public companies — such as all of our national banks — have their shares traded on the New York Stock Exchange or NASDAQ. Consequently, the SOX rules with respect to corporate governance, enhanced financial disclosures, auditors' independence, and so on apply to the Canadian companies in the same way.

Not-for-profit organizations pay particular attention to the public's perception of their financial reporting and integrity. They rely heavily on government grants and private donations to fund their activities.

WARNING

Based on our experience, smaller businesses tend to think that they're immune to embezzlement and fraud by their loyal and trusted employees. These are personal friends, after all. Yet, in fact, many small businesses are hit hard by fraud and usually can least afford the consequences. Most studies of fraud in small businesses have found that the average loss is well into six figures! You know, even in a friendly game of poker, we always cut the deck before dealing the cards around the table. Your business, too, should put checks and balances into place to discourage dishonest practices and to uncover any fraud and theft as soon as possible.

INTERNAL CONTROLS AGAINST MISTAKES AND THEFT

Accounting is characterized by a lot of paperwork; forms and procedures are plentiful. Most business managers and employees have their enthusiasm under control when it comes to the paperwork and procedures that the accounting department requires. One reason for this attitude, in our experience, is that non-accountants fail to appreciate the need for accounting controls.

These internal controls are designed to minimize errors in bookkeeping, which has to process a great deal of detailed information and data. Equally important, controls are necessary to deter employee fraud, embezzlement, and theft, as well as fraud and dishonest behaviour against the business from the outside. Every business is a target for fraud and theft, such as customers who shoplift; suppliers who deliberately ship less than the quantities invoiced to a business and hope that the business won't notice the difference (called *short-counts*); and even dishonest managers themselves, who might pad expense accounts or take kickbacks from suppliers or customers.

For these reasons a business should take steps to avoid being an easy target for dishonest behaviour by its employees, customers, and suppliers. Every business should institute and enforce certain control measures, many of which are integrated into the accounting process.

Here are five common examples of internal control procedures:

- Requiring a second authorization on cash disbursements over a certain dollar amount

- Matching up receiving reports based on actual counts and inspections of incoming shipments with purchase orders before cutting cheques for payment to suppliers

- Requiring both a sales manager's and another high-level manager's approval for write-offs of customers' overdue receivable balances (that is, closing the accounts on the assumption that they won't be collected), including a checklist of collection efforts that were undertaken

- Having auditors or employees who do not work in the warehouse take surprise counts of products stored in the company's warehouse and compare the counts with inventory records

- Requiring mandatory vacations by every employee, including bookkeepers and accountants, during which time someone else does that person's job (because a second person might notice irregularities or deviations from company policies)

WARNING

And then there's the growing specter of hacks into the information databases of businesses. These intrusions are referred to as *cyberthreats.* Hackers have broken into the computer information systems of many major companies, getting around the inadequate controls the businesses had in place. Interestingly, hackers haven't shown interest in accounting information *per se.* Rather, the hackers are after Social Insurance numbers, credit scores, home addresses, passwords, email addresses — mainly personal and private information. We don't know of a computer database break-in for the purpose of manipulating or destroying accounting information — but a hacker could alter accounting information after breaking into a company's information system. The topic of cybercrime is beyond the scope of this book, other than to warn you about this serious threat that requires a new set of internal controls. A class of forensic professionals called *cybercrime investigators* has emerged who advise and assist businesses in coming to grips with cyberthreats. These specialists include both accountants and IT (information technology) experts.

Double-Entry Accounting

Businesses and not-for-profit entities use *double-entry accounting.* But we've never met an individual who uses double-entry accounting in personal bookkeeping. Instead, individuals use single-entry accounting. For example, when you make a payment, either by cheque or by an online bank payment on your credit card balance, you make an entry to decrease your bank balance. And that's it. You make just one entry — to decrease your bank account balance. It wouldn't occur to you to make a second, companion entry to decrease your credit card liability balance. Why? Because you don't keep a liability account for what you owe on your credit card. You depend on the credit card company to make an entry to decrease your balance.

REMEMBER

Businesses and not-for-profit entities have to keep track of their liabilities as well as their assets. And they have to keep track of *all* sources of their assets. (Some part of their total assets comes from money invested by their owners, for example.) When a business writes a cheque to pay one of its liabilities, it makes a two-sided (or double) entry — one to decrease its cash balance and the second to decrease the liability. This is double-entry accounting in action. Double-entry does *not* mean a transaction is recorded twice; it means both sides of the transaction are recorded at the same time.

TIP

Double-entry accounting pivots off the accounting equation:

Total assets = Total liabilities + Total owners' equity

The accounting equation is a condensed version of the balance sheet. The balance sheet is the financial statement that summarizes a business's assets on the one side and its liabilities plus its owners' equity on the other side. Liabilities and owners' equity are the sources of its assets. Each source has different claims on the assets, which we explain in Chapter 7.

One main function of the bookkeeping system is to record all transactions of a business — every single last one. If you look at transactions through the lens of the accounting equation, there is a beautiful symmetry in transactions (well, beautiful to accountants at least). All transactions have a natural balance. The sum of financial effects on one side of a transaction equals the sum of financial effects on the other side. Thus, the name of the balance sheet — because in theory, the balance sheet should always be, well, in balance.

Suppose a business buys a new delivery truck for $65,000 and pays in cash. The truck asset account increases by the $65,000 cost of the truck, and cash decreases $65,000. Here's another example: A company borrows $2 million from its bank. Its cash increases $2 million, and the liability for its loan payable to the bank increases the same amount.

Just one more example: Suppose a business suffers a loss from a tornado because some of its assets were not insured. The assets destroyed by the tornado are written off (decreased to zero balances), and the amount of the loss decreases owners' equity the same amount. The loss works its way through the income statement but ends up as a decrease in owners' equity.

TIP

Virtually all business bookkeeping systems use *debits and credits* for making sure that both sides of transactions are recorded and for keeping the two sides of the accounting equation in balance. A change in an account is recorded as either a debit or a credit according to the following rules:

Assets	= Liabilities	+ Owners' Equity
+ Debit	+ Credit	+ Credit
– Credit	– Debit	– Debit

An increase in an asset is tagged as a debit; an increase in a liability or owners' equity account is tagged as a credit. Decreases are just the reverse. Following this scheme, the total of debits must equal the total of credits in recording every transaction. In brief: *Debits have to equal credits.* Debits and credits have been used for centuries. (A book published in 1494 described how business traders and merchants of the day used debits and credits in their bookkeeping.) *Note:* Sales revenue and expense accounts also follow debit and credit rules. Revenue increases owners' equity (thus is a credit), and an expense decreases owners' equity (thus is a debit).

Following the rules of debits and credits, asset accounts have debit balances, and liabilities and owners' equity accounts have credit balances. (Yes, a balance sheet account can have a wrong-way balance in unusual situations, such as cash having a credit balance because the business has made more payments than it has in its chequing account.) The total of accounts with debit balances should equal the total of accounts with credit balances. When the total of debit balance accounts equals the total of credit balance accounts, the *books are in balance.*

WARNING

Even when the books are in balance, errors are still possible. The bookkeeper might have recorded debits or credits in wrong accounts, or might have entered wrong amounts, or might have missed recording some transactions altogether. Having balanced books simply means that the total of accounts with debit balances equals the total of accounts with credit balances. The important thing is whether the books (the accounts) have *correct* balances, which depends on whether all transactions and other developments have been recorded correctly.

Juggling the Books to Conceal Embezzlement and Fraud

WARNING

Fraud and illegal practices occur in large corporations and in one-owner or one-manager-controlled small businesses — and in every size business in between. Some types of fraud are more common in small businesses, including *sales skimming* (not recording all sales revenue, to deflate the taxable income of the business and its owner) and the recording of personal expenses through the business (to make these expenses deductible for income tax). Some kinds of fraud are committed mainly by large businesses, including paying bribes to public officials and entering into illegal conspiracies to fix prices or divide the market. The purchasing managers in any size business can be tempted to accept kickbacks and under-the-table payoffs from vendors and suppliers.

You know that fraud and illegal practices happen in the business world. Our point in bringing up this unpleasant topic is that fraud and illegal practices require manipulation of a business's accounts. For example, if a business pays a bribe it does not record the amount in a bald-faced account called "bribery expense." Rather, the business disguises the payment by recording it in a legitimate expense account (such as repairs and maintenance expense, or legal expense). If a business records sales revenue before sales have taken place (a not uncommon type of fraud), it does not record the false revenue in a separate account called "fictional sales revenue." The bogus sales are recorded in the regular sales revenue account.

Money laundering, another example of an illegal practice, involves taking money from illegal sources (such as drug dealing) and passing it through a business to make it look legitimate — to give the money a false identity. This money can hardly be recorded as "revenue from drug sales" in the business's accounts. If an employee embezzles money from the business, they have to cover their tracks by making false entries in the accounts or by not making entries that should be recorded.

Manipulating accounts to conceal fraud, illegal activities, and embezzlement is generally called *juggling the accounts.* Another term you probably have heard is *cooking the books.* Although this term is sometimes used in the same sense of juggling the accounts, the term *cooking the books* more often refers to deliberate accounting fraud, in which the main purpose is to produce financial statements that tell a better story than is supported by the facts.

When the accounts have been juggled or the books have been cooked, the business's financial statements are distorted, incorrect, and misleading. Lenders, other creditors, and the owners who have capital invested in the business rely on the company's financial statements. Also, a business's managers and board of directors (the group of people who oversee a business corporation) might be misled — assuming that they're not a party to the fraud, of course — and might also have liability to third-party creditors and investors for their failure to catch the fraud. Creditors and investors who end up suffering losses have legal grounds to sue the managers and directors (and perhaps the independent auditors who did not catch the fraud) for damages suffered.

Persons who engage in fraud cheat on their income taxes; they don't declare the ill-gotten income. Needless to say, the CRA is on constant alert for fraud in income tax returns, both business and personal returns. The CRA has the authority to come in and audit the business's books and also the personal income tax returns of its managers and investors. Tax evasion is punishable by the courts, we might point out.

Chapter **4**

Accounting in the Digital Age

Over the past 15 years, the rate of change in technological advancements clearly has been nothing short of mind-numbing. The computing power now possessed in a mobile format (cellphones, tablets, laptops, and yes, even watches and glasses) that allows for real-time access to data, information, articles, content, videos, and just about everything else has transformed how businesses operate, assess financial performances, manage employees, and interact with customers. These technology trends have been further amplified and accelerated by the COVID-19 pandemic that hit the world in early 2020. The move toward remote working and learning has pushed what was once a luxury or nice-to-have (that is, "I can work from home once a week") to a must-have (employees demanding that employers provide work-from-home or remote-working solutions).

Nowhere is this trend more prevalent than in the heavy data processing and financial transaction side of businesses, including information technology operations (such as IT or MIS), financial analysis and planning, and accounting. This chapter is dedicated to covering critical topics related to performing and managing the accounting function in the digital age by evaluating the topics from two perspectives:

>> First, what are the latest technological trends or tools that are available to businesses to assist with managing the accounting functions more efficiently?

>> Second, what risks are present with these technological trends or tools, and how does the accounting function need to adapt or evolve to manage these risks?

Noting a Few Foundational Accounting Concepts Related to Technology

REMEMBER

Before we dive into the latest and greatest technological trends and tools, we draw your attention to these base accounting concepts that never go out of style and always remain the foundation of accounting:

>> **CART:** Every accounting system, whether 100 percent automated or still being maintained in the dark ages on green ledger sheets, should always strive to produce *complete, accurate, reliable,* and *timely* financial information on which to base sound business decisions. This has been, is, and will always be the primary goal and objective of accounting systems.

>> **SGA:** Accounting systems, whether maintained in the cloud or on the ground, must be designed, controlled, and managed to ensure that company assets are always safeguarded. Never has this been more important because SGA, which stands for *safeguarding assets,* relates to making sure physical assets are properly insured or access is restricted from theft, and more importantly, invaluable company digital data (such as vital customer sales and personal information) is protected from both criminals and competitors.

>> **GIGO or DIGO:** The old saying of *garbage in, garbage out* is more important now than ever before. This is why we offer the acronym DIGO, which stands for *data in, garbage out.* The tendency in the modern accounting era is to assume that if the data flowing into the accounting system has been digitized and/or is supported by blockchain-enabled digital ledgers, then the data is more apt to be correct and free of errors. Don't make this rookie mistake; errors are just as likely to occur with digitized business transactions and records, but if the flow of these records (through the accounting and financial information reporting system) is left unchecked, they can pollute a financial

reporting system very quickly and create even more damage if the output reaches decision-makers who ultimately base decisions on erroneous information.

>> **Art versus science:** The profession of accounting is governed by numerous organizations (for example, the International Accounting Standards Board, or IASB for public companies, and the Accounting Standards Board, or AcSB, for private companies) that have assisted with documenting guidelines and policies for accountants to utilize when preparing company financial information (that is, GAAP — generally accepted accounting principles). Further, universities, colleges, and other institutions attempt to educate accountants to apply the GAAP in a consistent manner. But don't forget that accounting still remains a profession that incorporates a significant number of opinions, subjectivity, and for lack of a better term, creativity (the art side of the equation) that technology most likely will never be able to replace.

REMEMBER

The advances made in technology and the digital economy have had a profound and positive impact on the accounting function. These advances have made life so much easier on so many fronts for accountants; one of the single biggest benefits has been allowing accountants to shift their focus and efforts from wasting time on processing data, paperwork, and financial transactions to being able to analyze and interpret accounting and financial reports and data. This is undoubtedly a huge benefit but one that can be achieved only by keeping in mind two critical concepts:

>> Data integrity has been, is, and will always be of utmost importance; in today's rapid-paced global economic environment, DIGO (data in, garbage out) is not acceptable and it can be fatal to a business.

>> Developing and implementing proper accounting controls, policies, and procedures to protect the security of all financial data and information has reached an entirely new level given the risks associated with digitizing source documents. As we note in the next section, security, security, and security are the critical buzzwords with accounting systems and software.

REMEMBER

As you work your way through the remainder of this chapter, we want to reinforce that the current technology-based tools available to accountants are absolutely wonderful to have and use, and they have, without question, made accounting systems more efficient. But these technology-based tools have added an entirely new layer of financial and operational management risks that must be proactively managed to achieve our two primary goals of CART and SGA. Remember the old saying "The more things change, the more things stay the same"? This certainly applies to the business accounting function today, tomorrow, or 20 years from now.

Using Accounting Software in the Cloud and on the Ground

It's possible, though not likely, that a very small business would keep its books the old-fashioned way: Record all transactions and do all the other steps of the bookkeeping cycle with pen and paper and by making handwritten entries using the old green ledger sheets. However, even a small business has a relatively large number of transactions that have to be recorded in journals and accounts, to say nothing about the end-of-period steps in the bookkeeping cycle (covered in Chapter 3).

A bewildering array of computer software packages is available today for small, medium, and large businesses. Some larger corporations develop and utilize their own computer-based accounting systems (that is, they write their own code), but more and more large companies are utilizing ERP (enterprise resource planning) systems to support their accounting requirements. Indeed, we identified over 1,700 accounting software systems listed on the Software Advice website; check out the current numbers at www.softwareadvice.com/accounting.

Many businesses do their accounting work in-house, on the ground at their own locations. They use on-the-premises computers, develop or buy accounting software, and control their own backup files. They may use an outside firm to handle certain accounting chores, particularly payroll. Alternatively, a business can do some or most of its accounting in the cloud. The term *cloud* refers to large-scale offsite computer servers that a business connects with over the Internet. The cloud can be used simply as the backup storage location for the company's accounting records. Cloud servers have the reputation of being very difficult to break into by hackers. Cloud providers offer a variety of accounting and business software and services that are too varied to discuss here. In short, a business can do almost all its accounting in the cloud. Of course, the business still needs very strong controls over the transmission of accounting information to and from the cloud. More and more businesses are switching to the cloud for doing more and more of their accounting tasks.

This has become an increasing trend during the COVID-19 pandemic, when many businesses were forced to close their offices and staff worked from home. Having data in the cloud has made it much more accessible to all who are responsible for that information and others who need access to it for strategic or other purposes. Most experts expect the trend of going to the cloud to continue.

Except for larger entities that employ their own accounting software and information technology experts, other businesses find that they need the consultation of outside IT (information technology) experts in choosing, implementing, upgrading, and replacing accounting software.

TIP

If we were giving a talk to owners/managers of small to medium-sized businesses, we would offer the following words of advice about accounting software:

>> Choose your accounting software carefully. It's hard to pull up stakes and switch to another software package. Changing even just one module, such as payroll or inventory, in your accounting software can be quite difficult.

>> In evaluating accounting software, you and your accountant should consider three main factors: ease of use, whether it has the particular features and functionalities you need, and the likelihood that the vendor will continue in business and be around to update and make improvements in the software.

>> In real estate, the prime concern is "location, location, location." The watchwords in accounting software are "security, security, security." You need very tight controls over all aspects of using the accounting software and over who is authorized to make changes in any of the modules of the accounting software.

>> Even when using advanced, sophisticated accounting software, a business must design the specialized reports it needs for its various managers and make sure that these reports are generated correctly from the accounting database.

>> Never forget "garbage in, garbage out" (see the previous section). Data-entry errors can be a serious problem in computer-based accounting systems. It's next to impossible to eliminate data-entry errors altogether. Even barcode readers make mistakes, and barcode tags themselves may have been tampered with. A business should adopt strong controls to minimize these input errors as well as strong internal controls for the verification of data entry.

>> Make sure your accounting software leaves good audit trails (which you need for management control) for your CPA when they audit your financial statements and for the Canada Revenue Agency (CRA) when it decides to audit your income tax returns. The lack of good audit trails looks very suspicious to the CRA.

>> Online accounting systems that permit remote input and access over the internet or a local area network with multiple users present special security problems. Think twice before putting any part of your accounting system online (and if you do, institute airtight controls).

TIP

Smaller businesses and even many medium-sized businesses don't have the budget to hire full-time information system and information technology (IT) specialists. They use consultants to help them select accounting software packages, install software, and get it up and running. Like other computer software, accounting programs are frequently revised and updated. A consultant can help keep a business's accounting software up to date, correct flaws and security weaknesses in the program, and take advantage of its latest features.

Controlling and Protecting Money Flows in the Electronic Age

For most businesses, the most targeted asset for theft is good old-fashioned cash. The reason is simple: It's the most liquid asset for criminals to steal and dispose of. Types of cash can range significantly:

» A small amount of currency that resides in a cash register at a retailer

» Currency that a bank keeps on hand in a bank teller's drawer

» Millions of dollars of cash that sits in a bank account (or accounts) of a major corporation

» Cryptocurrencies that are kept in a virtual wallet

Needless to say, the use of physical cash has been significantly reduced over the years as other forms of electronic payments replace the need to exchange physical cash. The use of cash saw another major decrease because of the COVID-19 pandemic, given the explosion in direct-to-consumer business models and direct delivery companies such as Amazon, Grubhub, and others.

The reason we highlight these trends is not to state the obvious but rather to emphasize that while the form in which payments are made is changing (from cash to electronic), the sheer volume of electronic payments has exploded over the past fifteen years. Every operating business has had to adapt and evolve to the changing landscape to process and receive electronic payments. This, in turn, has driven the requirement of companies to ensure they develop and implement proper policies and procedures to safeguard company assets because criminals are going to follow the cash; if they can't steal it from a retail store, they'll devise systems to steal money electronically.

All companies need to process payments on two fronts:

>> For cash inflows, companies must ensure that customers can remit payments for the goods or services purchased in the most efficient and friendly manner possible.

>> For cash outflows, companies must devise systems to ensure their vendors, suppliers, and employees are paid in an accurate and timely fashion.

For large businesses (think of Walmart and Amazon), the ebb and flow of payment processing (both inflows and outflows) can range in the tens of thousands of transactions daily, so these organizations have developed extremely sophisticated systems to track these payment flows. Small- to medium-sized businesses devise specific strategies and third-party relationships with their customers to assist with managing payment flows (and controlling risks). The control over the processing electronic payments is just as important and valuable to the customers as it is to the business. Find out more about digitally protecting money flows in the following sections.

Processing payroll

Most businesses rely on third-party payroll processing organizations to manage the task of paying employees. There are so many advantages to using third-party payroll processing organizations that the reasons are almost too many to list, but the primary pluses are centered in the following:

>> Ease in complying with payroll tax regulations by expert third parties

>> Processing direct deposit of payroll to the employees' bank account

>> Fast and accurate calculation of employees pay and deductions; can often be less costly than when carried out in-house

>> Direct online access to payroll records when pay rates, withholdings, and so on need to be changed

These days, you simply log on and update employee pay information in real time.

Controlling bank accounts

Bank account information needs to be provided to your customers (so they can process electronic payments to your business) and to vendors and suppliers (so they can receive payments from your business). With so much bank account information floating around in the cyberworld, it can be very helpful to set up unique bank accounts used for specific fund control purposes.

For example, a company may have a unique bank account set up for the sole purpose of receiving customer payments. This account is monitored every day and the excess funds are "swept" or consolidated into the company's primary operating account. The same concept holds for payroll accounts as well as vendor payment accounts because these may be funded with just enough money to cover the payments being made. The idea is to avoid concentrating funds in an account that may have more risk of being accessed from unwanted third parties or criminals. If a loss is realized, the loss can be minimized with only a limited amount of funds exposed at any time. The idea is to receive and sweep (customer payments) and remit and fund (vendor/supplier payments).

Surveying bank forms of electronic payments

Let's begin with processing payments via the traditional banking route, which includes using a wide range of options:

>> Completing transfers via bank wires (domestic or international)

>> Processing ACH (Automated Clearing House) transfers

>> Processing bank transfers (you and your vendor both use the same bank so you can transfer funds internally, within the bank)

>> Using bank-provided vendor pay-bill systems (a vendor wants to be paid with a cheque, which you process electronically online through the bank so it generates and distribute the physical cheque, alleviating the need for cheques to be generated in-house)

REMEMBER

Other forms of bank payments are available as well, but the general idea here is to leverage the extensive knowledge and security the bank has set up and implemented to process electronic payments in a tightly controlled and secure environment. Banks are highly regulated and operate in an industry that demands the highest level of trust from the public. Banks have, over the decades, devised payment processing systems that are some of the securest in the world, so why not utilize this expertise to protect your hard-earned cash?

Checking out non-bank forms of electronic payments

It seems that every day a new form of electronic payment is being devised. These include using credit cards, debit cards, PayPal, Apple Pay, Square, Amazon Pay,

Venmo, and similar types of electronic payment services. The reasons companies use these types of electronic payment services vary widely:

>> A small business handling any size of transaction with its customers and at a reduced risk compared to using cash

>> A customer paying with a credit card to earn "points" (for travel or cash back)

>> A business getting an automatic record of the sale

>> A large company such as Amazon making sure that every form of customer payment can be accepted to maximize the sales opportunity

The point is that non-bank forms of electronic payments are here to stay, and you can expect them to continue to increase in use as the world moves rapidly toward a cashless economy.

From a business perspective, it's almost impossible to build payment systems that don't incorporate the use of non-bank forms of payments because this has simply become the norm in today's economy. This doesn't mean that non-bank payments have no risk. Plenty of traps and problems may arise when using non-bank forms of electronic payments, including these:

>> Having to absorb merchant fees when accepting customer payments electronically (for example, PayPal charge the merchant 2.99 percent to process the payment)

>> Controlling consumer personal information (such as credit card numbers) that could possibly be stolen and exposed

>> Having to reconcile cash receipts from multiple electronic payment providers against your sales records (to match and properly apply cash receipts)

>> Maintaining agreements with multiple electronic payment providers

REMEMBER

The management and accounting issue is straightforward: The benefit of processing payments electronically must be analyzed and compared with the associated risks and costs. This may seem like a relatively simple cost-benefit analysis (on the surface), where the benefits of ease of customer payment are apparent, but the costs need to be thoroughly understood because they relate to not just a stated "processing fee" but also the risks a company takes with managing large amounts of data (and the company's responsibility to protect this data).

Using enhanced accounting controls

One important point we want to make on the electronic payments front is the need for businesses to develop, implement, and execute enhanced accounting controls, policies, and procedures to proactively manage this new environment. Here, we offer four examples of how companies have developed enhanced controls:

» **Using real-time reconciliations:** A direct-to-consumer company may generate hundreds of thousands of dollars of sales during a peak holiday season such as Black Friday. When this happens, literally hundreds of individual sales are processed with most payments coming from credit cards, debit cards, PayPal, and other sources. To ensure that all customer sales are matched with customer payments, real-time reconciliations (daily or even more frequently) are performed to ensure that all payments are received and recorded correctly.

» **Offloading data risks:** Companies may rely on front-end or consumer-facing computer platforms such as Shopify to act as a retail storefront on the web. On top of a company like Shopify providing a well-developed and sophisticated platform (which you don't have to create), Shopify can assist with processing the electronic payments so that vital customer personal information such as a full credit card number is maintained by Shopify (and protected with their security systems); your company doesn't have to maintain it. And since you don't maintain this information, the risk of data hacks or breaches is reduced, lowering your financial risk and exposure.

» **Monitoring frequency:** In the old days, a bank account could be reviewed and reconciled once a month. Not so today, as bank activity and transactions are constantly monitored for unusual or suspicious activity on a daily, hourly, or even real-time basis. Working closely with your bank and merchant account provider to develop systems to actively monitor financial transactions represents a big win for both parties.

» **Securing cyber-insurance:** Specific forms of insurance are now widely available for purchase to assist with the financial losses that may arise from data breaches, hacks, and so on. Simply put, a cyber-insurance policy, also referred to as "cyber-risk insurance" or "cyber-liability insurance" coverage, is a financial product that enables businesses to transfer the costs involved with recovery from a cyber-related security breach or similar events. Twenty years ago, this type of insurance was a "nice to have" item. Today, it's a must-have.

CONSIDERING THE FUTURE OF CRYPTOCURRENCIES

We would be remiss if we didn't include a brief discussion on the use of cryptocurrencies, such as Bitcoin and Ethereum (two of the more popular choices) and associated blockchain technology. The first item to consider is whether cryptocurrencies are even a currency; today, they are not considered currency but are referred to as an asset class (more appropriate in today's environment). Given that cryptocurrencies do not represent legal tender of a government or country, have highly volatile price environments, are subject to technology risks (because they basically represent ownership of a series of digits), are not widely accepted as a form of payment, don't have the global economic markets of well-established currencies (such as the U.S. dollar), and may be subject to significant government regulations, it's difficult, at the time of this book's publication, to classify cryptocurrencies as actual currencies on par with the Canadian dollar, Japanese yen, Chinese yuan, and the European euro. Rather, cryptocurrencies are still functioning at the capacity of a speculative asset class that is rapidly evolving in the new digital-based economy.

However, cryptocurrencies in one form or another will most likely find their footing down the road to become more widely accepted, stable, and able to operate within an equitable market (for buying, selling, and trading), thus eventually becoming a potential additional non-bank form of electronic payments (covered earlier in this chapter). Here's some advice on the cryptocurrency front:

- Educate yourself thoroughly on the pros and cons of using this form of electronic payment.

- Tread lightly to start; the cryptocurrency space most likely will remain volatile for the foreseeable future.

Managing the Accounting Function in the On-Demand World

To close this chapter, we cover a variety of items related to managing the accounting function in a world that now is built on accessing large amounts of data or information, efficiency in storing this data or information, speed in accessing the information, and widespread availability to the information. The topics highlighted in the following sections present a basic overview or sampling of the types of changes that are occurring at breakneck speed as the old days of the green eye-shaded bean counter give way to a tech-enabled financial information provider with access to vital information at the touch of a button.

Source documentation

In the olden days, most source documentation was stored in a "hard format" (such as paper-based storage systems that required large amounts of space). Not so today because the transition to paperless storage systems is now the norm rather than the exception. Companies actively maintain accounting records such as customer sales orders and invoices, shipping or packing slips, purchase orders, vendor/supplier invoices, employee wage records, third-party contracts, and the list goes on and on in a digital format. Basically, anything that was paper-based is now being stored in an electronic format (such as a PDF, JPEG, or PNG) or computer coded.

The good news is that the storage of source documentation is much more efficient, cheaper, and more readily accessible. The bad news is that with so much source documentation available electronically, if proper security and access controls have not been implemented, the risk of vital documents being accessed by unauthorized personnel or outside parties has become much more elevated (see the next section).

Data rooms

Data rooms or internal data centers are virtual locations where basically all digitized documentation resides. Companies such as Dropbox specialize in helping companies organize and safeguard almost any type of digital company data, ranging from simple customer orders or copies of vendor invoices to confidential company formation documentation, third-party agreements, and the like. Businesses have the option to outsource digital documentation storage to a company like Dropbox or manage this process internally by maintaining their own computer systems. Either way, convenience, security, and accessibility represent advantages of using data rooms because controls can be built in to give different parties access to different levels of company documentation. For example, a company may want to give its human resources manager access to employee contracts and pay records (in a specific subfolder maintained in the data room) but would not want to provide this person access to critical financing documentation.

WARNING

Well-developed and managed (we cannot emphasize this point enough) data rooms are now the norm, but a word of caution is warranted. Proactive management of data rooms is essential to ensure that only authorized personnel have access to the correct folder or subfolder of source documentation.

Financial reporting

Review and control of input and output is more important now than ever before. With online, cloud-based accounting systems, it can be tempting to simply push a button for a pre-formatted report, and voilà, just like that, out comes a financial report such as an income statement or balance sheet for review with the management team. We cannot tell you how many times we've seen underqualified or inexperienced parties access the accounting system, produce a financial report, and think they have become an expert because the accounting system is just so easy to use. Worse yet, they then distribute it to a third party without thinking about it twice. (Translation: This is a fatal error.)

REMEMBER

The problem is parties who are not qualified accountants or financial professionals may not understand that critical adjustments and/or financial transactions must be captured in the accounting system to ensure that CART (complete, accurate, reliable, and timely) financial reports are ready and available for management review. We cannot emphasize enough that tight controls must be maintained by a business to ensure that critical financial reports and statements are released at the appropriate time, after review by qualified parties, and distributed only to the right parties, supported by a reliable analysis (to assist with understanding the financial results).

Flash reports and KPIs

The real-time economy we live and operate in has resulted in an explosion of what are referred to as flash reports (targeted, high-frequency, compressed reports) that generally focus on highlighting a company's KPIs (key performance indicators). For example, a direct-to-consumer company may launch a new social media advertising campaign on Instagram over a three-hour period during a holiday shopping window and wants to have access to sales data from different advertising strategies instantaneously (in other words, a quick flash report). This real situation happens every day.

REMEMBER

What is important to remember about this type of reporting is that the financial and operational data doesn't always originate from the accounting system but may come from a consumer-facing sales technology platform or other type of company technology management system. Here, the accounting function needs to "extend" beyond the base accounting system to develop and implement controls that ensure that the financial information being reported from another source technology platform is consistent with the financial transactions being captured and reported in the accounting system. Again, we cannot tell you how many horror stories have resulted from two different technology systems not being properly monitored and reconciled to ensure consistency and accuracy of financial reporting. These days, financial information is seemingly anywhere and everywhere and easily accessible, which runs the risk of creating an exponential increase in reporting errors and mistakes (if proper controls and security have not been established).

Accounting and financial analysis tools

Countless financial and accounting technology tools, resources, platforms, systems, and the like are available today to assist companies with managing their business. These tools range from the likes of the ever-popular Excel or Google Docs to very specific software platforms that sit on top of accounting systems to help generate periodic financial statements. It would be pointless to attempt to list every financial or accounting technology-based tool available; by the time we prepared the list, a quarter of the systems would be gone, replaced by new solutions.

REMEMBER

These tools are very valuable to the accounting and financial groups within a business but must be managed closely for a couple of reasons:

>> First, the business financial information contained in these tools (such as an Excel spreadsheet used to house a company's financial forecasts) tends to be very confidential and needs to be tightly controlled.

>> Second, these tools often are very easy to use, update, change, edit, and so on (by multiple parties), and when changes are made, audit trails (the what and why and how of changes) are often sacrificed.

Disciplined accounting management of these tools is just as important as with the company's primary accounting system used to capture transactional and financial data.

IN THIS CHAPTER

» **Structuring the business to attract capital**

» **Partnering with others in business**

» **Looking out for number one in a sole proprietorship**

» **Choosing the best structure for income tax**

Chapter **5**

Deciding the Legal Structure for a Business

The obvious reason for investing in a business rather than putting your hard-earned money in a safer type of investment is the potential for greater rewards. Note the word *potential*. As one of the partners or shareowners of a business, you're entitled to your fair share of the business's profit — but at the same time, you're subject to the risk that the business could go down the tubes, taking your money with it.

Ignore the risks for a moment and look at just the rosy side of the picture: Suppose the doohickeys that your business sells become the hottest products of the year. Sales are booming, and you start looking at buying a five-bedroom mansion with an ocean view. Don't jump into that down payment just yet — you may not get as big a piece of the sales revenue pie as you're expecting. You may not see *any* profit until after all the claims on sales revenue are satisfied. And even if you do, the way the profit is divided among owners depends on the business's legal structure.

This chapter shows you how legal structure determines your share of the profit — and how changes beyond your control can make your share less valuable. It also explains how the legal structure determines whether the business as a separate entity pays income taxes.

Recognizing the Legal Roots of Business Entities

REMEMBER

One of the most important aspects of our legal system, from the business and economic point of view, is that the law enables *entities* to be created for conducting business activities. These entities are separate and distinct from the individual business owners. Business entities have many of the rights of individuals. Business entities can own property and enter into contracts, for example. In starting a business venture, one of the first things the founders have to do is select which type of structure to use — which usually requires the services of a lawyer who knows the federal and provincial laws. We also recommend that you consult with an accountant who will help you decide when it would be a good time to incorporate.

A business may have just one owner, or two or more owners. A one-owner unincorporated business may choose to operate as a *sole proprietorship*; a multi-owner business must choose to be a *corporation* or a *partnership*. The most common type of business is a corporation (although the number of sole proprietorships would be larger if you count part-time, self-employed persons in this category).

No legal structure is inherently better than another; which one is right for a particular business is something that the business's owners need to decide at the time of starting the business. The advice of a lawyer is usually needed. The following discussion focuses on the basic types of entities that owners can use for their business. Later, this chapter explains how the structure determines the income tax paid by the business and its owners, which is always an important consideration.

Studying the Sources of Business Capital

Every business needs capital. *Capital* provides the money for the assets a business needs to carry on its operations. Common examples of assets are the working cash balance a business needs for day-to-day activities, products held in inventory for sale, and long-life operating assets (buildings, machines, computers, office equipment, and so on). One of the first questions that sources of business capital ask is: How is the business entity organized legally? In other words, which specific form or legal structure is being used by the business? The different types of business legal entities present different risks and offer different rewards to business capital sources.

Before examining the different types of business entities in detail, it's useful to look at the basic sources of business capital. In other words, where does a business get capital? Regardless of the particular legal structure a business uses, the answer comes down to two basic sources: debt and equity. *Debt* refers to the money borrowed by a business, and *equity* refers to money invested in the business by owners. Making profit also provides equity capital. No matter which type of business entity form that it uses, every business needs a foundation of ownership (equity) capital to persuade people to loan money to the business.

In starting a new business from scratch, the founders typically must invest a lot of *sweat equity,* which refers to the gruelling effort and long hours to get the business off the ground and up and running. The founders don't get paid for their sweat equity, and it does not show up in the business's accounting records.

Tapping two sources of owners' equity

REMEMBER

The rights and risks of a business's owners are completely different than those of its debt holders. Whether you're a budding entrepreneur about to start up a new business venture or a seasoned business investor, you need to understand the fundamental differences between the debt holders and shareowners of a business. Every business — regardless of how big it is and whether it's publicly or privately owned — has owners; no business can get all the capital it needs just by borrowing. Every business needs a continuing base of ownership (equity) capital. Without the foundation of equity capital, a business wouldn't be able to get credit from its suppliers, and it couldn't borrow money. As they say in politics, the owners must have some skin in the game.

The equity capital in a business always carries the risk of loss to its owners. So, what do the owners expect and want from taking on this risk? Their expectations include the following:

>> They expect the business to earn profit on their equity capital in the business, and they expect to share in that profit by receiving cash distributions from profit and from increases in the value of their shares — with no guarantee of either.

>> They may expect to directly participate in the management of the business, or they may plan to hire someone else to manage the business. In smaller businesses, an owner may be one of the managers and may sit on the board of directors. In very large businesses, however, an owner is just one of thousands; they elect a representative board of directors to oversee the managers of the business and protect the interests of the non-manager owners.

>> Looking down the line to the eventual demise of the business, owners expect to receive a proportionate share of the proceeds if the business is sold or to receive a proportionate share of ownership when another business buys or merges with the business. They may end up with nothing if the business goes kaput and nothing remains after paying off the creditors of the business.

When owners invest money in a business, the accountant records the amount as an increase in the company's *cash* account. And, to keep things in balance, the amount invested in the business is also recorded as an increase in an *owners' equity* account. Owners' equity also increases when a business makes profit. (Refer to Chapters 6 and 9 for more on this subject.) Because of the two different reasons for increases, the owners' equity of an incorporated business is divided into two separate types of accounts:

>> **Invested capital:** This type of owners' equity account records the amounts of money that owners have invested in the business, which could have been many years ago. Owners may invest additional capital from time to time, but generally speaking they cannot be forced to put additional money in a business. *Note:* A business may keep two or more accounts for invested capital from its owners.

>> **Retained earnings:** The profit earned by a business over the years that has been retained and not distributed to its owners is accumulated in this account. If all profit had been distributed every year, retained earnings would have a zero balance. (If a business has never made a profit, its accumulated loss would cause retained earnings to have a negative balance, which generally is called a *deficit*.) If none of the annual profits of a business had been distributed to its owners, the balance in retained earnings would be the cumulative profit earned by the business since it opened its doors (net of any losses along the way).

Whether to retain part or all of annual net income is one of the most important decisions that a business makes; distributions from profit have to be decided at the highest level of a business. A growing business needs additional capital for expanding its assets, and increasing the debt load of the business usually cannot supply all the additional capital. So, the business *ploughs back* some of its profit for the year rather than giving it out to the owners. In the long run this may be the best course of action because it provides additional capital for growth.

Leveraging equity capital with debt

Suppose a business has $10 million in total assets (you find assets in the balance sheet). This doesn't mean that it has $10 million in owners' equity. Assuming the business has a good credit rating, it probably has some amount of trade credit, which is recorded in *accounts payable* and *accrued expenses payable* liability accounts (as we explain in Chapter 7). These are non-interest-bearing liabilities that originate from the normal operations of the business.

Let's say that the business's accounts payable and accrued expenses payable liabilities total $3 million. This leaves $7 million to account for. It's possible that all $7 million is provided by *equity capital* (that is, the sum of money invested by its owners plus the accumulated balance of retained earnings). But more likely, the business borrowed money, which is recorded in *notes payable* and similarly titled liability accounts.

The basic idea of borrowing money is to leverage the owners' equity capital. For example, suppose the $7 million is split between $2 million debt and $5 million owners' equity. The business has $2 debt capital for every $5 equity capital. The business is *leveraging*, or building on its equity capital; it's using its equity capital to increase the total capital of the business. How much debt should a business take on?

Some businesses depend on debt for more than half of their total capital. In contrast, some businesses have virtually no debt at all. You find many examples of both public and private companies that have no borrowed money. But as a general rule, most businesses carry some debt (and therefore have interest expense).

The debt decision isn't strictly an accounting responsibility — although after the decision to borrow money is made, the accountant is involved in recording debt and interest transactions. Deciding on debt is the responsibility of the chief financial officer (CFO) and chief executive officer of the business. In medium-sized and smaller businesses, the chief accounting officer (controller) may also serve as the CFO. In larger businesses, two different persons hold the top financial and accounting positions.

TIP

The loan contract between a business and its lender may prohibit the business from distributing profit to owners during the period of the loan. Or, the loan agreement may require that the business maintain a minimum cash balance. In general, the higher the ratio of debt to equity, the more likely a lender will charge higher interest rates and will insist on tougher conditions because the lender has higher risk that the business might default on the loan.

WARNING

When borrowing money, the president or another officer in their capacity as an official agent of the business signs a note payable document in favour of the bank or other lender. In addition, the bank (or other lender) may ask the major investors in a smaller, privately owned business to sign a loan guarantee or note payable *as individuals*, in their personal capacities — and it may ask their spouses to sign the note payable as well or a separate legal document of guarantee may be used. Definitely understand your personal obligations if you are inclined to sign a business's note payable. You take the risk that you may have to pay some part or perhaps the entire amount of the loan from your personal assets.

Incorporating a Business

The law views a *corporation* as a real, live person. Like an adult, a corporation is treated as a distinct and independent individual who has rights and responsibilities. (A corporation can't be sent to jail, but its officers can be put in the slammer if they are convicted of using the corporate entity for carrying out fraud.) A corporation's "birth certificate" is akin to its articles of incorporation, filed federally under the Canada Business Corporations Act or provincially under the terms of a provincial corporations act. A corporation must have a legal name, of course, like an individual. Some names cannot be used — Shopify, for example, because it is an existing company. Consult a lawyer on this point.

Just as a child is separate from their parents, a corporation is separate from its owners. The corporation is responsible for its own debts. The bank can't come after you if your neighbour defaults on their loan, and the bank can't come after you if the corporation you have invested money in goes belly up. If a corporation doesn't pay its debts, its creditors can seize only the corporation's assets, not the assets of the corporation's owners.

REMEMBER

This important legal distinction between the obligations of the business entity and its individual owners is known as *limited liability* — that is, the limited liability of the owners. Even if the owners have deep pockets, they have no legal exposure for the unpaid debts of the corporation (unless they've used the corporate shell to defraud creditors). So, when you invest money in a corporation as an owner, you know that the most you can lose is the amount you put in. You may lose every dollar you put in, but the corporation's creditors cannot reach through the corporate entity to grab your assets to pay off the business's liabilities. You may lose more than just your investment if you personally guaranteed debt to a creditor or a bank. (But, to be prudent, check with your lawyer on this issue — just to be sure.)

Issuing shares

When raising equity capital, a corporation issues ownership shares to persons who invest money in the business. These ownership shares are documented by share certificates, which state the name of the owner and how many shares are owned. The corporation has to keep a register of how many shares everyone owns, of course. (An owner can be an individual, another corporation, or any other legal entity such as a trust.) Actually, many public corporations use an independent agency to maintain their ownership records. In some situations shares are issued in *book entry form*, which means you get a formal letter (not a fancy engraved share certificate) attesting to the fact that you own so many shares. Your legal ownership is recorded in the official "books," or share register of the corporation.

The owners of a corporation are called *shareholders* because they own shares issued by the corporation. The shares are *negotiable*, meaning the owner can sell them at any time to anyone willing to buy them without having to get the approval of the corporation or other shareholders. *Publicly owned corporations* are those whose shares are traded in public markets, such as the Toronto Stock Exchange (TSX), New York Stock Exchange, and NASDAQ. A ready market exists for the buying and selling of shares.

The shareholders of a private business have the right to sell their shares, although they may enter into a binding agreement restricting this right. For example, suppose you own 20,000 of the 100,000 shares issued by the business. So, you have 20 percent of the voting power in the business (one share has one vote). You may agree to offer your shares to the other shareowners before offering the shares to someone else outside the present group of shareholders. Or, you may agree to offer the business itself the right to buy back the shares. In these ways, the continuing shareholders of the business control who owns its shares.

Offering different classes of shares

TIP

Before you invest in shares, you should ascertain whether the corporation has issued just one *class* of shares. A class is one group, or type, of shares all having identical rights; every share is the same as every other share. A corporation can issue two or more different classes of shares. For example, a business may offer Class A and Class B shares, where Class A shareholders get to vote in elections for the board of directors but Class B shareholders do not get a vote.

Federal and provincial incorporation statutes generally are liberal when it comes to allowing corporations to issue different classes of shares. The differences between classes of shares are significant and affect the value of the shares of each class.

Two classes of corporate shares are fundamentally different: *common shares* and *preferred shares*. Two basic differences are as follows:

>> Preferred shareholders are promised a certain amount of cash dividends each year (note we wrote *promised*, not *guaranteed*), but the corporation makes no such promises to its common shareholders. Each year, the board of directors must decide how much, if any, cash dividends to distribute to its common shareholders.

>> Common shareholders have the most risk. A business that ends up in deep financial trouble is obligated to pay off its liabilities first, and then its preferred shareholders. By the time the common shareholders get their turn, the business may have no money left to pay them.

Neither of these points makes common shares seem too attractive. But other considerations exist:

>> Preferred shares usually are promised a *fixed* (limited) dividend per year and typically don't have a claim to any profit beyond the stated amount of dividends. (Some corporations issue *participating* preferred shares, which give the preferred shareholders a contingent right to more than just their basic amount of dividends. This topic is too technical to explore further in this book.)

>> Preferred shareholders typically don't have voting rights. In other words, preferred shareholders usually do not participate in electing the corporation's board of directors or vote on other critical issues facing the corporation.

The main advantages of common shares, therefore, are the ability to vote in corporation elections and the unlimited *upside potential*: After a corporation's obligations to its preferred shares are satisfied, the rest of the profit it has earned accrues to the benefit of its common shareholders.

Here are some important things to understand about common shares:

>> Each share is equal to every other share in its class. This way, ownership rights are standardized, and the main difference between two shareholders is how many shares each owns.

>> The only time a business must return shareholders' capital to them is when the majority of shareholders vote to liquidate the business (in part or in total). Other than this, the business's managers don't have to worry about losing the shareholders' capital.

>> A shareholder can sell their shares at any time, without the approval of the other shareholders. However, as we mention earlier, the shareholders of a privately owned business may agree to certain restrictions on this right when they first became shareholders in the business.

>> Shareholders can put themselves in key management positions, or they may delegate the task of selecting top managers and officers to the *board of directors*, which is a small group of persons selected by the shareholders to set the business's policies and represent shareholders' interests.

Now, don't get the impression that if you buy 100 shares of Canadian Tire you can get yourself elected to its board of directors. On the other hand, if Warren Buffett bought 100 million shares of Canadian Tire, he could very well get himself on the board. The relative size of your ownership interest is key. If you put up more than half the money in a business, you can put yourself on the board and elect yourself president of the business. The shareholders who own 50 percent plus one share constitute the controlling group that decides who goes on the board of directors.

Note: The all-shares-are-created-equal aspect of corporations is a practical and simple way to divide ownership, but its inflexibility can be a hindrance, too. Suppose the shareholders want to delegate to one individual extraordinary power, or to give one person a share of profit out of proportion to their share ownership. The business can make special compensation arrangements for key executives and ask a lawyer for advice on the best way to implement the shareholders' intentions. Nevertheless, certain incorporating statutes require that certain voting matters be settled by a majority vote of shareholders. If enough shareholders oppose a certain arrangement, the other shareholders may have to buy them out to gain a controlling interest in the business.

Determining the market value of shares

If you want to sell your shares, how much can you get for them? A world of difference exists between owning shares of a public corporation and owning shares of a private corporation. *Public* means there is an active market in the shares of the business; the shares are *liquid*. They can be converted into cash in a flash by calling your stockbroker or going online to sell them. You can go to one of many websites (such as http://ca.finance.yahoo.com) that provide current market prices. But shares in privately owned businesses aren't publicly traded, so how can you determine the value of your shares in such a business?

Well, we don't mean to sidestep the question, but shareholders of a private business don't worry about the market value of their shares — until they are serious about selling their shares, or when something else happens that demands putting a value on the shares. If you divorce your spouse, a value is needed for the shares you own, as part of the divorce property settlement. When the business itself is put up for sale, a value is put on the business; dividing this value by the number of shares issued by the business gives the value per share.

Other than during events like these, which require that a value be put on the shares, the shareowners of a private business get along quite well without knowing a definite value for their shares. This doesn't mean they have no idea regarding the value of their business and what their shares are worth. They read the financial statements of their business, so they know its profit performance and financial condition. In the backs of their minds they should have a reasonably good estimate regarding how much a willing buyer might pay for the business and the price they would sell their shares for. So even though they don't know the exact market value of their shares, they are not completely in the dark about that value.

TIP

Space does not permit an extended discussion of business valuation methods here. Generally speaking, the value of ownership shares in a private business depends heavily on the recent profit performance and the current financial condition of the business, as reported in its latest financial statements. The financial statements may have to be "trued up," as they say, to bring some of the historical cost values in the balance sheet up to current replacement or market values.

REMEMBER

Business valuation is highly dependent on the specific circumstances of each business. The present owners may be eager to sell out, and they may be willing to accept a low price instead of taking the time to drive a better bargain. The potential buyers of the business may see opportunities that the present owners don't see or aren't willing to pursue. Even Warren Buffett, who has a well-deserved reputation for knowing how to value a business, admits that he's made some real blunders along the way.

Keeping alert for dilution of share value

WARNING

Watch out for developments that cause a *dilution effect* on the value of your shares — that is, that cause each share to drop in value. Keep in mind that sometimes the dilution effect may be the result of a good business decision, so even though your share of the business has decreased in the short term, the long-term profit performance of the business (and, therefore, your investment) may benefit. But you need to watch for these developments closely. The following situations cause a dilution effect:

>> A business issues additional shares at the going market value but doesn't really need the additional capital — the business is in no better profit-making position than it was before issuing the new shares. For example, a business may issue new shares to let a newly hired chief executive officer buy them. The immediate effect may be a dilution in the value per share. Over the long term, however, the new CEO may turn the business around and lead it to higher levels of profit that increase the shares' value.

>> A business issues new shares at a discount below its shares' current value. For example, the business may issue a new batch of shares at a price lower than the current market value to employees who take advantage of an employee share-purchase plan. Selling shares at a discount, by itself, has a dilution effect on the market value of the shares. But in the grand scheme of things, the share-purchase plan may motivate employees to achieve higher productivity levels, which can lead to superior profit performance of the business.

Now consider this: The main purpose of issuing additional shares is to deliberately dilute the market value per share. For example, a publicly owned corporation doubles its number of shares by issuing a two-for-one *stock split*. Each shareholder gets one new share for each share currently owned, without investing any additional money in the business. As you would expect, the market value of the stock drops in half — which is exactly the purpose of the split, because the lower share price is better for stock market trading (according to conventional wisdom).

Recognizing conflicts between shareholders and managers

Shareholders (including managers who own shares in the business) are primarily concerned with the business's profit performance; the dividends they receive and the value of their shares depend on it. Managers' jobs depend on living up to the business's profit goals. But although shareholders and managers have the common goal of optimizing profit, they have certain inherent conflicts of interest:

>> The more money that managers make in wages and benefits, the less shareholders see in bottom-line net income. Shareholders obviously want the best managers for the job, but they don't want to pay any more than they have to. In many corporations, top-level managers, for all practical purposes, set their own salaries and compensation packages.

REMEMBER

Most public business corporations establish a compensation committee consisting of *outside* directors that sets the salaries, incentive bonuses, and other forms of compensation of the top-level executives of the organization. An outside director is one who has no management position in the business and who, therefore, should be more objective and should not be beholden to the business's chief executive. This is good in theory, but it doesn't work out all that well in practice — mainly because the top-level executive of a large public business typically has the dominant voice in selecting the persons to serve on its board of directors. Being a director of a large public corporation is a prestigious position, to say nothing of the annual fees that are fairly substantial at most corporations.

>> The question of who should control the business — managers, who are hired for their competence and are intimately familiar with the business, or shareholders, who may have no experience relevant to running this business but whose money makes the business tick — can be tough to answer.

In ideal situations, the two sides respect each other's contributions to the business and use this tension constructively. Of course, the real world is far from ideal, and in some companies, managers control the board of directors rather than the other way around.

As an investor, be aware of these issues and how they affect the return on your investment in a business. If you don't like the way your business is run, you can sell your shares and invest your money elsewhere. (However, if the business is privately owned, possibly no ready market exists for its shares, which puts you between a rock and a hard place.)

WHERE PROFIT GOES IN A CORPORATION

Suppose that a private business earned $1.32 million net income for the year just ended and has issued 400,000 shares. Divide net income by the number of shares, and you come up with *earnings per share* of $3.30. Assume that the business paid $400,000 cash dividends during the year, or $1.00 per share. The retained earnings account thus increased $2.30 per share (earnings per share minus dividends per share). Although shareholders don't have the cash to show for it, their investment is better off by $2.30 per share, which shows up in the balance sheet as an increase in the retained earnings account. They can hope that the business will use the cash provided from profit to increase future profit, which should lead to higher cash dividends.

Now, suppose the business is a public company that is 1,000 times larger. It earned $1.32 billion on its 400 million shares and distributed $400 million in cash dividends. You may think that the market value should increase $2.30 per share, because the business earned this much per share that it retained in the business and did not distribute to its shareholders. Your thinking is quite logical: Profit is an increase in the net assets of a business (assets less liabilities, which is also called *net worth*). The business is $2.30 per share "richer" at the end of the year than it was at the start of the year, due to the profit it earned and retained.

Yet it's entirely possible that the market price of the shares actually *decreased* during the year. Market prices are governed by psychological, political, and economic factors that go beyond the information in the financial reports of a business. Financial statements are only one of the information sources that investors use in making their buy-and-sell decisions. Chapters 14 and 19 explain how investors use the information in financial reports.

Creating a Partnership

Suppose you're starting a new business with one or more other owners, but you don't want it to be a corporation. You can choose to create a *partnership*, which is the main alternative to the corporate form of business.

REMEMBER

A partnership is also called a *firm*. You don't see this term used to refer to a corporation nearly as often as you do to a partnership. The term *firm* connotes an association of a group of individuals working together in a business or professional practice.

Compared with the relatively rigid structure of corporations, a partnership allows the division of management authority, profit sharing, and ownership rights among the owners to be flexible. Partnerships avoid the two stages of taxation that corporations are subject to (see "Choosing the Best Structure for Income

Tax," later in this chapter, for details). Partnerships also differ from corporations with respect to owners' liability. A partnership's owners are in two categories:

>> **General partners** are subject to *unlimited liability*. If a business can't pay its debts, its creditors can reach into general partners' personal assets. General partners have the authority and responsibility to manage the business. They are roughly equivalent to the president and other high-level managers of a business corporation. The general partners usually divide authority and responsibility among themselves, and often they elect one member of their group as the senior general partner or elect a small executive committee to make major decisions.

>> **Limited partners** escape the unlimited liability that the general partners have hanging around their necks. Limited partners are not responsible, as individuals, for the liabilities of the partnership entity. These junior partners have ownership rights to the business's profit, but they don't generally participate in the high-level management of the business. A partnership must have one or more general partners; not all partners can be limited partners.

Many large partnerships copy some of the management features of the corporate form — for example, a senior partner who serves as chair of the general partners' executive committee acts in much the same way as the chair of a corporation's board of directors.

REMEMBER

Generally, a partner can't sell their interest to an outsider without the consent of all the other partners. You can't just buy your way into a partnership; the other partners have to approve your joining the partnership. In contrast, you can buy shares and thereby become part owner of a corporation without the approval of the other shareholders.

The partnership or LLP agreement (see the sidebar "Limited Liability: Partnerships and LLPs") specifies how to divide profit among the owners. Whereas owners of a corporation receive a share of profit directly proportional to the number of shares they own, a partnership or LLP does not have to divide profit according to how much each owner invested. Invested capital is only one of three factors that generally play into profit allocation in partnerships and LLPs:

>> **Treasure:** Owners may be rewarded according to how much of the *treasure* — invested capital — they contributed. So if Jane invested twice as much as Joe did, her cut of the profit may be twice as much as Joe's.

>> **Time:** Owners who invest more time in the business may receive more of the profit. Some partners or owners, for example, may generate more billable hours to clients than others, and the profit-sharing plan reflects this disparity. Some partners or owners may work only part-time, so the profit-sharing plan takes this factor into account.

LIMITED LIABILITY: PARTNERSHIPS AND LLPS

A *limited liability partnership* (LLP) is a general partnership where the partners, certain legislatively specified professionals, are not personally liable for the wrongful, negligent acts of their professional partners or the employees, agents, or representatives of the partnership. Partners, however, remain personally liable for other types of partnership debt. Lawyers and Chartered Professional Accountants (CPAs) are permitted to form an LLP.

These types of entities were created mainly in reaction to large damage awards in malpractice lawsuits against partners in the past. The professionals pleaded for protection from the unlimited liability of the partnership form of organization, which they had traditionally used. Until these new types of professional legal entities came along, the code of professional ethics of the various professions required that practitioners operate as a partnership (or as sole practitioners).

>> **Talent:** Regardless of capital and time, some partners bring more to the business than others. Maybe they have better business contacts, or they're better *rainmakers* (they have a knack for making deals happen), or they're celebrities whose names alone are worth a special share of the profit. Whatever it is that they do for the business, they contribute much more to the business's success than their capital or time suggests.

TIP

A partnership needs to maintain a separate capital (ownership) account for each partner. The total profit of the entity is allocated into these capital accounts, as spelled out in the partnership agreement. The agreement also specifies how much money each partner can withdraw from his capital account. For example, partners may be limited to withdrawing no more than 80 percent of their anticipated share of profit for the coming year, or they may be allowed to withdraw only a certain amount until they've built up their capital accounts.

Going It Alone: Sole Proprietorships

A *sole proprietorship* is, basically, the business arm of an individual who has decided not to carry on their business activity as a corporation or as a partnership. This is the default option. *Note:* Some of the features discussed previously, such as investors or shares, do not exist for sole proprietorships.

REMEMBER

This kind of business is not a separate legal entity, although it is a separate accounting entity. It's like the front porch of a house — attached to the house but a separate and distinct area. You may be a sole proprietor of a business without knowing it! An individual may do house repair work on a part-time basis or be a full-time barber who operates by themselves. Both are sole proprietorships. Anytime you regularly provide services for a fee, sell things at a flea market, or engage in any business activity whose primary purpose is to make profit, you are a sole proprietor. If you carry on business activity to make profit or income, the Canada Revenue Agency (CRA) requires that you file a separate schedule of business activity with your annual individual income tax return. This schedule summarizes your revenue and expenses from your sole proprietorship business.

As the sole owner (proprietor) you have *unlimited liability,* meaning that if your business can't pay all its liabilities, the creditors to whom your business owes money can come after your personal assets. Many part-time entrepreneurs may not know this or may put it out of their minds, but this is a big risk to take. We have friends who are part-time business consultants and they operate their consulting businesses as sole proprietorships. If they are sued for giving bad advice, all their personal assets are at risk — though they may be able to buy malpractice insurance to cover these losses.

Obviously, a sole proprietorship has no other owners to prepare financial statements for, but the proprietor should still prepare these statements to know how their business is doing. Banks usually require financial statements from sole proprietors who apply for loans.

TIP

One other piece of advice for sole proprietors: Although you don't have to separate invested capital from retained earnings on the balance sheet like corporations do, you should still show the changes in the fiscal year to your owner's equity — not only for the purpose of tracking the business but for the benefit of any future buyers of the business as well.

Choosing the Best Structure for Income Tax

While deciding which type of business structure is best for securing capital and managing their business, owners should also consider the dreaded income tax factor. They should know the key differences between the alternative kinds of business entities from the income tax point of view:

>> **Taxable-entity corporations:** Corporations are subject to income tax on their annual taxable income. Plus, their shareholders pay a second income tax on cash dividends that the business distributes to them from profit. To a large

extent, the tax laws provide lower tax rates to corporations on their taxable income and on taxable dividends so that the total amount of tax paid by the corporation and the shareholders is essentially the same as if the income were earned in a sole proprietorship. The owners (shareholders) of a corporation include the cash distributions from the after-tax profit that the business has paid to them in their individual income tax returns.

» **Pass-through entities — partnerships, proprietorships, and LLPs:** These entities do not pay income tax on their annual income; instead, they pass through their taxable income to their owners, who pick up their share of the taxable income on their individual tax returns. Depending on the number of partners, a *partnership return* must be filed with the CRA. In this partnership annual return, management informs the CRA how much income is allocated to each owner, and they send each owner a copy of this information to include with their individual income tax return.

REMEMBER

When two or more owners join together and invest money to start a business and don't incorporate and don't file legal papers to form an LLP, the law treats the business as a *de facto* partnership. Most partnerships are based on written agreements among the owners, but even without a formal, written agreement, a partnership exists in the eyes of the law.

WARNING

Once more, we must mention that choosing the best structure for a business is a complicated affair that goes beyond just the legal liability and income tax issues. You need to consider many other factors, such as the number of equity investors who will be active managers in the business, federal or provincial laws regarding the business's legal entities, and ease of transferring ownership shares. After you select a particular structure, changing it later is not easy. Asking the advice of a qualified professionals is well worth the money and can prevent costly mistakes.

Sometimes the search for the ideal structure that minimizes income tax and maximizes other benefits is like the search for the Holy Grail. Business owners should not expect to find the perfect answer — they have to compromise and balance the advantages and disadvantages. In its external financial reports, a business has to make clear which type of entity it is. The type of entity is an important factor to the business's lenders and other creditors, and of course to its owners.

2

Exploring Financial Statements

Get to know the ins and outs of the income statement, which summarizes the profit-making activities of the business and its bottom-line profit or loss for the period.

Understand how the balance sheet reports the financial condition of the business at a point in time — specifically on the last day of the profit period.

Expand your knowledge of what's included in the statement of cash flows, which reports the amount of cash produced from profits or consumed from losses, and how businesses identify and secure other sources of cash during the period and what the business did with this money (that is, what they used the cash for).

Make sure you're up to speed on the topic of adequate disclosure in external financial reports to the creditors and investors of a business. Business financial reports should reveal all the information that the creditors and investors are entitled to know.

IN THIS CHAPTER

» Looking at a typical income statement

» Becoming an active reader of income statements

» Understanding the substance of profit

» Handling out-of-the-ordinary gains and losses in the income statement

» Correcting misconceptions about profit

Chapter 6

Reporting Profit or Loss in the Income Statement

n this chapter, we lift up the hood and explain how the profit engine runs. Making a profit is the main financial goal of a business. (Not-for-profit organizations and government entities don't aim to make profit, but they should break even and avoid a deficit.) Accountants are the designated financial scorekeepers in the business world and are tasked with measuring the most important financial number of a business. We find profit accounting a fascinating challenge. For one thing, we have to understand how a business operates and its strategies to account for its profit.

REMEMBER

Of the three primary financial statements (the balance sheet, the income statement, and the statement of cash flows), the income statement is the financial statement that tends to be the most easily "manipulated" and the most targeted to, shall we say, embellish. The reason for this is that most external parties tend to focus their review or analysis first on the income statement with such questions as "How fast are top-line sales growing?" and "How much profit did the company generate?" (these are critical performance points of interest). Most companies make a concerted effort to prepare complete, accurate, reliable, and timely financial statements, including the income statement, that do not contain material misstatements, but it does pay to raise an eyebrow every now and then when a company's financial performance seems just a bit off or too good to be true.

Making a profit and accounting for it aren't nearly as simple as you may think. Managers have the demanding tasks of making sales and controlling expenses, and accountants have the tough tasks of measuring revenue and expenses and preparing reports that summarize the profit-making activities in a fair and reasonable fashion. Also, accountants are called on to help business managers analyze profit for decision making, which we explain in Chapters 15 and 16. And accountants prepare profit forecasts for management, which we cover in Chapter 17.

This chapter focuses on the financial consequences of making profit and how profit activities are reported in a business's external financial reports to its owners and lenders. Generally accepted accounting principles (GAAP) govern the recording and reporting of profit; see Chapter 2 for details about GAAP.

Presenting a Typical Income Statement

At the risk of oversimplification, we would say that businesses make profit three basic ways:

>> Selling *products* (with allied services) and controlling the cost of the products sold and other operating costs (for example, an auto manufacturer)

>> Selling *services* and controlling the cost of providing the services and other operating costs (such as a CPA or law firm)

>> *Investing* in assets that generate investment income and market value gains and controlling operating costs (banks, for example)

Obviously, this list isn't exhaustive, but it captures a large slice of business activity. In this chapter, we show you typical externally reported income statements for the different types of businesses. Products range from automobiles to computers to food to clothes to jewellery. The customers of a business may be the final consumers in the economic chain, or a business may sell to other businesses. Services range from transportation to entertainment to consulting, such as a CPA or law firms. Investment businesses range from mutual funds to banks to real estate development companies.

Looking at businesses that sell products

Figure 6-1 presents a typical profit report for a technology-based product-oriented business that also sells software and services; this report, called the *income statement*, would be sent to its outside (external) owners, creditors, and lenders. The report could just as easily be called the *net income statement* because the bottom-line profit term preferred by accountants is *net income*, but the word *net* is dropped off the title. Alternative titles for the external profit report include *statement of financial performance, earnings statement, operating statement, statement of operating results*, and *statement of earnings*. (Note that profit reports distributed to managers inside a business are usually called *P&L* [profit and loss] statements, but this moniker isn't used much in external financial reporting.)

QW Example Tech., Inc. Income Statement Sales of Both Products & Software Services for the Fiscal Year Ending 12/31/2024		
(all dollar amounts in thousands)	12/31/2023	12/31/2024
Sales Revenue, Net	$53,747	$71,064
Costs of Goods Sold	$23,314	$26,891
Gross Profit	$30,433	$44,173
Selling, General, & Administrative Expenses	$29,286	$36,678
Operating Income	$1,147	$7,495
Other Expenses (Income):		
Other Expenses & (Income)	$250	$250
Interest Expense	$400	$350
Total Other Expenses (Income)	$650	$600
Profit Before Income Taxes	$497	$6,895
Income Tax Expense	$174	$2,413
Net Income	$323	$4,482
Earnings Per Share	$0.32	$2.76

© John Wiley & Sons, Inc.

FIGURE 6-1: Typical income statement for a technology business.

The heading of an income statement identifies the business (which in this example is incorporated — thus the term "Inc." following the name), the financial statement title ("Income Statement"), and the time period summarized by the statement ("for the Fiscal Year Ended December 31, 2024"). We explain the legal organization structures of businesses in Chapter 5.

You may be tempted to start reading an income statement at the bottom line. But this financial report is designed for you to read from the top line (sales revenue) and proceed down to the last — the bottom line (net income). Each step down the ladder in an income statement involves the deduction of an expense. In Figure 6-1, five expenses are deducted from the sales revenue amount, and four profit lines are given:

>> **Gross profit (also called gross margin):** Sales revenue minus the cost of goods (products) sold expense but before operating and other expenses are considered

>> **Operating income (or loss):** Profit (or loss) before interest, other expenses and income tax expenses are deducted from gross profit

>> **Profit (or loss) before income tax:** Profit (or loss) after deducting interest expense and other expenses from operating earnings but before income tax expense

>> **Net income (or loss):** Final profit for the period after deducting all expenses from sales revenue, which is commonly called the *bottom line*

Although you see income statements with fewer than four profit lines, you seldom see an income statement with more.

The terminology in income statements varies from business to business, but you can usually determine the meaning of a term from its context and placement in the income statement.

TIP

Note in Figure 6-1 that below the net income line, the *earnings per share* (EPS) amount is reported. This important number equals net income divided by the number of ownership shares that the business corporation has issued and that are being held by its shareholders. All public corporations whose shares are traded in stock markets must report this key metric. EPS is compared to the current market price of the share to help judge whether the share is overpriced or underpriced. Private companies aren't required to report EPS, but they may decide to do so. If a private business decides to report its EPS, it should follow the accounting standard for calculating this number. We discuss the calculation of EPS in Chapter 12.

REMEMBER

The format for all businesses is to report two-year comparative financial statements in side-by-side columns — for the period just ended and for the same period one year ago. Some companies present three-year comparative financial statements. Two-year or three-year financial statements may be legally required, such as for public companies whose debt and shares are traded in a public market.

Looking at businesses that sell services

Figure 6-2 presents a typical income statement for a *service-oriented* business — in this example, one that operates a small-business consulting company.

Local Sample Service Co, Inc.
Income Statement
Sales of Services
for the Fiscal Year Ending
12/31/2024

	12/31/2024
Service Revenue, Net	$4,252,000
Direct Expenses	$2,625,000
Gross Profit	$1,627,000
Selling, General, & Administrative Expenses	$1,310,000
Operating Income	$317,000
Other Expenses (Income):	
Other Expenses & (Income)	$5,000
Interest Expense	$11,000
Total Other Expenses (Income)	$16,000
Profit Before Income Taxes	$301,000
Income Tax Expense	$800
Net Income	$300,200
Earnings Per Share	$3.00

© *John Wiley & Sons, Inc.*

FIGURE 6-2: Typical income statement for a business that sells services.

If a business sells services and does not sell products, it does not have a cost of goods sold expense (which reflects the costs of tangible products sold) but rather will often report a more generic costs of sales expense. Although not always required, almost all service-based businesses incur some type of direct expenses that vary with sales revenue. In our example, the direct expenses recorded as costs of sales include salaries, wages, employee benefits, travel, and similar types of expenses that are incurred as a direct result of generating consulting sales revenue. Service revenue less direct expenses equals gross profit. We should caution you that you'll find many variations on the basic income statement example in Figure 6-2. In particular, a business has a fair amount of latitude regarding the number of expense lines to disclose in its external income statement.

In Figure 6-2, the second profit line is *operating income* (or *operating earnings*), which is profit before interest expense, other expenses, and income tax expense. The service business example in Figure 6-2 discloses five broad types of expenses, similar to our technology company example in Figure 6-1.

TIP

The premise of financial reporting is that of *adequate disclosure*, but you find many variations in the reporting of expenses. A business — whether a product or service company — has fairly wide latitude regarding the number of expense lines to disclose in its external income statement. The owners of the company may not be satisfied that just three expenses provide enough detail about the operating activities of the business. Accounting standards do not dictate where particular expenses must be disclosed. The expenses can be disclosed on the income statement or in the notes to the financial statements.

Taking Care of Housekeeping Details

TIP

We want to point out a few things about income statements that accountants assume everyone knows but, in fact, are not obvious to many people. (Accountants do this a lot: They assume that the people using financial statements know a good deal about the customs and conventions of financial reporting, so they don't make things as clear as they could.) Here goes:

>> **Minus signs are missing.** Expenses are deductions from sales revenue, but you rarely see minus signs in front of expense amounts to indicate that they are deductions. Forget about minus signs in income statements and in other financial statements as well. Sometimes parentheses are put around a deduction to signal that it's a negative number, but that's the most you can expect to see.

>> **Your eye is drawn to the bottom line.** Putting a double underline under the final (bottom-line) profit number for emphasis is common practice but not

universal. Instead, net income might be shown in bold type. You generally don't see anything as garish as a fat arrow pointing to the profit number or a big smiley encircling the profit number — but again, tastes vary.

» **Profit isn't usually called** *profit.* As you see in Figures 6-1 and 6-2, bottom-line profit is called *net income.* Businesses use other terms as well, such as *net earnings* or just *earnings.* (Can't accountants agree on anything?) In this book, we use the terms *net income* and *profit* interchangeably.

» **You don't get details about sales revenue.** The sales revenue amount in an income statement is the combined total of all sales during the year. You can't tell how many different sales were made, how many different customers the company sold products to, or how the sales were distributed over the 12 months of the year. (Public companies are required to release quarterly income statements during the year, and they include a special summary of quarter-by-quarter results in their annual financial reports; private businesses may or may not release quarterly sales data.) Sales revenue does not include sales tax and GST/HST that the business collects from its customers and remits to the governments. Further, sales revenue is usually reported as a net figure, which includes gross sales less any deductions for sales returns, discounts, allowances, and the like.

Note: In addition to sales revenue from selling products and service revenue from selling services, a business may have income from other sources. For instance, a business may have earnings from investments in marketable securities. In its income statement, investment income goes on a separate line and is not commingled with sales revenue. Investment income would be reported as other income. (The businesses featured in Figures 6-1 and 6-2 do not have investment income.)

» **Gross margin matters.** The *cost of goods sold* expense is the cost of products sold to customers, the sales revenue of which is reported on the *sales revenue* line. The idea is to match up the sales revenue of goods sold with the cost of goods sold and show the *gross profit* (also called *gross margin*), which is the profit before other expenses are deducted. The other expenses could in total be more than gross margin, in which case the business would have a loss for the period.

A bottom-line loss usually has parentheses around it to emphasize that it's a negative number.

REMEMBER

» **Operating costs are lumped together.** The broad category *selling, general, and administrative expenses* (refer to Figure 6-1) consists of a wide variety of costs of operating the business and making sales. Some examples follow:

- Labour costs (wages, salaries, and benefits paid to employees)
- Marketing, advertising (social media, traditional print, and so on), selling, and promotional expenditures

- Insurance premiums

- Rent for using assets and/or property taxes on buildings and land

- Cost of utilities (such as gas and electric)

- Travel and entertainment costs

- Telecommunication and Internet charges

- Depreciation and amortization of operating assets that are used more than one year (including buildings, land improvements, cars and trucks, computers, office furniture, tools and machinery, and shelving)

- Legal and audit costs

As with sales revenue, you don't get much detail about operating expenses in a typical income statement as it's presented to the company's debtholders and shareholders. A business may disclose more information than you see in its income statement — mainly in the notes that are included with its financial statements. (We explain notes in Chapter 10.)

Knowing Your Job: Asking Questions!

The worst thing you can do when presented with an income statement is to be a passive reader. You should be inquisitive. An income statement is not fulfilling its purpose unless you grab it by its numbers and start asking questions.

For example, you should be curious regarding the business's size. Another question to ask is: How does profit compare with sales revenue for the year? Profit (net income) equals what's left over from sales revenue after you deduct all expenses. The business featured in Figure 6-1 produced $4.482 million profit from its $71.064 million sales revenue for the year, which equals 6.3 percent. This ratio of profit to sales revenue, often referred to as *profit margin*, means expenses absorbed 93.7 percent of sales revenue. Although it may seem rather thin, a 6.3 percent profit margin on sales is quite acceptable for many businesses. (Some businesses consistently make a bottom-line profit of 10 to 20 percent of sales, and others are satisfied with a 1 or 2 percent profit margin on sales revenue.) Profit ratios on sales vary widely from industry to industry.

REMEMBER

GAAP are relatively silent regarding which expenses have to be disclosed on the face of an income statement or elsewhere in a financial report. For example, the amount a business spends on advertising does not have to be disclosed. On the other hand, GAAP require disclosure of certain expenses, such as amortization and depreciation as well as interest and income tax expense on the income statement or in the notes to the financial statements.

In the example shown in Figure 6-1, expenses such as labour costs and advertising expenditures are buried in the all-inclusive *selling, general, and administrative expenses* line. (If the business manufactures the products it sells instead of buying them from another business, a good part of its annual labour cost is included in its *cost of goods sold* expense line.) Some companies disclose specific expenses such as advertising and marketing costs, research and development costs, and other significant expenses. In short, income statement expense disclosure practices vary considerably from business to business.

Another set of questions you should ask in reading an income statement concerns the business's *profit performance*. Refer again to the company's profit performance report (see Figure 6-1). Profit-wise, how did the business do? Underneath this question is the implicit question: Relative to what? Generally speaking, four sorts of benchmarks are used for evaluating profit performance:

>> Comparisons with broad, industry-wide performance averages

>> Comparisons with immediate competitors' performances

>> Comparisons with the business's performance in recent years

>> Comparisons with the internal forecast

Deconstructing Profit

Now that you've had the opportunity to read an income statement (see Figures 6-1 and 6-2), let us ask you a question: What *is* profit? We guess that your answer is, "Profit is revenue less expenses." That answer is correct, as far as it goes, but it doesn't go far enough. It doesn't tell us what profit consists of or the substance of profit.

In this section, we explain the anatomy of profit. Having read the product company's income statement, you now know that the business earned net income for the year ending December 31, 2024 (see Figure 6-1). Where's the profit? If you had to put your finger on the profit, where would you touch?

Recording profit works like a pair of scissors: You have a positive revenue blade and a negative expenses blade. Revenue and expenses have opposite effects. This leads to two questions: What is a revenue? And what is an expense?

Figure 6-3 summarizes the financial natures of revenue and expenses in terms of effects on assets and liabilities. Note the symmetrical framework of revenue and expenses. It's beautiful in its own way, don't you think? In any case, this summary framework is helpful for understanding the financial effects of revenue and expenses.

FIGURE 6-3:
Fundamental
natures of
revenue and
expenses.

	Asset	Liability
Revenue	+	−
Expense	−	+

© John Wiley & Sons Inc.

Revenue and expense effects on assets and liabilities

Here's the gist of the two-by-two matrix shown in Figure 6-3. In recording a sale, the bookkeeper increases a revenue account. The revenue account accumulates sale after sale during the period. So, at the end of the period, the total sales revenue for the period is the balance in the account. This amount is the cumulative end-of-period total of all sales during the period. All sales revenue accounts are combined for the period, and one grand total is reported in the income statement on the top line. As each sale (or other type of revenue event) is recorded, either an asset account is increased or a liability account is decreased.

TIP

We're sure that you follow that revenue increases an asset. For example, if all sales are made for cash, the company's cash account increases accordingly. However, you may have trouble understanding that certain revenue transactions are recorded with a decrease in a liability. Here's why: Customers may pay in advance for a product or service to be delivered later (examples are prepaying for airline tickets and making a down payment for future delivery of products). In recording such advance payments from customers, the business increases cash, of course, and increases a liability account usually called *deferred revenue*. The term *deferred* simply means postponed. When the product or service is delivered to the customer — and not before then — the bookkeeper records the amount of revenue that has now been earned *and* decreases the deferred revenue liability by the same amount.

Recording expenses is straightforward. When an expense is recorded, a specific expense account is increased, and either an asset account is decreased or a liability account is increased the same amount. For example, to record the cost of goods sold, the expense with this name is increased, say, $35,000, and in the same entry, the inventory asset account is decreased $35,000. Alternatively, an expense entry may involve a liability account instead of an asset account. For example, suppose the business receives a $10,000 bill from its CPA auditor that it will pay later. In recording the bill from the CPA, the audit expense account is increased $10,000 and a liability account called *accounts payable* is increased $10,000.

The summary framework of Figure 6-3 has no exceptions. Recording revenue and expenses (as well as gains and losses) always follows these rules. So where does this leave you for understanding profit? Profit itself doesn't show up in Figure 6-3, does it? Profit depends on amounts recorded for revenue and expenses.

REMEMBER

Revenue and expenses are originally recorded as increases or decreases in different asset and liability accounts. Cash is just one asset. We explain the other assets and the liabilities in the later section "Pinpointing the Assets and Liabilities Used to Record Revenue and Expenses."

Some businesses make sales for cash; cash is received at the time of the sale. In recording these sales, a revenue account is increased and the cash account is increased. Some expenses are recorded at the time of cutting a cheque to pay the expense. In recording these expenses, an appropriate expense account is increased and the cash asset account is decreased. However, for most businesses, the majority of their revenue and expense transactions do not simultaneously affect cash.

For most businesses, cash comes into play before or after revenue and expenses are recorded. For example, a business buys product from its supplier that it will sell sometime later to its customers. The purchase is paid for before the goods are sold. No expense is recorded until products are sold. Here's another example: A business makes sales on credit to its customers. In recording credit sales, a sales revenue account is increased and an asset account called *accounts receivable* is increased. Sometime later, the receivables are collected in cash. The amount of cash actually collected through the end of the period may be less than the amount of sales revenue recorded.

REMEMBER

Cash inflow from revenue is almost always different from revenue for the period. Furthermore, cash outflow for expenses is almost always different from expenses for the period. The lesson is this: Do not equate revenue with cash inflow, and do not equate expenses with cash outflows. The net cash flow from profit for the period — revenue inflow minus expense outflow — is bound to be higher or lower than the accounting-based measure of profit for the period. The income statement does not report cash flows!

This chapter lays the foundation for Chapter 8, where we explain cash flow from profit. Cash flow is an enormously important topic in every business. We're sure even Apple, with its huge treasure of marketable investments, worries about its cash flow.

Folding profit into retained earnings

The business in the Figure 6-1 example earned $4.482 million profit for the year. Therefore, its retained earnings account increased by this amount, because the bottom-line amount of net income for the period is recorded in this account. We know this for sure. But what we can't tell from the income statement is how the business's assets and liabilities were affected by its sale and expense activities during the period. One possible scenario is the following (in thousands of dollars):

$$\text{Assets} = \text{Liabilities} + \frac{\text{Owners' equity}}{\text{Invested capital} + \text{Retained earnings}}$$

$$+\$7,482 = +\$3,000 + \qquad\qquad \$4,482$$

This scenario works because the sum of the right-side changes ($3 million increase in liabilities plus $4.482 million increase in retained earnings) equals the $7.482 million increase in assets.

REMEMBER

After profit is determined for the period, which means that all revenue and expenses have been recorded for the period, the profit amount is entered as an increase in *retained earnings*. The $4.482 million net income for the year (refer to Figure 6-1) gets closed into retained earnings. (We discuss closing the books in Chapter 3.) Doing this keeps the accounting equation in balance.

In most situations, not all annual profit is distributed to owners; some is retained in the business. Unfortunately, the retained earnings account sounds like an asset in the minds of many people. It isn't! It's a source-of-assets account, not an asset account. It's on the right side of the accounting equation; assets are on the left side.

To summarize, the company's $4.482 million net income resulted in some combination of changes in its assets and liabilities, such that its shareholders' equity (specifically, its retained earnings) increased $4.482 million.

TIP

The financial gyrations in assets and liabilities from profit-making activities is especially important for business managers to understand and pay attention to, because they have to manage and control the changes. It would be dangerous simply to assume that making a profit has only beneficial effects on assets and liabilities. One of the main purposes of the statement of cash flows, which we discuss in Chapter 8, is to summarize the financial changes caused by the business's profit activities during the year.

Pinpointing the Assets and Liabilities Used to Record Revenue and Expenses

The sales and expense activities of a business involve inflows and outflows of cash, as we're sure you know. What you may not know, however, is that the profit-making process also involves four other basic assets and three basic types of liabilities. Cash is the pivotal asset. Revenue and expenses, sooner or later, lead to cash. But in the meantime, other asset and liability accounts are used to record the flow of profit activity. The following sections explain the main assets and liabilities used in recording revenue and expenses.

Making sales: Accounts receivable and deferred revenue

REMEMBER

Many businesses allow their customers to buy their products or services on credit. They use an asset account called *accounts receivable* to record the total amount owed to the business by its customers who have made purchases "on the cuff" and haven't paid yet. In most cases, a business doesn't collect all its receivables by the end of the year, especially for credit sales that occur in the last weeks of the year. It records the sales revenue and the cost of goods sold expense for these sales as soon as a sale is completed and products are delivered to the customers. This is one feature of the *accrual basis of accounting,* which records revenue when sales are made and records expenses when these costs are incurred. When sales are made on credit, the accounts receivable asset account is increased; later, when cash is received from the customer, cash is increased and the accounts receivable account is decreased. Collecting the cash is the follow-up transaction trailing along after the sale is recorded. In most cases, a business doesn't collect all of its credit sales by the end of the year, so it reports a balance for its accounts receivable in its end-of-period balance sheet (see Chapter 7).

In contrast to making sales on credit, some businesses collect cash before they deliver their products or services to customers. An example is concert tickets, where you buy and pay for a ticket days or weeks ahead of the performance. When a business receives advance payments from customers, it increases cash (of course) and increases a liability account called *deferred revenue*. Sales revenue isn't recorded until the product or service is delivered to the customer. When delivered sales revenue or service revenue is increased, the liability account is decreased, which reflects that part of the liability has been paid down by delivery of the product or service.

REMEMBER

Increases or decreases in the asset account *accounts receivable* and the liability account *deferred revenue* affect cash flow during the year of the profit-making activities of the business. We explain cash flow in Chapter 8. Until then, keep in mind that the balance of accounts receivable at the end of the year is the amount of sales revenue that has not yet been converted into cash. Accounts receivable represents cash waiting in the wings to be collected in the near future, and deferred revenue is the amount of money collected in advance from customers. The two accounts appear in the balance sheet, which we discuss in Chapter 7.

Selling products: Inventory

The *cost of goods sold* is one of the primary expenses of businesses that sell products. (In Figure 6-1, note that this expense equals roughly 38 percent of the sales revenue for the year ended December 31, 2024, calculated as $26,891 ÷ $71,064.) This expense is just what its name implies: the cost that a business pays for the products it sells to customers. A business makes profit by setting its sales prices high enough to cover the actual costs of products sold, the costs of operating the business, interest on borrowed money, and income taxes, with something left over for profit.

When the business acquires a product, the cost of the product goes into an *inventory asset* account (and the cost is either deducted from the cash account or added to the accounts payable liability account, depending on whether the business pays with cash or buys on credit). When a customer buys that product, the business transfers the cost of the product from the inventory asset account to the *cost of goods sold* expense account because the product is no longer in the business's inventory; the product has been delivered to the customer.

The first step in the income statement is deducting the cost of goods sold expense from the sales revenue for the goods sold. All businesses that sell products usually report the cost of goods sold as a separate expense in their income statements, as you see in Figure 6-1.

REMEMBER

A business that sells products needs to have some products on hand for ready sale to its customers. When you drive by an auto dealer and see all the cars, SUVs, and pickup trucks waiting to be sold, remember that these products are inventory. The cost of unsold products (goods held in inventory) is not yet an expense; only after the products are actually sold does the cost get listed as an expense. In this way, the cost of goods sold expense is correctly matched against the sales revenue from the goods sold. Correctly matching expenses against sales revenue is the essential starting point of accounting for profit.

Prepaying operating costs: Prepaid expenses

Prepaid expenses are the opposite of unpaid expenses. For example, a business buys fire insurance and general liability insurance (in case a customer who slips on a wet floor sues the business). Insurance premiums must be paid ahead of time, before coverage starts. The premium cost is allocated to expense in the actual period benefited. At the end of the year, the business may be only halfway through the insurance coverage period, so it charges off only half the premium cost as an expense. (For a six-month policy, you charge one-sixth of the premium cost to each of the six months covered.) At the time the premium is paid, the entire amount is recorded in the prepaid expenses asset account, and for each period of coverage, the appropriate fraction of the cost is recorded as a decrease in the asset account and as an increase in the insurance expense account.

Another example of something initially put in the prepaid expenses asset account occurs when a business pays cash to stock up on office supplies that it may not use for several months. The cost is recorded in the prepaid expenses asset account at the time of purchase; when the supplies are used, the appropriate amount is subtracted from the prepaid expenses asset account and recorded in the office supplies expense account.

TIP

Using the prepaid expenses asset account is not so much for the purpose of reporting all the assets of a business, because the balance in the account compared with other assets and total assets is typically small. Rather, using this account is an example of allocating costs to expenses in the period benefited by the costs, which isn't always the same period in which the business pays those costs. The prepayment of these expenses lays the groundwork for continuing operations seamlessly into the next year.

Understanding fixed assets: Depreciation expense

Long-term operating assets that are not held for sale in the ordinary course of business are called *property, plant, and equipment* or *fixed assets*; these include buildings, machinery, office equipment, vehicles, computers and data-processing equipment, and so on. *Depreciation* refers to spreading out the cost of a fixed asset over the years of its useful life to a business, instead of charging the entire cost to expense in the year of purchase. That way, each year of use bears a share of the total cost. For example, autos and light trucks are typically depreciated over five years; the idea is to charge a fraction of the total cost to depreciation expense during each of the five years. (The actual fraction each year depends on the method of depreciation used, which we explain in Chapter 9.)

TIP

Depreciation is a real expense but not a cash outlay expense in the year it is recorded. The cash outlay occurs when the fixed asset is acquired. See "The Positive Effect of Depreciation on Cash Flow" sidebar for more information.

Take another look back at the technology company income statement example in Figure 6-1. From the information supplied in its income statement, we don't know how much depreciation expense the business recorded in 2024. However, as required by GAAP, the notes to the business's financial statements reveal this amount. In 2024, the business recorded $1.239 million of depreciation expense. Basically, this expense decreases the book value (the recorded value) of its depreciable assets. *Book value* equals original cost minus the accumulated depreciation recorded so far. Book value may be different — indeed, quite a bit different — compared with the current replacement value of fixed assets.

THE POSITIVE EFFECT OF DEPRECIATION ON CASH FLOW

Depreciation and amortization are good news for cash flow. This concept gets a little complex, so stay with us here. To start with, fixed assets wear out and lose their economic usefulness over time. Some fixed assets last many years, such as office furniture and buildings. Other fixed assets last just a few years, such as delivery trucks and computers. Accountants argue, quite logically, that the cost of a fixed asset should be spread out or allocated over its predicted useful life to the business. Depreciation methods are rather arbitrary, but any reasonable method is much better than the alternative of charging off the entire cost of a fixed asset in the year it is acquired.

A business has to pass the cost of its fixed assets through to its customers and recover the cost of its fixed assets through sales revenue. A good example to illustrate this critical point is a taxicab driver who owns their cab. They set their fares high enough to pay for their time; to pay for the insurance, licence, gas, and oil; and to recover the cost of the cab. Included in each fare is a tiny fraction of the cost of the cab, which over the course of the year adds up to the depreciation expense that they passed on to their passengers and collected in fares. At the end of the year, they have collected a certain amount of money that pays them back for part of the cost of the cab.

In summary, fixed assets are gradually *sold off and* turned back into cash, each year. Part of sales revenue recovers some of the cost of fixed assets, which is why the decrease in the fixed assets account to record depreciation expense has the effect of increasing cash (assuming your sales revenue is collected in cash during the year). What the company does with this cash recovery is another matter. Sooner or later, you need to replace fixed assets to continue in business.

Figuring unpaid expenses: Accounts payable, accrued expenses payable, and income taxes payable

A typical business pays many expenses *after* the period in which the expenses are recorded. Following are some common examples:

>> A business pays its employees in arrears, which means that at any point in time, wages and salaries are owed to employees.

>> A business hires a law firm that does a lot of legal work during the year, but the company doesn't pay the bill until the following year.

>> A business has unpaid bills for telephone and Internet service, gas, electricity, and water that it used during the year.

Accountants use three different types of liability accounts to record a business's unpaid expenses:

>> **Accounts payable:** This account is used for items that the business buys on credit and for which it receives an invoice (a bill). For example, your business receives an invoice from its lawyers for legal work done. As soon as you receive the invoice, you record in the accounts payable liability account the amount that you owe. Later, when you pay the invoice, you subtract that amount from the accounts payable account, and your cash goes down by the same amount.

>> **Accrued expenses payable:** A business has to make estimates for several unpaid costs at the end of the year because it hasn't yet received invoices for them. Examples of accrued expenses include the following:

  • Unpaid wages, unused vacation and sick days that employees carry over to the following year, which the business has to pay for in the coming year

  • Unpaid bonuses or commissions to salespeople

  • The cost of future repairs and part replacements (warranties) on products that customers have bought and haven't yet returned for repair under warranty

  • The daily accumulation of interest on borrowed money that won't be paid until the next interest due date

  Without invoices to refer to, you have to examine your business operations carefully to determine which liabilities of this sort to record.

>> **Income taxes payable:** This account is used for income taxes that a business still owes to the federal and provincial governments at the end of the year. Canada Revenue Agency administers all provincial and territorial corporate income taxes except for the provinces of Quebec and Alberta. The income tax expense for the year is the total amount based on the taxable income for the entire year. Your business may not pay 100 percent of its income tax expense during the year; it may owe a small fraction to the governments at year's end. You record the unpaid amount in the income taxes payable account.

Note: A business may be unincorporated and be a *proprietorship* or *partnership*. In that case, its income is taxable in the hands of its owners and so there would be no income tax expense appearing on the income statement. Chapter 5 explains proprietorship and partnership types of business entities; the business we refer to here is an ordinary corporation that pays income tax.

Reporting Gains and Losses

We have a small confession to make: The income statement example shown in Figure 6-1 is a sanitized version as compared with actual income statements in external financial reports. If you took the trouble to read a hundred or so income statements, you'd be surprised at the wide range of things you'd find in these statements. But we do know one thing for certain you would discover.

REMEMBER

Many businesses report *gains and losses* in addition to their usual revenue and expenses. In these situations, the income statement is divided into two sections:

>> The first section presents the *ordinary, continuing sales, income, and expense from operations* of the business for the year, as well as gains and losses which are highlighted by headings on the income statement such as *other revenues and gains*, and *other expenses and losses*.

>> The second section presents any *unusual gains or losses* and gains or losses from *discontinued operations* that the business recorded in the year.

Unusual gains and losses

Occasionally, a business will suffer some losses or experience some gains that are not caused by day-to-day operations. These losses or gains might be related to the sale of an investment or even a charge against the business for something over which the business has little or no control. These events are considered outside of the business's main operations and yet they clearly must be included on the income statement. These *unusual gains and losses* are shown separately.

Some additional examples of items that would be listed under unusual gains and losses include:

>> **Settling lawsuits and other legal actions:** Damages and fines that you pay — as well as damages that you receive in a favourable ruling — are unusual gains and losses.

>> **Writing down (also called *writing off*) damaged and impaired assets:** If products become damaged and unsellable, or fixed assets are destroyed unexpectedly, you need to remove these items from the asset accounts. Even when certain assets are in good physical condition, if they lose their capability to generate future sales or other benefits to the business, accounting rules say that the assets have to be taken off the books.

>> **Relocating or reorganizing the business:** Some one-time charges are paid by the business to address a major shift in customer demand or tackle an economic downturn.

Discontinued operations

The second section of the income statement that deserves even more prominence is the one for discontinued operations of the business.

Some examples of discontinued operations include the following:

>> **Selling a segment of the business:** Layoffs require severance pay or trigger early retirement costs; selling the fixed assets of the segment may cause large gains or losses.

>> **Abandoning product lines:** When you decide to discontinue selling a line of products, you lose at least some of the money that you paid for obtaining or manufacturing the products, either because you sell the products for less than you paid or because you just dump the products you can't sell. So long as the product line was operated as a separate business segment, the costs connected with the abandonment qualify for treatment as discontinued operations.

According to financial reporting standards (GAAP), which we explain in Chapter 2, a business must make these one-time events very visible in its income statement. So, in addition to the main part of the income statement that reports normal profit activities, a business with discontinued operations must add a second layer to the income statement to disclose these happenings.

If a business has no discontinued operations in the year, its income statement ends with one bottom line, usually called *net income* (which is the situation shown in Figure 6-1). When an income statement includes a second layer, that line becomes a subtotal called *income from continuing operations*, as shown in the following:

Income from continuing operations	$267,000,000
Discontinued operations, net of income taxes	(20,000,000)
Net income	$247,000,000

You will note that discontinued operations are shown net of income taxes. You can therefore tell exactly what are all of the effects, even that of the taxes, of the decision to discontinue the particular operations.

Statement of Retained Earnings

In this chapter, we show you that income is the main source of increase to retained earnings. But other events or transactions can also change this account, which holds the equity belonging to the owners. What if something happens and it's too late to report the transaction on the statement of income? By "too late" we mean that this event or transaction belongs to an earlier year and that year is already over and done with.

WARNING

Canadian GAAP deal with addressing changes in accounting policy and correcting errors that occurred in previous years. Imagine you discover an error in recording the amount of amortization or depreciation in a past year. You might be tempted to charge the current-year income statement with the effect of this error. This would not be allowed under Canadian and international GAAP, because the expense of the current year would be incorrect as well. Two wrongs don't make a right, even when intended to correct for a past error.

Following are the two main items that cannot be recorded to the income statement:

>> **Changing accounting policy:** A business may decide to use a different method for recording revenue and expenses than it did in the past, in some cases because the accounting rules (set by the authoritative accounting governing bodies — see Chapter 1) have changed. Often, the new method requires a business to record a one-time cumulative effect caused by the switch in accounting policy. These special items can be huge. Because the

effect of the change must appear on the financial statements as though it had been adopted retroactively as soon as possible, the effect on the previous year's income statement has to be applied to the retained earnings balance, net of any tax effect. It is too late to go to the previous years' income statements because these periods are now closed. We discuss the closing of the books in Chapter 3.

» **Correcting errors from previous financial reports:** If you or your accountant discovers that a past financial report had an accounting error, you make a catch-up correction entry, which means that you record an increase or decrease as an adjustment to the retained earnings, net of any tax effect. This error has nothing to do with your financial performance this year and therefore should not appear in the current year's income statement.

The statement of retained earnings is the fourth financial statement in the typical set of financial statements. It is sometimes very short. Its purpose is to show what happened to retained earnings in the year, outlining how much profit the business made and also the dividends that the business paid the shareholders. In a way it is the link between the statement of income and the balance sheet. Because it is so short, a lot of accountants combine it with the statement of income.

WARNING

The statement of retained earnings is used by private enterprises in Canada. Public companies, following International Financial Reporting Standards (IFRS), use an expanded version of the statement of retained earnings called the *statement of changes in equity*. All information found on a statement of retained earnings is included in the statement of changes in equity, along with the details of any increases or decreases to the public company's other equity accounts for the reporting period. We discuss some of the differences between IFRS and Accounting Standards for Private Enterprises (ASPE) in Chapter 2.

Closing Comments

The income statement occupies centre stage; the bright spotlight is on this financial statement because it reports profit or loss for the period. But remember that a business reports three primary financial statements — the other two being the balance sheet and the statement of cash flows, which we discuss in the next two chapters. The three statements are like a three-ring circus. The income statement may draw the most attention, but you have to watch what's going on in all three places. As important as profit is to the financial success of a business, the income statement is not an island unto itself.

TIP

Keep in mind that financial statements are supplemented with notes and contain other commentary from the business's executives. If the financial statements have been audited, the CPA firm includes a short report stating whether the financial statements have been prepared in conformity with GAAP.

We don't like closing this chapter on a sour note, but we must point out that an income statement you read and rely on — as a business manager, an investor, or a lender — may not be true and accurate. In the large majority of cases, businesses prepare their financial statements in good faith, and their profit accounting is honest. They may bend the rules a little, but basically their accounting methods are within the boundaries of GAAP even though the businesses put a favourable spin on their profit number.

WARNING

But some businesses resort to accounting fraud and deliberately distort their profit numbers. In this case, an income statement reports false and misleading sales revenue or expenses or both to make the bottom-line profit appear to be better than the facts would support. If the fraud is discovered at a later time, the business puts out revised financial statements. Basically, the business in this situation rewrites its profit history. We wish we could say that this doesn't happen often, but the number of high-profile accounting fraud cases in the past has been alarming. Nortel Networks Corporation had to reissue its financial statements three times. The auditors did not catch the accounting fraud, even though to do so is one purpose of an audit. Investors who relied on the fraudulent income statements ended up suffering large losses.

Anytime we read a financial report, we keep in mind the risk that the financial statements may be stage managed to some extent to make year-to-year reported profit look a little smoother and less erratic and to make the business's financial position appear a little better. Regrettably, financial statements don't always tell it like it is. Rather, the business's chief executive and chief accountant fiddle with the financial statements to some extent. We say much more about this tweaking of a business's financial statements in later chapters.

IN THIS CHAPTER

» **Interpreting the balance sheet**

» **Categorizing business transactions**

» **Connecting revenue and expenses with their assets and liabilities**

» **Examining where businesses go for capital**

» **Understanding values in balance sheets**

Chapter **7**

Reporting Financial Condition on the Balance Sheet

This chapter explores one of the three primary financial statements that businesses report — the *balance sheet*, which is also called the *statement of financial condition* and the *statement of financial position*. This financial statement is a summary at a point in time of the assets of a business on the one hand, and the liabilities and owners' equity sources of the business on the other hand. The format is usually assets at the top and liabilities and owners' equity at the bottom of the statement.

REMEMBER

The balance sheet may seem to stand alone because it's presented on a separate page in a financial report. But keep in mind that the assets and liabilities reported in a balance sheet are the results of the business's activities, or transactions. *Transactions* are economic exchanges between the business and the parties it deals with: customers, employees, vendors, government agencies, and sources of capital. The other two financial statements — the income statement (see Chapter 6) and the statement of cash flows (see Chapter 8) — report transactions over a period of time (for example, 30 days), whereas the balance sheet reports values at an instant in time (for example, as of December 31, 2024). The balance sheet is almost always prepared as of the last day of the income statement period.

Unlike the income statement, the balance sheet doesn't have a natural bottom line, or one key figure that's the focus of attention. The balance sheet reports various assets, liabilities, and sources of owners' equity. Cash is a very important asset, but other assets are equally important as well, including accounts receivable; inventory; property, plant, and equipment; intangible assets; and company investments. The balance sheet, as explained in this chapter, has to be read as a whole — you can't focus only on one or two items in this financial summary of the business. You shouldn't put on blinders in reading a balance sheet by looking only at two or three items. You might miss important information by not perusing the whole balance sheet.

Expanding the Accounting Equation

The *accounting equation*, discussed in Chapter 1, is a very condensed version of a balance sheet. In its most concise form, the accounting equation is as follows:

$$\text{Assets} = \text{Liabilities} + \text{Owners' Equity}$$

Figure 7-1 expands the accounting equation to identify the basic accounts reported in a balance sheet. Many of the balance sheet accounts you see in Figure 7-1 are introduced in Chapter 6, which explains the income statement and the profit-making activities of a business. In fact, most balance sheet accounts are driven by profit-making transactions.

REMEMBER

Certain balance sheet accounts are not involved in recording the profit-making transactions of a business. Short- and long-term debt accounts aren't used in recording revenue and expenses, and neither is the invested capital account, which records the investment of capital from the owners of the business. Transactions involving debt and owners' invested capital accounts have to do with *financing* the business — that is, securing the capital needed to run the business.

Assets =	Liabilities +	Owners' Equity
Cash & Equivalents	Accounts Payable	Retained Earnings
		Invested Capital
Accounts Receivable	Accrued Liabilities	Account
Inventory	Income Taxes Payable	Other Equity
Prepaid Expenses	Other Current Liabilities	
Property, Plant, and Equipment, Net	Short-Term Debt	
Intangible & Other, Net	Long-Term Debt	

FIGURE 7-1: Expanded accounting equation.

© John Wiley & Sons, Inc.

Presenting a Proper Balance Sheet

Figure 7-2 presents a two-year, comparative balance sheet for the business example that we introduce in Chapter 6. This technology business sells products and services and makes sales on credit to its customers. Its income statement for the year just ended is shown in Figure 6-1. The balance sheet is at the close of business, December 31, 2023 and 2024. In most cases financial statements are not completed and released until a few weeks after the balance sheet date. Therefore, by the time you would read this financial statement it's already out of date, because the business has continued to engage in transactions since December 31, 2024. When substantial changes have occurred in the interim, a business should disclose these developments in notes to the financial statements.

The balance sheet in Figure 7-2 is in the vertical (portrait) layout, with assets on top and liabilities and shareholders' equity on the bottom. Alternatively, a balance sheet may be in the horizontal (landscape) mode, with liabilities and shareholders' equity on the right side and assets on the left.

REMEMBER

The financial statement in Figure 7-2 is called a *classified* balance sheet because certain accounts are grouped into classes (groups). Although the accounts in the class are different, they have common characteristics. Two such classes are *current assets* and *current liabilities.* Notice that subtotals are provided for each class. We discuss the reasons for reporting these classes of accounts later in this chapter (see the section "Current assets and liabilities"). The total amount of assets and the total amount of liabilities plus shareholders' equity are given at the bottom of the columns for each year. We probably don't have to remind you that these two amounts should be equal; otherwise, the company's books aren't in balance.

QW Example Tech., Inc. Statement of Financial Position at December 31, 2023 and 2024			
(all dollar amounts in thousands)	12/31/2023	12/31/2024	Change
Assets			
Current Assets:			
Cash & Equivalents	$788	$11,281	$10,493
Accounts Receivable, Net	6,718	8,883	2,165
Inventory, LC&NRV	4,061	1,733	(2,328)
Prepaid Expenses	300	325	25
Total Current Assets	11,867	22,222	10,355
Long-Term Operating & Other Assets:			
Property, Plant, & Equipment	7,920	8,670	750
Accumulated Depreciation	(3,081)	(4,320)	(1,239)
Net Property, Plant, & Equipment	4,839	4,350	(489)
Other Assets:			
Intangible Assets, Net	1,000	500	(500)
Goodwill	100	100	0
Total Long-Term Operating & Other Assets	5,939	4,950	(989)
Total Assets	$17,806	$27,172	$9,366
Liabilities			
Current Liabilities:			
Accounts Payable	$1,654	$1,929	$275
Accrued Liabilities	667	830	163
Current Portion of Debt	1,000	1,000	0
Other Current Liabilities & Deferred Revenue	408	1,204	796
Total Current Liabilities	3,729	4,963	1,234
Long-Term Liabilities:			
Notes Payable & Other Long-Term Debt	7,200	6,250	(950)
Total Liabilities	10,929	11,213	284
Shareholders' Equity			
Share Capital — Common	5,000	5,000	0
Share Capital — Preferred	0	5,000	5,000
Retained Earnings	1,877	5,959	4,082
Total Shareholders' Equity	6,877	15,959	9,082
Total Liabilities & Shareholders' Equity	$17,806	$27,172	$9,366

FIGURE 7-2: Illustrative two-year comparative balance sheet for a technology business.

© John Wiley & Sons, Inc.

WARNING

If a business doesn't release its annual financial report within a few weeks after the close of its fiscal year, you should be alarmed. The reasons for such a delay are all bad. One reason might be that the business's accounting system is not functioning well and the controller (chief accounting officer) has to do a lot of work at year-end to get the accounts up-to-date and accurate for preparing the financial statements. Another reason is that the business is facing serious problems and can't decide on how to account for the problems. Perhaps a business may be delaying the reporting of bad news. Or the business may have a serious dispute with its independent CPA auditor that has not been resolved.

REMEMBER

The balance sheet in Figure 7-2 includes a column for *changes* in the assets, liabilities, and owners' equity over the year (from year-end 2023 through year-end 2024). Including these changes is not required by financial reporting standards, and in fact most businesses do not include the changes. It's certainly acceptable to report balance sheet changes, but it's not mandated, and most companies don't. We include the changes for ease of reference in this chapter. Transactions generate changes in assets, liabilities, and owners' equity, which we summarize later in this chapter (see the section "Understanding That Transactions Drive the Balance Sheet").

Doing an initial reading of the balance sheet

Now suppose you own the business whose balance sheet is in Figure 7-2. (Most likely, you wouldn't own 100 percent of the ownership shares of the business; you'd own the majority of shares, giving you working control of the business.) You've already digested your most recent annual income statement (refer to Figure 6-1), which reports that you earned $4,482,000 net income on annual sales of $71,064,000. What more do you need to know? Well, you need to check your financial condition, which is reported on the balance sheet.

Is your financial condition viable and sustainable to continue your profit-making endeavor? The balance sheet helps answer this critical question. Perhaps you're on the edge of going bankrupt, even though you're making a profit. Your balance sheet is where to look for signs of possible financial troubles.

In reading through a balance sheet such as the one shown in Figure 7-2, you may notice that it doesn't have a punch line like the income statement does. The income statement's punch line is the net income line, which is rarely humorous to the business itself but can cause some snickers among analysts. (Earnings per share is also important for public corporations.) You can't look at just one item on the balance sheet, murmur an appreciative "ah-ha," and rush home to watch the game. You have to read the entire thing (sigh) and make comparisons among the items. Chapters 11 and 12 offer more information on interpreting financial statements.

At first glance, you might be somewhat amazed that your cash balance increased by $10,493,000 during the year (refer to Figure 7-2) when your profit of $4,482,000 was less than half of this figure. Why would your cash balance increase so much? Well, think about it. Many other transactions affect your cash balance. For example, did you sell some intangible assets? Yes, you did, as a matter of fact. The intangible assets decreased $500,000 during the year. Another source of cash came from the issuance of preferred shares in the amount of $5,000,000. We discuss the source and use of cash in more detail in Chapter 8.

Overall, your total assets increased $9,366,000. All assets increased during the year except inventory and other long-term assets. One big reason is the $4,082,000 increase in your retained earnings (which is derived from your net income of $4,482,000 less a dividend paid of $400,000). We explain in Chapter 6 that earning profit increases retained earnings. Profit was $4,482,000 for the year, but retained earnings increased only $4,082,000. Therefore, part of profit was distributed to the owners via issuing a $400,000 dividend, decreasing retained earnings. We discuss these things and other balance sheet interpretations as you move through this chapter. For now, the preliminary read of the balance sheet doesn't indicate any earth-shattering financial problems facing your business.

TIP

The balance sheet of a service business and a product business look pretty much the same as our technology business (see Figure 7-2) — except a service business doesn't report an inventory of products held for sale. If it sells on credit, a service business has an accounts receivable asset, just like a product company that sells on credit. The size of its total assets relative to annual sales revenue for a service business varies greatly from industry to industry, depending on whether or not the service industry is *capital intensive*. Some service businesses, such as airlines, utility companies, and hotel chains, need to make heavy investments in long-term operating assets. Other service businesses do not.

REMEMBER

The balance sheet is unlike the income and cash flow statements, which report flows over a period of time (such as sales revenue that is the cumulative amount of all sales during the period). The balance sheet presents the *balances* (amounts) of a company's assets, liabilities, and owners' equity at an instant in time. Note the two quite different meanings of the term *balance*. As used in *balance sheet*, the term refers to the equality of the two opposing sides of a business — total assets on the one side and total liabilities and owners' equity on the other side, like a scale with equal weights on both sides. In contrast, the *balance* of an account (asset, liability, owners' equity, revenue, and expense) refers to the amount in the account after recording increases and decreases in the account — the net amount after all additions and subtractions have been entered. Usually, the meaning of the term is clear in context.

An accountant can prepare a balance sheet any time a manager wants to know how things stand financially. Some businesses — particularly financial institutions such as banks, mutual funds, and securities brokers — need balance sheets at the end of each day, to track their day-to-day financial situation. For most businesses, however, balance sheets are prepared only at the end of each month, quarter, and year. A balance sheet is always prepared at the close of business on the last day of the profit period. In other words, the balance sheet should be in sync with the income statement.

Kicking balance sheets out into the real world

The statement of financial position, or balance sheet, shown in Figure 7-2 is about as lean and mean as you'll ever read. In the real world, many businesses are fat and complex. Also, we should make clear that Figure 7-2 shows the content and format for an *external* balance sheet, which means a balance sheet included in a financial report released outside a business to its owners and creditors. Balance sheets that stay within a business can be quite different.

Internal balance sheets

REMEMBER

For internal reporting of financial condition to managers, balance sheets include much more detail, either in the body of the financial statement itself or, more likely, in supporting schedules. For example, Figure 7-2 shows just one cash account, but the chief financial officer of a business needs to know the balances on deposit in each of the business's chequing accounts.

As another example, the balance sheet in Figure 7-2 includes just one total amount for accounts receivable, but managers need details on which customers owe money and whether any major amounts are past due. Greater detail allows for better control, analysis, and decision making. Internal balance sheets and their supporting schedules should provide all the detail that managers need to make good business decisions. See Chapter 13 for more detail on how business managers use financial reports.

External balance sheets

Balance sheets presented in external financial reports (which go out to investors and lenders) do not include much more detail than the balance sheet in Figure 7-2.

We want to make it clear that CSIS (Canadian Security Intelligence Service) and the RCMP (Royal Canadian Mounted Police) do not vet balance sheets to keep secrets from being disclosed that would harm national security. The term *classified*, when applied to a balance sheet, does not mean restricted or top secret; rather, the term means that assets and liabilities are sorted into basic classes, or groups, for external reporting. Classifying certain assets and liabilities into *current* categories is done mainly to help readers of a balance sheet more easily compare current assets with current liabilities for the purpose of judging the short-term liquidity and solvency of a business. Generally, an accountant classifies an asset as current if the business expects to use it up in operations in the next 12 months. A liability is current if the business expects to pay it in the next 12 months.

Judging liquidity and solvency

REMEMBER

Liquidity refers to the business's capability to pay its current liabilities when they are due. *Solvency*, on the other hand, refers to the business's capability to pay all of its liabilities on time. Delays in paying liabilities on time can cause serious problems for a business. In extreme cases, a business can be thrown into *involuntary bankruptcy*. Even the threat of bankruptcy can cause serious disruptions in the normal operations of a business, and profit performance is bound to suffer. If current liabilities become too high relative to current assets — which constitute the first line of defence for paying current liabilities — managers should move quickly to resolve the problem. A perceived shortage of current assets relative to current liabilities could ring alarm bells in the minds of the company's creditors and owners.

Therefore, note in Figure 7-2 the following groupings (dollar amounts refer to year-end 2024):

>> **Current assets:** The first four asset accounts (cash and equivalents, accounts receivable, inventory, and prepaid expenses) are added to give the $22.222 million subtotal for *current assets.*

>> **Current liabilities:** The first four liability accounts (accounts payable, accrued liabilities, current portion of debt, and other current liabilities and deferred revenue) are added to give the $4.963 million subtotal for *current liabilities.*

>> **Notes payable:** The total interest-bearing debt of the business is separated between $1 million in *short-term* notes payable, or portion of a note payable (those due in one year or sooner) and $6.250 million in *long-term* notes payable or long-term portion of a note payable and other long-term liabilities (those due after one year).

The following sections offer more detail about current assets and liabilities.

Current assets and liabilities

Short-term, or *current*, assets are as follows:

>> Cash

>> Marketable securities that can be converted into cash

>> Assets converted into cash or used in operations within one operating cycle, the main components being accounts receivable and inventory

The *operating cycle* refers to the repetitive process of putting cash into inventory, holding products in inventory until they are sold, selling products on credit (which generates accounts receivable), and collecting the receivables in cash. In other words, the operating cycle is the "from cash through inventory and accounts receivable and back to cash" sequence. The operating cycles of businesses vary from a few weeks to several months, depending on how long inventory is held before being sold and how long it takes to collect cash from sales made on credit.

Short-term, or *current*, liabilities include non-interest-bearing liabilities that arise from the business's operating (sales and expense) activities. A typical business keeps many accounts for these liabilities — a separate account for each vendor, for instance. In an external balance sheet you usually find only three or four operating liabilities, and they are not labelled as non-interest-bearing. It is assumed that the reader knows that these operating liabilities don't bear interest (unless the liability is seriously overdue and the creditor has started charging interest because of the delay in paying the liability).

TIP

The balance sheet example shown in Figure 7-2 discloses three operating liabilities: accounts payable, accrued liabilities, and other current liabilities and deferred revenue. Be warned that the terminology for these short-term operating liabilities varies from business to business.

In addition to operating liabilities, interest-bearing notes payable that have maturity dates one year or less from the balance sheet date are included in the current liabilities section. The current liabilities section may also include certain other liabilities that must be paid in the short run (which are too varied and technical to discuss here).

Current and quick ratio

The sources of cash for paying current liabilities are the company's current assets. That is, current assets are the first source of money to pay current liabilities when these liabilities come due. Remember that current assets consist of cash and assets that will be converted into cash in the short run. To size up current assets against total current liabilities, the *current ratio* is calculated. Using information from the company's balance sheet (refer to Figure 7-2), you calculate its year-end 2024 current ratio as follows:

$22.222 million current assets ÷ $4.963 million current liabilities = 4.48 current ratio

Generally, businesses do not provide their current ratio on the face of their balance sheets or in the notes to their financial statements — they leave it to the reader to calculate this number. On the other hand, many businesses present a financial highlights section in their financial report, which often includes the current ratio.

The *quick ratio* is more restrictive. Only cash and assets that can be quickly converted into cash are included, which excludes inventory and prepaid expenses. The business in this example doesn't have any short-term marketable investments that could be sold on a moment's notice. You calculate the quick ratio as follows (see Figure 7-2):

$20.164 million quick assets ÷ $4.963 million current liabilities = 4.06 quick ratio

TIP

Folklore has it that a company's current ratio should be at least 2.0. However, business managers know that an acceptable current ratio depends a great deal on general practices in the industry for short-term borrowing. Some businesses do well with a current ratio less than 2.0 and quick ratios less than 1.0, so take the 2.0 benchmark with a grain of salt. Retailers with high inventory turnover such as Loblaw or Wal-Mart have low current ratios. A lower current ratio does not necessarily mean that the business won't be able to pay its short-term (current) liabilities on time. Chapters 11 and 12 explain liquidity and solvency in more detail.

Understanding That Transactions Drive the Balance Sheet

REMEMBER

A balance sheet is a snapshot of the financial condition of a business at an instant in time — the most important moment in time being at the end of the last day of the income statement period. The *fiscal*, or accounting, year of the business ends on December 31. So, its balance sheet is prepared at the close of business at midnight December 31. (A company should end its fiscal year at the close of its natural business year or at the close of a quarter — September 30, for example.)

This freeze-frame nature of a balance sheet may make it appear that a balance sheet is static. Nothing is further from the truth. A business does not shut down to prepare its balance sheet. The financial condition of a business is in constant motion because the business's activities go on non-stop.

The activities, or transactions, of a business fall into three basic types:

>> **Operating activities, which also can be called profit-making activities:** This category refers to making sales and incurring expenses, and also includes the allied transactions that are part and parcel of making sales and incurring expenses. For example, a business records sales revenue when sales are made on credit, and then, later, records cash collections from customers. Another example: A business purchases products that are placed in its inventory (its stock of products awaiting sale), at which time it records an entry for the purchase. The expense (the cost of goods sold) is not recorded until the products are actually sold to customers. Keep in mind that the term *operating activities* includes the allied transactions that precede or are subsequent to the recording of sales and expense transactions.

>> **Investing activities:** This term refers to making investments in long-term assets and (eventually) disposing of the assets when the business no longer needs them. The primary examples of investing activities for businesses that sell products and services are *capital expenditures,* which are the amounts spent to modernize, expand, and replace the long-term operating assets of a business. A business may also invest in *financial assets,* such as bonds and shares or other types of debt and equity instruments. Purchases and sales of financial assets are also included in this category of transactions.

>> **Financing activities:** These activities include securing money from debt and equity sources of capital, returning capital to these sources, and making distributions from profit to owners. Note that distributing profit to owners is treated as a financing transaction. The decision of whether to distribute some of its profit depends on whether the business needs more capital from its owners to grow the business or to strengthen its solvency. Retaining part or all of the profit for the year is one way of increasing the owners' equity in the business. We discuss this topic later in "Financing a Business: Sources of Cash and Capital."

Figure 7-3 presents a summary of changes in assets, liabilities, and owners' equity during the year for the business example we introduce in Chapter 6 and continue in this chapter. Notice the middle three columns, which show each of the three basic types of transactions of a business. One column is for changes caused by its revenue and expenses and their connected transactions during the year, which collectively are called *operating activities* (although we prefer to call them profit-making activities). The second column is for changes caused by its *investing activities* during the year. The third column is for the changes caused by its *financing activities.*

(all dollar amounts in thousands)	Beg. Balance 12/31/2023	Operating Activities	Investing Activities	Financing Activities	Change	End. Balance 12/31/2024
QW Example Tech., Inc. **Statement of Financial Position** **at December 31, 2023 and 2024**						
Assets						
Current Assets:						
Cash & Equivalents	$788	$7,593	($750)	$3,650	$10,493	$11,281
Accounts Receivable, Net	$6,718	($2,165)	$0	$0	($2,165)	$8,883
Inventory, LC&NRV	$4,061	$2,328	$0	$0	$2,328	$1,733
Prepaid Expenses	$300	($25)	$0	$0	($25)	$325
Total Current Assets	$11,867	$7,731	($750)	$3,650	$10,631	$22,222
Long-Term Operating & Other Assets:						
Property, Plant, & Equipment	$7,920	$0	$750	$0	$750	$8,670
Accumulated Depreciation	($3,081)	$1,239	$0	$0	$1,239	($4,320)
Net Property, Plant, & Equipment	$4,839	$1,239	$750	$0	$1,989	$4,350
Other Assets:						
Intangible Assets, Net	$1,000	$500	$0	$0	$500	$500
Goodwill	$100	$0	$0	$0	$0	$100
Total Long-Term Operating & Other Assets	$5,939	$1,739	$750	$0	$2,489	$4,950
Total Assets	$17,806	$9,470	$0	$3,650	$13,120	$27,172
Liabilities						
Current Liabilities:						
Accounts Payable	$1,654	$275	$0	$0	$275	$1,929
Accrued Liabilities	$667	$163	$0	$0	$163	$830
Current Portion of Debt	$1,000	$0	$0	$0	$0	$1,000
Other Current Liabilities & Deferred Revenue	$408	$796	$0	$0	$796	$1,204
Total Current Liabilities	$3,729	$1,234	$0	$0	$1,234	$4,963
Long-Term Liabilities:						
Notes Payable & Other Long-Term Debt	$7,200	$0	$0	($950)	($950)	$6,250
Total Liabilities	$10,929	$1,234	$0	($950)	$284	$11,213
Shareholders' Equity						
Share Capital — Common	$5,000	$0	$0	$0	$0	$5,000
Share Capital — Preferred	$0	$0	$0	$5,000	$5,000	$5,000
Retained Earnings	$1,877	$4,482	$0	($400)	$4,082	$5,959
Total Shareholders' Equity	$6,877	$4,482	$0	$4,600	$9,082	$15,959
Total Liabilities & Shareholders' Equity	$17,806	$5,716	$0	$3,650	$9,366	$27,172

FIGURE 7-3: Summary of changes in assets, liabilities, and owners' equity during the year according to basic types of transactions.

© *John Wiley & Sons, Inc.*

Note: Figure 7-3 includes subtotals for current assets and liabilities; the formal balance sheet for this business is in Figure 7-2. Businesses don't report a summary of changes in their assets, liabilities, and owners' equity (though we think such a summary would be helpful to users of financial reports). The purpose of Figure 7-3 is to demonstrate how the three major types of transactions during the year change the assets, liabilities, and owners' equity accounts of the business during the year.

The 2024 income statement of the business is shown in Figure 6-1. You may want to flip back to this financial statement in Chapter 6. On sales revenue of $71.064 million, the business earned $4.482 million bottom-line profit (net income) for the year. The sales and expense transactions of the business during the year plus the associated transactions connected with sales and expenses cause the changes shown in the operating-activities column in Figure 7-3. You can see that the $4.482 million net income has increased the business's owners' equity–retained earnings by the same amount. (The business paid $400,000 distributions from profit in the form of a dividend to its owners during the year, which decreases the balance in retained earnings.)

TIP

The operating-activities column in Figure 7-3 is worth lingering over for a few moments because the financial outcomes of making profit are seen in this column. In our experience, most people see a profit number, such as the $4.482 million in this example, and stop thinking any further about the financial outcomes of making the profit. This is like going to a movie because you like its title, without knowing anything about the plot and characters. You probably noticed that the $7.593 million increase in cash in this operating-activities column differs from the $4.482 million net income figure for the year. The cash effect of making profit (which includes the associated transactions connected with sales and expenses) is almost always different from the net income amount for the year. Chapter 8 explains this difference.

REMEMBER

The summary of changes in Figure 7-3 gives you a sense of the balance sheet in motion, or how the business got from the start of the year to the end of the year. Having a good sense of how transactions propel the balance sheet is important. This kind of summary of balance sheet changes can be helpful to business managers who plan and control changes in the assets and liabilities of the business. Managers need a solid understanding of how the three basic types of transactions change assets and liabilities. Figure 7-3 also provides a useful platform for the statement of cash flow in Chapter 8.

Sizing Up Assets and Liabilities

TIP

When you first read the balance sheet in Figure 7-2, did you wonder about the size of the company's assets, liabilities, and owners' equities? Did you ask, "Are the balance sheet accounts about the right size?" The balances in a company's balance sheet accounts should be compared with the sales revenue size of the business. The amount of assets needed to carry on the profit-making transactions of a business depend mainly on the size of its annual revenue. And the sizes of its assets, in turn, largely determine the sizes of its liabilities — which, in turn, determines the size of its owners' equity accounts (although the ratio of liabilities and owners' equity depends on other factors as well).

Although the business example we use in this chapter is hypothetical, we didn't use random numbers. For the example, we use a modest-sized business that has $71.064 million in annual sales revenue. The other numbers in its income statement and balance sheet are realistic relative to each other. We assume that the business earns 62 percent gross margin ($44.173 million gross margin ÷ $71.064 million sales revenue = 62 percent), which means its cost of goods sold expense is 38 percent of sales revenue. The sizes of particular assets and liabilities compared with their relevant income statement numbers vary from industry to industry, and even from business to business in the same industry.

Based on its history and operating policies, the managers of a business can estimate what the size of each asset and liability should be; these estimates provide useful *control benchmarks* against which the actual balances of the assets and liabilities are compared. Assets (and liabilities, too) can be too high or too low relative to the sales revenue and expenses that drive them, and these deviations can cause problems that managers should try to correct.

For example, based on the credit terms extended to its customers and the company's policies regarding how aggressively it acts in collecting past-due receivables, a manager determines the range for the proper, or within-the-boundaries, balance of accounts receivable. This figure is the control benchmark. If the actual balance is reasonably close to this control benchmark, accounts receivable is under control. If not, the manager should investigate why accounts receivable is smaller or larger than it should be.

The following sections discuss the relative sizes of the assets and liabilities in the balance sheet that result from sales and expenses (for the fiscal year 2024). The sales and expenses are the *drivers*, or causes, of the assets and liabilities. If a business earned profit simply by investing in shares and bonds, it would not need all the various assets and liabilities explained in this chapter. Such a business — a mutual fund, for example — would have just one income-producing asset: investments in securities. This chapter focuses on merchandising businesses that sell products on credit.

Sales revenue and accounts receivable

Annual sales revenue for the year 2024 is $71.064 million in our example (see Figure 6-1 in Chapter 6). The year-end accounts receivable is one-eighth of this, or $8.883 million (see Figure 7-2). The average customer's credit period is roughly 46 days: 365 days in the year times the 12.5 percent ratio of accounts receivable balance to annual sales revenue. Of course, some customers' balances are past 46 days, and some are quite new; you want to focus on the average. The key question is whether a customer credit period averaging 46 days is reasonable.

REMEMBER

Suppose that the business offers all customers a 30-day credit period, which is fairly common in business-to-business selling (although not for a retailer selling to individual consumers). The relatively small deviation of about 15 days (45 days average credit period versus 30 days normal credit terms) probably is not a significant cause for concern. But suppose that, the average accounts receivable had been $12.9 million, which is 18 percent of annual sales, or about a 66-day average credit period. Such an abnormally high balance should raise a red flag; the responsible manager should look into the reasons for the abnormally high accounts receivable balance. Perhaps several customers are seriously late in paying and should not be extended new credit until they pay up.

Cost of goods sold expense and inventory

In Figure 7-3, the cost of goods sold expense for the year 2024 is $26.891 million, of which we have assumed $10.395 million relates strictly to product sales and the balance of $16.496 million relates to software service sales. The year-end inventory is $1.733 million, or about 16.7 percent. In rough terms, the average product's inventory holding period is 61 days — 365 days in the year times the 16.7 percent ratio of ending inventory to annual cost of goods sold for products only. Of course, some products may remain in inventory longer than the 61-day average, and some products may sell in a much shorter period than 61 days. You need to focus on the overall average. Is a 61-day average inventory holding period reasonable?

One thing that should immediately jump out in our example is this: Why did the inventory balance decrease so drastically on a year-over-year basis (from $4.061 million to $1.733 million)? The answer lies in the change in strategy that this technology company is pivoting its business from being *product focused* (that is, selling tangible computers and technology) to selling more software and services (which is labour intensive).

REMEMBER

The "correct" average inventory holding period varies from industry to industry. In some industries, especially heavy equipment manufacturing, the inventory holding period is three months or longer. The opposite is true for high-volume retailers, such as retail supermarkets, that depend on getting products off the shelves as quickly as possible. The 61-day average holding period in the example is reasonable for many businesses but would be too high for others.

The managers should know what the company's average inventory holding period should be — they should know the control benchmark for the inventory holding period. If inventory is much above this control benchmark, managers should take prompt action to get inventory back in line (which is easier said than done, of course). If inventory is at abnormally low levels, this should be investigated as well. Perhaps some products are out of stock and should be immediately restocked to avoid lost sales.

Fixed assets and depreciation expense

Depreciation is like other expenses in that all expenses are deducted from sales revenue to determine profit. Other than this, however, depreciation is different from other expenses. (Amortization expense, which we get to later, is closely related to depreciation.) When a business buys or builds a long-term operating asset, the cash outlay for the asset is recorded in a fixed asset account which we more formally call *property, plant, and equipment*. The cost of a fixed asset is spread out, or allocated, over its expected useful life to the business. The depreciation expense recorded in the period doesn't require any further cash outlay during the period. (The cash outlay occurred when the fixed asset was acquired.) Rather, depreciation expense for the period is that portion of the total cost of a business's fixed assets that is allocated to the period to record the cost of using the assets during the period. Depreciation depends on which method is used to allocate the cost of fixed assets over their estimated useful lives. We explain different depreciation methods in Chapter 9.

The higher the total cost of its fixed assets (called *property, plant, and equipment* in a formal balance sheet), the higher a business's depreciation expense. However, no standard ratio of depreciation expense to the cost of fixed assets exists. Either the depreciation expense for the year is reported as a separate expense in the income statement, or the amount is disclosed in a note to the financial statements.

REMEMBER

Because depreciation is based on the gradual charging off, or writing-down, of the cost of a fixed asset, the balance sheet reports not one but two numbers: the original (historical) cost of its fixed assets and the *accumulated depreciation* amount (the total amount of depreciation that has been charged to expense from the time of acquiring the fixed assets to the current balance sheet date). The purpose isn't to confuse you by giving you even more numbers to deal with. Seeing both numbers gives you an idea of how old the fixed assets are and also tells you how much these fixed assets originally cost and when they will likely need replacing. By the way, GAAP (generally accepted accounting principles) rules require the disclosure of these amounts. In the example we're working with in this chapter, the business has, over several years, invested $8.67 million in its fixed assets (that it still owns and uses), and it has recorded total depreciation of $4.32 through the end of the most recent fiscal year, December 31, 2024. The business recorded $1.239 million of depreciation expense in its most recent year.

You can tell that the company's collection of fixed assets includes some old assets because the company has recorded $4.32 million total depreciation since assets were bought — a fairly sizable percentage of original cost (roughly half). But many businesses use accelerated depreciation methods that pile up a lot of the depreciation expense in the early years and less in the later years (see Chapter 9 for more details), so estimating the average age of the company's assets is hard.

A business could discuss the actual ages of its fixed assets in the notes to its financial statements, but hardly any businesses disclose this information — although they do identify which depreciation methods they are using.

Operating expenses and their balance sheet accounts

The sales, general, and administrative (SG&A) expenses connect with three balance sheet accounts: prepaid expenses, accounts payable, and accrued liabilities account (see Figure 7-2). The broad SG&A expense category includes many different types of expenses in making sales and operating the business. (Separate expense accounts are maintained for specific expenses; depending on the business's size and the needs of its various managers, hundreds or thousands of specific expense accounts are established.)

For bookkeeping convenience, a business records many expenses when the expense is paid. For example, wage and salary expenses are recorded on payday. However, this "record as you pay" method does not work for many expenses. For instance, insurance and office supplies costs are *prepaid,* and then released to expense gradually over time. The cost is initially put in the *prepaid expenses* asset account. (Yes, we know that "prepaid expenses" doesn't sound like an asset account, but it is.) Other expenses are not paid until weeks after the expenses are recorded. The amounts owed for these unpaid expenses are recorded in an *accounts payable* or in an *accrued expenses payable* liability account.

REMEMBER

For more details, take a look at Chapter 6. Remember that the accounting objective is to match expenses with sales revenue for the year, and only in this way can the amount of profit be measured for the year. So expenses recorded for the year should be the correct amounts, regardless of when they're paid.

Intangible assets, goodwill, and amortization expense

Our business example includes a small investment in intangible assets of approximately $500,000 at the end of 2024. *Intangible* means without physical existence, in contrast to buildings, vehicles, and computers. For example:

>> A business might purchase the customer list of another company that is going out of business.

>> A business might buy patent rights from the inventor of a new product or process.

>> A business might buy another business lock, stock, and barrel and pay more than the total of the individual assets of the company being bought are worth — even after adjusting the particular assets to their current values. The extra amount is for *goodwill,* which may consist of a trained and efficient workforce, an established product with a reputation for high quality, or a valuable location. Goodwill is reported separately from intangible assets on the balance sheet.

REMEMBER

Most intangible assets that are used by a business are purchased and recorded by that business. To be recognized in the accounts, goodwill must have been purchased. Building up a good reputation with customers or establishing a well-known brand is not recorded as goodwill. You can imagine the value of Coca-Cola's brand name, but this "asset" is not recorded on the company's books. (However, Coca-Cola protects its brand name with all the legal means at its disposal to maintain the competitive advantage it enjoys from name recognition.)

The cost of an intangible asset is put in the appropriate asset account, just like the cost of a tangible asset is recorded in a fixed asset account. And, like a fixed asset account (with the exception of land), the cost of an intangible asset that has a limited useful economic life is allocated over its estimated useful life. (*Note:* Certain intangible assets are viewed as having more or less perpetual useful lives.) The allocation of the cost of an intangible asset over its estimated economic life is called *amortization.* Amortization expense is similar to depreciation expense.

For intangible assets and goodwill with unlimited useful lives, instead of recording amortization, accounting guidelines dictate that these assets be tested for any impairment in their capability to help produce income. Should they be determined to be impaired, an impairment loss is recorded. Impairment losses on the income statement can be huge.

Debt and interest expense

Look back at the balance sheet shown in Figure 7-2. Note that the sum of this business's short-term (current) and long-term notes payable at year-end 2024 is $7.25 million. From its income statement in Figure 7-3, we see that its interest expense for the year was $350,000. Based on the amount of debt, the annual interest rate is about 4.8 percent. (The business may have had more or less borrowed at certain times during the year, of course, and the actual interest rate depends on the debt levels from month to month.)

A business's cash account consists of the money it has in its chequing accounts plus the money that it keeps on hand. Cash is the essential lubricant of business activity. Sooner or later, virtually all business transactions pass through the cash account. Every business needs to maintain a working cash balance as a buffer against fluctuations in day-to-day cash receipts and payments. You can't really get by with a zero cash balance, hoping that enough customers will provide enough cash to cover all the cash payments that you need to make that day.

At year-end 2024, the cash balance of the business whose balance sheet is presented in Figure 7-2 is $11.281 million, which equals a little more than eight weeks of annual sales revenue. How large a cash balance should a business maintain? This question has no simple answer. A business needs to determine how large a cash safety reserve it's comfortable with to meet unexpected demands on cash while keeping the following points in mind:

- Excess cash balances are unproductive and don't earn any profit for the business.
- Insufficient cash balances can cause the business to miss taking advantage of opportunities that require quick action, such as snatching up a prized piece of real estate that just came on the market or buying out a competitor.

For most businesses, a small part of their total annual interest is unpaid at year-end; the unpaid part is recorded to bring interest expense up to the correct total amount for the year. In Figure 7-3, the accrued amount of interest is included in the *accrued liabilities* account. In most balance sheets you don't find accrued interest payable on a separate line; rather, it's included in the accrued expenses payable liability account. However, if unpaid interest at year-end happens to be a rather large amount, or if the business is seriously behind in paying interest on its debt, it should report the accrued interest payable as a separate liability.

Income tax expense and income tax payable

In its 2024 income statement, the business reports $6.895 million earnings before income tax — after deducting interest and all other expenses from sales revenue. The actual taxable income of the business for the year probably is different than this amount because of the many complexities in the income tax law. In the example, we use a realistic 35 percent tax rate, so the income tax expense is $2.413 million of the pre-tax income of $6.895 million as shown in Figure 6-1 in Chapter 6.

A large part of the income tax amount for the year must be paid to the Canada Revenue Agency in monthly instalments before the end of the year. But a small part is usually still owed at the end of the year. The unpaid part is recorded in the *income tax payable* liability account which has been consolidated in the other current liability account balance of $1.204 million in Figure 7-2. In the example, let us assume that the unpaid part is $804,000 of the total $2.413 million income tax for the year, but we don't mean to suggest that this ratio is typical. Generally, the unpaid income tax at the end of the year is fairly small, but just how small depends on several technical factors.

Net income and cash dividends (if any)

A business may have other sources of income during the year, such as interest income on investments. In this example, however, the business has only sales revenue, which is gross income from the sale of products and services. All expenses — starting with cost of goods sold down to and including income tax — are deducted from sales revenue to arrive at the last, or bottom, line of the income statement. The preferred term for bottom-line profit is *net income*, as you see in Figure 6-1.

The $4.482 million net income for the year (see Figure 6-1) increases the owners' equity account *retained earnings* by the same amount. The $4.482 million profit (here we go again using the term *profit* instead of *net income*) either stays in the business or some of it is paid out and divided among the business's owners. This business paid out $400,000 total cash distributions from profit during the year, and the total of these cash payments to its owners (shareholders) is recorded as a decrease in retained earnings. As we discuss in Chapter 4, you have to look at the statement of retained earnings if you are a private enterprise, or the statement of changes in equity if you are a public corporation. You can't tell from the income statement or the balance sheet the amount of cash dividends. You could also look in the statement of cash flows for this information (which we explain in Chapter 8).

Financing a Business: Sources of Cash and Capital

REMEMBER

To run a business, you need financial backing, otherwise known as *capital*. In broad overview, a business raises capital needed for its assets by buying things on credit, waiting to pay some expenses, borrowing money, getting owners to invest money in the business, and making profit that is retained in the business.

Borrowed money is known as *debt*; capital invested in the business by its owners and retained profits are the two sources of *owners' equity*.

How did the business whose balance sheet is shown in Figure 7-2 finance its assets? Its total assets are $27.172 million at year-end 2024. The company's profit-making activities generated three liabilities — accounts payable, accrued expenses payable, and income tax payable and other current liabilities (including income tax payable as previously noted) — and in total these three liabilities provided $3.963 million of the business's total assets. Debt provided $7.25 million, and the three sources of owners' equity provided the other $15.959 million. All three sources add up to $27.172 million, which equals total assets, of course. Otherwise, its books would be out of balance, which is a definite no-no.

Accounts payable, accrued liabilities, other current liabilities, and income tax payable are short-term, non-interest-bearing liabilities that are sometimes called *spontaneous liabilities* because they arise directly from a business's expense activities. They aren't the result of borrowing money but rather are the result of buying things on credit or delaying payment of certain expenses.

Avoiding these three liabilities in running a business is hard; they are generated naturally in the process of carrying on operations. In contrast, the mix of debt (interest-bearing liabilities) and equity (invested owners' capital and retained earnings) requires careful thought and high-level decisions by a business. There's no natural or automatic answer to the debt-versus-equity question. The business in the example has a large amount of debt relative to its owners' equity, which would make many business owners uncomfortable.

Debt is both good and bad, and in extreme situations it can get ugly. The advantages of debt follow:

>> Most businesses can't raise all the capital they need from owners' equity sources, and debt offers another source of capital (though, of course, many lenders are willing to provide only part of the capital that a business needs).

>> Interest rates charged by lenders are lower than rates of return expected by owners. Owners expect a higher rate of return because they're taking a greater risk with their money — the business is not required to pay them back the same way that it's required to pay back a lender. For example, a business may pay 6 percent annual interest on its debt and be expected to earn a 12 percent annual rate of return on its owners' equity.

WARNING

Here are the disadvantages of debt:

>> A business must pay the agreed-upon rate of interest for the period even if it suffers a loss for the period or earns a lower rate of return on its assets.

>> A business must be ready to pay back the debt on the specified due date, which can cause some pressure on the business to come up with the money on time. (Of course, a business may be able to *roll over*, or renew, its debt, meaning that it replaces its old debt with an equivalent amount of new debt, but the lender has the right to demand that the old debt be paid and not rolled over.)

WARNING

If a business defaults on its debt contract — it doesn't pay the interest on time or doesn't pay back the debt on the due date — it faces some major unpleasantness. In extreme cases, a lender can force it to shut down and liquidate its assets (that is, sell off everything it owns for cash) to pay off the debt and unpaid interest. Just as you can lose your home if you don't pay your home mortgage, a business can be forced into involuntary bankruptcy if it doesn't pay its debts. A lender may allow the business to try to work out its financial crisis through bankruptcy procedures, but bankruptcy is a nasty affair that invariably causes many problems and can cripple or terminate a business.

Recognizing the Hodgepodge of Values Reported in a Balance Sheet

In our experience, the values for assets reported in a balance sheet can be a source of confusion for both business managers and investors, who tend to put all dollar amounts on the same value basis. In their minds, a dollar is a dollar, whether it's in accounts receivable, inventory, fixed assets, accounts payable, or retained earnings. But some dollars are much older than other dollars.

The dollar amounts reported in a balance sheet are the result of the transactions recorded in the assets, liabilities, and owners' equity accounts. (Hmm, where have you heard this before?) Some transactions from years ago may still have life in the present balances of certain assets. For example, the land owned by a business that is reported in the balance sheet goes back to the transaction for the purchase of the land, which could be 20 or 30 years ago. The balance in the land asset is standing in the same asset column, for example, as the balance in the accounts receivable asset, which likely is only one or two months old.

REMEMBER

Book values (sometimes referred to as *carrying amounts*) are the amounts recorded in the accounting process and reported in financial statements. Don't assume that the book values reported in a balance sheet necessarily equal the current market values. Book values are based on the accounting methods used by a business. Generally speaking, the amounts reported for cash, accounts receivable, and liabilities are equal to or are close to their current market or settlement values. For example, accounts receivable will be turned into cash for the amount recorded on the balance sheet, and liabilities will be paid off at the amounts reported in the balance sheet. The book values of inventory and fixed assets, as well as any other assets in which the business invested some time ago, are most likely lower than current replacement values.

Also, keep in mind that a business may have unrecorded assets. These off-balance-sheet assets include a well-known reputation for quality products and excellent service, secret formulas (think Coca-Cola), patents that are the result of its research and development over the years, and a better trained workforce than its competitors. The business did not purchase these intangible assets from outside sources but rather accumulated them over the years through its own efforts. These assets, though not reported in the balance sheet, should show up in better-than-average profit performance in the business's income statement.

WARNING

The current replacement values of a company's fixed assets may be quite a bit higher than the recorded costs of these assets, in particular for buildings, land, heavy machinery, and equipment. For example, the aircraft fleet of Air Canada, as reported in its balance sheet, is hundreds of millions of dollars less than the current cost it would have to pay to replace the planes. Complicating matters is the fact that many of its older planes are not being produced anymore, and Air Canada would replace the older planes with newer models.

Private businesses in Canada using Accounting Standards for Private Enterprises (ASPE) are not permitted to write up the book values of their assets to current market or replacement values. On the other hand, investments in marketable securities have to be written up, or down, for all companies in Canada. Investment property or rental real estate may be revalued to fair value when following IFRS. Some accountants believe that although recording market values has intuitive appeal, a market-to-market valuation model is not practical or appropriate for businesses that sell products and services. They believe that these businesses do not stand ready to sell their assets (other than inventory); they need their assets for operating the business into the future. At the end of their useful lives, assets are sold for their disposable or residual values (or traded in for new assets).

TIP

Don't think that the market value of a business is simply equal to its owners' equity reported in its most recent balance sheet. Putting a value on a business depends on several factors in addition to the latest balance sheet of the business.

IN THIS CHAPTER

» Clarifying why the statement of cash
flows is reported

» Earning profit versus generating
cash flow

» Presenting the statement of cash
flows in two flavours

» Reading lines and between the lines
in the statement of cash flows

» Gaining insights into cash flows

Chapter **8**

Reporting Cash Flows

You could argue that the income statement (see Chapter 6) and balance sheet (see Chapter 7) are enough to meet an owner's needs. These two financial statements answer the most important questions about the financial affairs of a business. The income statement discloses revenue and how much profit the business squeezed from its revenue, and the balance sheet discloses the amounts of assets being used to make sales and profit, as well as its capital sources. What more do you need to know? Well, it's also helpful to know about the cash flows of the business.

This chapter explains the third primary financial statement reported by businesses: the *statement of cash flows*. This financial statement has two purposes: It explains why cash flow from profit differs from bottom-line profit, and it summarizes the investing and financing activities of the business during the period. This may seem like an odd mix to put into one financial statement, but it makes sense. Earning profit (net income) generates net cash inflow (at least, it should normally). Making profit is a primary source of cash to a business. The investing and financing transactions of a business hinge on its cash flow from profit. All sources and uses of cash hang together and should be managed in an integrated manner.

REMEMBER

To further emphasize the importance of the statement of cash flows, we offer this bit of important advice: When reading the financial statements, always make sure you *understand* the income statement, *trust* the balance sheet, but most importantly, *rely* on the statement of cash flows. While the statement of cash flows is generally the most difficult of the financial statements to understand and analyze, it also provides invaluable information as it relates to how a business *generates* (comes up with) and *consumes* (uses) its all-important lifeline: cash! It's one thing for the management team of a business to explain why sales revenue came in below forecasts or an anticipated profit turned into an actual loss. These discussions are painful enough but do not even compare to having to explain why a business actually ran out of cash. Trust us when we say that this is one conversation that a business owner absolutely does not want to have with investors or creditors. The statement of cash flows represents critical financial information to assist businesses with always ensuring they have enough cash to support ongoing operations. In short, the importance of cash flow in showing the financial health of a business is often misunderstood but can't be overestimated.

Meeting the Statement of Cash Flows

The income statement (see Chapter 6) has a natural structure:

Revenue – Expenses = Profit (Net Income)

So does the balance sheet (see Chapter 7):

Assets = Liabilities + Owners' Equity

The statement of cash flows doesn't have an obvious natural structure, so the accounting rule-making body had to decide on the basic format for the statement. They settled on the following structure:

± Cash Flow from Operating Activities

± Cash Flow from Investing Activities

± Cash Flow from Financing Activities

= Cash Increase or Decrease during Period

+ Beginning Cash Balance

= Ending Cash Balance

The plus-minus sign means that the cash flow could be positive or negative. Generally, the cash flow from the investing activities of product businesses is negative, which means that the business spent more on new investments in long-term assets than cash received from disposals of previous investments. And generally, the cash flow from operating activities (profit-making activities) should be positive, unless the business spent more in cash than it took in during the year and drained cash out of the business.

TIP

The threefold classification of activities (transactions) reported in the statement of cash flows — operating, investing, and financing — are the same ones we introduce in Chapter 7, in which we explain the balance sheet. Figure 7-3 summarizes these transactions for the technology company example that we continue in this chapter.

In the company example, the business's cash balance increases by $10.493 million during the year ending December 31, 2024. You see this increase in the company's balance sheets for the years ended December 31, 2023 and 2024 (see Figure 7-2). The business started the year with $788,000 cash and ended the year with $11.281 million. What does the balance sheet, by itself, tell you about the reasons for the cash increase? The two-year comparative balance sheet provides some clues about the reasons for the cash increase. What you need is a clear answer. However, answering such a question isn't the purpose of a balance sheet.

Presenting the direct method

REMEMBER

The statement of cash flows begins with the cash from making profit, or *cash flow from operating activities*, as accountants call it. *Operating activities* is the term accountants adopted for sales and expenses, which are the "operations" that a business carries out to earn profit. Furthermore, the term *operating activities* also includes the transactions associated with sales and expenses. For example, making a sale on credit is an operating activity, and so is collecting the cash from the customer at a later time. Recording sales and expenses can be thought of as primary operating activities because they affect profit. Their associated transactions are secondary operating activities because they don't affect profit. However, they do affect cash flow, which we explain in this chapter.

Figure 8-1 presents the statement of cash flows for the product business example we introduce in Chapters 6 and 7. What you see in the first section of the statement of cash flows is called the *direct method* for reporting cash flow from operating activities. The dollar amounts are the cash flows connected with sales and expenses. For example, the business collected $68,949,000 from customers during the year, which is the direct result of making sales. The company paid $24,288,000 for the products it sells, some of which went toward maintaining the inventory of products awaiting sale next period.

QW Example Tech., Inc. Statement of Cash Flows for the Fiscal Year Ending 12/31/2024		
(all dollar amounts in thousands)	12/31/2023	12/31/2024
Cash Inflows, Collections from Sales	$53,051	$68,949
Cash Outflows:		
Payments for Products & Other Costs of Goods Sold	($23,053)	($24,288)
Payments for General, Selling, & Admin. Expenses	($27,646)	($34,801)
Payments for Other Expenses	($250)	($250)
Payments for Interest Expense	($400)	($350)
Payments for Income Tax Expense	($211)	($1,667)
Net Cash Flow from Operating Activities	$1,491	$7,593
Investing Activities, Cash Provided (Used):		
Increase in Property, Plant, & Equipment and Intangible Assets	($720)	($750)
Net Cash Flow from Investing Activities	($720)	($750)
Financing Activities, Cash Provided (Used):		
Dividends or Distributions Paid	$0	($400)
Sale of Preferred Shares	$0	$5,000
Repayments of Long-Term Debt	($1,000)	($950)
Other Financing Activities	$50	$0
Net Cash Flow from Financing Activities	($950)	$3,650
Net Increase (Decrease) in Cash & Equivalents	($179)	$10,493
Beginning Cash & Equivalents Balance	$967	$788
Ending Cash & Equivalents Balance	$788	$11,281

© John Wiley & Sons, Inc.

FIGURE 8-1:
The statement of cash flows — illustrating the *direct method* for cash flow from operating activities.

Note: Because we use the same business example in this chapter that we use in Chapters 6 and 7, you may want to take a moment to review its 2024 income statement in Figure 6-1. And you may want to review Figure 7-3, which summarizes how the three types of activities changed its assets, liabilities, and owners' equity accounts during the year 2024. (Go ahead, we'll wait.)

TIP

The basic idea of the direct method is to present the sales revenue and expenses of the business on a cash basis, in contrast to the amounts reported in the income statement, which are on the accrual basis for recording revenue and expenses. *Accrual basis* accounting is real-time accounting that records transactions when economic events happen: Accountants record sales on credit when the sales take place, even though cash isn't collected from customers until sometime later. Cash payments for expenses occur before or after the expenses are recorded. *Cash basis* accounting is just what it says: Transactions aren't recorded until there's actual cash flow (in or out).

The revenue and expense cash flows you see in Figure 8-1 differ from the amounts you see in the accrual accounting basis income statement (refer to Figure 6-1). Herein lies a problem with the direct method. If you, a conscientious reader of the financial statements of a business, compare the revenues and expenses reported in the income statement with the cash flow amounts reported in the statement of cash flows, you may get confused. Which set of numbers is the correct one? Well, both are. The numbers in the income statement are the true numbers for measuring profit for the period. The numbers in the statement of cash flows are additional information for you to ponder.

Opting for the indirect method

A business can use the alternative method or format for reporting cash flow from operating activities. The alternative method starts with net income, and then makes adjustments to reconcile cash flow from operating activities with net income. This alternative method is called the *indirect method,* which we show in Figure 8-2. Although use of the direct method is strongly encouraged by the standard setters internationally and in Canada, in practice the indirect format is used more often. We think this is because of the public's resistance to change, rather than an expression of a real preference.

The indirect method for reporting cash flow from operating activities focuses on the *changes* during the year in the assets and liabilities that are connected with sales and expenses. We explain these connections in Chapter 6. (You can also trace these changes back to Figure 7-2 in Chapter 7.)

Although obvious differences exist in the first section of the statement of cash flows between the two methods for reporting cash flow from operating activities, the other two sections of the statement — cash flow from investing activities and cash flow from financing activities — are the same. The level of detail disclosed in these two sections varies from business to business. For example, some companies report one amount for all capital expenditures (investments in new long-term operating assets), whereas others give a more detailed breakdown by type of asset.

QW Example Tech., Inc.		
Statement of Cash Flows		
for the Fiscal Year Ending		
12/31/2024		
(all dollar amounts in thousands)	12/31/2023	12/31/2024
Net Profit	$323	$4,482
Operating Activities, Cash Provided (Used):		
Depreciation & Amortization	$1,631	$1,739
Decrease (Increase) in Accounts Receivable	($746)	($2,165)
Decrease (Increase) in Inventory	$150	$2,328
Decrease (Increase) in Other Current Assets	($50)	($25)
Increase (Decrease) in Accounts Payable	$111	$275
Increase (Decrease) in Accrued Liabilities	$59	$163
Increase (Decrease) in Other Liabilities	$13	$796
Net Cash Flow from Operating Activities	$1,491	$7,593
Investing Activities, Cash Provided (Used):		
Increase in Property, Plant, & Equipment and Intangible Assets	($720)	($750)
Net Cash Flow from Investing Activities	($720)	($750)
Financing Activities, Cash Provided (Used):		
Dividends or Distributions Paid	$0	($400)
Sale of Preferred Shares	$0	$5,000
Repayments of Long-Term Debt	($1,000)	($950)
Other Financing Activities	$50	$0
Net Cash Flow from Financing Activities	($950)	$3,650
Net Increase (Decrease) in Cash & Equivalents	($179)	$10,493
Beginning Cash & Equivalents Balance	$967	$788
Ending Cash & Equivalents Balance	$788	$11,281

© John Wiley & Sons, Inc.

FIGURE 8-2:
The statement of cash flows — illustrating the *indirect method* for presenting cash flow from operating activities.

Explaining the Variance between Cash Flow and Net Income

TIP

A positive cash flow from operating activities is the amount of cash generated by a business's profit-making operations during the year, exclusive of its other sources of cash during the year. Cash flow from operating activities indicates a business's capability to turn profit into available cash — cash in the bank that can be used for the needs of business. As you see in Figure 8-1 or Figure 8-2 (take your pick), the business in our example generated $7,593,000 cash from its profit-making activities in the year. The business also experienced a strong growth in sales for the year in the amount of $17.317 million.

The following sections explain how the asset and liability changes affect cash flow from operating activities. As a business manager, keep a close watch on the changes in each of your assets and liabilities and understand the cash flow effects caused by these changes. Investors focus on the business's capability to generate a healthy cash flow from operating activities, so investors are also equally concerned about these changes. In some situations, these changes can signal serious problems!

TIP

We realize that you may not be too interested in the details of these changes, so at the start of each section, we present the punch line. If you want, you can just read this short explanation and move on (though the details are fascinating — well, at least to accountants).

Note: Instead of using the full phrase *cash flow from operating activities* every time, we use the shorter phrase *cash flow* in the following sections. All data for assets and liabilities are found in the two-year balance sheet of the business (refer to Figure 7-2).

Accounts receivable change

Punch Line: An increase in accounts receivable hurts cash flow; a decrease helps cash flow.

REMEMBER

The accounts receivable asset shows how much money customers who bought products on credit still owe the business. This asset is a promise of cash that the business will receive. Basically, accounts receivable is the amount of uncollected sales revenue at the end of the period. Cash doesn't increase until the business collects money from its customers.

The business started the year with $6.718 million and ended the year with $8.883 million in accounts receivable. The beginning balance was collected during the year, but the ending balance had not been collected at the end of the year. Thus, the *net* effect is a shortfall in cash inflow of $2.165 million. The key point is that you need to keep an eye on the increase or decrease in accounts receivable from the beginning of the period to the end of the period. Here's what to look for:

>> If the amount of credit sales you made during the period is greater than what you collected from customers during the period, your accounts receivable

increased over the period, and you need to *subtract* from net income that difference between start-of-period accounts receivable and end-of-period accounts receivable. In short, an increase in accounts receivable hurts cash flow by the amount of the increase.

>> If the amount you collected from customers during the period is greater than the credit sales you made during the period, your accounts receivable *decreased* over the period, and you need to *add* to net income that difference between start-of-period accounts receivable and end-of-period accounts receivable. In short, a decrease in accounts receivable helps cash flow by the amount of the decrease. Reducing the amount that customers owe the business is good news from the cash flows perspective.

In our business example, accounts receivable increased $2.165 million. Cash collections from sales were $2.165 million less than sales revenue. Ouch! The business increased its sales substantially over the last period, so you shouldn't be surprised that its accounts receivable increased. The higher sales revenue was good for profit but bad for cash flow.

REMEMBER

The lagging behind effect of cash flow is the price of growth — managers and investors need to understand this point. Increasing sales without increasing accounts receivable is a happy situation for cash flow, but in the real world you usually can't have one increase without the other.

Inventory change

Punch Line: An increase in inventory hurts cash flow; a decrease helps cash flow.

Inventory is usually the largest short-term, or *current*, asset of businesses that sell products. If the inventory account is greater at the end of the period than at the start of the period — because unit costs increased or because the quantity of products increased — the amount the business actually paid out in cash for inventory purchases (or for manufacturing products) is more than what the business recorded in the cost of goods sold expense for the period.

In our business example, inventory decreased $2.328 from start-of-year to end-of-year as a result of the company pivoting from selling just products to focus on selling software and related services. In our business example, the company was actually able to reduce the amount of inventory it owned as it was able to successfully liquidate a number of product lines that were not replaced. So the company was able to turn $2.328 million into cash by not having to replace these items. Thus, this was a very nice bump to cash flow as the money spent in previous years to invest in inventory was instead turned into cash via aggressively selling or liquidating older or discontinued product lines.

Prepaid expenses change

Punch Line: An increase in prepaid expenses (an asset account) hurts cash flow; a decrease helps cash flow.

A change in the prepaid expenses asset account works the same way as a change in inventory and accounts receivable, although changes in prepaid expenses are usually much smaller than changes in those other two asset accounts.

The beginning balance of prepaid expenses is charged to expense this year, but the cash for this amount was actually paid out last year. This period (the year 2024 in our example), the business pays cash for next period's prepaid expenses, which affects this period's cash flow but doesn't affect net income until next period. In short, the $25,000 increase in prepaid expenses in this business example has a negative cash flow effect.

REMEMBER

As it grows, a business needs to increase its prepaid expenses for such things as insurance (premiums have to be paid in advance of the insurance coverage) property taxes and its inventory of office and data processing supplies. Increases in accounts receivable, inventory, and prepaid expenses are the cash flow price a business has to pay for growth. Rarely do you find a business that can increase its sales revenue without increasing these assets.

Depreciation: Real but non-cash expense

Punch Line: Recording depreciation expense decreases the book value of long-term operating (fixed) assets. No cash outlay occurs when recording depreciation expense. Each year the business converts in an indirect way part of the total cost invested in its fixed assets into cash. It recovers this amount through cash collections from sales. Thus, depreciation is a positive cash flow factor.

The original costs of fixed assets are recorded in a *property, plant, and equipment* type account. Depreciation is recorded in an *accumulated depreciation* account, which is a so-called *contra* account because its balance is deducted from the balance in the fixed asset account (see Figure 7-2). Recording depreciation increases the accumulated depreciation account, which decreases the book value of the fixed asset.

The amount of depreciation expense recorded in the period is a portion of the original cost of the business's fixed assets, most of which were bought and paid for years ago. (Chapters 6 and 7 explain more about depreciation.) Because the depreciation expense is not a cash outlay this period, the amount is added to net income to determine cash flow from operating activities (refer to Figure 8-2). Depreciation is just one adjustment factor to get from net income reported in the income statement to cash flow from operating activities reported in the statement of cash flows.

For measuring profit, depreciation is definitely an expense — no doubt about it. Buildings, machinery, equipment, tools, vehicles, computers, and office furniture are all on an irreversible journey to the junk heap (although buildings usually take a long time to get there). Fixed assets (except for land) have a limited, finite life of usefulness to a business; depreciation is the accounting method that allocates the total cost of fixed assets to each year of their use in helping the business generate sales revenue. In our example, the business recorded $1.239 million of depreciation expense for the year. Notice that the total amount recorded in the statement of cash flows is $1.739 million, or $500,000 higher. The reason for this difference is that the company also recorded $500,000 of amortization expense during the year (to reduce the value of certain intangible assets). The combination of these two items amounts to the $1.739 million figure in the statement of cash flows.

TIP

Instead of looking at depreciation as only an expense, consider the investment-recovery cycle of fixed assets. A business invests money in its fixed assets that are then used for several or many years. Over the life of a fixed asset, a business has to recover through sales revenue the cost invested in the fixed asset (ignoring any residual value at the end of its useful life). In a real sense, a business "sells" some of its fixed assets each period to its customers — it factors the cost of fixed assets into the sales prices that it charges its customers.

For example, when you go to a supermarket, a small slice of the price you pay for that litre of milk goes toward the cost of the building, the shelves, the refrigeration equipment, and so on. (No wonder they charge so much!) Each period, a business recoups part of the cost invested in its fixed assets. In the example, $1.739 million of sales revenue went toward reimbursing the business for the use of its fixed and intangible assets during the year.

Changes in operating liabilities

Punch Line: An increase in a short-term operating liability helps cash flow; a decrease hurts cash flow.

The business in our example, like almost all businesses, has four basic liabilities inextricably intertwined with its expenses: accounts payable, accrued liabilities, other current liabilities and deferred revenue and income tax payable. When the beginning balance of one of these liability accounts is the same as its ending balance (not too likely, of course), the business breaks even on cash flow for that account. When the end-of-period balance is higher than the start-of-period balance, the business did not pay out as much money as was recorded as an expense in the year. Refer back to the company's comparative balance sheet of the business in Figure 7-2 to compare the beginning and ending balances of these three liability accounts.

In our business example, the business disbursed $1.654 million to pay off last year's accounts payable balance. (This $1.654 million was the accounts payable balance at December 31, 2023, the end of the previous fiscal year.) Its cash this year decreased $1.654 million because of these payments. But this year's ending balance sheet (at December 31, 2024) shows accounts payable of $1.929 million that the business will not pay until the following year. This $1.929 million amount was recorded to expense in the year 2024. So, the amount of expense was $275,000 more than the cash outlay for the year; or, in reverse, the cash outlay was $275,000 less than the expense. An increase in accounts payable benefits cash flow for the year. In other words, an increase in accounts payable has a positive cash flow effect. Increases in accrued liabilities, other current liabilities and deferred revenue and income tax payable work the same way.

REMEMBER

In short, liability increases are favourable to cash flow — in a sense the business ran up more on credit than it paid off. Such an increase means that the business delayed paying cash for certain things until next year. So you need to add the increases in the three liabilities to net income to determine cash flow, as you see in the statement of cash flows (refer to Figure 8-2). The business avoided cash outlays to the extent of the increases in these three liabilities. In some cases, of course, the ending balance of an operating liability may be lower than its beginning balance, which means that the business paid out more cash than the corresponding expenses for the period. In this case, the decrease is a negative cash flow factor.

Putting the cash flow pieces together

Taking into account all the adjustments to net income, the bottom line (oops, we shouldn't use that term when referring to cash flow) is that the company's cash balance increased $7.593 million from its operating activities during the year. The first section in the statement of cash flows (refer to Figure 8-2) shows the stepping stones from net income to the amount of cash flow from operating activities.

Recall that the business experienced sales growth during this period mainly by increasing service revenue. The downside of sales growth is that assets and liabilities also grow — the business needs higher sales level and also has higher accounts receivable and would usually also have higher inventory. In our example the company has less inventory because it has generated its growth by increasing service revenue which does not involve inventory. The business's prepaid expenses and liabilities also increased, although not nearly as much as accounts receivable.

Still, the business had $7.593 million cash at its disposal. What did the business do with this $7.593 million of available cash? You have to look to the remainder of the cash flow statement to answer this important question.

Sailing Through the Rest of the Statement of Cash Flows

After you get past the first section of the statement of cash flows, the remainder is a breeze. Well, to be fair, you *could* encounter some rough seas in the remaining two sections. But, generally speaking, the information in these sections is not too difficult to understand. The last two sections of the statement report on the other sources of cash to the business and the uses the business made of its cash during the year.

Understanding investing activities

The second section of the statement of cash flows (refer to Figure 8-1 or 8-2) reports the investment actions that a business's managers took during the year. Investments, like tea leaves, serve as indicators regarding what the future may hold for the company. Major new investments are the sure signs of expanding or modernizing the production and distribution facilities and capacity of the business. Major disposals of long-term assets and shedding off a major part of the business could be good news or bad news for the business, depending on many factors. Different investors may interpret this information differently, but all would agree that the information in this section of the cash flow statement is important.

Certain long-lived operating assets are required for doing business. For example, FedEx and UPS wouldn't be terribly successful if they didn't have airplanes and trucks for delivering packages and computers for tracking deliveries. When these assets wear out, the business needs to replace them. Also, to remain competitive, a business may need to upgrade its equipment to take advantage of the latest technology or to provide for growth. These investments in long-lived, tangible, productive assets, which are called *property, plant, and equipment* or *fixed assets* for short, are critical to the business's future. In fact, these cash outlays are called *capital expenditures* to stress that capital is being invested for the long haul.

One of the first claims on cash flow from operating activities is for capital expenditures. Note that the business spent $750,000 on fixed assets, which are referred to more formally as *property, plant, and equipment* in the cash flow statement (to keep the terminology consistent with account titles used in the balance sheet — the term *fixed assets* is rather informal).

A typical statement of cash flows doesn't go into much detail regarding exactly what specific types of fixed assets the business purchased (or constructed): how many additional square feet of space the business acquired, how many new drill presses it bought, and so on. Some businesses do leave a clearer trail of their investments, though. For example, in the notes or elsewhere in their financial reports, airlines describe how many new aircraft of each kind were purchased to replace old equipment or to expand their fleets.

REMEMBER

Usually, a business disposes of some of its fixed assets every year because they reached the end of their useful lives and will no longer be used. These fixed assets are sent to the junkyard, traded in on new fixed assets, or sold for relatively small amounts of money. The value of a fixed asset at the end of its useful life is called its *residual value*. The disposal proceeds from selling fixed assets are reported as a source of cash in the investing activities section of the statement of cash flows. Usually, these amounts are fairly small. Also, a business may sell off fixed assets because it's downsizing or abandoning a major segment of its business; these cash proceeds can be fairly large, particularly in the case of discontinued operations. We discuss discontinued operations in Chapter 6.

Looking at financing activities

Note in the annual statement of cash flows for the business example (refer to Figure 8-1 or 8-2) that cash flow from operating activities is a positive $7.593 million and the negative cash flow from investing activities is $750,000. The result to this point, therefore, is a net cash increase of $6.843 million, which would have increased the company's cash balance this much if the business had no financing activities during the year. However, the business decreased its long-term debt during the year, its owners invested additional money in the business, and it distributed some of its profit to shareholders. The third section of the cash flow statement summarizes the *financing activities* over the period.

REMEMBER

The managers did not have to go outside the business for the $7.593 million cash increase generated from its operating activities for the year. Cash flow from operating activities is an *internal* source of money generated by the business itself, in contrast to *external* money that the business raises from lenders and owners. A business does not have to go hat in hand for external money when its internal cash flow is sufficient to provide for its growth. Making profit is the cash flow spigot that should always be turned on.

A business that earns a profit could, nevertheless, have a *negative* cash flow from operating activities — meaning that despite posting a net income for the period, the changes in the company's assets and liabilities cause its cash balance to decrease. In reverse, a business could report a bottom-line *loss* for the year, yet it could have a *positive* cash flow from its operating activities. The cash recovery from depreciation plus the cash benefits from decreases in its accounts receivable and inventory could be more than the amount of loss. More realistically, a loss usually leads to negative cash flow, or little positive cash flow.

The term *financing* refers to a business raising capital from debt and equity sources — by borrowing money from banks and other sources willing to loan money to the business and by its owners putting additional money in the business. The term also includes the flip side — that is, making principal payments on debt and returning capital to owners. The term *financing* also includes cash distributions by the business from profit to its owners in the form of dividends. By the way, keep in mind that interest on debt is an expense that is reported in the income statement. Dividends, on the other hand, are not expenses reported in the income statement. Dividends are deductions from retained earnings. We discuss the statement of retained earnings in Chapter 6.

Most businesses borrow money for the short term (generally defined as less than one year), as well as for longer terms (generally defined as more than one year). In other words, a typical business has both short-term and long-term debt.

The business in our example has both short-term and long-term debt. Although this is not a hard-and-fast rule, most cash flow statements report just the *net* increase or decrease in short-term debt, generally with financial institutions, not the total amounts borrowed and total payments on short-term debt during the period. In contrast, both the total amounts of borrowing from and repayments on long-term debt during the year are generally reported in the statement of cash flows — the numbers are reported gross, instead of net.

In our example, $950,000 of long-term debt was paid down during the year, but short-term debt was paid off during the year and replaced with new short-term notes payable. However, no net increase is reported in the cash flow statement, as the amount didn't change.

The financing section of the cash flow statement also reports the flow of cash between the business and its owners (the shareholders of a corporation). Owners can be both a *source* of a business's cash (capital invested by owners) and a *use* of a business's cash (profit distributed to owners). The financing activities section of the cash flow statement reports additional capital raised from its owners, if any, as well as any capital returned to the owners. In the cash flow statement, note that the business issued preferred shares for $5 million during the year, and it paid a total of $400,000 cash dividends from profit to its owners.

Speaking of cash dividends from profit to shareholders, you might note that we deduct the $400,000 cash dividends directly from the $7,593,000 cash flow from profit for the year, which leaves $7,193,000 for other business purposes. You might think that we should deduct the $400,000 in cash dividends from operating activities to better "match up" the cash flow from profit (operating activities) and how much of this amount was distributed to the owners. In our view, this is a natural comparison to make. However, the official financial reporting standard for private companies in Canada (Accounting Standards for Private Enterprises) says that cash distributions from profit should be put in the financing activities section of the statement of cash flows, as you see in Figures 8-1 and 8-2. As for international standards used by public companies (International Financial Reporting Standards), dividends paid can be reported as either operating or financing cash flows. For further discussion on this point, see the next section, "Being an Active Reader."

WARNING

Besides the difference in the treatment of dividends paid when comparing cash flow statements of companies following ASPE and those following IFRS, we have to warn you of another potential difference. This difference is for the classification of interest and dividends received. For private companies using ASPE, interest and dividends received are revenues and so they increase profit. Consequently, they are included as operating cash flows. For IFRS they can be reported either as operating or investing inflows of cash since they consist of returns on investments. When it comes to interest paid by the business, the distinction between ASPE and IFRS is the same as the description above concerning dividends paid. ASPE requires the reporting of interest payments as operating cash flows, while IFRS gives a choice between showing these as financing or operating cash outflows.

Being an Active Reader

As a business lender or investor, your job is to ask questions (at least in your own mind) when reading a financial statement. You should be an active reader, not a ho-hum passive reader, in reading the statement of cash flows. You should mull over certain questions to get full value out of the financial statement.

The statement of cash flows reveals what financial decisions the business's managers made during the period. Of course, management decisions are always subject to second-guessing and criticizing. And passing judgment based on reading a financial statement isn't totally fair, because it doesn't capture the pressures the managers faced during the period. Maybe they made the best possible decisions in the circumstances. Then again, maybe not.

One issue comes to the forefront in reading the company's statement of cash flows. The business in our example (refer to Figure 8-1 or 8-2) distributed $400,000 cash from profit to its owners — a 9 percent *payout ratio* (which equals the $400,000 distribution divided by its $4.482 million net income). In analyzing whether the payout ratio is too high, too low, or just about right, you need to look at the broader context of the business's sources of and needs for cash.

The company's $7.593 million cash flow from operating activities is enough to cover the business's $750,000 capital expenditures during the year well as the $950,000 of debt repayments, and still leave a very healthy $5.893 million available. The owners also kicked in another $5 million during the year, for a grand total of $10,893,000. If we were on the board of directors of this business, we certainly would ask the chief executive why cash dividends to shareowners were limited to $400,000, given the significant increase in cash.

Trying to Pin Down Free Cash Flow

A term has emerged in the lexicon of finance: free cash flow. This is not — we repeat, not — an officially defined term by any authoritative accounting rule-making body. Furthermore, the term does not appear in cash flow statements reported by businesses. Rather, *free cash flow* is street language; the term appears on some finance Internet sites. Securities brokers and investment analysts use the term freely (pun intended). Unfortunately, free cash flow hasn't settled into one universal meaning, although most usages have something to do with cash flow from operating activities.

TIP

The term *free cash flow* refers to the following:

» Net income plus depreciation expense, plus any other expense recorded during the period that does not involve the outlay of cash — such as amortization of costs of the intangible assets of a business, and other asset write-downs and impairments that don't require cash outlay

» Cash flow from operating activities as reported in the statement of cash flows, although the very use of a different term (*free cash flow*) suggests a different meaning is intended

» Cash flow from operating activities minus the amount spent on capital expenditures during the year (purchases or construction of property, plant, and equipment)

>> Earnings before interest, tax, depreciation, and amortization (EBITDA) — although this definition ignores the cash flow effects of changes in the short-term assets and liabilities directly involved in sales and expenses, and it obviously ignores that most of interest and income tax expenses are paid in cash during the period

WARNING

In the strongest possible terms, we advise you to be clear about which definition of free cash flow a speaker or writer is using. Unfortunately, you can't always determine what the term means even in context. Be careful out there!

One definition of free cash flow, in our view, is quite useful: cash flow from operating activities minus capital expenditures for the year. The idea is that a business needs to make capital expenditures to stay in business and thrive. And to make capital expenditures, the business needs cash. Only after paying for its capital expenditures does a business have "free" cash flow that it can use as it likes. In the example in this chapter, the free cash flow according to this definition is:

$7.593 million cash flow from operating activities – $750,000 capital expenditures = $6.843 million free cash flow

In many cases, cash flow from operating activities falls short of the money needed for capital expenditures. To close the gap, a business has to borrow more money, persuade its owners to invest more money in the business or dip into its cash reserve. Should a business in this situation distribute any of its profit to owners? After all, it has a cash *deficit* after paying for capital expenditures. But, in fact, many businesses make cash distributions from profit to their owners even when they don't have any free cash flow.

IN THIS CHAPTER

» **Disclosing changes in owners' equity**

» **Realizing that accounting is as much an art form as a science**

» **Grasping the impacts of alternative accounting methods in recording profit**

» **Taking a closer look at cost of goods sold expense and depreciation expenses**

» **Monitoring hot topics within sales revenue and expenses**

» **Using the statement of cash flows as a sanity check**

Chapter **9**

Choosing Accounting Methods

ccounting is a constantly changing profession that strives to adhere to a simple mandate of providing complete, accurate, reliable, and timely financial information on which to base business and economic decisions. The importance of this concept is how we begin this chapter, because understanding just how dynamic accounting environments have become and the associated disclosures that should come along with all the "numbers" should be kept in mind at all times.

To start, we raise the topic of disclosure in external financial reports to a business's creditors and investors. Accountants prefer the term *adequate disclosure* and don't like the term *full disclosure*, which could involve a high legal standard that might require providing highly sensitive information. Businesses don't have to reveal everything in their external financial reports — they're justified in protecting their competitive advantages by withholding disclosure about some matters. At the same time, business financial reports should reveal all the information that creditors and investors are entitled to know about the business (hence the term *adequate disclosure*).

The three primary financial statements — income statement, balance sheet, and statement of cash flow (see Chapters 6, 7, and 8) — constitute the bedrock disclosure by a business. Public companies are subject to many rules regarding the disclosure of information in addition to their three basic financial statements. Virtually all businesses include (or should include) notes to their financial statements, which we discuss in Chapter 10.

One thing businesses do not have to disclose is how different their profit and financial condition would have been had they used alternative accounting methods. In recording revenue, expenses, and other business transactions, the accountant must choose among different methods for recording the economic reality of the transactions. You may think that accountants are in agreement on the exact ways of recording business transactions, but this isn't the case.

REMEMBER

As you dive into this chapter, remember that accounting is a constantly evolving profession that is almost always in a perpetual state of playing catch-up with the dizzying rate of change occurring throughout the global economic, tax, and financial landscape.

Reporting Changes in Shareholders' Equity

Although the three primary financial statements (income statement, balance sheet, and statement of cash flows) are important, they can't convey all the information that a business's lenders and investors want to know and are entitled to know, so a business should include additional information. One prime example is the *statement of changes in shareholders' equity*. This statement supplements the information disclosed in the shareholders' equity section of the balance sheet. The statement provides a *continuity schedule*, which is a summary of the activities during the year that changed the shareholders' equity accounts.

Figure 9-1 presents the statement of changes in shareholders' equity for the technology company example we use in Chapters 6, 7, and 8. The company in the example had various transactions occur during the year involving its shareholders' equity accounts, including rolling $4.482 million of net income into retained earnings, raising $5 million of new equity in the form of preferred shares, and paying a dividend of $400,000. Presenting the statement of changes in shareholders' equity is convenient for the financial report reader.

QW Example Tech., Inc. Statement of Changes in Shareholders' Equity for the Fiscal Year Ending 12/31/2024						
Description	Common Shares	Common Shares Amount	Preferred Shares	Preferred Shares Amount	Retained Earnings	Total
Balance, January 1, 2024	1,000,000	$5,000,000	0	$0	$1,877,000	$6,877,000
Sale of Preferred Shares			500,000	$5,000,000		$5,000,000
Net Income					$4,482,000	$4,482,000
Dividends					($400,000)	($400,000)
Balance, December 31, 2024	1,000,000	$5,000,000	500,000	$5,000,000	$5,959,000	$15,959,000

© John Wiley & Sons, Inc.

FIGURE 9-1: Example of a statement of changes in shareholders' equity.

In Canada, private businesses that follow Accounting Standards for Private Enterprises (ASPE) prepare a statement of retained earnings. A statement of retained earnings looks similar to Figure 9-1 because it shows only the retained earnings column. Because the capital structure of private businesses is often simple, there is less need for further details.

Larger businesses generally have more complicated ownership structures than smaller and medium-size companies. Larger businesses are most often organized as corporations. (We discuss the legal organization of a business in Chapter 5.) Corporations can issue more than one class of shares, and many do. If one class has preference over the other class, it is called *preferred shares*. A corporation may have both voting and nonvoting shares.

We could go on and on, but the main point is that many businesses, especially larger public companies, engage in a broad range of activities during the year involving changes in their shareholders' equity components. These shareholders' equity activities can be important but tend to get lost in a comparative balance sheet and in the statement of cash flows. Therefore, the business prepares a separate statement of changes in shareholders' equity covering the same periods as its income statement. Some of these statements are monsters, with upwards of ten columns for the elements of shareholders' equity.

TIP

The general format of the statement of changes in shareholders' equity includes columns for each class of shares, retained earnings, and the accumulated other comprehensive income element of shareholders' equity. Professional stock analysts have to pore over these statements. Average financial report readers quickly turn the page when they see this statement, but it's worth a quick glance if nothing else.

Recognizing Reasons for Accounting Differences

The financial statements reported by a business are just one version of its financial history and position. Different accountants and different managers for the business could have presented different versions that would have told a different story, at least to some extent. The income statement and balance sheet depend on which accounting methods a business chooses. Moreover, on orders from management, financial statements can be tweaked to make them look better. We discuss how businesses can (and do!) put spin on their financial statements in Chapters 10 and 14.

The dollar amounts reported in the financial statements of a business aren't simply facts that depend only on good bookkeeping. Here's why different accountants record transactions differently. The accountant:

>> Must make choices among different accounting methods for recording the amounts of revenue and expenses.

>> Can select between pessimistic and optimistic estimates and forecasts when recording certain revenue and expenses.

>> Has some wiggle room in implementing accounting methods, especially regarding the precise timing of when to record sales and expenses.

>> Can carry out certain tactics at year-end to put a more favourable spin on the financial statements, usually under the orders or tacit approval of top management. (We discuss these manipulations in Chapter 10.)

REMEMBER A popular notion is that accounting is an exact science and that the amounts reported in financial statements are true and accurate down to the last dollar. When people see a dollar amount reported to the last digit in a financial statement, they get the impression of exactitude and precision. However, in the real world of business, the accountant has to make many arbitrary choices between ways of recording revenue and expenses and of recording changes in their corresponding assets and liabilities. (In Chapter 6, we explain that revenue and expenses are coupled with assets and liabilities.)

We don't discuss accounting errors in this chapter. It's always possible that the accountant doesn't fully understand the transaction being recorded or relies on misleading information, with the result that the entry for the transaction is wrong. And bookkeeping processing slip-ups happen. The term *error* generally refers to honest mistakes; there's no intention of manipulating the financial statements. Unfortunately, if a business does not detect accounting mistakes, its financial statements end up being misleading. (We point out in Chapter 3 that a business should institute effective internal controls to prevent accounting errors.)

Looking at a More Conservative Version of the Company's Income Statement

TIP

Everyone having a financial stake in a business should understand and keep in mind the bias or tilt of the financial statements they're reading. Using a baseball analogy, the version of financial statements in your hands may be in left field, right field, or centre field. All versions are in the ballpark of generally accepted accounting principles or GAAP, which define the playing field but don't dictate that every business has to play straight down the middle. In their financial reports, businesses don't comment on whether their financial statements as a whole are liberal, conservative, or somewhere in between. However, a business does have to disclose in the notes to its statements which accounting methods it uses. (See Chapter 10 for getting a financial report ready for release.)

Presenting an alternative income statement

REMEMBER

Only one set of financial statements is included in a business's financial report: one income statement, one balance sheet, one statement of cash flows, and one statement of changes in shareholders' equity. A business does not provide a second alternative set of financial statements that would have been generated if the business had used different accounting methods and if the business had not tweaked its financial statements. The company's financial statements would have been different if alternative accounting methods had been used to record sales revenue and expenses and if the business had not engaged in certain end-of-period manoeuvres to make its financial statements look better.

Figure 9-2 shows a comparison that you never see in real-life financial reports. The Actual column presents the income statement reported by the business. The Alternative column reveals an income statement for the year that the business could have reported (but didn't) if it had used alternative but acceptable accounting methods. The Difference column shows the effect on profit between the two methods. For example, sales revenue is less by $750,000 in the alternative column. Combined with higher cost of goods sold by $150,000 and higher operating expenses by $100,000, this produces a negative $1 million difference in operating income. In the Alternative scenario, income tax expense is lower as a result of the decrease in operating income and thus net income has been reduced by $650,000, which you see as a negative number.

	QW Example Tech., Inc. Two Income Statements for the Fiscal Year Ending 12/31/2024		
(all dollar amounts in thousands except earnings per share)	ACTUAL FYE 12/31/2024	ALTERNATIVE FYE 12/31/2024	DIFFERENCE FYE 12/31/2024
Sales Revenue, Net	$71,064	$70,314	($750)
Costs of Goods Sold	$26,891	$27,041	$150
Gross Profit	$44,173	$43,273	($900)
Selling, General, & Administrative Expenses	$36,678	$36,778	$100
Operating Income	$7,495	$6,495	($1,000)
Other Expenses (Income):			
Other Expenses & (Income)	$250	$250	$0
Interest Expense	$350	$350	$0
Total Other Expenses (Income)	$600	$600	$0
Profit Before Income Taxes	$6,895	$5,895	($1,000)
Income Tax Expense (Benefit)	$2,413	$2,063	($350)
Net Income	$4,482	$3,832	($650)
Earnings Per Share (Fully Diluted)	$2.76	$2.36	($0.40)

© John Wiley & Sons, Inc.

FIGURE 9-2: Actual versus Alternative income statements for a company.

REMEMBER

Assuming you've read Chapter 6, the Actual account balances in the income statement should be familiar — these are the same numbers from the financial statements we explain in that chapter. The dollar amounts in the Alternative column are the amounts that could have been recorded using different accounting methods. You don't need the statement of cash flows here, because cash flow from profit (operating activities) is the same amount under both accounting scenarios and because the cash flows from investing and financing activities are the same. Keep in mind these important points.

The business in our example adopted accounting methods that were more aggressive and resulted in strong profits. Some businesses go in the opposite direction. They adopt conservative accounting methods for recording profit performance, and they wouldn't think of tinkering with their financial statements at the end of the year, even when their profit performance falls short of expectations and their financial condition has some trouble spots. The Alternative column in Figure 9-2 reports the results of conservative accounting methods. As you see, using the Alternative accounting methods results in a lower bottom line. Net income would have been $650,000 smaller, resulting in a decrease in earnings per share of $0.40 or approximately 14 percent lower.

Now, you may very well ask, "Where did you get the numbers for the Alternative financial statements?" The dollar amounts are our best estimates of the conservative and cautious numbers for this business — a company that has been in business for several years, has made a profit most years, and has not gone through bankruptcy. Both the Actual and the Alternative income statements are hypothetical but realistic and are not dishonest or deceitful.

Spotting significant differences

It's a little jarring to see a second set of numbers for the income statement. You're bound to raise your eyebrows when we say that both sets of accounting numbers are true and correct yet different. Financial report users have been conditioned to accept one version for financial statements without thinking about what alternative financial statements would look like. Seeing an alternative scenario takes a little time to get used to, like learning how to drive on the left side of the road in Great Britain. An alternative set of numbers is always lurking in the shadows, even though you don't get to see them.

TIP

The differences in revenue and expenses don't look that big, until you get to the bottom line. In the Alternative scenario, net income is $650,000 lower, which is 14.5 percent smaller. In putting a market value on the business, suppose that you use the earnings multiple method. Further suppose that you are willing to pay six times the most recent annual profit of the business. Using the Actual financial statements, you would offer $26.892 million for the business ($4.482 million net income × 6 = $26.892 million). If the Alternative accounting methods were used, you'd offer only $22.992 million ($3.832 million net income × 6 = $22.992 million). If the business had used the more conservative accounting methods, you would offer $3.9 million less for the business!

Explaining the Differences

REMEMBER

Keep in mind the following points about revenue and expenses (from Chapter 6):

>> Recording sales revenue increases an asset (or decreases a liability in some cases).

>> Recording an expense decreases an asset or increases a liability.

Therefore, assets are lower or liabilities are higher or both if you used conservative accounting methods, and collectively these differences should equal the difference in retained earnings.

This section briefly explains some of the reasons for each of the differences shown in Figure 9-2. We keep the explanations succinct and to the point. The idea is to give you a taste of some of the most important reasons for the differences.

Accounts receivable and sales revenue

Here are some common reasons why sales revenue and accounts receivable are lower when conservative accounting methods are adopted:

>> A business waits a little longer to record sales made on credit, to be more certain that all aspects of delivering products and the acceptance by customers are finalized and there is little chance of customers returning the merchandise. This delay in recording sales results in a slightly lower accounts receivable balance because some credit sales in December weren't yet recorded because they were still in the process of final acceptance by the customers. (Of course, the cost of goods sold for these sales wouldn't have been recorded.)

If products are returnable and the deal between the seller and buyer does not satisfy normal conditions for a completed sale, the recording of sales revenue should be postponed until the return privilege no longer exists. For example, some products are sold *on approval,* which means the customer takes the product and tries it out for a few days or longer to see if they really want it. International Financial Reporting Standards (IFRS) accounting rules require that a reasonable estimate of regular returns be recognized as a liability when the sale is recorded. At the same time, an estimate of the cost of the goods that are expected to be returned are recognized as an asset. The technical term for this revenue recognition rule is the *contract-based approach.* For small businesses in Canada that follow ASPE, this rule does not apply and the business follows the earnings approach, in which the effect of the return is usually recorded when the return takes place.

REMEMBER

Businesses should be consistent from year to year regarding when they record sales. For some businesses, the timing of recording sales revenue is a major problem — especially when the final acceptance by the customer depends on performance tests or other conditions that the business must satisfy. Some businesses engage in *channel stuffing* by forcing their dealers or customers to take delivery of more products than they want to buy. A good rule to follow is to read the company's financial statement notes that explain its revenue recognition policy or method, and see if anything seems unusual. If the note is vague, be careful!

>> A business may be quicker in recognizing a customer's past due balance as uncollectible. After a reasonable effort to collect a debt, a business creates an allowance for doubtful account by recording a *bad debts* expense. The amount recorded is based on the estimates reflecting past patterns or current trends. The allowance for doubtful accounts decreases the past due accounts receivable balance to zero or a substantially reduced amount. In contrast, a business could wait much longer to allow for a customer's past due accounts. Both accounting methods end up writing off a customer's debt if it has been outstanding too long and has become uncollectible — but a company could wait until the last minute to record a bad debt expense.

Inventory and cost of goods sold expense

The business in the example sells products, mainly to other businesses. A business either manufactures the products it sells or purchases products for resale to customers. (Chapter 16 explains the determination of product costs for manufacturing businesses.) For this discussion, it isn't too important whether the business manufactures or purchases the products it sells. The costs of its products have drifted upward over time because of inflation and other factors. Therefore, the business has had to increase its sales prices to keep up with product cost increases.

Product cost inflation can be dealt with in two ways:

>> Follow the chronological order of acquisition and let the older product costs go out to cost of goods sold before the more recent product costs are charged out to expense.

>> Use a method of charging out inventory to cost of goods sold expense that does not follow the chronological order of acquisition.

We explain these different methods in the section "Calculating Cost of Goods Sold and Cost of Inventory."

In Figure 9-2, the Actual scenario uses the method that minimizes the cost of goods sold expense and maximizes the cost of ending inventory. The Alternative scenario, in contrast, uses the method that maximizes the cost of goods sold expense and minimizes the cost of ending inventory. The Alternative scenario's cost of goods sold expense for the year is $150,000 higher.

Fixed assets and depreciation expense

Most accountants agree that the costs of long-term operating assets that have limited useful lives to a business should be spread out over those predicted useful lives instead of being charged off entirely to expense in the year of acquisition. These long-lived operating assets are labelled *property, plant, and equipment* and less formally are called *fixed assets*. (The cost of land owned by a business is not depreciated because land is a property right that has perpetual life.) The allocation of the cost of a fixed asset over its estimated useful economic life to a business is called *depreciation*. The principle of depreciation is beyond criticism, but the devil is in the detail.

REMEMBER

The original costs of fixed assets should theoretically include certain costs in addition to their purchase or construction costs. However, in practice, these fringe costs are not always included in the original cost of fixed assets. For example, it is theoretically correct to include installation costs of putting into place and connecting electrical and other power sources of heavy machinery and equipment. It is correct to include the cost of painting logos on the sides of delivery trucks. The cost of an older building just purchased by a business should include the preparatory clean-up costs and the safety inspection cost. But in practice, a business may not include such additional costs in the original costs of its fixed assets on the basis that the amounts are not significant.

In the Actual accounting scenario, the business does include most of these additional costs in the original costs of its fixed assets, which means that the cost balances of its fixed assets are higher compared with the Alternative, conservative scenario. These additional costs aren't expensed immediately but are included in the total amount to be depreciated over future years. Also, in the Actual scenario, the business uses *straight-line depreciation* (discussed later in this chapter), which spreads out the cost of a fixed asset evenly over the years of its useful life to the business.

In contrast, in the Alternative (conservative) scenario, the business in its fixed asset accounts doesn't include any costs other than purchase or construction costs, which means these additional costs are charged to expense immediately. Also, and most importantly, the business uses *accelerated depreciation* (discussed later in this chapter) for allocating the cost of its fixed assets to expense. Higher amounts are allocated to early years, and smaller amounts to later years. The result is that the accumulated depreciation amount in the Alternative scenario is higher, which signals that a lot more depreciation expense has been recorded over the years.

Accrued expenses payable, income tax payable, and expenses

REMEMBER

A typical business at the end of the year has certain costs that will not be paid until sometime in the future — costs that are an outgrowth of the current year's operating activities. For example, a business should *accrue* (calculate and record) the amount it owes to its employees for vacation and sick pay. A business may not have received its property tax bill yet, but it should estimate the amount of tax to be assessed and record the proper portion of the annual property tax expense for the current year. One expense accrual is easy to calculate: the accumulated interest on notes payable that hasn't been paid yet at the end of the year. Calculating this amount is straightforward because the amount borrowed and the interest rate are definite.

Most businesses sell products with expressed or implied warranties and guarantees. Even if good quality controls are in place, some products sold by a business don't perform up to promises, and the customers want the problems fixed. A business has to estimate the cost of these future obligations and record this amount as an expense in the same period that the goods are sold (along with the cost of goods sold expense, of course). It should not wait until customers return products for repair or replacement. If the business waits to record the cost, some of the expense for the guarantee work won't be recorded until the following year. After being in business a few years, a company can forecast with reasonable accuracy the percentage of products sold that will be returned for repair or replacement under the guarantees and warranties offered to its customers. However, brand-new products that have no track record may be a serious problem in this regard.

In the Actual scenario, the business doesn't estimate future product warranty and guarantee costs and certain other costs that should be accrued on the basis that the amounts are insignificant. It records these costs on a when-paid basis. It waits until it incurs these costs to record an expense. The company has decided that although its liabilities are understated, the amount is not significant. In the Alternative scenario, on the other hand, the business takes the high road and goes to the trouble of estimating future costs that should be matched against sales revenue for the year. Therefore, its accrued expenses payable liability account is higher.

In the Alternative, conservative scenario (see Figure 9-2), we assume that the business can use the same accounting methods for income tax, which gives a lower taxable income and income tax for the year. Accordingly, the income tax expense for the year is $350,000 lower, and the year-end balance of income tax payable is lower. A business makes instalment payments during the year on its estimated income tax for the year, so only a fraction of the annual income tax is still unpaid at the end of the year. A business is required by the Canada Revenue Agency (CRA) to use the same accounting methods for income tax that it does for recording its transactions. However, CRA has several exceptions which leads to complexities we don't go into here.

Wrapping things up

Figure 9-2 presents just one alternative scenario regarding how different accounting methods cause differences in the financial statements of a company. The differences in Figure 9-2 are not unrealistic in our opinion. Businesses keep only one set of books. Even a business itself doesn't know how different its financial statements would be if it had used different accounting policies or methods. You can read the financial statement notes describing the accounting policies a business follows to determine whether liberal or conservative accounting methods are being used. We warn you that accounting policy notes are not easy to read. Plus, they don't allow you to determine what profit would have been and how the balance sheet amounts would be different if alternative accounting policies or methods had been used.

TIP

If you own or manage a business, we urge you to get involved in deciding which accounting policies and methods to use for measuring your profit and how these methods are implemented. Chapter 18 explains that a manager has to answer questions about their financial reports on many occasions, so you should know which accounting methods your business uses to prepare the financial statements. However, "get involved" does not mean manipulating the amounts of sales revenue and expenses recorded in the year — to make profit look higher, to smooth fluctuations in profit from year to year, or to improve the amounts of assets and liabilities reported in your ending balance sheet. You shouldn't even consider doing these things. (Of course, these manipulations go on in the real world. Some people also drive under the influence, but that doesn't mean you should.)

Calculating Cost of Goods Sold Expense and Inventory Cost

One main accounting decision that companies that sell products must make is which method to use for recording the cost of goods sold expense, which is the sum of the costs of the products sold to customers during the period. You deduct cost of goods sold from sales revenue to determine *gross profit* — the first profit line on the income statement (refer to Figure 9-2). Cost of goods sold is an important figure because if gross margin is wrong, bottom-line profit (net income) is wrong.

A business acquires products either by buying them (retailers and distributors) or by producing them (manufacturers). Chapter 16 explains how manufacturers determine product cost; for retailers, product cost is simply purchase cost. (Well, it's not entirely this simple, but you get the point.) A business enters product cost in the inventory asset account and holds it there until the products are sold.

When a product is sold, but not before, you take the product cost out of inventory and record it in the cost of goods sold expense account. You must be absolutely clear on this point.

Likewise, not until the business sells products does it have a cost of goods sold expense. When you write a cheque or make an online payment, you know how much it's for — you have no doubt about the amount of the expense. But when a business withdraws products from its inventory and records a cost of goods sold expense, the expense amount is in some doubt. The amount of expense depends on which accounting policy or method the business selects. The business needs to adopt a cost flow formula or assumption concerning how the inventory is going to go from being asset to an expense. The assumption of the flow of inventory chosen by the business does not have to match the sequence in which the inventory physically moves in and out of the warehouse or store.

A business can choose among three methods to record its cost of goods sold and the cost balance that remains in its inventory asset account:

>> First-in, first-out (FIFO) cost method

>> Average cost method

>> Specific identification method

WARNING

You enter product costs in the inventory asset account in the order acquired, but you don't necessarily take costs out of the inventory asset account in this order. The different methods refer to the order in which product costs are *taken out* of the inventory asset account. You may think that only one method is appropriate — that the sequence in should be the sequence out. However, GAAP permit alternative methods based on accounting policy choices made by management. You can adopt whatever cost flow formula you want, as long as you consistently apply the same method from year to year.

REMEMBER

The choice among the three available accounting methods does *not* depend on the physical flow of products. For some types of inventory, such as gasoline, tracking the physical flow of products wouldn't even be possible. Generally speaking, products are delivered to customers in the order the business bought or manufactured the products — one reason is that a business does not want to keep products in inventory too long because the products might deteriorate or show their age.

So, products generally move into and out of inventory in a first-in, first-out sequence. Nevertheless, a business may choose another accounting method because it is a better match of the costs of goods sold expense to the sales revenue.

The FIFO (first-in, first-out) method

With the FIFO method, you charge out product costs to cost of goods sold expense in the chronological order in which you acquired the goods. At least, the assumption is that you do. The procedure is that simple, just like how the first people in line to see a movie get in the theatre first. The ticket-taker collects the tickets in the order in which they were bought.

Suppose that you acquire four units of a product during a period, one unit at a time, with unit costs as follows (in the order in which you acquire the items): $100, $102, $104, and $106. By the end of the period, you have sold three of these units. Using FIFO, you calculate the cost of goods sold expense as follows:

$$\$100 + \$102 + \$104 = \$306$$

In short, you use the first three units to calculate the cost of goods sold expense.

The cost of the ending inventory asset, then, is $106, which is the cost of the most recent acquisition. The $412 total cost of the four units is divided between the $306 cost of goods sold expense for the three units sold and the $106 cost of the one unit in ending inventory. The total cost has been accounted for; nothing has fallen between the cracks.

FIFO works well for two reasons:

>> **Products generally move into and out of inventory in a first-in, first-out sequence.** The earlier acquired products are delivered to customers before the later acquired products are delivered, so the most recently purchased products are the ones still in ending inventory to be delivered in the future. Using FIFO, the inventory asset reported in the balance sheet at the end of the period reflects recent purchase (or manufacturing) costs, which means the balance in the asset is close to the current *replacement costs* of the products.

Many grocers arrange food products on the shelf in such a way that forces customers to implement FIFO. (You've probably foiled that plan while grocery shopping, however, by checking the "best before" date on dairy or bakery products to buy the freshest food. So much for FIFO!)

TIP

>> **When product costs are steadily increasing, many (but not all) businesses follow a first-in, first-out sales price strategy and hold off raising sales prices as long as possible.** They delay raising sales prices until they have sold their lower-cost products. Only when they start selling from the next batch of products, acquired at a higher cost, do they raise sales prices. We favour using the FIFO cost of goods sold expense method when a business follows this basic sales pricing policy, because both the expense and the sales revenue are better matched for determining gross margin. We realize that sales pricing is complex and may not follow such a simple process, but the main point is that many businesses use a FIFO-based sales pricing approach. If your business is one of them, we urge you to use the FIFO expense method to be consistent with your sales pricing.

The average cost method

Without getting into the mechanics of how the computer software does this, we can say that the *average cost method* seems to offer the least amount of bias in choosing a cost formula. As the name implies, the cost of goods sold expense is based on the weighted average of the cost of the inventory purchased. The costs of many things in the business world fluctuate, and business managers tend to focus on the average product cost over a time period. Also, the averaging of product costs over a period of time has a desirable smoothing effect that prevents cost of goods sold from being overly dependent on wild swings of one or two acquisitions.

The specific identification method

Another acceptable cost formula is the *specific identification method*. As the title implies, you have to be able to specifically identify the inventory item that is being sold to assign the exact amount you paid for that inventory as a cost of goods sold expense. You would think that this would lead to the most accurate method. Maybe so, but you can't count on its use being possible. The item of inventory would have to be unique to distinguish it from all other items in inventory. Consequently, you would have to use something such as a serial number to tell you which particular item you're selling. A great example is a car. A car dealer might have two otherwise identical cars on the lot, but the serial numbers make each car unique and the cost of buying the two cars could be different.

Recording Inventory Losses under the Lower of Cost and Net Realizable Value (LC&NRV) Rule

Acquiring and holding an inventory of products involves certain unavoidable economic risks:

>> **Deterioration, damage, and theft risk:** Some products are perishable or otherwise deteriorate over time, which may be accelerated under certain conditions that are not under the control of the business (such as the air conditioning going on the blink). Most products are subject to damage when they're handled, stored, and moved (for example, when the forklift operator misses the slots in the pallet and punctures the container). Products may be stolen (by employees and outsiders).

>> **Replacement cost risk:** After you purchase or manufacture a product, its replacement cost may drop permanently below the amount you paid (which usually also affects the amount you can charge customers for the products).

>> **Sales demand risk:** Demand for a product may drop off permanently, forcing you to sell the products below cost just to get rid of them.

Regardless of which cost formula a business uses (such as FIFO) to record cost of goods sold and inventory cost, it must apply the *lower of cost and net realizable value* (LC&NRV) test to inventory. A business should regularly inspect its inventory carefully to determine loss due to theft, damage, and deterioration. And the business should go through the LC&NRV routine at least once a year, usually near or at year-end.

The process consists of comparing the cost of every product in inventory — meaning the cost that's recorded for each product in the inventory asset account according to whichever cost method or formula the company uses — with that product's *net realizable value* (NRV) (how much the business can sell the product for). If a product's cost on the books is higher than NRV, an accounting entry is made to decrease product cost to the lower value of NRV. In other words, inventory losses are recognized *now* rather than *later*, when the products are sold. The inventory cost value on the balance sheet is more realistic and not an inflated value that cannot be realized in a future sale.

Appreciating Depreciation Methods

In theory, depreciation expense accounting is straightforward: You divide the cost of a fixed asset (except land) among the number of years that the business expects to use the asset. In other words, instead of having a huge lump-sum expense in the year that you make the purchase, you charge a fraction of the cost to expense for each year of the asset's lifetime. Using this method is much easier on your bottom line in the year of purchase, of course.

WARNING

Theories are rarely as simple in real life as they are on paper, and this one is no exception. Do you divide the cost *evenly* across the asset's lifetime, or do you charge more to certain years than others? Furthermore, when it eventually comes time to dispose of fixed assets, the assets may have some *residual*, or *salvage*, value. In theory, only cost minus the residual value should be depreciated. But in practice, most companies ignore residual value and the total cost of a fixed asset is depreciated.

The CRA does not allow you to take a tax deduction for depreciation in the calculation of your taxable income. On the other hand, it does allow you to deduct the equivalent of depreciation, which it calls *capital cost allowance* (CCA). The tax deduction percentage rates in the CCA calculation allowed by the CRA are specifically listed by asset class. In turn, each asset class has a percentage rate that is allowed in the calculation of CCA using a technique that resembles the double-declining balance method used in accounting, which we are about to explain.

REMEMBER

Hundreds of books have been written on depreciation, but the book that counts when it's time to calculate your taxes is the Income Tax Act. Don't expect tax rules to be too logical. The tax laws have their own set of goals that don't coincide with the goals of accounting. That's why businesses keep one depreciation (CCA) schedule for income tax and a second for preparing financial statements.

The two main accounting methods for recording depreciation follow:

>> **Straight-line depreciation:** With this method, you divide the cost evenly among the years of the asset's estimated useful lifetime. Buildings typically are depreciated this way. Assume that a building purchased by a business cost $390,000, and its useful life is 39 years. The depreciation expense is $10,000 (1/39 of the cost) for each of the 39 years. After you start using this method for a particular asset, you shouldn't switch to another depreciation method later. Consistency is an important quality in the presentation of accounting information. You can compare the depreciation expenses best when the technique in calculating the expenses is consistent from year to year.

» **Accelerated depreciation:** This term is a generic catchall for several different kinds of methods. What they all have in common is that they're *front-loading* methods, meaning that you charge a larger amount of depreciation expense in the early years and a smaller amount in the later years.

One popular accelerated method is the *double-declining balance* (DDB) depreciation method. With this method, you calculate the straight-line depreciation rate, and then you double that percentage. You apply that doubled percentage to the declining balance over the course of the asset's depreciation time line.

You ignore the *residual value* of fixed assets in the first years of the life of the asset when calculating depreciation using the declining and double-declining methods of depreciation. You stop recording depreciation when book value of the fixed asset reaches its residual value. (Recall that *book value* is equal to original cost minus the balance in the accumulated depreciation account.)

REMEMBER

When you calculate depreciation for income tax (CCA), you also ignore the residual value of fixed assets under all conditions. Consequently, the asset's tax value — *undepreciated capital cost* (UCC) — will never be zero. This is the case because the CCA calculation is always taking a percentage of a balance, never the remaining balance.

Fully depreciated fixed assets are grouped with all other fixed assets in external balance sheets. All these long-term resources of a business are reported in one asset account called *property, plant, and equipment* (usually not "fixed assets"). If all its fixed assets were fully depreciated, the balance sheet of a company would look rather peculiar — the cost of its fixed assets would be offset by its accumulated depreciation. Keep in mind that the cost of land (as opposed to the structures on the land) is not depreciated. The original cost of land stays on the books as long as the business owns the property.

The straight-line depreciation method has strong advantages: It's easy to understand, and it stabilizes the depreciation expense from year to year. Nevertheless, many business managers and accountants favour adopting an accelerated depreciation method. By doing so, the decreasing charge for depreciation is counterbalanced with the increasing repair and maintenance costs the business invariably experiences at the later stages of the life of the asset. The end result is an even pattern of expense over the life of the asset. Keep in mind, however, that the depreciation expense in the annual income statement is higher in the early years when you use an accelerated depreciation method, and so bottom-line profit is lower. Many accountants and businesses like accelerated depreciation because it paints a more conservative (a lower or more moderate) picture of profit performance in the early years. Who knows — fixed assets may lose their economic usefulness to a business sooner than expected. When this happens, using the accelerated depreciation method looks very wise in hindsight.

REMEMBER

Except for new enterprises, a business typically has a mix of fixed assets — some in their early years of depreciation, some in their middle years, and some in their later years. So, the overall depreciation expense for the year may not be that different than if the business had been using straight-line depreciation for all its depreciable fixed assets. A business does *not* have to disclose in its external financial report what its depreciation expense would have been if it had been using an alternative method. Readers of the financial statements cannot tell how much difference the choice of accounting methods would have caused in depreciation expense that year. GAAP only require that the business mention the policies or methods it is using in the financial statement's notes.

REMEMBER

Depreciation is not about cash flow. It's a technique to allocate the cost of a long-term asset over the years you intend to use it to help generate revenue. The available techniques or methods for calculating depreciation are loaded with a bunch of estimates. You need to estimate how long you are going to use the asset. You need to estimate what kind of residual value you expect to get at the end of the useful life of the asset. Finally, you must try to choose the best depreciation method for your particular asset and business. Pick a method that will properly reflect the pace or rate at which you intend to use the asset. That way, the expense makes sense in relation to the particular revenue and to the asset. Don't be intimidated about arriving at estimates. Your estimates are bound to change. That's just the nature of estimates — and of accounting, for that matter.

Scanning the Revenue and Expense Horizon

Recording sales revenue and other income can present some hairy accounting problems. As a matter of fact, the standard setters around the globe — including the Canadian Accounting Standards Board (AcSB), the International Accounting Standards Board (IASB), and the U.S. Financial Accounting Standards Board (FASB) — rank revenue recognition as a major problem area. A good part of the reason for putting revenue recognition high on the list of accounting problems is that many high-profile financial accounting frauds have involved recording bogus sales revenue that had no economic reality. Sales revenue accounting presents challenging problems in some situations. But, in our view, the accounting for many key expenses is equally important. Frankly, it's difficult to measure expenses on a year-by-year basis.

We could write a book on expense accounting, which would have at least 20 or 30 major chapters. All we can do here is call your attention to a few major expense accounting issues.

>> **Asset impairment write-downs:** Inventory shrinkage and lower of cost and net realizable value, bad debts, and depreciation by their very nature are asset write-downs. Other asset write-downs are required when an asset becomes *impaired*, which means that it has lost some or all of its economic utility to the business. An asset write-down reduces the book (recorded) value of an asset (and at the same time records an expense or loss of the same amount). A *write-off* reduces the asset's book value to zero and removes it from the accounts, and the entire amount becomes an expense.

>> **Employee-defined benefits pension plans and other post-retirement benefits:** The GAAP rule on this expense is complex. The business must make several key estimates, including, for example, the expected rate of return on the investment portfolio set aside for these future obligations. This and other estimates affect the amount of expense recorded. In some cases, a business uses an unrealistically high rate of return to minimize the amount of this expense.

>> **Certain discretionary operating expenses:** Many operating expenses involve timing problems or serious estimation problems or both. Furthermore, some expenses are discretionary, which means how much to spend during the year depends almost entirely on the discretion of managers. Managers can defer or accelerate these expenses to manipulate the amount of expense recorded in the period. For this reason, publicly held companies filing financial reports with securities commissions are required to disclose some of these particular expenses.

>> **Income tax expense:** Public companies following IFRS can use different accounting methods for some of the expenses reported in the income statement than they use for calculating taxable income. Oh, boy! You calculate the hypothetical amount of taxable income as though the accounting methods the income statement uses were also used in the tax return; then you figure the income tax based on this hypothetical taxable income. This is the income tax expense that the income statement reports. You reconcile this amount with the actual amount of income tax owed based on the accounting method used for income tax purposes. A rather technical note to the financial statements provides a reconciliation of the two different income tax amounts. A second method, allowed only under ASPE, is called the taxes payable method. This method allows a business to record income tax expense purely on the basis of the amount of income tax the business pays.

>> **Management stock options:** A *stock option* is a contract between an executive and the business that gives the executive the option to purchase a certain number of the corporation's shares at a fixed price (called the *exercise* or *strike* price) after certain conditions are satisfied. Usually, a stock option does not vest until the executive has been with the business for a certain number of years. GAAP rules require that a value (measured using an appropriate options pricing model) be put on stock options when they are issued and that this amount be recorded as an expense.

Please don't think that the preceding short list does justice to all the expense accounting problems of businesses. Canadian businesses — large and small, public and private — operate in a highly developed and sophisticated economy. One result is that expense accounting has become complicated and confusing.

WARNING

As if accountants didn't already have enough problems in measuring profit, a growing trend among public corporations is to undercut their own income statements. In press releases and meetings with stock analysts, it seems an increasing number of public companies promote a version of adjusted earnings, on the grounds that these alternative concepts of profit are better guides to the future of the business. It's difficult to tell whether private businesses are following this trend. Private companies with few exceptions do not issue press releases or meet with stock analysts. Their communications and dealings with their sources of capital are private, of course.

In particular, many public companies use the metric of earnings before interest, tax, depreciation, and amortization (EBITDA) as a useful measure of their profit. You don't have to read far between the lines to see that these companies want to draw attention away from their income statements to put their profit performance in a more favourable light. We admit that EBITDA has a use in the management analysis of profit performance, but it's not the final, all-things-considered measure of profit that investors should focus on. Net income, not EBITDA, is the bottom line.

3

Understanding Financial Reports, Financial Statements, and Financial Information

Develop a basis for the inside story of how business financial reports are produced. (It's not as bad as making sausage, but there are several messy details.)

Discover how to dig deeper into a financial report, decipher operating performance summaries provided by management, and identify "devil in the detail" issues of importance.

Find out how both internal and external parties use financial statement analysis techniques and ratio calculations to interpret and better understand the financial performance of a company.

Get the lowdown on the more detailed and highly confidential accounting information that company executives, managers, and owners (in other words, the insiders) of the business need for identifying problems and opportunities — in short, for running the business.

Find out the current trends in financial reporting and discover how companies utilize "financial engineering" to help tell their stories.

IN THIS CHAPTER

» Reviewing the purposes of financial reports

» Keeping up to date on accounting and financial reporting standards

» Ensuring that disclosure is adequate

» Nudging the numbers to make profit and solvency look better

» Comparing the financial reports of public and private companies

» Dealing with information overload in financial reports

Chapter **10**

Producing Financial Reports

Financial statements are the core content of a financial report. But the term *financial report* connotes more content than the basic set of financial statements. To start this chapter, we briefly review the three primary business financial statements. Then we move on to a broader view of the contents of a financial report.

Lest you think that accountants prepare the whole of a financial report, we explain the role of top management in preparing the financial report of a business. Accountants are the main actors in whipping together the financial statements of the business. That's their job. Then the top-level managers of the business take over. The managers are the primary actors in deciding the additional content to put in the financial report, from the letter to the shareholders to the historical summary of the key financial data of the business.

We also call your attention to the seamy side of financial reporting. The company's managers may put a spin on the financial statement numbers generated by the accountant. Also, we compare the financial reports of the typical public corporation with those of private and smaller businesses.

Quickly Reviewing the Theory of Financial Reporting

Business managers, creditors, and investors rely on financial reports because they provide information regarding how the business is doing and where it stands financially. Like newspapers, financial reports deliver financial news about the business. One big difference between newspapers and financial reports is that businesses themselves, not independent reporters, decide what goes into their financial reports. If you read financial information on websites, such as Google Finance, keep in mind that the information comes from the financial reports prepared and issued by the business.

Starting with financial statements

In Chapters 6, 7, and 8, we explain the three primary financial statements of a business. Head to those chapters for more detail, but here's a brief overview:

>> **Income statement:** Summarizes sales revenue and other revenue and gains (if any) and expenses and losses (if any) for the period. It ends with the bottom-line profit for the period, which most commonly is called *net income* or *net earnings*. Inside a business, this profit performance statement is commonly called the *Profit & Loss,* or *P&L, report.*

>> **Balance sheet:** Summarizes the financial position at the end of the period, consisting of amounts for assets, liabilities, and owners' equity at the closing date of the income statement period (and at other times as needed by managers). Its more formal name is the *statement of financial position.*

>> **Statement of cash flows:** Reports the cash increase or decrease during the period from profit-making operating activities (revenue and expenses) and the reasons this key figure is different than bottom-line net income. It also summarizes other cash flows during the period from investing and financing activities.

These three statements, plus the notes to the financials and other content, are packaged into annual financial reports so a business's investors, lenders, and other interested parties can keep tabs on the business's financial health and performance. Abbreviated versions of their annual reports are distributed quarterly by public companies. Private companies do not have to provide interim financial reports, though many do. In this chapter, we shine a light on the preparation process so you can recognize the types of decisions that must be made before a financial report hits the streets.

Keeping in mind the reasons for financial reports

A financial report is designed to answer certain basic financial questions:

>> Is the business making a profit or suffering a loss, and how much?

>> Is the business's sales revenue increasing or decreasing?

>> How do assets stack up against liabilities?

>> Where did the business get its capital, and is it making good use of the money?

>> What is the cash flow from the profit or loss for the period?

>> Did the business reinvest all its profit or distribute some of the profit to owners?

>> Does the business have enough capital for future growth?

>> Does the business have enough liquidity to pay its bills, and is it solvent?

TIP

People should read a financial report like a road map: to point the way and check how the trip is going. Managing and putting money in a business is a financial journey. A manager is like the driver and must pay attention to all the road signs; investors and lenders are like the passengers who watch the same road signs. Some of the most important road signs are the ratios between sales revenue and expenses and their related assets and liabilities in the balance sheet.

In short, the purpose of financial reporting is to deliver important information that the lenders and owners of the business need and are entitled to receive. Financial reporting is part of the essential contract between a business and its lenders and investors. Although lawyers may not like this, the contract can be stated in a few words:

> Give us your money, and we'll give you the information you need to know regarding how we're doing with your money.

Financial reporting is governed by statutory and common law, and it should abide by ethical standards. Unfortunately, financial reporting sometimes falls short of both legal and ethical standards.

WARNING

Businesses assume that the readers of the financial statements and other information in their financial reports are knowledgeable about business and finance in general and understand basic accounting terminology and measurement methods. Financial reporting practices, in other words, take a lot for granted about readers of financial reports. Don't expect to find friendly hand-holding and helpful explanations in financial reports. Reading financial reports is not for the faint of heart. You need to be prepared for serious concentration.

Recognizing Management's Role

The *annual financial report* of a business consists of the three primary financial statements (mentioned earlier in this chapter) with their associated footnotes and a variety of additional content, such as photographs of executives, vision statements, highlights of key financial performance measures, letters to shareholders from top management, MDORs or MD&As (that is, management discussion of operating results or management discussion and analysis), and more. Public companies provide considerably more content than private companies. Much of the additional content falls outside the realm of financial accounting and to a large extent is at the discretion of the business.

The business's top managers assisted by their top lieutenants play an essential role in the preparation of the financial reports of the company — which they (and outside investors and lenders) should understand. The managers perform certain critical steps before the financial report of the company is released to the outside world:

1. **Confer with the company's chief financial officer and controller (chief accountant) to make sure that the latest accounting and financial reporting standards and requirements under generally accepted accounting principles (GAAP) are applied in its financial report.**

    A smaller business may consult with an independent CPA on these matters.

    With the adoption of the International Financial Reporting Standards (IFRS) for public companies and Accounting Standards for Private Enterprises (ASPE), we all have experienced a high degree of flux in accounting and financial reporting standards and requirements. The Accounting Standards Board (AcSB) and its international counterpart, the International Accounting Standards Board (IASB), have been and continue to be very busy.

REMEMBER

A business and its independent CPA auditors cannot simply assume that the accounting methods and financial reporting practices that have been used for many years are still correct and adequate. A business *must* check carefully whether it is in full compliance with current accounting standards and financial reporting requirements.

2. **Carefully review the disclosures in the financial report.**

The top managers and financial officers must make sure that the *disclosures* — all information other than the financial statements — are adequate according to financial reporting standards and that all the disclosure elements are truthful but, at the same time, not damaging to the business. Ideally, the disclosures should be written in clear language.

TIP

This disclosure review can be compared with the notion of *due diligence,* which is done to make certain that all relevant information is collected, that the information is accurate and reliable, and that all relevant requirements and regulations are being complied with. This step is especially important for public corporations whose securities (shares and debt instruments) are traded on securities exchanges. Public businesses fall under the jurisdiction of several securities laws, which require technical and detailed filings with the Canadian Securities Administrators (CSA).

3. **Consider whether additional information or explanations are needed in the annual report to the shareholders.**

The annual report contains two distinct sections — the financial statements and an unaudited section containing MD&A. The MD&A section of the annual report gives the top managers a platform for explaining major events that have occurred during the year reported. In addition, the top managers will also discuss how the business has or has not achieved the plans put forward in past annual reports. You will also find in the MD&A section outlines of management's future goals.

WARNING

When we discuss the third step later in this chapter, we're venturing into a grey area that accountants don't much like to talk about. The manager has to strike a balance between the business's interests on the one hand and the interests of the shareholder owners (investors) and creditors of the business on the other. The best analogy we can think of is business advertising. Advertising should be truthful but, as we're sure you know, businesses have a lot of leeway regarding how to advertise their products and have been known to engage in hyperbole. Managers exercise the same freedoms in putting together their annual reports. Annual reports may have some hype, and managers may put as much positive spin on bad news as possible without making deceitful and deliberately misleading comments. See the later section "Putting a Spin on the Numbers (Short of Cooking the Books)" for details.

The management spin used to describe events or transactions of the past or even concerning plans for the future is fair game in the MD&A portion of the annual report. You expect to see a pitch made for keeping you interested and hoping for a good return on your investment. Don't forget, that portion of the annual report is not audited, so take what management says with a grain of salt.

Keeping Current with Financial Accounting and Reporting Standards

REMEMBER

Standards and requirements for accounting and financial reporting don't stand still. For many years, changes in accounting and financial reporting standards moved like glaciers — slowly and not too far. But, just as the climate has warmed, the activity of the accounting and financial reporting authorities has heated up. In fact, it's hard to keep up with the changes.

Without a doubt, the rash of accounting and financial reporting scandals over the last few decades or so was one major reason for the step-up in activity by the standard setters. In the United States, the Enron accounting fraud not only brought down a major international CPA firm (Arthur Andersen) but also led to passage of the Sarbanes-Oxley Act of 2002 and its demanding requirements on public companies regarding establishing and reporting on internal controls to prevent financial reporting fraud.

Canada had its own home-grown accounting scandals. Nortel Networks Corporation, viewed by shareholders as Canada's darling, came down like a tonne of bricks.

The other major reason for the heightened pace of activity by the standard setters is, in our opinion, the increasing complexity of doing business. When you look at how business is being conducted these days, you find more and more complexity — for example, the use of financial derivative contracts and instruments. The legal exposure of businesses has expanded, especially in respect to environmental laws and regulations. Canada has stepped up and adopted international standards (IFRS) for its public companies. The United States is next to join the internationalization of accounting and financial reporting standards, as we discuss in Chapter 2.

REMEMBER

In our view, the standard setters should be given a lot of credit for their attempts to deal with the problems that have emerged in recent decades and for trying to prevent repetition of the accounting scandals of the past. But the price of doing so has been a rather steep increase in the range and rapidity of changes in accounting and financial reporting standards and requirements. Top-level managers of businesses have to make sure that the business's top-level financial and accounting officers are keeping up with these changes and that their financial reports follow all current rules and regulations of GAAP. Managers lean heavily on their chief financial officers and controllers for keeping in full compliance with accounting and financial reporting standards.

Making Sure Disclosure Is Adequate

The financial statements are the backbone of the financial report section of the annual report. In fact, a financial report is not deserving of the name if the financial statements aren't included. But a financial report is much more than just the financial statements; a financial report needs *disclosures.* Of course, the financial statements themselves provide disclosure of important financial information about the business. The term *disclosures,* however, usually refers to additional information provided in a financial report.

The CEO of a public corporation, the president of a private corporation, or the managing partner of a partnership has the primary responsibility to make sure that the financial statements are prepared according to GAAP — ASPE or IFRS, as the case may be — and that the financial report provides adequate disclosure. They work with the business's chief financial officer and controller to make sure that the financial report meets the standard of adequate disclosure. (Many smaller businesses hire an independent CPA to advise them on their financial reports.)

REMEMBER

For a quick survey of disclosures in financial reports, the following distinctions are helpful:

>> **Notes** provide additional information about the basic figures included in the financial statements. Virtually all financial statements need notes to provide additional information for several of the account balances.

>> **Supplementary financial schedules and tables** to the financial statements provide more details than can be included in the body of financial statements.

>> A wide variety of **other information** is presented, some of which is required if the business is a public corporation. Other information is voluntary and not strictly required legally or according to GAAP.

Notes: Nettlesome but needed

Notes appear at the end of the financial statements. Within the financial statements, you see references to particular notes. And at the bottom of each financial statement, you often find the following sentence (or words to this effect): "The notes are integral to the financial statements." Read all notes for a full understanding of the financial statements, although we should mention that some notes are dense and technical. For example, read the note that explains how a public corporation put the value on its management stock options to record the expense for this component of management compensation. Then take two aspirin to get rid of your headache.

Notes come in two types:

>> **One or more notes are included to identify the major accounting policies and methods that the business uses.** (Chapter 9 explains that a business must choose among alternative accounting methods for recording revenue and expenses, and for their corresponding assets and liabilities.) The business must reveal which accounting methods it uses for booking its revenue and expenses. In particular, the business must identify its cost of goods sold expense (and inventory) method and its depreciation methods. Some businesses have unusual problems regarding the timing for recording sales revenue, and a note should clarify their revenue recognition method. Other accounting methods that have a material effect on the financial statements are disclosed in notes as well.

>> **Other notes provide additional information and details for many assets and liabilities.** For example, Canadian resource companies describe how they have taken care of recording liabilities for decommissioning and reclamation costs of mining sites. Details about stock option plans for executives are the main type of note to the share account in the owners' equity section of the balance sheet.

REMEMBER

Some notes are always required; a financial report would be naked without them. Deciding whether a note is needed (after you get beyond the obvious ones disclosing the business's accounting policies and methods) and how to write the note is largely a matter of judgment and opinion, although certain standards apply:

>> Because of dual GAAP (IFRS and ASPE) in Canada, the notes and related auditors' report must be clear and state the set of standards that were followed in the preparation of the financial statements and the disclosure requirements that apply.

>> For public companies that are listed on the U.S. stock exchanges (an example is Shopify Inc. which is also listed on the Toronto Stock Exchange (TSX), an

Annual Information Form prepared in accordance with U.S. generally accepted accounting principles as issued by the Financial Accounting Standards Board (FASB) would apply.

>> Canadian securities regulators require disclosure of a broad range of information for publicly owned corporations.

All this is quite a smorgasbord of disclosure requirements, to say the least.

REMEMBER

You may wonder how different the company's annual profits would have been if an alternative accounting method had been in use. A business's managers can ask its accounting department to do this analysis. But, as an outside investor, you would have to compute these amounts yourself (assuming you had all the necessary information). Businesses disclose which accounting methods they use, but they do not disclose how different annual profits would have been if an alternative method had been used.

Other disclosures in financial reports

The following discussion includes a fairly comprehensive list of the various types of disclosures (other than notes) found in annual financial reports of *publicly owned* businesses. A few caveats are in order:

>> Not every public corporation includes every one of the following items, although the disclosures are fairly common.

>> The level of disclosure by private businesses — after you get beyond the financial statements and notes — is generally much less than in public corporations. A private business may include any or all of the following disclosures, but by and large it is not required to do so (and, in our experience, few do).

>> Tracking the actual disclosure practices of private businesses is difficult because their annual financial reports are circulated only to their owners and lenders. In other words, a private business keeps its financial report as private as possible.

In addition to the financial statements and notes to the financials, public corporations typically include the following disclosures in their annual reports to their shareholders:

>> **Cover (or transmittal) letter:** A letter from the business's chief executive to the shareholders, which usually takes credit for good news and blames bad news on big government, unfavourable world political developments, a poor economy, or some other thing beyond management's control.

>> **Management's report on internal control over financial reporting:** An assertion by the chief executive officer and chief financial officer regarding their satisfaction with the effectiveness of the business's internal controls, which are designed to ensure the reliability of its financial reports and to prevent financial and accounting fraud.

>> **Highlights table:** A table that presents key performance indicators or figures from the financial statements, such as sales revenue, total assets, profit, total debt, owners' equity, number of employees, and number of units sold (such as the number of vehicles sold by an automobile manufacturer, or the number of "revenue seat miles" flown by an airline, meaning one airplane seat occupied by a paying customer for one mile). The idea is to give the shareholder a financial thumbnail sketch of the business.

>> **Management discussion and analysis:** The major developments and changes during the year that affected the business's financial performance and situation.

>> **Segment information:** A report of the sales revenue and operating profits (before interest and income tax, and perhaps before certain costs that cannot be allocated among different segments) for the major divisions of the organization, or for its different markets (international versus domestic, for example).

>> **Historical summaries:** A financial history that extends back beyond the years (usually three) included in the financial statements.

>> **Graphics:** Bar charts, trend charts, and pie charts representing financial conditions; photos of key people and products.

>> **Promotional material:** Information about the company, its products, its employees, and its managers, often stressing an overarching theme for the year. Most companies use their annual financial report as an advertising opportunity or a public relations opportunity.

>> **Profiles:** Information about members of top management and the board of directors. Of course, everyone appears to be well qualified for their position. Negative information (such as prior brushes with the law) is not reported.

>> **Quarterly summaries of profit performance and share prices:** Financial performance for all four quarters in the year and share price ranges for each quarter.

>> **Management's responsibility statement:** A short statement indicating that management has primary responsibility for the accounting methods used to prepare the financial statements, for writing the notes to the statements, and for providing the other disclosures in the financial report. Usually, this statement appears in the auditor's report.

>> **Independent auditor's report:** The report from the CPA firm that performed the audit, expressing an opinion on the financial statements and accompanying disclosures and their adherence to Canadian GAAP. Public corporations are required to have audits; private businesses may or may not have their annual financial statements audited.

>> **Company contact information:** Information on how to contact the company, including its web address.

We should mention that annual financial reports have virtually no humour — no cartoons, no one-liners, and no jokes. (Well, the CEO's letter to shareholders may have some humorous comments, even when the CEO doesn't mean to be funny.) Financial reports are written in a sombre and serious vein. The tone of most annual financial reports is that the fate of the Western world depends on the financial performance of the company. Come on!

Managers of public corporations rely on lawyers, auditors, and their financial and accounting officers to make sure that everything that should be disclosed in the business's annual financial reports is included, and that the exact wording of the disclosures is not misleading, inaccurate, or incomplete. This is a tall order. The field of financial reporting disclosure changes constantly.

WARNING

Both federal and provincial statutes, as well as authoritative accounting standards, have to be observed in financial report disclosures. Inadequate disclosure is just as serious as using wrong accounting methods for measuring profit and for determining values for assets, liabilities, and owners' equity. A financial report can be misleading because of improper accounting methods or because of inadequate or misleading disclosure. Both types of deficiencies can lead to nasty lawsuits against the business and its managers.

Putting a Spin on the Numbers (Short of Cooking the Books)

This section discusses two accounting tricks that involve manipulating, or massaging, the accounting numbers. We don't endorse either technique, but you should be aware of both so that you can watch out for them when reading financial statements. In some situations, the financial statement numbers don't come out exactly the way the business prefers. With the connivance of top management, accountants can use certain tricks of the trade — some would say sleight of hand, or shenanigans — to move the numbers closer to what the business prefers. One trick improves the appearance of the business's *short-term liquidity* and the cash balance reported in the balance sheet at the end of the year. The other device shifts some profit from one year to the next to report a smoother trend of net income from year to year. Nortel Networks Corporation used this last trick to its own demise.

WARNING

We don't mean to suggest that all businesses engage in these accounting machinations, but many do. The extent of use of these schemes is hard to pin down because no business would openly admit to using them. The evidence is fairly convincing, however, that many businesses massage their numbers to some degree. We're sure you've heard the term *loopholes* applied to income tax. Well, some loopholes exist in financial statement accounting as well.

Window dressing: Pumping up ending cash balance and cash flow

Suppose you manage a business and your controller has just submitted for your review the *preliminary*, or first draft, of the year-end balance sheet. (Chapter 7 explains the balance sheet, and Figure 7-2 shows a complete balance sheet for a business.) Figure 10-1 shows the current assets and current liabilities sections of the balance sheet draft.

FIGURE 10-1:
Current assets and current liabilities of a business, before window dressing.

Statement of Financial Position (AKA Balance Sheet)			
Current Assets:	12/31/2024	Current Liabilities:	12/31/2024
Cash & Equivalents	$30,000	Accounts Payable	$235,000
Accounts Receivable, Net	$486,000	Accrued Expenses	$187,000
Inventory, LC&NRV	$844,000	Income Taxes Payable	$58,000
Prepaid Expenses	$72,000	Short-Term Debt	$200,000
Total Current Assets	$1,432,000		$680,000

© John Wiley & Sons, Inc.

Wait a minute: a $30,000 cash balance? How can that be? Maybe your business has been having some cash flow problems and you've intended to increase your short-term borrowing and speed up collection of accounts receivable to help the cash balance. Folks generally don't like to see such a low cash balance — it makes them kind of nervous, to put it mildly, no matter how you try to cushion it. So what do you do to avoid setting off alarm bells?

Your controller is probably aware of a technique called *window dressing*, a simple method for making the cash balance look better. Suppose your fiscal year-end is

October 31. Your controller takes the cash collections from customers paying their accounts receivable that are actually received on November 1, 2, and 3, and records them as if these cash collections had been received on October 31. After all, the argument can be made that the customers' cheques were in the mail — that money is yours, as far as the customers are concerned.

WARNING

Window dressing reduces the balance in accounts receivable and increases the cash by the same amount — it has no effect on your profit figure for the period. It just makes your cash balance look a touch better. Window dressing can also be used to improve other accounts' balances, which we don't go into here. All these techniques involve holding the books open — to record certain events that take place after the end of the fiscal year (the ending balance sheet date) to make things look better than they were at the close of business on the last day of the year.

Sounds like everybody wins, doesn't it? You look like you've done a better job as manager, and your lenders and investors don't panic. Right? Wrong! Window dressing is deceptive to your creditors and investors, who have every right to expect that the end of your fiscal year as stated on your financial reports is truly the end of your fiscal year. Auditors who discover this type of treatment have to decide if this treatment materially affects the financial statements, and advise management to undo the window dressing. You can see in this situation how the auditor's judgment comes into play.

WARNING

Window dressing can be the first step on a slippery slope. A little window dressing today, and who knows what tomorrow? Maybe giving the numbers a nudge now will lead to more serious accounting deceptions, such as profit-smoothing techniques (discussed next), or even out-and-out accounting fraud. Moreover, when a business commits some accounting hanky-panky, should the business's chief executive brief its directors on the accounting manipulation? Things get messy, to say the least!

Be aware that window dressing improves cash flow from operating activities, which is an important number in the statement of cash flows that creditors and investors closely watch. (We discuss the statement of cash flows and cash flow from operating activities in Chapter 8.) Suppose, for example, that a business holds open its cash receipts journal for several days after the close of its fiscal year. As a result, its ending cash balance is reported $3.25 million higher than the business had in its chequing accounts on the balance sheet date. Also, its accounts receivable balance is reported $3.25 million lower than was true at the end of its fiscal year. This makes cash flow from profit (operating activities) $3.25 million higher, which could be the main reason in the decision to do some window dressing.

Smoothing the rough edges off year-to-year profit fluctuations

You shouldn't be surprised when we tell you that business managers are under tremendous pressure to make profit every year and to keep profit on the up escalator year after year. Managers strive to make their numbers and to hit the milestone markers set for the business. Reporting a loss for the year, or even a dip below the profit trend line, is a red flag that stock analysts and investors view with alarm. Everyone likes to see a steady upward trend line for profit; no one likes to see a profit curve that looks like a roller coaster.

Managers can do certain things to deflate or inflate profit (net income) recorded in the year, which are referred to as *profit-smoothing* techniques. Other names for these techniques are *income smoothing* and *earnings management.* Profit smoothing is like a white lie told for the good of the business and perhaps for the good of managers as well. Managers know that the accounting system always makes some noise. Profit smoothing muffles the noise.

REMEMBER

The general view in the financial community is that profit smoothing is not nearly as serious as *cooking the books,* or *juggling the books.* These terms refer to deliberate, fraudulent accounting practices such as recording sales revenue that has not happened or not recording expenses that have happened. Nevertheless, profit smoothing is still serious and if carried too far could be interpreted as accounting fraud. Managers can and do go to jail for fraudulent financial statements.

WARNING

Fraud is meant to deceive and may not be found by auditors. An audit by a CPA firm should root out any significant accounting fraud when the business is knowingly perpetrating the fraud or when it's an innocent victim of fraud against the business. But we continue to see many embarrassing cases in which a CPA auditor failed to discover major fraud by or against the business. Several books have been published on this topic, which you can find by typing *accounting fraud* or *cooking the books* in your search engine. We recommend *Forensic Accounting For Dummies* (John Wiley & Sons, Inc., 2011) by Frimette Kass-Shraibman and Vijay Sampath.

The pressure on public companies

Managers of publicly owned corporations whose shares are actively traded are under intense pressure to keep profits steadily rising. Security analysts who follow a particular company make profit forecasts for the business, and they base their buy/hold/sell recommendations largely on these earnings forecasts. If a business fails to meet its own profit forecast or falls short of stock analysts' forecasts, the market price of its shares usually takes a hit. Stock option and bonus incentive compensation plans are also strong motivations for achieving the profit goals set for the business.

WARNING

The evidence is fairly strong that publicly owned businesses engage in some degree of profit smoothing. Frankly, it's much harder to know whether private businesses do so. Private businesses don't face the public scrutiny and expectations that public corporations do. On the other hand, key managers in a private business may have bonus arrangements that depend on recorded profit. In any case, business investors and managers should know about profit smoothing and how it's done.

Compensatory effects

Most profit smoothing involves pushing some amount of revenue and expenses or both into years other than those in which they would normally be recorded. For example, if the president of a business wants to report more profit for the year, they can instruct the chief accountant to accelerate the recording of some sales revenue that normally wouldn't be recorded until next year, or to delay the recording of some expenses until next year that normally would be recorded this year.

Chapter 9 explains that managers choose among alternative accounting methods for several important expenses (and for revenue as well). After making these key choices, the managers should let the accountants do their jobs and let the chips fall where they may. If bottom-line profit for the year turns out to be a little short of the forecast or target for the period, so be it. This hands-off approach to profit accounting is the ideal way. However, managers often use a hands-on approach — they intercede (one could say interfere) and override the normal accounting for sales revenue or expenses.

TIP

Both managers who do profit smoothing and investors who rely on financial statements in which profit smoothing has been done must understand one thing: These techniques have compensatory effects. The effects next year offset and cancel out the effects this year. Less expense this year is counterbalanced by more expense next year. Sales revenue recorded this year means less sales revenue recorded next year. Of course, the compensatory effects work the other way as well: If a business depresses its current year's recorded profit, its profit next year benefits. In short, a certain amount of profit can be brought forward into the current year or delayed until the following year.

WARNING

A business can go only so far in smoothing profit. If a business has a particularly bad year, all the profit-smoothing tricks in the world won't close the gap. And if managers are used to profit smoothing, they may be tempted in this situation to resort to accounting fraud, or cooking the books.

Management discretion in the timing of revenue and expenses

Several smoothing techniques are available for filling the potholes and straightening the curves on the profit highway. Most profit-smoothing techniques require one essential ingredient: management discretion in deciding *when* to record expenses or *when* to record sales.

Many small business contractors whose contracts do not extend over several months or who are unable to estimate the progress toward completion on contracts are allowed to use the *completed contract method* for recording sales revenue. Not until the job is totally complete does the company book the sales revenue and deduct all costs to determine the gross margin from the job (in other words, from the contract). In most cases, the company has to return a few weeks after a job is finished for final touch-up work or to satisfy customer complaints. In the past, the company waited for this final visit before calling a job complete. However, in one case, the company was falling short of its profit goals, so the president decided to move up the point at which a job was called complete. The company decided not to wait for the final visit, which rarely involved more than a few minor expenses. Thus the company completed more jobs during the year, recorded more sales revenue and higher gross margin in the year, and the company met its profit goals.

The *completed contract method* calls for the recognition of revenue when the job is substantially complete. If reasonable estimates of progress can be established, the percentage of completion method must be used to account for all contracts.

You might be interested to know that the completed contract method for recognizing revenue in construction accounting is not allowed under IFRS. Instead, the *zero-profit method* is allowed which has the same bottom-line result as the completed contract method. You don't need to guess to understand why.

A common technique for profit smoothing is to delay normal maintenance and repairs, which is referred to as *deferred maintenance.* Many routine and recurring maintenance costs required for autos, trucks, machines, equipment, and buildings can be put off, or deferred, until later. These costs are not recorded to expense until the actual maintenance is done, so putting off the work means delaying recording the expense.

A few other techniques used include the following:

>> A business that spends a fair amount of money for employee training and development may delay these programs until next year so the expense this year is lower.

>> A company can cut back on its current year's outlays for market research and product development (though this could have serious long-term effects).

- » A business can reduce the amount of the estimated bad debts to record in a year. The percentage of accounts receivable viewed as uncollectible are reduced, decreasing its *bad debts*. The business can, therefore, put off recording some of its bad debts expense until next year.

- » A fixed asset out of active use may have little or no future value to a business. But instead of writing off the undepreciated cost of the *impaired asset* as a loss this year, the business may use some discretion and delay the write-off until next year under ASPE. However, impairments must be dealt with every year under IFRS.

Keep in mind that most of these costs will be incurred next year, so the effect is to rob Peter (make next year absorb the cost) to pay Paul (let this year escape the cost).

WARNING

Clearly, managers have a fair amount of discretion over the timing of some expenses, so certain expenses can be accelerated into this year or deferred to next year to make for a smoother year-to-year profit trend. But a business does not divulge in its external financial report the extent to which it has engaged in profit smoothing. Nor does the independent auditor comment on the use of profit-smoothing techniques by the business — unless the auditor thinks that the company has gone too far in massaging the numbers and that its financial statements are downright misleading.

FINANCIAL REPORTING ON THE INTERNET

The vast majority of public companies put their financial reports on their websites. For example, you can go to www.suncor.com and navigate to Suncor Energy Inc.'s investors relations, where you can locate its annual report to shareholders. Each company's website is different, but usually you can figure out fairly easily how to download its annual and quarterly financial reports. You can sometimes get the annual report broken down into its main components, such as management discussion & analysis and financials, which are strictly the financial statements with notes. You will find it easy to drill down to exactly what you want to see.

Alternatively (and this is far more involved, mind you), you can go to the SEDAR (System for Electronic Document Analysis and Retrieval) filing system and database at www.sedar.com. SEDAR is maintained by the Canadian Securities Administrators (CSA). EDGAR (Electronic Data Gathering, Analysis, and Retrieval), maintained by the Securities and Exchange Commission (SEC), is the corresponding system for the U.S. public companies. Finding a particular filing is relatively easy when you know which one you want to see.

Comparing Public and Private Companies

Suppose you had the inclination (and the time!) to compare 100 annual financial statements of publicly owned corporations with 100 annual financial statements of privately owned businesses (assuming you could assemble 100 private company financial reports). You'd see many differences. Public companies are generally much larger (in terms of annual sales and total assets) than private companies, as you would expect. Furthermore, public companies generally are more complex — concerning employee compensation, financing instruments, multinational operations, laws that effect big business, legal exposure, and so on.

REMEMBER

Private and public corporations are bound by GAAP for measuring profit and for valuing assets, liabilities, and owners' equity, and for disclosures in their financial reports. (To be more precise, private companies usually follow ASPE and are exempt from some accounting rules of the IFRS, particularly concerning disclosure.) By and large, private companies do not have too many serious accounting issues.

As we mention in Chapter 2, the accounting profession has taken initiatives with the goal of better recognizing the different needs of private companies and the constituents of financial reporting by private companies. Well, this is the party line. In our view, the main purpose is to lighten the accounting and financial reporting burden on private companies, which generally don't have the time or the accounting expertise to comply with the large number of complex standards on the books.

Reports from publicly owned companies

Around 1,500 publicly owned corporations have their shares traded on the TSX. In the United States, the figure is close to 7,000 corporations that are traded on the New York Stock Exchange, NASDAQ, or other stock markets. Publicly owned companies must file annual financial reports with the securities commissions. These companies' filings are available to the public on the SEDAR database (refer to the sidebar "Financial Reporting on the Internet").

The annual financial reports of publicly owned corporations include all or most of the disclosure items we list earlier in the chapter (see the section "Making Sure Disclosure Is Adequate"). As a result, annual reports published by large publicly owned corporations run to 30, 40, or 50 pages (or more). The large majority of public companies put their annual reports on their websites. Many public companies also present condensed versions of their financial reports — see the section "Recognizing condensed versions" later in this chapter.

Annual reports from public companies generally are well done — the quality of the production work and graphics is excellent; the colour scheme, layout, and design have good eye appeal. But be warned that the volume of detail in their financial reports is overwhelming. (See the next section for advice on dealing with the information overload in annual financial reports.)

Although private companies that follow ASPE are cut some slack when it comes to reporting certain financial information — such as earnings per share — the requirements for publicly owned businesses are more stringent. When a company goes public with an IPO (initial public offering of shares), it gives up a lot of the privacy that a closely held business enjoys. A public company is required to have its annual financial statements audited by an outside, independent CPA firm. The auditor passes judgment on the company's accounting methods, adequacy of disclosure, and information in the financial statements. The auditor's report also states whether or not the company has prepared its financial statements in accordance with the appropriate Canadian GAAP. The CPA auditor has a heavy responsibility to evaluate and report on the adequacy of the client's internal controls.

Reports from private businesses

Compared with their public brothers and sisters, private businesses following ASPE generally provide reduced disclosure in their annual financial reports. Their primary financial statements with the accompanying notes are pretty much it. Often, their financial reports may be printed on plain paper and stapled together. A privately held company may have few shareholders, and typically one or more of the shareholders are active managers of the business, who already know a great deal about the business. We suppose that a private company could email its annual financial report to its lenders and shareowners.

WARNING

Private corporations could provide all the disclosures we mention in this chapter — there's certainly no law against doing so. But they generally don't. Investors in private businesses can request confidential reports from managers at the annual shareholders' meetings (which is not practical for a shareholder in a large public corporation). And major lenders to a private business can demand that certain items of information be disclosed to them as a condition of the loan.

A private business may have its financial statements audited by a CPA firm but generally is not required by law to do so. In the case of public companies following IFRS, the stock market prices are extremely important, and full disclosure of information should be made publicly available so that market prices are fairly determined. On the other hand, the ownership shares of privately owned businesses are not traded, so there's no need for a complete package of information.

Dealing with Information Overload

As a general rule, the larger a business becomes the longer its annual financial report. We've seen annual financial reports of small, privately owned businesses that you could read in 30 minutes to an hour. In contrast, the annual reports of large, publicly owned business corporations are typically 30, 40, or 50 pages (or more). You would need two hours to do a quick read of the entire annual financial report, without trying to digest its details.

TIP

If you did try to digest the details of an annual financial report, which is a long, dense document not unlike a lengthy legal contract, you would need many hours (perhaps the whole day) to do so. For one thing, an annual financial report contains many, many numbers. We've never taken the time to count how many distinct numbers an average annual financial report contains. But we can guarantee the average report has at least hundreds of numbers, and reports for large, diversified, global, conglomerate businesses likely have more than a thousand.

Browsing based on your interests

How do investors in a business deal with the information overload of annual financial reports? Few people take the time to plough through every sentence, every word, every detail, and every number on every page — except for those professional accountants, lawyers, and auditors directly involved in the preparation and review of the financial report. It's hard to say how most managers, investors, creditors, and others interested in annual financial reports go about dealing with the massive amount of information — little research has been done on this subject. But we have some observations to share with you.

TIP

An annual financial report is like the Sunday edition of a newspaper, such as the *National Post*. Hardly anyone reads every sentence on every page of these Sunday papers, much less every word in the advertisements — most people pick and choose what they want to read. They browse their way through the paper, stopping to read only the particular articles or topics they're interested in. Some people just skim through the paper. Some glance at the headlines. We think most investors read annual financial reports like they read Sunday newspapers. The complete information is there if you really want to read it, but most readers choose which information they have time to read in depth.

Annual financial reports are designed for *archival purposes*, not for a quick read. Instead of addressing the needs of investors and others who want to know about the business's profit performance and financial position — but have only a limited amount of time available — accountants produce an annual financial report that is a voluminous financial history of the business. Accountants leave it to the users of annual reports to extract the main points. So, financial statement readers use certain key ratios and other tests to get a feel for the business's financial performance and position. (Chapters 12 and 19 explain how readers of financial reports get a fix on the financial performance and position of a business.)

Recognizing condensed versions

TIP

Here's a well-kept secret: Many public businesses and non-profit organizations don't send a complete annual financial report to their shareholders or members. They know that few people have the time or the technical background to read thoroughly the full-scale financial statements, notes, and other disclosures in their comprehensive financial reports. So, they present relatively brief summaries that are boiled-down versions of their complete financial reports.

Typically, these summaries — called *condensed financial statements* — do not provide notes or the other disclosures that are included in the complete and comprehensive annual financial reports. If you really want to see the official financial report of the organization, you retrieve it from the company's website or you can ask its headquarters to send you a copy — refer to the sidebar "Financial Reporting on the Internet."

Using other sources of business information

Keep in mind that annual financial reports are only one of several sources of information to owners, creditors, and others who have a financial interest in the business. Annual financial reports, of course, come out only once a year — usually two months or so after the end of the company's fiscal (accounting) year. You have to keep abreast of developments during the year by reading quarterly reports of the business, financial newspapers or by listening to BNN Bloomberg (Business News Network) on TV. And it's a good idea to keep up with blogs about the companies on the Internet, subscribe to newsletters, and so on. Financial reports present the sanitized version of events; they don't divulge scandals or other negative news about the business.

REMEMBER

Not everything you may like to know as an investor is included in the annual financial report. For example, information about salaries and incentive compensation arrangements with the business's top-level managers is disclosed in a management information circular, not in the annual financial report. A proxy statement is the means by which the corporation solicits the vote of shareholders on issues that require shareholder approval — one of which is compensation packages of top-level managers. Proxy statements are also available on the SEDAR database.

IN THIS CHAPTER

» **Looking after your investments**

» **Evaluating and managing investment opportunities**

» **Tapping into other sources of invaluable business information**

» **Scanning notes and focusing on which ones are important**

» **Looking at the auditor's report**

Chapter **11**

Deciphering a Financial Report

This chapter focuses on the *external* financial report that a business sends to its lenders and shareholders. Many topics explained in the chapter apply to not-for-profit (NFP) entities as well, but the main focus is reading the financial reports of profit-motivated business entities. External financial reports are designed for the *non-manager* stakeholders in the business. The business's managers should definitely understand how to read and analyze its external financial statements, and managers should do additional financial analysis, which we discuss in Chapter 13. This additional financial analysis by managers uses confidential accounting information that is not circulated outside the business.

This chapter ventures into the field of financial statement analysis. Some argue that this topic is in the realm of finance and investments, not accounting. Well, our answer is this: We assume one of your reasons for reading this book is to understand and learn how to read financial statements. From this perspective, this chapter definitely should be included, whether or not the topics fit into a strict definition of accounting.

Some years ago, a private business needed additional capital to continue its growth. Its shareholders could not come up with all the additional capital the business needed. So they decided to solicit several people to invest money in the company, including us. We studied the business's most recent financial report. We had an advantage that you'll have too if you read this chapter: We know how to read a financial report and what to look for.

After studying the financial report, we concluded that the profit prospects of this business looked promising and that we probably would receive reasonable cash dividends on his investment. We also thought the business might be bought out by a bigger business someday, and we would make a gain. That proved to be correct: The business was bought out a few years later, and we doubled our money (and earned dividends along the way).

Not all investment stories have a happy ending, of course. As you know, stock market prices go up *and* down. A business may go bankrupt, causing its lenders and shareholders large losses. This chapter isn't about guiding you toward or away from making specific types of investments. Our purpose is to explain basic tools lenders and investors use for getting the most information value out of a business's financial reports — to help you become a more intelligent lender and investor.

Knowing the Rules of the Game

When you invest money in a business venture or lend money to a business, you should receive regular financial reports from the business. The basic premise of financial reporting is *accountability* — to inform the sources of a business's ownership and debt capital about the business's financial performance and condition. For public companies, brief financial reports are sent to owners and lenders quarterly (every three months). A full and comprehensive financial report is sent annually. This chapter focuses on the annual financial report. The ratios and techniques of analysis that we explain in the chapter are useful for both quarterly and annual financial reports.

REMEMBER

Financial reports have both written rules and unwritten rules. The main written rules in Canada and elsewhere are called *generally accepted accounting principles* (GAAP). The unwritten rules don't have a name. For instance, no explicit rule prohibits the use of swear words and vulgar expressions in financial reports. Yet, quite clearly, a strict unwritten rule prevents improper language in financial reports. You should understand one unwritten rule in particular: A financial report is not a confessional. A business does not have to lay bare all its problems in its financial reports. A business cannot resort to accounting fraud to cover up its problems, of course, but it does not comment on its difficulties and sensitive issues in reporting its financial affairs to the outside world.

Making Savvy Investment Choices

An investment opportunity in a private business won't show up on your doorstep every day. However, if you make it known that you have money to invest as an equity shareholder, you may be surprised at how many offers come your way. Alternatively, you can invest in publicly traded *securities*, those shares and bonds listed every day in major securities markets. Your stockbroker would be delighted to execute a buy order for 100 shares of, say, Bell Canada Enterprises Inc. (BCE) for you. You could even do some investing online using a discount broker. (Most Canadian banks offer discount brokerage services. Individuals deciding to manage their own Registered Retirement Savings Plan (RRSP) investments through self-directed RRSP accounts find these services attractive, because the brokerage fees can be low on trades.) You could also have a trading account for your Tax-Free Savings Account (TFSA). Keep in mind that your money does not go to BCE; the company is not raising additional money. Your money goes to the seller of the 100 shares. You're investing in the *secondary capital market* — the trading in shares by buyers and sellers after the shares were originally issued some time ago. In contrast, those investors approached by private business invested in the *primary capital market*, which means that their money goes directly to the business.

A growing tactic for raising money is *crowdfunding*, which is done over the Internet. On a website, a new or early-stage business invites anyone with money to join in the venture and become a shareholder. Usually, you can invest a relatively small amount of money in a crowdfunding appeal. The business seeking the money is counting on a large number of people or legal entities to invest money in the opportunity.

Managing investments alone or using a third party

You may choose not to manage your securities investments or your RRSP investments yourself. But remember that, when managing your investments directly, for lack of a better term, "the buck stops with you." That is, when you make decisions to buy, sell, or trade any type of investment security, the decision is yours (and is not being supported by a professional advisor). Instead, you can put your money in one or more of the thousands of mutual funds available today, or in an exchange-traded fund (ETF), in closed-end investment companies, in unit investment trusts, and so on, all of which are managed by third-party professionals. You can read other books to gain an understanding of the choices you have for investing your money and managing your investments. Be careful about books that promise spectacular investment results with no risk and little effort. One practical, well-written, and level-headed book is *Investing For Canadians For Dummies*, 4th Edition, by Eric Tyson and Tony Martin (John Wiley & Sons, Inc., 2018).

Finding and understanding information sources

TIP

Investors in a private business have one main source of financial information about the business they've put their hard-earned money in: its financial reports. Investors should read these reports carefully and look for the vital signs of progress and problems. The financial statement ratios that we explain in Chapter 12 point the way — like signposts on the financial information highway.

Investors in securities of public businesses have many sources of information at their disposal. They can read the financial reports of the businesses they have invested in and those they are thinking of investing in. Instead of thoroughly reading these financial reports, they may rely on stockbrokers, the financial press, stock analysts' reports, and other sources of information. Many individual investors turn to their stockbrokers for investment advice. Brokerage firms put out all sorts of analyses and publications, and they participate in the placement of new shares and bond securities issued by public businesses. A broker will be glad to provide you information from companies' latest financial reports. So, why should you bother reading this chapter if you can rely on other sources of investment information?

REMEMBER

The more you know about interpreting a financial report, the better prepared you are to evaluate the commentary and advice of stock analysts and other investment experts. If you can at least nod intelligently while your stockbroker talks about a business's P/E and EPS, you look like a savvy investor — and you may get favourable treatment. P/E (Price/Earnings) and EPS (Earnings Per Share), by the way, are two of the key ratios explained later in Chapter 12. The ratios explained in Chapter 12 are frequently mentioned in the media. A business may include one or more of the ratios in its financial report (public companies have to disclose EPS).

Chapter 12 covers financial statement ratios that you should understand, as well as warning signs to look out for in the audit reports. (Part 2 of this book explains the three primary financial statements that are the core of every financial report: the income statement, the balance sheet, and the statement of cash flows.)

Contrasting Reading Financial Reports of Private Versus Public Businesses

Most public companies make their financial reports available to the public at large; they don't limit distribution only to their present shareholders and lenders. For instance, we don't happen to own any shares of BCE. So, how did we get its annual financial report? We simply went to BCE's website. In contrast, private companies generally keep their financial reports private — they distribute their financial reports only to their shareholders and lenders. Even if you were a close friend of the president of a private business, we doubt that the president would let you see a copy of its latest financial report. You may as well ask to see the president's latest personal income tax return. (You're not going to see that either.)

REMEMBER

As we explain in Chapters 2 and 10, the accounting profession currently has two sets of GAAP. Private companies that use ASPE (Accounting Standards for Private Enterprises) have been relieved of the onerous burdens imposed by certain accounting and financial reporting standards that apply to public companies required to use IFRS (International Financial Reporting Standards).

The annual financial reports of private businesses are generally bare bones. They include the primary financial statements (balance sheet, income statement, statement of retained earnings, and statement of cash flows), plus some notes — and that's about it.

TIP

Besides having to follow IFRS, public businesses are saddled with the additional layer of requirements issued by the various securities and exchange commissions. (These agencies have no jurisdiction over private businesses.) You can find the financial reports and other forms filed with the Canadian Securities Administrators (CSA) in the SEDAR (System for Electronic Document Analysis and Retrieval) filing system. You can access the system through www.sedar.com. The objective in making the filed information public is to enhance investor awareness and to promote confidence in the transparent operation of capital markets in Canada.

Many publicly owned businesses present very different annual financial reports to their shareholders than their filings with the CSA. A large number of public companies include only *condensed* financial information in their annual shareholder reports (not their full-blown and complete financial statements as would be filed with the CSA). The financial information in the two documents can't differ in any material way. In essence, an investor can choose from two levels of information — one condensed and the other very technical.

A typical annual financial report by a public company to its shareholders is a glossy booklet with excellent art and graphic design, including high-quality photographs. The company promotes its products and features its people in glowing terms that describe teamwork, creativity, and innovation — you get the picture. In contrast, the reports to the CSA are more formal and structured. We strongly recommend that professional investors and investment managers read not just the financial statements but the whole annual report, which contains the *management discussion and analysis* (MD&A) and the annual information form discussing the business's history, its main markets and competitors, bond ratings, environment matters, and so on.

Understanding the Role of MDORs and MD&As

Almost every public company produces what's commonly referred to as a *management discussion of operating results* or MDOR, generally located at the beginning of its annual financial report. The MDOR, also sometimes referred to as the MD&A, is a section of a business's financial report that is generally reserved for management to provide an assessment or overview of key operating results, market trends, industry data, strategies, and so on. This overview is what management believes would be beneficial for external parties to know to help them more fully understand the operating results of a business.

TIP

The MDOR is usually located at the front of the periodically prepared externally distributed financial report and quite often starts with a shareholder or investor letter prepared by the company's chair of the board or CEO.

REMEMBER

No doubt, the MDOR can provide useful information to external parties, but it should be noted that the information provided in the MDOR generally has not been audited by the independent CPA firm (but rather represents information being presented by a company's management team). This means that the MDOR tends to include a broader range of business information that has been internally prepared by the company and incorporates more opinions and perspectives than audited financial statements (which tend to stay factual in nature). We're not saying that the information provided in the MDOR is not valuable, because some very interesting topics can be covered along with supporting data (and we encourage you to thoroughly read the information presented). However, it's important to understand the role of the MDOR, the source of the information presented, and the fact that it can be "skewed" somewhat to direct a reader to topics that only tell a portion of the financial performance story.

Frolicking through the Notes

In contrast to MDOR disclosures (see the previous section), *financial statement notes* are part of the audited financial statements, prepared by an independent CPA firm (with support from company financial executives and legal counsel). They're most often located toward the back of the externally prepared financial report, just after the financial statements.

Reading the notes in annual financial reports is no walk in the park. The investment pros read them because in providing consultation to their clients they are required to comply with due diligence standards — or because of their legal duties and responsibilities of managing other people's money. As CPAs, we have to stay on top of financial reporting; every year we read a sample of annual financial reports to keep up with current practices. But beyond the group of people who get paid to read financial reports, does anyone read notes?

TIP

For a company you've invested in (or are considering investing in), we suggest that you do a quick read-through of the notes and identify the ones that seem to have the most significance. Generally, the most important notes are those dealing with the following matters:

>> **Stock options or other equity incentives awarded by the business to its executives:** The additional shares issued under stock options *dilute* (thin out) the business's earnings per share, which in turn puts downside pressure on the market value of its shares, assuming everything else remains the same.

>> **Pending lawsuits, litigation, and investigations by government agencies:** These intrusions into the normal affairs of the can have enormous consequences and always should be clearly understood.

>> **Revenue recognition policies, procedures, and guidelines:** Companies have come under increased scrutiny about how they report earned sales revenue in the income statement because using overly aggressive reporting techniques has become a focal point of potential fraud. Companies are pulling forward earned sales revenue to help enhance the operating results.

>> **Employee retirement and other post-retirement benefit plans:** Your main concerns here should be whether these future obligations of the business are seriously underfunded. We have to warn you: This particular note is one of the most complex pieces of communication you'll ever encounter.

>> **Intangible assets:** The economy has shifted dramatically over the past 30-plus years into the "information and digital age." Data, intellectual property, computer software code, goodwill, trade secrets, original content, and the like are now just as valuable an asset as a building, manufacturing machine and equipment, and good old-fashioned hard or tangible assets. The accounting for these *intangible assets* is evolving and relatively subjective, so you may want to pay extra attention to notes that focus specifically on how these assets are valued and amortized.

>> **Debt problems:** It's not unusual for companies to get into problems with their debt. Debt contracts with lenders can be complex and are financial straitjackets in some ways. A business may fall behind in making interest and principal payments on one or more of its debts, which triggers provisions in the debt contracts that give its lenders various options to protect their rights. Some debt problems are normal, but in certain cases lenders can threaten drastic action against a business, which should be discussed in its notes.

>> **Segment information for the business:** Public businesses have to report information for the major segments of the organization — sales and operating profit by territories or product lines. This gives a better glimpse of the different parts making up the entire business. (Segment information may be reported elsewhere in an annual financial report than in the notes.)

>> **Subsequent events:** The notes might reveal that an event that occurred after the end of the fiscal year has a direct effect on the business's capability to perform at an adequate pace in the future. An example is a business that reports a fire at one of its business plants.

Stay alert for other critical matters that a business may disclose in its notes. We suggest scanning each and every note for potentially important information. Finding a note that discusses a major lawsuit against the business, for example, may make that company's shares too risky for your stock portfolio.

Checking Out the Auditor's Report

All public companies are required by securities laws to have annual audits. Private companies follow ASPE and aren't covered by these laws and generally don't have regular audits. Audits by CPAs are expensive, and smaller businesses simply can't afford them. On the other hand, many privately owned businesses have audits done even though it is expensive because an audit report adds credibility to their financial report.

For larger private companies that have raised large amounts of capital, are envisioning going public, or need to establish a higher level of credibility, audits are completed because they know that an audit report adds credibility to their financial report, even though the audit is expensive.

If a private business's financial report doesn't include an audit report, you have to trust that the business has prepared accurate financial statements according to applicable accounting and financial reporting standards and that the notes to the financial statements cover all important points and issues. One thing you could do is to find out the qualifications of the company's chief accountant. Is the accountant a CPA? Does the accountant have a university degree with a major in accounting? Does the financial report have any obvious deficiencies?

In the following sections, we focus on why audits are so important and the general mechanics of an audit.

Why audits?

The top managers, along with their finance and accounting officers, oversee the preparation of the company's financial statements and notes (see Chapter 10 for details). These executives have a vested interest in the profit performance and financial condition of the business; their yearly bonuses usually depend on recorded profit, for example. This situation is somewhat like the batter in a baseball game calling the strikes and balls. Where's the umpire? Independent CPA auditors are like umpires in the financial reporting game. The licenced CPA comes in, does an audit of the business's accounting system and methods, critically examines the financial statements, and gives a report that's attached to the company's financial statements.

We hope we're not the first people to point this out to you, but the business world is not like Sunday school. A financial report can be wrong and misleading because of innocent, unintentional *errors* or because of deliberate, cold-blooded *fraud*. Errors can happen because of incompetence and carelessness. Audits are one means of keeping misleading financial reporting to a minimum. The CPA auditor should definitely catch all major errors. The auditor's responsibility for discovering fraud isn't as clear-cut. You may think catching fraud is the purpose of an audit, but we're sorry to tell you it's not as simple as that.

WARNING

Sometimes the auditor fails to discover major accounting fraud. Furthermore, the implementation of accounting methods is fairly flexible, leaving room for interpretation and creativity that's just short of *cooking the books* (deliberately defrauding and misleading readers of the financial report). Some massaging of the numbers is tolerated by auditors, which may mean that what you see on the financial report isn't exactly an untarnished picture of the business. We explain *window dressing* and *profit smoothing* — two common examples of massaging the numbers — in Chapter 10.

What's in an auditor's report?

REMEMBER

The large majority of financial statement audit reports give the business a clean bill of health, or what's called a *clean opinion*. (The technical term for this opinion is an *unmodified opinion*, which means that the auditor doesn't qualify or restrict their opinion regarding any significant matter.) At the other end of the spectrum, the auditor may state that the financial statements are misleading and shouldn't be relied upon. This negative, disapproving audit report is called an *adverse opinion*. That's the big stick that auditors carry: They have the power to give a company's financial statements a thumbs-down opinion, and no business wants that.

The threat of an adverse opinion almost always motivates a business to give way to the auditor and change its accounting or disclosure to avoid getting the kiss of death of an adverse opinion. An adverse audit opinion says that the financial statements of the business are misleading. The securities commission doesn't tolerate adverse opinions by auditors of public businesses; it would suspend trading in a company's securities if the company received an adverse opinion from its CPA auditor.

If the auditor finds no serious problems, the CPA firm gives the business's financial report an *unmodified* or *clean* opinion. The key phrase auditors love to use is that the financial statements *present fairly* the financial position and performance of the business. However, we should warn you that the standard audit report has enough defensive, legalistic language to make even a seasoned accountant blush. If you have any doubts, go to the website of any public corporation and look at its most recent financial statements, particularly the auditor's report. A clean audit report has predicable content; any deviation from a clean report involves significant technical jargon, outlining why the report is modified and not clean as to its opinion.

TIP

The following summary cuts through the jargon and explains what the clean audit report really says:

Audit Report (Unmodified or Clean Opinion)

1st section	We did an audit of the financial report of the business at the date and for the periods covered by the financial statements (which are specifically named).
2nd section	We express an opinion. The company's financial statements present fairly in all material respects the financial position, performance, and cash flows in accordance with the financial reporting standards.
3rd section	We describe the auditor's responsibilities, including ethical and independence requirements, and state that we obtained sufficient evidence to express our opinion.
4th section	We draw your attention to key audit matters.
5th section	We provide a description of management's primary responsibility for the financial statements, including enforcing internal controls for the preparation of the financial statements and assessing whether the company will continue as a going concern.
6th section	We carried out audit procedures that provide us a reasonable basis for expressing our opinion, but we didn't necessarily catch everything.
7th section	We followed the legal and regulatory requirements of the particular jurisdiction and we provide the name of the engagement partner on the audit along with their signature.

WARNING

Unfortunately, auditors' reports have become increasingly difficult to read. Even seasoned stock analysts have trouble figuring out the nuances of wording in an audit opinion. Much of this creeping obfuscation of audit report language has been caused by the legal responsibilities imposed on CPA auditors. In any case, be prepared to struggle through the language in reading an audit report. Sorry, but that's how it is in our litigation-prone society.

An audit report that does *not* give a clean opinion may look similar to a clean-opinion audit report to the untrained eye. Some investors see the name of a CPA firm next to the financial statements and assume that everything is okay — after all, if the auditor had seen a problem, the RCMP would have pounced on the business and put everyone in jail, right? Well, not exactly. For example, the auditor's report may point out a flaw in the company's financial statements but not a fatal flaw that would require an adverse opinion. In this situation, the CPA issues a *modified opinion*. The auditor includes a short explanation of the reasons for the modification. You don't see this type of audit opinion that often, but you should read the auditor's report to be sure.

WARNING

One type of an auditor's report is very serious — when the CPA expresses substantial doubts about the capability of the business to continue as a going concern. A *going concern* is a business that has sufficient financial wherewithal and momentum to continue its normal operations into the foreseeable future and that would be able to absorb a bad turn of events without having to default on its liabilities. A business could be under some financial distress but overall still be judged a going concern. Unless evidence to the contrary exists, the CPA auditor assumes that the business is a going concern.

Discovering fraud, or not

Auditors have trouble discovering fraud for several reasons. The most important reason, in our view, is that those managers who are willing to commit fraud understand that they must do a good job of concealing it. Managers bent on fraud are clever in devising schemes that look legitimate, and they're good at generating false evidence to hide the fraud. These managers think nothing of lying to their auditors. Also, they're aware of the standard audit procedures used by CPAs and design their fraud schemes to avoid audit scrutiny as much as possible.

Over the years, the auditing profession has taken somewhat of a wishy-washy position on the issue of whether auditors are responsible for discovering accounting and financial reporting fraud. The general public is confused because CPAs seem to want to have it both ways. CPAs don't mind giving the impression to the general public that they catch fraud, or at least catch fraud in most situations. However, when a CPA firm is sued because it didn't catch fraud, the CPA pleads that an audit conducted according to generally accepted auditing standards doesn't necessarily discover fraud in all cases.

In the court of public opinion, it's clear that people think that auditors should discover material accounting fraud — and, for that matter, auditors should discover any other fraud against the business by its managers, employees, vendors, or customers. CPAs refer to the difference between their responsibility for fraud detection (as they define it) and the responsibility of auditors perceived by the general public as the *expectations gap*. CPAs want to close the gap — not by taking on more responsibility for fraud detection but by lowering the expectations of the public regarding their responsibility.

You'd have to be a lawyer to understand in detail the case law on auditors' legal liability for fraud detection, and we're not lawyers. But quite clearly, CPAs are liable for gross negligence in the conduct of an audit. If the judge or jury concludes that gross negligence was the reason the CPA failed to discover fraud, the CPA is held liable. (CPA firms have paid millions and millions of dollars in malpractice lawsuit damages.)

REMEMBER

In a nutshell, standard audit procedures don't always uncover fraud, except when the perpetrators of the fraud are particularly inept at covering their tracks. Using tough-minded forensic audit procedures would put auditors in adversarial relationships with their clients, and CPA auditors want to maintain working relationships with clients that are cooperative and friendly. A friendly auditor, some would argue, is an oxymoron. Also, there's the cost factor. Audits are already expensive. The CPA audit team spends many hours carrying out many audit procedures.

An audit would cost a lot more if extensive fraud detection procedures were used in addition to normal audit procedures. To minimize their audit costs, businesses assume the risk of not discovering fraud. They adopt internal controls (see Chapter 3) that are designed to minimize the incidence of fraud. But they know that clever fraudsters can circumvent the controls. They view fraud as a cost of doing business (so long as it doesn't get out of hand).

One last point: In many accounting fraud cases that have been reported in the financial press, the auditor knew about the accounting methods of the client but didn't object to the misleading accounting — you may call this an *audit judgment failure.* In these cases, the auditor was overly tolerant of questionable accounting methods used by the client. Perhaps the auditor had serious objections to the accounting methods, but the client persuaded the CPA to go along with the methods.

In many respects, the failure to object to bad accounting is more serious than the failure to discover accounting fraud, because it strikes at the integrity and backbone of the auditor. CPA ethical standards demand that a CPA resign from an audit if the CPA judges that the accounting or financial reporting by the client is seriously misleading.

Chapter **12**

Analyzing Financial Information with Ratios

Whether from an internal or external perspective, financial ratio analysis represents an invaluable tool to help assess how a company is performing financially.

External parties rely heavily on completing detailed financial ratio analyses to evaluate the financial performance of a company but deal with two limiting factors:

» First, external parties generally can complete their analyses only on an annual or quarterly basis (when financial reports are issued).

» Second, and more importantly, external parties don't have access to the same amount of confidential or detailed financial information as internal management (which enables internal management to complete a more thorough and informative analysis).

Internal management can dig deeper and complete financial ratio analyses more frequently, but make no mistake — these tools are essential for both internal and external parties!

Understanding the Importance of Using Ratios to Digest Financial Statements

Financial statements have lots of numbers in them. (Duh!) All these numbers can seem overwhelming when you're trying to see the big picture and make general conclusions about the financial performance and condition of the business. Instead of actually reading your way through the financial statements — that is, carefully reading every line reported in all the financial statements — one alternative is to compute certain ratios to extract the main messages from the financial statements. Many financial report readers go directly to ratios and don't bother reading everything in the financial statements. In fact, five to ten ratios can tell you so much about a business.

REMEMBER

Financial statement ratios enable you to compare a business's current performance with its past performance or with another business's performance, regardless of whether sales revenue or net income was bigger or smaller for the other years or the other business. In other words, using ratios cancels out size differences. (We bet you knew that, didn't you?)

As a rule, you don't find too many ratios in financial reports. Publicly owned businesses are required to report just one ratio (earnings per share, or EPS, covered later in this chapter), and privately owned businesses generally don't report any ratios. Generally accepted accounting principles (GAAP) don't demand that any ratios be reported (except EPS for publicly owned companies). However, you still see and hear about ratios all the time, especially from stockbrokers and other financial professionals, so you should know what the ratios mean, even if you never go to the trouble of computing them yourself.

Improving Your Knowledge of Financial Language

Before we provide a listing of what are considered the standard or basic financial ratio analyses in the rest of this chapter, it's helpful to walk through a list of commonly used financial and accounting terminology (to ensure that you're well versed with financial lingo):

>> **Top Line:** A company's net sales revenue generated over a period of time (for example, for a 12-month period). This is found at the top of the income statement.

>> **COGS and COS:** Acronyms for costs of goods sold (for a product-based business) and costs of sales (for a service-based business). COGS or COS tend to vary directly (or in a linear fashion) with the top-line sales revenue.

>> **Gross Profit and Margin:** Sometimes used interchangeably, gross profit equals your top line less your COGS or COS. The gross margin (a percentage calculation) is determined by dividing your gross profit by the top line.

>> **Op Ex:** A rather broad term short for operating expenses, which may include selling, general, administrative, corporate overhead, and other related expenses. Unlike COGS or COS, Op Ex tends to be fixed in nature and does not vary directly with the top-line sales revenue.

>> **SG&A:** Selling, general, and administrative expenses. Companies may distinguish between Op Ex and SG&A to assist parties with understanding the expense structure of its operations in more detail.

>> **Bottom Line:** A company's net profit or loss after all expenses have been deducted from net sales revenue. Being in the *black* indicates that a net profit is present, and being in the *red* indicates that a net loss was generated. This information can usually be found at the end of the income statement.

>> **Breakeven:** The operating level where a company generates zero in profit or loss as it *broke even* (the amount of sales revenue that needs to be generated to cover all COGS/COS and Op Ex).

>> **Contribution Margin:** The profit generated by a specific operating unit or division of a company (but not for the company as a whole). Most larger companies have multiple operating units or divisions, so the profit (or loss) of each operating unit or division is calculated to determine how much that specific unit or division "contributed" to the overall performance of the entire company.

>> **Cap Ex:** Stands for capital expenditures and is a calculation of how much a company invested in tangible or intangible assets during a given period (for equipment, machinery, new buildings, investments in intangible assets, and so on).

>> **YTD, QTD, MTD:** Acronyms for year to date, quarter to date, and month to date. For example, a flash report may present QTD sales for the period of 10/1/24 through 11/15/24 (so management can evaluate sales levels through the middle of a quarter).

>> **FYE and QE:** Acronyms for fiscal year-end and quarter-end. Most companies utilize a fiscal year-end that is consistent with a calendar year-end of 12/31/xx (which would make their quarter-ends 3/31/xx, 6/30/xx, 9/30/xx, and 12/31/xx).

TIP

Please note that several companies utilize FYEs that are different than a calendar year-end to match their business cycle with that of a specific industry. For example, companies that operate ski resorts may use a FYE of 6/30/xx to coincide with the typical operating year (which tend to run from 7/1/xx through 6/30/xx).

REMEMBER

One thing that you find when completing ratio analysis is that financial professionals often use a variety of rather unique terms and "lingo" (for lack of a better term) associated with the financial and accounting profession so the better versed you are from the start, the more effective your ratio analysis will be.

Starting with Sample Company Financial Statements

Figures 12-1, 12-2, and 12-3 present an income statement, a balance sheet, and a statement of cash flows for a business that serves as the example for the rest of the chapter. We don't present the notes to the company's financial statements, but we discuss reading notes in Chapter 11. In short, the following discussion focuses on ratios from the income statement, balance sheet, and statement of cash flows.

TECHNICAL
STUFF

This chapter does not pretend to cover the field of *securities analysis* (that is, the analysis of shares and debt instruments issued by corporations), but this is a topic touched on in Chapters 10 and 11. The broad field of securities analysis includes the analysis of competitive advantages and disadvantages of a business, domestic and international economic developments, business combination possibilities, general economic conditions, and much more. The key ratios explained in this chapter are basic building blocks in securities analysis.

QW Example Tech., Inc. Income Statement for the Fiscal Year Ending 12/31/2024	
(all dollar amounts in thousands)	12/31/2024
Sales Revenue, Net	$71,064
Costs of Goods Sold	$26,891
Gross Profit	$44,173
Selling, General, & Administrative Expenses	$36,678
Operating Income — EBIT	$7,495
Other Expenses (Income):	
Other Expenses & (Income)	$250
Interest Expense	$350
Total Other Expenses (Income)	$600
Profit Before Income Taxes	$6,895
Income Tax Expense	$2,413
Net Income	$4,482
Earnings Per Share (Basic)	$4.08
Earnings Per Share (Fully Diluted)	$2.76

FIGURE 12-1:
Base income statement for sample company.

© John Wiley & Sons, Inc.

TECHNICAL STUFF

Also, this chapter does not discuss *trend analysis*, which involves comparing a company's latest financial statements with its previous years' statements to identify important year-to-year changes. For example, investors and lenders are extremely interested in the sales growth or decline of a business, and the resulting impact on profit performance, cash flow, and financial condition. The concept of trend analysis is touched on in Chapters 13 and 17.

This chapter has a more modest objective: to explain basic ratios used in financial statement analysis and what those ratios indicate about a business. Only a handful of ratios are discussed in the chapter, but they are fundamentally important and represent the most widely used by industry professionals.

```
                    QW Example Tech., Inc.
                    Statement of Financial Position
                    (AKA Balance Sheet)
                    12/31/2024
```

(all dollar amounts in thousands)	12/31/2024
Assets	
Current Assets:	
Cash & Equivalents	$11,281
Accounts Receivable, Net	$8,883
Inventory, LC&NRV	$1,733
Prepaid Expenses	$325
Total Current Assets	$22,222
Long-Term Operating & Other Assets:	
Property, Plant, & Equipment	$8,670
Accumulated Depreciation	($4,320)
Net Property, Plant, & Equipment	$4,350
Other Assets:	
Intangible Assets, Net	$500
Goodwill	$100
Total Long-Term Operating & Other Assets	$4,950
Total Assets	$27,172
Liabilities	
Current Liabilities:	
Accounts Payable	$1,929
Accrued Liabilities	$830
Current Portion of Debt	$1,000
Other Current Liabilities & Deferred Revenue	$1,204
Total Current Liabilities	$4,963
Long-Term Liabilities:	
Notes Payable & Other Long-Term Debt	$6,250
Total Liabilities	$11,213
Shareholders' Equity	
Share Capital — Common	$5,000
Share Capital — Preferred	$5,000
Retained Earnings	$5,959
Total Shareholders' Equity	$15,959
Total Liabilities & Shareholders' Equity	$27,172

© John Wiley & Sons, Inc.

FIGURE 12-2:
Base balance
sheet for sample
company.

QW Example Tech., Inc.
Statement of Cash Flows
for the Fiscal Year Ending
12/31/2024

(all dollar amounts in thousands)	12/31/2024
Net Profit (Loss)	$4,482
Operating Activities, Cash Provided (Used):	
Depreciation & Amortization	$1,739
Decrease (Increase) in Accounts Receivable	($2,165)
Decrease (Increase) in Inventory	$2,328
Decrease (Increase) in Prepaid Expenses	($25)
Increase (Decrease) in Accounts Payable	$275
Increase (Decrease) in Accrued Liabilities	$163
Increase (Decrease) in Other Current Liabilities & Deferred Revenue	$796
Net Cash Flow from Operating Activities	$7,593
Investing Activities, Cash Provided (Used):	
Increases in Property, Plant & Equipment and Intangible Assets	($750)
Net Cash Flow from Investing Activities	($750)
Financing Activities, Cash Provided (Used):	
Dividends or Distributions Paid	($400)
Sale of Preferred Shares	$5,000
Repayments of Long-Term Debt	($950)
Net Cash Flow from Financing Activities	$3,650
Net Increase (Decrease) in Cash & Equivalents	$10,493
Beginning Cash & Equivalents Balance	$788
Ending Cash & Equivalents Balance	$11,281

FIGURE 12-3:
Base statement
of cash flows for
sample company.

© John Wiley & Sons, Inc.

On opening a company's financial report, probably one of the first things most investors do is to give the financial statements a once-over; they do a quick scan of the financial statements. What do most financial report readers first look for? In our experience, they look first at the bottom line of the income statement, to see whether the business made a profit or suffered a loss for the year. As one sports celebrity put it when explaining how they keep tabs on their various business investments, they look first to see if the bottom line has "parentheses around it." The business in our example does not; it made a profit. Its income statement reports that the business earned $4.482 million (rounded; see Figure 12-1) net income, or bottom-line profit for the year. Is this profit performance good, mediocre, or poor? Ratios help answer this question.

After reading the income statement, most financial statement readers probably then take a quick look at the company's assets and compare them with the liabilities of the business. Are the assets adequate to the demands of the company's liabilities? Again, ratios help answer this question.

Benchmark Financial Ratios: Financial Strength and Solvency

Stock analysts, investment managers, individual investors, investment bankers, economists, company directors and executive management teams, and many others are interested in the fundamental financial aspects of a business. Ratios are a big help in analyzing the financial situation and performance of a business. To start our discussion on financial ratio analysis, you might anticipate that we'll begin with profit analysis. No, we start with something more important — solvency and liquidity.

REMEMBER

Solvency and liquidity refer to the ability of a business to pay its liabilities when they come due. If a business is insolvent and cannot pay its liabilities on time, its very continuance is at stake. In many respects, solvency comes first and profit second (as the first rule in business is to never run out of cash to operate). The ability to earn a profit rests on the ability of the business to continue on course and avoid being shut down or interfered with by its lenders. In short, earning a profit demands that a business remain solvent. Maintaining solvency (its debt-paying ability) is essential for every business. If a business defaults on its debt obligations, it becomes vulnerable to legal proceedings that could stop the company in its tracks, or at least could interfere with its normal operations.

Bankers and other lenders, when deciding whether to make and renew loans to a business, direct their attention to certain key financial statement ratios to help them evaluate the solvency situation and prospects of the business. These ratios provide a useful financial profile of the business in assessing its creditworthiness and for judging the ability of the business to pay interest and to repay the principal of its loans on time and in full.

REMEMBER

One additional concept that is important to understand is the difference between solvency and liquidity. In certain cases, you may evaluate a business that appears solvent (that is, assets are greater than liabilities with ample shareholders' equity) yet is not liquid. This situation can occur when a business mismanages its cash resources, which come under stress (it may have over invested in fixed assets and is running short on cash to pay current bills). The financial ratio analyses provided address both solvency and liquidity issues for our fictitious company.

See Figure 12-4 for an analysis of all the ratios in the following sections.

QW Example Tech., Inc. Financial Ratio Analysis: Strength and Solvency at 12/31/2024	
(all dollar amounts in thousands)	
Current Ratio	31-Dec-2024
Total Current Assets	$22,222
Total Current Liabilities	$4,963
Current Ratio	4.48
Net Working Capital	31-Dec-2024
Total Current Assets	$22,222
Total Current Liabilities	$4,963
Net Working Capital	$17,259
Quick or Acid Test Ratio	31-Dec-2024
Total Current Assets	$22,222
Less: Inventory & Prepaid Expenses	($2,058)
Net Current Assets	$20,164
Current Liabilities	$4,963
Quick or Acid Test Ratio	4.06
Debt-to-Equity Ratio	31-Dec-2024
Total Debt (i.e., Liabilities)	$11,213
Total Owners' Equity	$15,959
Debt-to-Equity Ratio	0.70
Debt-to-Tangible Net Equity Ratio	31-Dec-2024
Total Liabilities	$11,213
Total Owners' Equity	$15,959
Less: Intangible Assets and Goodwill	($600)
Tangible Net Equity	$15,359
Debt-to-Tangible Net Equity Ratio	0.73

FIGURE 12-4: Solvency ratios for sample company.

© John Wiley & Sons, Inc.

Current ratio

REMEMBER

The *current ratio* tests the short-term liability-paying ability of a business. It is calculated by dividing total current assets by total current liabilities in a company's most recent balance sheet. The current ratio for the company is computed as follows:

Current assets ÷ Current liabilities = Current ratio

The current ratio is hardly ever expressed as a percent (which would be 348 percent for our example company at 12/31/24). The current ratio for the business example is stated as 4.48 to 1.00, or more simply just as 4.48.

TIP

The common opinion is that the current ratio for a business should be 2 to 1 or higher (although this depends on the type of industry the company operates within as in some instances, current ratios closer to 1.25 to 1.00 are acceptable). Most businesses find that their creditors expect this minimum current ratio. In other words, short-term creditors generally like to see a business limit its current liabilities to one-half or less of its current assets.

Why do short-term creditors put this limit on a business? The main reason is to provide a safety cushion of protection for the payment of the company's short-term liabilities. A current ratio of 2 to 1 means there is $2 of cash and current assets that should be converted into cash during the near future that will be available to pay each $1 of current liabilities that come due in roughly the same time period. Each dollar of short-term liabilities is backed up with $2 of cash on hand or near-term cash inflows. The extra dollar of current assets provides a margin of safety for the creditors.

A company may be able to pay its liabilities on time with a current ratio of less than 2 to 1, or perhaps even if its current ratio were as low as 1 to 1. In our business example, the company has borrowed $1 million using short-term notes payable, which equals 4.5 percent of its total current assets (see Figure 12-2). In this situation, the company's lenders would probably be willing to provide short-term loans to the business given its solid current ratio, relatively low short-term borrowing ratio to current assets (of 4.5 percent), and its solid profitability (in 2024).

Net working capital

We also want to note that the company's net working capital (defined as total current assets less total current liabilities) amounts to approximately $17.259 million at 12/31/24. The reason we present net working capital right after the current ratio is that lenders often incorporate loan covenants that state a business must maintain net working capital of X millions of dollars (to ensure ample internal liquidity is maintained). Here's the ratio:

Current assets – Current liabilities = Net working capital

REMEMBER

In summary, short-term sources of credit generally like to see a company's current assets be double its current liabilities (again, depending on the industry) along with maintaining strong levels of net working capital. After all, creditors are not owners — they do not share in the profit earned by the business. The income on their loans is limited to the interest they charge (and collect). As creditors, they quite properly minimize their loan risks; as limited-income (fixed-income) investors, they are not compensated to take on much risk.

Acid test ratio (aka quick ratio)

REMEMBER

Inventory is many weeks or months away from conversion into cash. Products are typically held two, three, or four months before being sold. If sales are made on credit, which is normal when one business sells to another business (that is, a B-to-B business model), there is a second waiting period before the receivables are collected. In short, inventory is not nearly as liquid as accounts receivable; it takes much longer to convert inventory first into sales and then into cash. Furthermore, there is no guarantee that all the products in inventory will be sold, because inventory can become obsolete, spoiled, lost/stolen, and so on.

A more severe measure of the short-term liability-paying ability of a business is the *acid test ratio* (also known as *quick ratio*), which excludes inventory (and prepaid expenses). Only cash, short-term marketable securities investments (if any), and accounts receivable are counted as sources to pay the current liabilities of the business.

This ratio is also called the quick ratio because only cash and assets quickly convertible into cash are included in the amount available for paying current liabilities; it is more in the nature of a liquidity ratio that focuses on how much cash and near-cash assets a business possesses to pay its short-term liabilities.

In this example, the company's acid test ratio is calculated as follows (the business has no investments in marketable securities):

Liquid assets ÷ Current liabilities = Acid test ratio

The general rule is that a company's acid test ratio should be 1 to 1 or better, although there are many exceptions. In our sample company, its quick ratio amounts to 4.06 to 1.00 — again a very healthy ratio and one that indicates financial strength.

Debt-to-equity ratio

Some debt is generally good, but too much debt is dangerous. The *debt-to-equity ratio* is an indicator of whether a company is using debt prudently, or perhaps has gone too far and is overburdened with debt that may cause problems. For this example, the company's debt-to-equity ratio calculation is as follows:

Total debt ÷ Total owners' equity = Debt-to-equity ratio

This ratio tells us that the company is using $0.70 of liabilities in addition to each $1 of shareholders' equity in the business. Notice that all liabilities (non-interest-bearing as well as interest-bearing, and both short-term and long-term) are included in this ratio, and that all owners' equity (invested share capital and retained earnings) is included.

This business, with its 0.70 debt-to-equity ratio, would be viewed as moderately leveraged. *Leverage* refers to using the equity capital base to raise additional capital from nonowner sources. In other words, the business is using $.70 of debt total capital for every $1 of equity capital.

Historically, most businesses have tended to stay below a 1-to-1 debt-to-equity ratio. They don't want to take on too much debt, or they cannot convince lenders to put up more than one-half of their assets. However, some capital-intensive (asset-heavy) businesses such as public utilities and financial institutions operate with debt-to-equity ratios much higher than 1 to 1. In other words, they are highly leveraged.

But a word of caution in today's world (which we address more fully in Chapter 14). Over the decade and a half since the Great Recession of 2007–2009, the world was flooded with massive cash infusions from global central banks by undertaking highly accommodative monetary policies and driving interest rates down. By some estimates, over $20 trillion of cash/currency has been injected into the global economy by the world's leading central banks, which was amplified by the global COVID-19 pandemic starting in 2020. This resulted in a drastic decline in interest rates that, unbelievable as it may sound, led to over $15 trillion of global debt generating negative interest rates (yes, you heard us right).

WARNING

These policy changes have encouraged businesses to secure new and unbelievably cheap debt to be used for business purposes ranging from investing in capital equipment to repurchasing its issued shares, helping drive up earnings per share (EPS, covered later in this chapter). This so-called "easy" monetary environment has unfortunately also produced two unwanted side effects:

>> First, debt-to-equity ratio historical "norms" (for lack of a better term) of, let's say, less than 1-to-1 (as previously noted) have been sacrificed in the name of debt that is cheap (low interest rates), abundant (large amounts of fresh/new capital), and easy (limited financial performance covenant requirements). So not only are companies becoming more and more leveraged, the quality of the debt, via establishing performance covenants to ensure that a company's performance is acceptable, is being reduced or in some cases eliminated. It doesn't take a genius to quickly conclude that a more leveraged company with lower-quality debt is generally a recipe for disaster.

>> Second, when companies use debt to repurchase their own shares (a very common practice over the past few years), the number of shares outstanding when calculating its EPS decreases (for example, Company XYZ had 1 million shares outstanding and elected to repurchase 100,000, leaving 900,000 shares remaining as outstanding). With fewer outstanding shares and a relatively constant net profit, the company provides the appearance, or some may say illusion, that its EPS is increasing even though its net profit did not change. This concept is a perfect example of what is commonly referred to as *financial engineering* — a topic that we dig into in Chapter 14 and that is something extremely important to understand in today's world economy.

Debt-to-tangible net equity

This financial ratio analysis takes the debt-to-net worth (or debt-to-equity) analysis one step further by extracting intangible assets from the calculation. Intangible assets represent a broad range of assets including software development costs, capitalized intellectual property (such as patents), content creation, and similar types of assets that are not tangible in nature.

REMEMBER

The reason this calculation is important to lenders is that in today's rapidly moving economy, especially for technology-based companies, what may be of value today could be completely worthless in two years. Thus, by stripping out the intangible assets and goodwill from the debt-to-equity ratio, a lender has a better view of a company's real financial leverage.

The debt-to-tangible net equity for our sample company tells an interesting story as follows:

Total debt ÷ (Total owners' equity less intangible assets and goodwill) = Debt-to-tangible net equity ratio

For our sample company, the debt-to-tangible net equity ratio of 0.73 to 1.00 is approximately the same as the debt-to-equity ratio of 0.70, which indicates that the company's financial strength is not being significantly influenced by intangible assets and goodwill. However, and a word of caution, this ratio is very important to monitor as companies that aggressively expand operations via buying or investing in "soft" or intangible assets may be viewed as being higher risk due to the fickle nature of valuing intangible assets.

Benchmark Financial Ratios: Financial Performance

Shifting gears somewhat, we now turn our attention to presenting ratio analysis that is centered on analyzing financial information that is derived from both the income statement and balance sheet. The general idea with these ratios is to evaluate how a company is performing in relation to its total investment in assets and capital required to operate the business (debt and equity). See Figure 12-5 for an analysis of all the ratios in the following sections.

Return on sales (ROS)

Generating sales while controlling expenses is how a business makes profit. The profit residual slice of a company's total sales revenue pie is expressed by the *return on sales ratio*, which is net income divided by sales revenue for the period. This ratio is sometimes referred to as a *profit margin*. The company's return on sales ratio for its latest two years is as follows:

Net income ÷ Sales revenue = Return on sales (ROS)

There is another way of explaining the return on sales ratio. For the FYE 12/31/24, each $100 of sales revenue the business earned generated $6.31 of net income and expenses of $93.69. Return on sales varies quite markedly from one industry to another. Some businesses do well with only a 2–4 percent return on sales; others need more than 20 percent to justify the large amount of capital invested in their assets. For a company operating in the technology market, especially with a focus on software, return on sales far north of 10 percent is now the norm (so this company appears to be underperforming compared to its peers).

```
┌──────────────────────────────────────────────────────────┐
│                    QW Example Tech., Inc.                   │
│         Financial Ratio Analysis: Financial Performance     │
│                   for the Fiscal Year Ending                │
│                          12/31/2024                         │
├──────────────────────────────────────────────────────────┤
```

(all dollar amounts and number of shares in thousands)	
Return on Sales — FYE:	31-Dec-2024
Net Income	$4,482
Revenue, Net	$71,064
Return on Sales	6.31%
Return on Equity — FYE:	31-Dec-2024
End-of-Year Total Shareholders' Equity	$15,959
Net Income	$4,482
Return on Average Equity	28.08%
Return on Assets — FYE:	31-Dec-2024
End-of-Year Total Assets	$27,172
Net Income Before Interest & Income Taxes	$7,245
Return on Average Assets	26.66%
Earnings Per Share, Fully Diluted — FYE:	31-Dec-2024
Net Income	$4,482
Shares Outstanding, Fully Diluted (#)	1,625
Earnings Per Share, Fully Diluted	$2.76
Earnings Per Share, Basic — FYE:	31-Dec-2024
Net Income	$4,482
Less: Preferred Dividends	($400)
Earnings Available for Common	$4,082
Shares Outstanding, Basic	1,000
Earnings Per Share, Basic	$4.08
Price/Earnings Ratio — FYE:	31-Dec-2024
Market Value Per Share (not in thousands)	$70.00
Earnings Per Share, Fully Diluted	$2.76
Price-Earnings Ratio	25.36
Debt Service Coverage Ratio — FYE:	31-Dec-2024
Net Income	$4,482
Income Tax Expense	$2,413
Interest Expense	$350
Depreciation & Amortization Expense	$1,739
Adjusted Debt Service Cash Flow	$8,984
Interest Expense	$350
Loan Principal Payments Due, 1 Year	$1,000
Total Debt Service Payments, 1 Year	$1,350
Debt Service Coverage Ratio	6.65

© John Wiley & Sons, Inc.

FIGURE 12-5:
Financial
performance
ratios for sample
company.

Return on equity (ROE)

Owners take the risk of whether their business can earn a net income and sustain its profit performance over the years. How much would you pay for a business that consistently suffers a loss? The value of the owners' investment depends first and foremost on the past and potential future profit performance of the business — or not just profit, we should say, but profit relative to the capital invested to earn that profit.

For instance, suppose a business earns $100,000 annual net income for its shareholders. If its shareholders' equity is $250,000, then its profit performance relative to the shareholders' capital used to make that profit is 40 percent, which is very good indeed. If, however, shareholders' equity is $2,500,000, then the company's profit performance equals only 4 percent of owners' equity, which is weak relative to the owners' capital used to earn that profit.

REMEMBER

In short, profit should be compared with the amount of capital invested to earn that profit. Net income for a period divided by the amount of capital invested to earn that profit is generally called *return on investment* (ROI). ROI is a broad concept that applies to almost any sort of investment of capital.

The owners' historical investment in a business is the total of the owners' equity accounts in the company's balance sheet. Their profit is bottom-line net income for the period — well, maybe not all net income. A business corporation may issue *preferred shares*, on which a fixed amount of dividends must be paid each year. The preferred shares have the first claim on dividends from net income. Therefore, preferred share dividends are subtracted from net income to determine the *net income available for the common shareholders*. Our company has issued preferred shares, so not all net income "belongs" to its common shareholders. However, for simplicity in displaying this calculation, we assume that all the net income earned by the company is available to all the equity owners (both common and preferred).

Dividing annual net income by shareholders' equity gives the *return on equity* (ROE) ratio. The calculation for the company's ROE in this example is as follows:

Net income ÷ Shareholders' equity = Return on equity (ROE)

TIP

We use the ending balance of shareholders' equity to simplify the calculation. Alternatively, the average during the year could be used, and should be if there have been significant changes during the year.

By most standards, this company's 28.08 percent annual ROE for the FYE 12/31/24 would be considered very strong, but then again, technology companies often generate these types of returns. However, everything is relative. ROE should be compared with industry-wide averages and with investment alternatives. Also, the risk factor is important: Just how risky is the shareholders' capital investment in the business?

We need to know much more about the history and prospects of the business to reach a conclusion regarding whether it's 28.08 percent ROE is good, mediocre, or poor. Also, we should consider the *opportunity cost of capital* — that is, the ROI the shareholders could have earned on the next-best use of their capital. Furthermore, we have not considered the personal income tax on dividends paid to its individual shareholders. In summary, judging ROE is not a simple matter!

Return on assets (ROA)

Here is another useful profit performance ratio:

$$\text{EBIT} \div \text{Total assets} = \text{Return on assets (ROA)}$$

The *return on assets* (ROA) ratio reveals that the business earned $26.66 before interest and income tax expenses on each $100 of assets. The ROA is compared with the annual interest rate on the company's borrowed money. In this example, the company's annual interest rate on its short-term and long-term debt is approximately 5.0 percent. The business earned 26.66 percent on the money borrowed, as measured by the ROA. The difference or spread between the two rates is a favorable spread equal to 21.66 percentage points, which increases the earnings after interest for shareholders. This source of profit enhancement is called *financial leverage gain*. In contrast, if a company's ROA is less than its interest rate, it suffers a financial leverage loss.

REMEMBER

Ratios do not provide final answers — they're helpful indicators, and that's it. For example, if you're in the market for a house, you may consider cost per square foot (the total cost divided by total square feet) as a way of comparing the prices of the houses you're looking at. But you have to put that ratio in context: Maybe one neighborhood is closer to public transportation than another, and maybe one house needs more repairs than another. In short, the ratio isn't the only factor in your decision.

Earnings per share (EPS), basic and fully diluted

Publicly owned businesses, according to GAAP, report earnings per share below the net income line in their income statements — giving EPS a certain distinction among ratios. Why is EPS considered so important? Because it gives investors a means of determining the amount the business earned on their share investments: EPS tells you how much net income the business earned for each share you own. The essential equation for EPS is as follows:

Net income less preferred dividends ÷ Total number of common shares = Earnings per share (EPS)

For the example in Figures 12-1 and 12-2, the company's $4.482 million net income is divided by the 1.625 million shares the business has issued to compute its fully diluted $2.76 EPS. If its basic EPS is calculated, the resulting figure would be $4.08. (Refer to Figure 12-5 for the math.)

The computation based on the higher number of shares is called the *diluted* earnings per share. (*Diluted* means thinned out or spread over a larger number of shares.) The computation based on the number of shares issued and outstanding is called *basic* earnings per share. Both are reported at the bottom of the income statement (see Figure 12-1).

REMEMBER

EPS is extraordinarily important to the shareholders of businesses whose shares are publicly traded. These shareholders pay close attention to market price per share. They want the net income of the business to be communicated to them on a per-share basis so they can easily compare it with the market price of their shares. The shares of privately owned corporations aren't actively traded, so there's no readily available market value for the shares. Private businesses don't have to report EPS. The thinking behind this exemption is that their shareholders don't focus on per-share values and are more interested in the business's total net income.

WARNING

Publicly owned businesses report two EPS figures — unless they have a *simple capital structure* that doesn't require the business to issue additional shares in the future. In this case, the caption is "Basic and fully diluted earnings per share." Generally, publicly owned corporations have *complex* capital structures and must report two EPS figures, as you see in Figure 12-1. Sometimes it's not clear which of the two EPS figures is being used in press releases and in articles in the financial press. You must be careful to determine which EPS ratio is being used — and which is being used in the calculation of the P/E ratio (explained in the next section). The more conservative approach is to use diluted EPS, although this calculation includes a hypothetical number of shares that may or may not actually be issued in the future.

Price/earnings (P/E) ratio

The price/earnings (P/E) ratio is another ratio that's of particular interest to investors in public businesses. The P/E ratio gives you an idea of how much you're paying in the current price for shares for each dollar of earnings (the net income being earned by the business). Remember that earnings prop up the market value of shares.

TIP

The P/E ratio is, in one sense, a reality check on just how high the current market price is in relation to the underlying profit that the business is earning. Extraordinarily high P/E ratios are justified when investors think that the company's EPS has lots of upside potential in the future.

The P/E ratio is calculated as follows:

Current market price of shares ÷ Most recent trailing 12 months diluted EPS = P/E ratio

Note: If the business has a simple capital structure and doesn't report a diluted EPS, its basic EPS is used for calculating its P/E ratio (see the preceding section).

Suppose the common shares of the business in our example are trading at $70, and its fully diluted EPS for the latest year is $2.76. *Note:* For the remainder of this section, we use the term EPS; we assume you understand that it refers to fully diluted EPS for businesses with complex capital structures or to basic EPS for businesses with simple capital structures.

Share prices of public companies bounce around day to day and are subject to big changes on short notice. To illustrate the P/E ratio, we use the $70 price, which is the closing price on the latest trading day in the stock market. This market price means that investors trading in the shares think that the shares are worth about 25.4 times EPS ($70 market price ÷ $2.76 EPS = 25.36, rounded up to 25.4). This P/E ratio should be compared with the average stock market P/E for the applicable industry of the business, to gauge whether the business is selling above or below the market average.

TECHNICAL STUFF

Over the last century, average P/E ratios have fluctuated more than you may think. We remember when the average P/E ratio was less than 10 and a time when it was more than 20. Also, P/E ratios vary from business to business, industry to industry, and year to year. One dollar of EPS may command only a $12 market value for a mature business in a no-growth industry, whereas a dollar of EPS for dynamic businesses in high-growth industries may be rewarded with a $35 market value per dollar of earnings (net income).

Debt service coverage ratio

Thus far, the ratios provided and associated analyses have tended to focus on the income statement and balance sheet (ignoring the cash flow statement). This is traditionally where most parties focus their attention, because the information gleaned from the calculations is especially useful. But cash flow ratios and analyses are just as informative and in today's world have become mainstays when evaluating a company's operating performance and financial viability. Here, we present a basic solvency ratio and analysis tool that is widely used in the market: the debt service coverage ratio.

The goal with the debt service coverage ratio (DSCR) is to ensure that the company can not only cover its interest expense but in addition make all necessary debt principal payments as well. For our sample company, here is the calculation:

Net income + Income tax expense + Interest expense + Depreciation and amortization expense ÷ Interest expense + Loan principal payments due in one year = Debt service coverage ratio

For our sample company, here is how the math would work (all figures expressed in thousands of dollars):

» $4,482 + $2,413 + $350 + $1,739 = $8,984
» $8,984 ÷ ($350 + $1,000) = 6.65

It goes without saying that this ratio needs to be north of 1.00 to 1.00 with most lenders demanding a minimum ratio of at least 1.50 to 1.00 (and often higher) to ensure there is a cushion available to cover any potential cash flow problems or hiccups. So, the good news for our example company for the FYE 12/31/24 is that their 6.65 DSCR is well above the target of 1.50 — but it does highlight the importance of managing available cash flow in relation to both total interest expense and debt principal payments due.

You should also note that no adjustment has been made for the $400,000 of annual preferred share dividends. The reason is that the company's lenders sit in a senior position to the preferred shareholders and are most interested in the company being able to cover the total debt service prior to any preferred share dividends. In fact, experienced lenders often incorporate a covenant in the loan agreement that states that preferred dividends cannot be paid unless the DSCR is above 2.00.

Making Time for Additional Ratios (If Needed)

The list of ratios earlier in this chapter is bare bones; it covers the hardcore, everyday tools for interpreting financial statements. You could certainly calculate many more ratios from the financial statements, such as the inventory turnover ratio. (Chapter 13 explains additional ratios that managers of a business use based on internal information that's not revealed in its external financial statements.) How many ratios to calculate is a matter of judgment and is limited by the time you have for reading a financial report.

Computer-based databases are at our disposal, and it's relatively easy to find many other financial statement ratios. Which of these additional ratios provide valuable insight?

REMEMBER

Be careful about wasting time on ratios that don't really add anything to the picture you get from the basic ratios explained in this chapter. Almost any financial statement ratio is interesting, we suppose. For instance, you could calculate the ratio of inventory divided by retained earnings to see what percent of retained earnings is tied up in the inventory asset. (This ratio isn't generally computed in financial statement analysis.) But we'd advise you to limit your attention to the handful of ratios that play a central role in looking after your investments.

IN THIS CHAPTER

» Recognizing the managerial limits of external financial statements

» Understanding the primary differences between internal and external financial information

» Examining the additional information needed for managing assets and liabilities

» Identifying the in-depth information needed for managing profit

» Providing additional information for managing cash flow

» Steering clear of rookie mistakes with internal financial information

Chapter **13**

Generating Internal Financial Information for Management Use

I f you're a business manager, we strongly suggest that you read Chapters 11 and 12 before continuing with this one. Chapter 11 discusses how a business's external, nonmanagerial lenders and investors read external financial reports. These stakeholders are entitled to regular financial reports so they can determine whether the business is making good use of their money. Chapter 12 explains key ratios that the external stakeholders use for interpreting the financial position and the profit performance of a business — which are equally relevant for the managers of the business.

TIP

Business managers should understand the financial statement ratios in Chapter 12. Every ratio does double duty; it's useful to outside lenders and investors and equally useful to internal managers. For example, the profit ratio and return on assets ratio are extraordinarily important to both the external stakeholders and the managers of a business — the first measures the profit yield from sales revenue, and the second measures profit on the assets employed by the business.

As important as they are, the external financial statements don't provide all the accounting information that managers need to plan and control the financial affairs of a business. Managers who look no further than these statements really don't have all the information they need to do their jobs. This additional information, which is largely confidential, is available from the accounting system of the business (or should be).

The accounts reported in external financial statements are like the table of contents of a book; each account is like a chapter title. Managers need to do more than skim chapter titles — they have to read the rest of the story. This chapter looks behind the accounts reported in the external financial statements. We explain the types of additional accounting information that managers need to control financial position and performance, and to plan the financial future of a business.

Building on the Foundation of External Financial Statements

REMEMBER

Managers are problem solvers. Every business has some problems, perhaps even some serious ones. However, external financial statements are not designed to highlight those problems. Except in extreme cases — in which the business is obviously in dire financial straits — you'd never learn about its problems just from reading its external financial statements. To borrow lyrics from an old Bing Crosby song, external financial statements are designed to "accentuate the positive, eliminate the negative . . . [and] don't mess with Mister In-Between."

Seeking out problems and opportunities

REMEMBER

Business managers need more accounting information than what's disclosed in external financial statements for two basic purposes:

>> **To alert them to problems** that exist or may be emerging that threaten the business's profit performance, cash flow, and financial position

>> **To suggest opportunities** for improving the business's financial performance and health

A popular expression these days is "mining the data." The accounting system of a business is a rich mother lode of management information, but you have to dig that information out of the accounting database. Working with the controller (chief accountant), a manager should decide what information is needed beyond what is reported in the external financial statements.

Avoiding information overload

Business managers are busy people. Nothing is more frustrating than getting reams of information that you have no use for. For that reason, the controller should guard carefully against information overload. While some types of accounting information should stream to business managers on a regular basis, other types should be provided only as needed.

Ideally, the controller reads the mind of every manager and provides exactly the accounting information that each manager needs. In practice, that can't always happen, of course. A manager may not be certain about which information is needed and which they don't. The flow of information has to be worked out over time.

Furthermore, *how* to communicate the information is open to debate and individual preferences. Some of the additional management information can be put in the main body of an accounting report, but most is communicated in supplemental schedules, graphs, and commentary. The information may be delivered to the manager's computer, or the manager may be given the option to call up selected information from the business's accounting database.

REMEMBER

Our point is simply this: Managers and controllers must communicate — early and often — to make sure managers get the information nuggets they need without being swamped with unnecessary data. No one wants to waste precious time compiling reports that are never read. So before a controller begins the process of compiling accounting information for managers' eyes only, be sure there's ample communication about what each manager needs.

Distinguishing Internal and External Financial Statements

Here's a spoiler alert, which should be both obvious and logical: The results of a financial statement, be it a balance sheet, an income statement, or a statement of cash flows, are the exact same between the internal and external financial statements; that is, total assets reported in the balance sheet are the same, the net profit or loss reported in the income statement is the same, and the ending cash balance reported in the statement of cash flows is the same. What is different basically boils down to understanding five key items — format, detail, confidentiality, timeliness, and completeness.

REMEMBER

Internally produced financial information must be presented in a manner that assists your target audience with efficiently and effectively interpreting critical financial data and results. We can't emphasize enough the importance of this function — the ability for accountants and financial types to effectively communicate complex information to other professionals and management team members is often the Achilles heel of the so-called "numbers people." Do the numbers people know debits, credits, generally accepted accounting principles (GAAP), the International Accounting Standards Board (IASB) rules (IFRS), the Accounting Standards for Private Enterprises (ASPE), and how to communicate to external numbers people? Yes. But what really separates the best-in-class companies from the pack is having their numbers people be extremely strong communicators and educators as well.

Format

The format should be much more user- and management-friendly (to drive home key points) as dictated by the company and not driven by external guidelines, such as those of the Securities and Exchange Commission (SEC). We want to strike a proper balance between providing too much information (pushing the user toward "getting lost in the forest") versus not enough; the idea is to give the reviewing party what they ask for and need (based on their level of responsibility).

REMEMBER

Further, we do not want to divulge data that a party does not need or understand, that confuses them, and/or that is confidential (translation: above their security clearance, so to speak). Most readers are not sophisticated accounting and financial professionals, but they do understand basic math, so the goal with the format is to provide financial information in the easiest-to-understand and reliable manner.

Detail

Obviously, the level of detail presented is far greater. For example, when internal financial statements are prepared, marketing, selling, advertising, and promotional expenses are often presented in a split format between direct operating expenses and corporate costs. The difference between these two expense groups is that direct operating advertising and selling expenses capture what are commonly referred to as *call to action expenses* that are designed to turn a prospect into an actual customer (by placing an order). Corporate marketing and branding expenses, on the other hand, represent a broader range of costs designed to help build awareness of the business and enhance its brand. For most businesses, understanding the difference between these two expense groups is especially important.

Confidentiality

WARNING

The information presented in internally prepared financial statements is highly confidential and must be controlled and safeguarded from external parties and prying eyes (for example, a competitor) and from internal parties who may not understand the financial information and accidently disclose it to an unwanted party. Companies must manage the delicate balance between disclosing confidential, valuable, and sensitive information to external parties (who can help them accurately assess the operating results) and not providing too much detail.

Timeliness

REMEMBER

Strength in accuracy is critical; speed in reporting is dependent on highly accurate information.

With internal financial information, quick is not an option; however, company management team members need access to financial statements that are prepared, distributed, and analyzed well in advance of issuing external financial statements and reports. This is done for two reasons:

>> Key management team members have an opportunity to evaluate the results and identify any potential errors, mistakes, or omissions.

>> If either good or bad news needs to be delivered to external parties, the management team has an opportunity to prepare for the inevitable grilling that is forthcoming.

Speed in reporting goes well beyond the financial statements; different types of flash reports are produced daily, hourly, and even by the minute as heavily data-dependent businesses (such as retailers) can now monitor the effectiveness of a new advertising campaign within minutes of its being launched (thanks to digital information and technology).

Completeness

The concept of completeness lies in the eye of beholder, or rather is based on the specific needs of the target audience. For example, a general manager of a manufacturing plant needs a complete income statement for that plant, but not necessarily for the entire company. Further, the income statement should include all relevant financial information, including prior-year comparisons, a budget-to-actual-variance analysis, key performance indicators (KPIs), and so on. Another example is a sales team manager who is focused on top-line sales for a region through the gross profit or margin generated, which may be compared against the budget or even other regions' performances. If that person does not have bottom-line responsibility, there is no need to provide a complete income statement.

Gathering Financial Position Information

The balance sheet — one of three primary financial statements included in a financial report — summarizes the business's financial position (see Chapter 7 for details). Figure 13-1 presents an example of an externally reported balance sheet. A business may report more than the accounts included in the example. For example, a business may invest in marketable securities or have receivables from loans made to officers of the business. A business corporation may issue more than one class of shares and would report a separate account for each class. And so on.

The idea of the figure is to focus on the *core* assets and liabilities of a typical business. Note two assets in the balance sheet: accounts receivable and inventory. These two accounts in the balance sheet tell you that the business sells products and makes sales on credit to its customers. Businesses that sell services don't have an inventory asset account, and businesses that sell only for cash and cash equivalents (credit/debit cards) don't report accounts receivable. A balance sheet reflects the nature and practices of the business entity, of course.

Note that in Figure 13-1 the balance sheet is for last year and this year (the fiscal year just ended). And the balance sheet includes a column for changes in each account during the year. For example, you may notice that the company's cash balance actually increased $10.493 million during the year. Don't hit the overjoyed button just yet. An increase in cash doesn't mean that the business produced a record profit for the year. Indeed, Figure 13-2 shows that the business made a nice profit for the year, but the cash increase was far greater.

The following sections walk down the balance sheet — assets first, liabilities next, and owners' equity accounts last — stressing what sorts of inside financial information managers need to carry out their job.

QW Example Tech., Inc. Statement of Financial Position (aka Balance Sheet) 12/31/2024			
(all dollar amounts in thousands)	12/31/2023	12/31/2024	Change
Assets			
Current Assets:			
Cash and Equivalents	$788	$11,281	$10,493
Accounts Receivable, Net	$6,718	$8,883	$2,165
Inventory, LC&NRV	$4,061	$1,733	($2,328)
Prepaid Expenses	$300	$325	$25
Total Current Assets	$11,867	$22,222	$10,355
Long-Term Operating and Other Assets:			
Property, Plant, & Equipment	$7,920	$8,670	$750
Accumulated Depreciation	($3,081)	($4,320)	($1,239)
Net Property, Plant, & Equipment	$4,839	$4,350	($489)
Other Assets:			
Intangible Assets, Net	$1,000	$500	($500)
Goodwill	$100	$100	$0
Total Long-Term Operating & Other Assets	$5,939	$4,950	($989)
Total Assets	$17,806	$27,172	$9,366
Liabilities			
Current Liabilities:			
Accounts Payable	$1,654	$1,929	$275
Accrued Liabilities	$667	$830	$163
Current Portion of Debt	$1,000	$1,000	$0
Other Current Liabilities and Deferred Revenue	$408	$1,204	$796
Total Current Liabilities	$3,729	$4,963	$1,234
Long-Term Liabilities:			
Notes Payable and Other Long-Term Debt	$7,200	$6,250	($950)
Total Liabilities	$10,929	$11,213	$284
Shareholders' Equity			
Share Capital — Common	$5,000	$5,000	$0
Share Capital — Preferred	$0	$5,000	$5,000
Retained Earnings	$1,877	$5,959	$4,082
Total Shareholders' Equity	$6,877	$15,959	$9,082
Total Liabilities and Shareholders' Equity	$17,806	$27,172	$9,366

Confidential — Property of QW Example Tech., Inc.

© John Wiley & Sons, Inc.

FIGURE 13-1:
Balance sheet example.

QW Example Tech., Inc. Income Statement for the Fiscal Year Ending 12/31/2024	
(all dollar amounts in thousands)	12/31/2024
Sales Revenue, Net	$71,064
Costs of Goods Sold	($26,891)
Gross Profit	$44,173
Selling, General, and Administrative Expenses	($34,939)
Depreciation and Amortization Expense	($1,739)
Operating Income Before Income Taxes and Interest	$7,495
Other Expenses:	
Other Expenses	($250)
Interest Expense	($350)
Total Other Expenses	($600)
Profit Before Income Taxes	$6,895
Income Tax Expense	($2,413)
Net Income	$4,482
Cash Flow from Operating Activity	$7,593
Confidential — Property of QW Example Tech., Inc.	

FIGURE 13-2:
Income
statement
example.

© John Wiley & Sons, Inc.

Cash

The external balance sheet (shown in Figure 13-1) reports just one cash account. But many businesses keep several bank chequing and deposit accounts, and some (such as gambling casinos and food supermarkets) keep a fair amount of currency on hand. A business may have foreign bank deposits in U.S. dollars, euros, English pounds, or other currencies.

REMEMBER

Managers should monitor the balances in every cash account to control and optimize the deployment of their cash resources. Therefore, information about each bank account should be reported to the manager.

Managers should ask these questions regarding cash:

>> Is the ending balance of cash the actual amount at the balance sheet date, or did the business engage in window dressing to inflate its ending cash balance? *Window dressing* refers to holding the books open after the ending balance sheet date to record additional cash inflow as if the cash were received on the last day of the period. Window dressing is not uncommon. (For details, see Chapter 10.) If window dressing has gone on, the manager should know the true, actual ending cash balance of the business.

>> Were there any *cash zero days* during the year? In other words, did the company's cash balance fall to zero (or near zero) during the year? How often did this happen? Is there a seasonal fluctuation in cash flow that causes "low tide" for cash, or are the cash zero days due to running the business with too little cash?

>> Are there any limitations on the uses of cash imposed by loan covenants by the company's lenders? Do any of the loans require compensatory balances that require that the business keep a minimum balance relative to the loan balance? In this situation, the cash balance is not fully available for general operating purposes.

>> Are there any out-of-the-ordinary demands on cash? For example, a business may have entered into buyout agreements with a key shareholder or with a vendor to escape the terms of an unfavourable contract. Any looming demands on cash should be reported to managers.

Accounts receivable

A business that makes sales on credit has the accounts receivable asset — unless it has collected all its customers' receivables by the end of the year, which is not likely. To be more correct, the business has hundreds or thousands of individual accounts receivable from its credit customers. In its external balance sheet, a business reports just one summary amount for all its accounts receivable. However, this total amount is not nearly enough information for the business manager.

A manager should ask these questions about accounts receivable:

>> Of the total amount of accounts receivable, how much is current (within the normal credit terms offered to customers), slightly past due, and seriously past due? A past due receivable causes a delay in cash flow and increases the risk of it becoming a *bad debt* (a receivable that ends up being partially or wholly uncollectible).

>> Has an adequate amount been recorded for bad debts? Is the company's method for determining its bad debts expense consistent year to year? Was the estimate

of bad debts this period tweaked to boost or dampen profit for the period? Has the CRA (Canada Revenue Agency) raised any questions about the company's method for writing off bad debts? (Chapter 9 discusses bad debts expense.)

>> Who owes the most money to the business? (The manager should receive a schedule of customers that shows this information.) Which customers are the slowest payers? Do the sales prices to these customers take into account that they typically do not pay on time?

It's also useful to know which customers pay quickly to take advantage of prompt payment discounts. In short, the payment profiles of credit customers are important information for managers.

>> Are there stray receivables buried in the accounts receivable total? A business may loan money to its managers and employees or to other businesses. Good business reasons may exist for such loans. In any case, these receivables shouldn't be included with accounts receivable, which should be reserved for receivables from credit sales to customers. Other receivables should be listed in a separate schedule.

Inventory

For businesses that sell products, inventory is typically a major asset. It's also typically the most problematic asset from both the management and accounting points of view. First off, the manager should understand the accounting method being used to determine the cost of inventory and the cost of goods sold expense. (You may want to quickly review the section in Chapter 9 that covers this topic.) In particular, the manager should have a good feel regarding whether the accounting method results in conservative or liberal profit measures.

Managers should ask these questions regarding inventory:

>> How long, on average, do products remain in storage before they are sold? The manager should receive a *turnover analysis* of inventory that clearly exposes the holding periods of products. Slow-moving products cause nothing but problems. The manager should ferret out products that have been held in inventory too long. The cost of these sluggish products may have to be written down or written off, and the manager has to authorize these accounting entries. The manager should review the sales demand for slow-moving products, of course.

>> Have there been any stock outs during the period? A stock out occurs when the turnover of inventory is so fast that no merchandise is available when a customer wants to buy. Managing inventory levels is tricky. You must have enough inventory, and not too much.

The manager should also request these reports:

>> Inventory reports that include side-by-side comparison of the costs and the sales prices of products (or at least the major products sold by the business). It's helpful to include the mark-up percentage for each product, which allows the manager to focus on mark-up percentage differences from product to product.

>> Regular reports summarizing major product cost changes during the period, and forecasts of near-term changes. It may be useful to report the current replacement cost of inventory assuming it's feasible to determine this amount.

Fixed assets less accumulated depreciation

REMEMBER

Fixed assets is the all-inclusive term for the wide range of long-term operating assets used by a business — from buildings and heavy machinery to office furniture. Except for the cost of land, the cost of a fixed asset is spread over its estimated useful life to the business; the amount allocated to each period is called *depreciation expense*. The manager should know the company's accounting policy regarding which fixed assets are *capitalized* (the cost is recorded in a fixed asset account) and which are *expensed* immediately (the cost is recorded entirely to expense at the time of purchase).

Most businesses adopt a cost limit below which minor fixed assets (a screwdriver, stapler, or wastebasket, for example) are recorded to expense instead of being depreciated over some number of years. The controller should alert the manager if an unusually high number of these small-cost fixed assets were charged off to expense during the year, which could have a significant effect on the bottom line.

The manager should be aware of the business's general accounting policies regarding estimating useful lives of fixed assets and whether the straight-line or accelerated methods of allocation are used. Indeed, the manager should have a major voice in deciding these policies, and not simply defer to the controller. In Chapter 9, we explain these accounting issues.

Using accelerated depreciation methods may result in certain fixed assets that are fully depreciated but are still in active use. These assets should be reported to the manager — even though they have a zero book value — so the manager is aware that these fixed assets are still being used but no depreciation expense is being recorded for their use.

TIP

Generally, the manager does not need to know the current replacement costs of *all* fixed assets — just those that will be replaced in the near future. At the same time, it is useful for the manager to get a status report on the company's fixed assets, which takes more of an engineering approach than an accounting approach. The status report includes information on the capacity, operating efficiency, and projected remaining life of each major fixed asset. The status report should include leased assets.

The manager needs an *insurance summary report* for all fixed assets that are (or should be) insured for fire and other casualty losses, which lists the types of coverage on each major fixed asset, deductibles, claims during the year, and so on. Also, the manager needs a list of the various liability risks of owning and using the fixed assets. The manager has to decide whether the risks should be insured.

Intangible assets

The balance sheet in Figure 13-1 reveals that the company has $1 million invested in intangible assets as of the fiscal year ending (FYE) December 31, 2023, which decreased to $500,000 as of the FYE December 31, 2024. Intangible assets can include a wide variety of things. The cost of acquiring the legal rights for using a patent or trademark could be in this asset account.

Accounting for these types of assets is tricky. In any case, the costs that are recorded in the intangible assets account should be justified on the grounds that the costs will provide profit one way or another. The business should be better off owning the intangible asset versus not owning it.

After acquiring intangible assets, the business should regularly take a hard look at the items making up the balance in its intangible assets account to test whether the items continue to have value to the business or perhaps have deteriorated in terms of their profit payoff. The accountants refer to this as testing for the possible *impairment* of value of intangible assets. The appropriate managers — most likely including marketing managers — should receive reports about each component of the balance of the intangible assets account. Managers, in most cases, are the ones to initiate a hard look at whether there's been impairment of one or more of the intangible assets of the business.

Accounts payable

As you know, individuals have a credit rating or credit score that affects their ability to borrow money and the interest rates they have to pay. Likewise, businesses have similar ratings. If a business has a really bad credit rating, it may not be able to buy on credit and may have to pay steep interest rates. We don't have space here to go into the details of how credit rankings are developed for businesses. Suffice it to say that a business should pay its bills on time. If a business consistently pays its accounts payable late, this behaviour gets reported to a credit rating agency (such as Equifax or Dun & Bradstreet).

The manager needs a schedule of accounts payable that are *past due* (beyond the credit terms given by the vendors and suppliers). Of course, the manager should know the reasons that the accounts have become overdue. The manager may have to personally contact these creditors and convince them to continue offering credit to the business.

REMEMBER

Frankly, some businesses operate on the principle of paying late. Their standard operating procedure is to pay their accounts payable two, three, or more weeks after the due dates. This could be due to not having adequate cash balances or wanting to hang on to their cash as long as possible. Years ago, IBM was notorious for paying late, but it got away with this policy because its credit rating was unimpeachable.

Accrued expenses payable

The controller should prepare a schedule for the manager that lists the major items making up the balance of the accrued liabilities account. Many operating liabilities accumulate — or, as accountants prefer to say, *accrue* — during the course of the year that are not paid until sometime later. One main example is employee vacation and sick pay; an employee may work for almost a year before being entitled to take two weeks' vacation with pay. The accountant records an expense each payroll period for this employee benefit, and it accumulates in the liability account until the liability is paid (the employee takes his vacation). Another payroll-based expense that accrues is the cost of Employment Insurance and Canada Pension Plan withholdings on employee wages and salaries.

WARNING

Accrued expenses payable can be a tricky liability from the accounting point of view. A lot of room exists for management discretion (or manipulation, depending on how you look at it) regarding which particular operating liabilities to record as expense during the year, and which not to record as expense until they are paid. The basic choice is whether to expense as you go or expense later. If you decide to record the expense as you go through the year, the accountant has to make estimates and assumptions, which are subject to error. Then there's the question of expediency. Employee vacation and sick pay may seem to be an obvious expense to accrue, but in fact many businesses do not accrue the expense on the grounds that it's simply too time consuming and because employees take the same holidays at pretty much the same time of the year. By not accruing, the liabilities are understated and the retained earnings on the balance sheet are overstated because of the missing vacation expense on the income statement.

Many businesses guarantee the products they sell for a certain period of time, such as 90 days or one year. The customer has the right to return the product for repair (or replacement) during the guarantee period. For example, when a customer returns an iPod for repair, Apple should have already recorded in a liability account the estimated cost of repairing iPods that will be returned after the point of sale. Businesses have more "creeping" liabilities than you might imagine. With a little work, we could list 20 or 30 of them, but we'll spare you the details. Our main point is that the manager should know what's in the accrued expenses liability account, and what's not. Also, the manager should have a good fix on when these liabilities will be paid.

Income tax payable

REMEMBER

It takes an income tax professional to comply with federal and provincial income tax laws on business. The manager should make certain that the accountant responsible for its tax returns is qualified and up to date.

The CRA requires businesses to make tax instalment payments, either monthly or quarterly depending on the size of the business. Failing to make these payments will trigger penalties and interest charged by the CRA when the current year's tax return is assessed. To motivate taxpayers to comply with this requirement, the tax rules prohibit the business from taking a tax deduction for any penalty or interest payment on deficient or late tax instalments. If the business expects to have a large increase in taxable income in the current year compared to the previous year, you don't have to pay the additional tax that will apply immediately through instalments, but you should accrue the additional tax. Such a situation would lead to a high balance in the income tax payable account, which needs to be explained to the manager.

The manager should also know how the business stands with the CRA, and whether the CRA has raised objections to the business's tax returns. The business may be filing an objection concerning how it was assessed in a previous year, or the business is in the middle of legal proceedings with the CRA — which the manager should be briefed on, of course. The chief executive officer (CEO) and perhaps other top-level managers should be given a frank appraisal of how things may turn out and whether the business is facing any additional tax payments and penalties. Needless to say, this is sensitive information.

WARNING

The CEO working closely with the controller should decide how aggressive to be on income tax issues and alternatives. Keep in mind that tax avoidance is legal, but tax evasion is illegal. As you probably know, the income tax law is exceedingly complex, but ignorance of the law is no excuse. The controller should make abundantly clear to the manager whether the business is walking on thin ice in its income tax returns.

Interest-bearing debt

In Figure 13-1, the balance sheet reports two interest-bearing liabilities: one for notes payable and one for long-term debt. The reason that financial reporting standards require that external balance sheets report the current portion of the debt as *current liabilities* is so the reader can compare this amount of short-term liabilities against the total of *current assets* (cash and assets that will be converted into cash in the short term). Interest-bearing debt that is due in one year or less is included in the current liabilities section of the balance sheet. (See Chapter 7 for more details.)

The amounts of the short-term and long-term debt accounts reported in the external balance sheet are not enough information for the manager.

TIP

The best practice is to lay out in one comprehensive schedule for the manager *all* the business's interest-bearing obligations. The obligations should be organized according to their due (maturity) dates, and the schedule should include other relevant information such as the lender, the interest rate on each debt, the plans to roll over the debt (or not), the collateral, and the main covenants and restrictions on the business imposed by the lender.

Recall that debt is one of the two sources of capital to a business (the other being owners' equity, which we get to next). The sustainability of a business depends on the sustainability of its sources of capital. The more a business depends on debt capital, the more important it is to manage its debt well and maintain excellent relations with its lenders.

Raising and using debt and equity capital, referred to as *financial management* or *corporate finance*, is a broad subject that extends beyond the scope of this book.

Owners' equity

REMEMBER

External balance sheets report two kinds of ownership accounts: one for *capital invested* by the owners in the business and one for *retained earnings* (profit that has not been distributed to shareowners). In Figure 13-1, two invested capital accounts are shown in the owners' equity section, one for common equity and the other for preferred equity. In fact, corporations, partnerships, and other types of business legal entities can have complex ownership structures. The owners' equity sections in their balance sheets report several invested capital accounts — one for each class of ownership interest in the business.

Broadly speaking, the manager faces three basic issues regarding the business's owners' equity:

>> Is more capital needed from the owners or other investors?

>> If more capital is needed, what terms should be provided to the parties providing capital, including any preferences or other beneficial terms?

>> Should some capital be returned to the owners?

>> Can and should the business make a cash distribution from profit to the owners and, if so, how much?

These questions belong in the field of financial management and extend beyond the scope of this book. However, we should mention that the external financial statements are useful in deciding these key financial management issues. For example, the manager needs to know how much total capital is needed to support the business's sales level. For every $100 of sales revenue, how much total assets does the business need? The *asset turnover ratio* (annual sales revenue divided by total assets) provides a good touchstone for determining the amount of capital that is needed for sales.

TIP

The external financial report of a business doesn't disclose the business's individual shareowners and the number of shares each person or institution owns. The manager may want to know this information. Any major change in the business's ownership usually is important information to the manager.

Culling Profit Information

REMEMBER

The sales (and other income, if any) and expenses of a business over a period of time are summarized in a financial statement called the *income statement*. Profit (sales revenue minus expenses) is the bottom line of the income statement. Chapter 6 explains the externally reported income statement, as well as how sales revenue and expenses are interconnected with the business's operating assets and liabilities. The income statement fits hand in glove with the balance sheet.

Chapter 15 explains internal profit reports to managers, which are called P&L (profit and loss) reports. P&L reports should be designed to help managers in their profit analysis and decision making.

Presenting an income statement for managers

Figure 13-2 presents the most recent annual income statement of the business whose balance sheet is shown in Figure 13-1. The two financial statements go together, of course. The income statement in Figure 13-2 is prepared according to GAAP that have been established for external financial reporting. No EPS (earnings per share) is reported because this income statement is prepared for managers.

REMEMBER

In Figure 13-2, we made one significant modification to the standard external income statement. We added a line for cash flow from operating activities, or cash flow from profit, as we prefer to call it. So, you see two "bottom lines." They are:

>> Net income based on the accrual-basis accounting methods for recording revenue and expenses during the period, according to GAAP

>> Cash flow from the profit-making (operating) activities for the period

Why two bottom lines? Not only do business managers have to make profit, but they also have to convert that profit into cash flow as soon as possible.

TIP

Managers should track cash flow as well as their profit performance. It's dangerous to simply assume that if profit is okay, then cash flow is okay. As Chapter 8 explains, cash flow deviates from profit, possibly by quite a bit. In reporting profit performance to managers, we think it's a good idea to keep accrual-basis profit and the cash flow from profit side by side in the income statement to managers, as in Figure 13-2.

Calculating cash flow on the back of an envelope

In the income statement (Figure 13-2), note that cash flow from profit (operating activities) is higher than profit for the year: $7.593 million cash flow – $4.482 million net income = $3.111 higher cash flow. This difference, which is fairly significant, deserves an explanation.

When it comes to explaining the difference between profit (net income) and cash flow, we think accountants do a lousy job, as we argue in Chapter 8. For one thing, cash flow from profit (operating activities) is reported in a separate financial statement — the statement of cash flows — instead of being placed next to net income in the income statement. Furthermore, accountants present a complicated schedule that shows how they determined cash flow instead of explaining the difference in a brief summary.

We suggest that managers get in the habit of doing a quick calculation of cash flow, one they could do on the back of an envelope. Doing such a calculation would reinforce the manager's understanding of and comfort level with cash flow.

Why is cash flow $3.111 million higher than profit for the year? The sidebar "Cash Flow Characteristics of Sales and Expenses" offers a short review of the differences between accrual-basis profit accounting and cash flow from revenue and for expenses. The numbers in the following calculation come from the balance sheet (Figure 13-1) and income statement (Figure 13-2).

In our business example, the difference between net income and cash flow can be summarized as follows:

$1.739 million depreciation and amortization expense for the year

$138,000 decrease in short-term operating assets, primarily from a large decrease in inventory offset by a large increase in trade accounts receivables .

$1.234 million increase in short-term operating liabilities

= $3.111 million excess of cash flow over net income

The $1.739 million of depreciation and amortization expense recorded for the year is not a cash outlay; indeed, it's just the opposite. The amount of depreciation and amortization has been recovered through sales revenue cash flow and thus is a positive cash flow factor. Accounts receivable and prepaid expenses both increased during the year but inventory decreased. The net of these asset decreases have the effect of increasing cash flow from profit by $138,000 during the year. Accounts payable, accrued expenses payable, and income tax payable all increase during the year; the total of these three positive factors is $1,234 million. Adding the three lines gives you the $3.111 million cash overflow.

You may automatically think that it's good that cash flow is more than profit. Well, not so fast. Cash flow has many aspects, and in some situations, a cash flow lower than profit is just what the doctor ordered.

CASH FLOW CHARACTERISTICS OF SALES AND EXPENSES

When reading internal income statements (also called profit and loss or P&L reports, managers should keep in mind that the accountant records sales revenue when sales are made — regardless of when cash is received from customers. Also, the accountant records expenses to match expenses with sales revenue and to put expenses in the period where they belong — regardless of when cash is paid for the expenses. The manager should not assume that sales revenue equals cash inflow, and that expenses equal cash outflow.

The cash flow characteristics of sales and expenses are summarized as follows:

- Cash sales generate immediate cash inflow. Keep in mind that sales returns and sales price adjustments after the point of sale reduce cash flow.

- Credit sales do not generate immediate cash inflow. No cash flow occurs until the customers' receivables are actually collected. A cash flow lag occurs from credit sales.

- Many operating costs are not paid until several weeks (or months) after they are recorded as expense; a few operating costs are paid before the costs are charged to expense.

- Depreciation expense is recorded by reducing the book value of a fixed asset and does not involve a cash outlay in the period when it is recorded. The business paid out cash when the asset was acquired. (Amortization expense on intangible assets is the same.)

Managing operating cash flows

REMEMBER

In a small, one-owner or one-manager business, one person has to manage both profit and cash flow from profit. In larger businesses, managers who have profit responsibility may or may not have cash flow responsibility. The profit manager may ignore the cash flow aspects of his sales and expense activities. The responsibility for controlling cash flow falls on some other manager. Of course, someone should manage the cash flows of sales and expenses.

As the calculation in the preceding section shows, the net cash flow during the period from carrying on profit-making operations depends on the changes in the operating assets and liabilities directly connected with sales revenue and expenses. Changes in these accounts during the year determine the cash flow from operating activities. In other words, changes in these accounts boost or crimp cash flow. One or more managers should closely monitor the changes in operating assets and liabilities. Controlling cash flow from profit (operating activities) means controlling changes in the operating assets and liabilities of making sales and incurring expenses — there's no getting around this fact of business life.

TIP

A good general rule is that each operating asset and liability should change about the same percent as the percent change in the sales activity of the business. If sales revenue increases, say, 10 percent, then operating assets and liabilities should increase *about* 10 percent. The percents of increase in the operating assets and liabilities (in particular, accounts receivable, inventory, accounts payable, and accrued expenses payable) should be emphasized in the cash flow report to the manager.

Scrutinizing sales revenue and expenses

In this section, we offer examples of sales revenue and expense information that managers need that is not reported in the external income statement of a business. Given the broad range of different businesses and different circumstances, we can't offer much detail.

Here's a sampling of the kinds of accounting information that business managers need either in their internal income statements (P&L reports) or in supplementary schedules and analyses:

>> **Sales volumes** (quantities sold) for all sources of sales revenue.

>> **List sales prices** and **discounts, allowances, and rebates** against list sales prices. For many businesses (but not all), sales pricing is a two-sided affair that starts with list prices (such as manufacturer's suggested retail price) and includes deductions of all sorts from the list prices.

>> **Sales returns** — products that were bought but later returned by customers.

>> **Special incentive offers** by suppliers that effectively reduce the purchase cost of products.

>> **Cost per acquisition or customer acquisition cost (CPA or CAC)** — how much a company spends on digital and social media advertising campaigns.

>> Significant **variations in discretionary expenses** from year to year, such as repair and maintenance, employee training costs, and advertising.

- » **Illegal payments** to secure business, including bribes, kickbacks, and other under-the-table payments. Keep in mind that businesses are not willing to admit to making such payments, much less report them in internal communications. Therefore, the manager should know how these payments are disguised in the business's accounts.

- » Sales revenue and margin for **new products.**

- » Significant **changes in fixed costs** and reasons for the changes.

- » **Expenses that surged** much more than increases in sales volume or sales revenue.

- » **New expenses** that show up for the first time.

- » **Accounting changes** (if any) regarding when sales revenue and expenses are recorded.

REMEMBER

The preceding list is not exhaustive, but it does cover many important types of information that managers need to interpret their P&L reports and to plan profit improvements in the future. Analyzing profit is an open-ended process. Many ways to slice and dice sales and expense data exist. Managers have only so much time at their disposal, but they should take the time to understand and analyze the main factors that drive profit.

Avoiding Rookie Mistakes

REMEMBER

Aspiring accountants — whether currently employed in an accounting role, looking to join the profession, or simply attempting to expand their knowledge of accounting and financial reporting — will find these four pearls of wisdom helpful for understanding and managing internal financial statements, reports, and information:

- » Never confuse internal financial information with external financial reporting. These two have vastly different uses, purposes, and audiences.

- » Never just hit the Send button. Although tempting, any financial information distributed to external parties should always be reviewed and approved by all appropriate personnel and management.

- » Assumption is the mother of all mistakes. If financial statements are requested, by internal or external parties (especially external), your policy should be loud and clear. The financial information is always reviewed and scrubbed by the appropriate company personnel before it is distributed. Do not assume that you can push a couple of buttons and print a report from accounting systems such as QuickBooks, Sage 50, or NetSuite, and then distribute this information. This can be a fatal mistake and almost always leads to far more questions and problems than it solves.

>> All financial information distributed — whether to external parties or for internal use — should clearly note two key items: that the financial information is either audited or unaudited, and that the financial information is confidential and the property of the company. Even for companies that have the best safeguards installed to protect their internal financial information, at some point this information is going to end up outside the organization, so it is always helpful (from a legal perspective) to have clear disclosures as to the confidential nature of the information.

IN THIS CHAPTER

» **Heeding a word of warning: Financial engineering does not mean accounting fraud**

» **Checking out commonly used financial engineering strategies**

» **Discovering how companies manufacture profits and losses**

» **Recognizing trends that may not be your friend**

Chapter **14**

Applying Tricks and Treats to Engineer Financial Results

The title of this chapter makes a gesture to Halloween; we all know that this is the yearly event when you go house to house with your kids and hopefully receive free treats. To a certain extent, the same logic applies with Bay Street because recently it seems that they can hand out all types of free "treats" when companies report financial results. While on the surface, the financial treat may appear to be very appealing, the tricks should be closely watched and understood to ensure you're not getting a rotten apple in your bag.

With this edition of *Accounting For Canadians For Dummies*, we felt it was important to include a chapter that specifically addresses how businesses can massage, manipulate, tweak, and/or package financial results to achieve specific or desired results (when presenting operating results to external parties). In a nutshell, we refer to this strategy simply as *financial engineering.*

REMEMBER

We should note that financial engineering is not to be confused with what is commonly referred to as "cooking the books" or the intentional and willful attempt to present fraudulent financial information to deceive external parties. This represents a completely different subject matter, which we touch on throughout this book. Rather, financial engineering is a broader concept that, whether utilized by Bay Street or Main Street (that is, private businesses), offers a lesson on how businesses can massage, tweak, adjust, and, for lack of a better term, manipulate financial information and results to present a financial story that helps achieve a specific goal or objective (which usually involves increasing a company's valuation).

Knowing What Financial Engineering Is Not

Before we dive into the concept of financial engineering and what it entails later in this chapter, it is helpful to identify what financial engineering is *not*. We want to put out of your mind any preconceived notions about the topics of fraudulent financial reporting or heavy-handed manipulation of accounting and other deliberately misleading information put into financial reports.

REMEMBER

There are two specific points that are important to understand:

>> Financial engineering does *not* refer to the intentional misreporting and misleading presentation of accounting transactions and financial operating results. It does not refer to cooking the books. While we would love to recall some of the great accounting frauds of the past (for example, Enron or Nortel), this subject would warrant a whole book to itself. We just point out here that almost all "great" accounting frauds were supported by executive-level management collusion. Multiple members of the executive management team worked in complicity to report financial information with the willful intent to deceive and mislead.

Be on the lookout for any signs of executive-level collusion, such as boards of directors that are not truly independent. Be careful if the CPA auditor of the financial report is relatively unknown. Finally, be extra careful of tightly controlled insider-operated businesses, which are more conducive to accounting and financial reporting abuse.

>> Financial engineering usually does *not* refer to companies adopting aggressive accounting methods and highly favourable estimates for recording

transactions and reporting financial operating results. Using aggressive accounting methods by itself does not represent a fraudulent activity so long as the accounting methods fall within the guidelines of generally accepted accounting principles (GAAP). The use of one accounting method over another is a decision best left for the company's management team, board of directors, and independent auditors to resolve and agree upon.

With this said, we would offer a tip as it relates to sniffing out companies that may be utilizing more aggressive accounting methods than are justified: Aggressive accounting methods can be used to accelerate sales revenue and defer expenses, thereby inflating earnings. While this makes the income statement look good and gives the appearance of strong profits, do not forget that the income statement (see Chapter 6) is generally the easiest of the three fundamental financial statements to manipulate. This is one reason we emphasize the importance of understanding how cash is generated and consumed in a business, which can readily be found in the cash flows statement (see Chapter 8).

Defining What Financial Engineering Is

When you know what financial engineering is not (see the preceding section), you can explore what financial engineering refers to. However, we encounter a problem right off the bat. The term has more than one meaning. Broadly speaking, it refers to the use of highly sophisticated mathematical methods and computer-based algorithms for analyzing financial reports data.

REMEMBER

Here we use the term *financial engineering* in an important but much more limited sense. In the rest of this chapter, we use the term to refer to going a step beyond simple ratios to use other techniques for analyzing and reconfiguring financial report information. This additional layer of analysis may very well sway or shift the reader's sentiment about a company's operating performance and financial position. The primary goal of financial engineering, as we use the term in this chapter, is to assist external parties with gaining a better understanding of a business's reported operating results and financial position.

One example of how businesses utilize financial engineering strategies directly in their financial reports concerns the issue of *unusual gains and losses*. Unusual gains and losses can be captured as a one-time loss reported as *other revenues* or *other expenses* in the income statement (below the operating income level). By carving out this rather unusual expense, an external reader of the financial statements could clearly and efficiently understand why the company incurred such a large loss, allowing them to focus on the remaining base operations to evaluate the company's financial performance.

Up to this point, we agree that presenting more complete, accurate, and revealing financial operating results in the financial statements is warranted and beneficial to outside parties. But it is also at this point where the concept of modern-day financial engineering needs to be appreciated and that accounting as an "art" form versus a science needs to be clearly understood by defining financial engineering in the simplest form.

REMEMBER

Financial engineering is based in the idea of taking GAAP financial statements and accounting information (as presented) and then engineering or rearranging the information into a different format, structure, comparison, and so on. The *engineered* data should offer invaluable additional information and perspectives for the purpose of allowing users to make better-informed business decisions. Without the engineered information, external parties may depend solely on a financial report, which can manipulate or distort information that could lead external parties to different conclusions on a company's financial performance and position.

TIP

When undertaking financial engineering, you take GAAP financial information and reconfigure it into a different financial framework. In doing this, you'll start to notice a series of rather commonly used terms and expressions frequently associated with companies that present financially engineered information. These terms usually abbreviated with acronyms, include non-GAAP, adjusted GAAP, EBITDA (earnings before interest, taxes, depreciation and amortization expense), adjusted EBITDA, proforma results, and free cash flow. The list goes on and on. Your antennae should definitely be raised, and you should plan to apply additional scrutiny to the information when this type of terminology appears.

WARNING

The risk of the information not being in compliance with GAAP increases because consistency and comparability may be lacking when it comes to how companies define, interpret, and present this information. Furthermore, companies may be much more selective in the type of information they present (to influence/direct a reader toward a specific conclusion). In short, financially engineered information, by itself, is not fraudulent in nature but rather a somewhat subjective method of reporting financial results that warrants additional scrutiny from external parties.

Ultimately, it is up to the financial report reader to decide how important the financially engineered information is, how credible it is, and whether it should be relied upon. There is no real school for this other than knowledge and experience, which we hope to help you build, at least a little bit, with our book and specifically this chapter.

Identifying Commonly Used "Tricks of the Trade" outside the realm of GAAP

In this section, we provide three examples of what we will call the *real* or *pure* financial engineering strategies that are outside the scope of GAAP but are frequently utilized by companies.

EBITDA and addbacks

First, we need to ask the question as to why EBITDA is important. Simply put, EBITDA is a measurement of profitability (a) used to evaluate a company's ability to service debt or support distributions/dividends and (b) relied upon as a basis for valuing a business (for example, when one company is looking to buy another business). It should make sense that a higher EBITDA generally translates into the ability for a company to support higher debt levels. It also indicates that the company's value is higher.

We need to emphasize that the concept of EBITDA is subjective and for the most part beyond the scope of GAAP (so it needs to be taken with a grain of salt). But where the real fun begins with EBITDA is when companies start to discuss or disclose *adjusted* EBITDA with operating performance addbacks. "What are addbacks?" you may ask. Addbacks as such are really nothing more than management's assessment of either increased revenue (that should have been earned but for some reason was not) or decreased expenses (that will be nonrecurring) that should be included or added back in calculating adjusted EBITDA to support a valuation analysis, debt service calculation, and so on.

WARNING

At this point, it should be abundantly clear just how badly not only EBITDA but addbacks can be abused to inflate earnings and company valuations to achieve a financial objective. Countless examples of the aggressive use of addbacks to inflate EBITDA could be provided, but the general concept we are driving home is that adjusting EBITDA is a very common strategy and a negotiating point when negotiating a financial transaction that can be manipulated beyond belief.

Sales revenue recognition

One of the hottest and most important topics in GAAP relates to recognizing sales and determining when the earnings process is complete. More than a few accountants and authoritative groups have weighed in on this subject as, with so many types of sales transactions utilized in the global economy today, there is no shortage of opinions and fact patterns available to help guide a company with recognizing sales revenue. Furthermore, several subjective elements must be taken into consideration when recognizing sales revenue, ranging from the validity of the sale to begin with (at the initial point of sales) through to the ultimate collectability of the sale (can the customer even pay).

REMEMBER

What companies have begun to do on a more frequent basis is to present a non-GAAP sales revenue to reflect, for example, just how many bookings they have (but have not yet delivered to the market or have not satisfied the tests to fully realize the sales revenue in the current period). Is this useful information? Absolutely. But does it mean the company has earned the revenue/sales? Absolutely not! So take care to understand the difference between GAAP-recognized sales revenue and the countless other forms of non-GAAP sales revenue that a company may disclose.

Pro forma operating results

Another quite common non-GAAP financial disclosure and analysis companies like to provide relates to presenting *pro forma* operating results. For example, a company may undertake a major acquisition toward the end of the year. Suppose the acquisition holds the promise of significant expense reductions being realized over the next two to three years with the combined operations because economies of scale are realized with large personnel expense reductions anticipated. So a company may take actual, audited GAAP-based financial results for both companies and then present a hypothetical combination of the two entities as if they were operating together and just how many costs/expenses could be eliminated.

WARNING

Again, this information may be interesting, but is it 100 percent factual and supported by an audit? No, as it is 100 percent non-compliant with GAAP. The information is highly dependent on management assessments and estimates that are based on forward-looking statements that may or may not come to fruition.

Manufacturing Imaginary Profits (and, Yes, Losses)

We start our discussion on how companies can manufacture profits by referring you back to the beginning of this chapter, where the concept of financial engineering is first discussed, as to what it is and what it is not, and we take this opportunity to expand our presentation on how profits can be "manufactured" by using accounting strategies. In effect, this represents a form or type of financial engineering that is more technical in nature as it closely relates to applying GAAP.

REMEMBER

Again, we would also like to be perfectly clear that the content provided in this section should not be confused with accounting or financial fraud. Rather, the concepts highlighted here originate from companies adjusting or changing specific accounting policies, procedures, use of estimates, and so on over several years as business conditions or operating circumstances change. These are legitimate (per GAAP) but warrant a closer look by both internal and external parties when companies move down this path.

Reviewing examples of "manufacturing" profits

We provide three examples for you to chew (or maybe the more appropriate word would be gag) on:

>> **Change in estimate:** Companies generally need to make periodic investments in various assets, tangible and intangible, to support their ongoing operations. When making investments in assets, the company must select appropriate depreciation, amortization, or depletion estimates (to appropriately expense the consumption of an asset over a period of time). Companies may elect to revise these estimates based on changes to their operating environment.

For example, if an asset was originally anticipated to be fully consumed and depreciated over a five-year period but, based on revised management estimates that indicate the asset has a longer life, the life was extended to seven years, then the period depreciation expense would naturally decrease, because the asset would be depreciated over a longer period. The same logic could be used when amortizing intellectual property (for example, the value assigned to a customer list that was purchased), but the point is that a simple change in an estimate from, say, five years to seven years could impact operating performance significantly. Other examples would be a company changing an estimate for potential sales returns or future warranty-related costs as they "scrub" operating results to be more accurate. We will let you decide whether a company scrubbing operating results is being done so legitimately or to achieve a specific performance target, but calculating accounting estimates is always an area that should demand attention.

>> **Change in policy:** A change in accounting estimate should not be confused with a change in accounting policy. For example, a company may change its policy on

how to track inventory costs from weighted average to first-in, first-out (FIFO) because it believes that this method would provide a more relevant presentation in the financial statements. (We discuss weighted average and FIFO inventory methods in Chapter 9.) In times of rising prices, which is normal due to inflation, net income is improved by this change. The change has to be applied retroactively and retained earnings would be increased.

>> **Cleaning house:** The two previous examples focused on how a company may inflate operating profits and earnings. The concept of cleaning house does the exact opposite; a common strategy companies use when bad news needs to be delivered (to the market or investors) is to deliver all the bad news at once. Or, simply put, let us clean house with all potential write-offs, adjustments, losses, and so on in one time period to sacrifice the current year to build a clean basis to drive profits in future years.

Mind you, no cash changes hands with these types of events; rather, the balance sheet is simply adjusted to eliminate the garbage (for lack of a better term) that has accumulated on the balance sheet over a period of time (for example, worthless inventory, unsupportable assets, quickly fading IP/content, and so on).

Keeping critical points in mind

REMEMBER

We would like to emphasize two important points as related to manufacturing profits:

>> In the three examples provided in the preceding section, no cash changes hands. None, zero, zip! This is to say that the related expenses or losses are not real, as somewhere in the past cash was impacted by either investing in a long-term asset or buying inventory (to provide two examples). Yes, the expenses and losses are very much real and the company's management team needs to be held accountable for any performance issues. But the adjustments noted earlier represent somewhat of a sleight of accounting hand to move expenses or costs between the balance sheet and income statement in a manner that is, for lack of a better term, desirable (to achieve certain goals or confirm a story).

>> Nothing is inherently wrong with these strategies, especially when a company's external CPA auditor has agreed to the changes and confirms that the changes comply with GAAP. But you should always watch for these items in relation to the size of adjustments, the frequency, and the reasoning/validity, because they may indicate either a management effort to "massage" the financial results or, worse yet, weaknesses in the company's internal accounting system and financial information reporting.

Looking Out for Particular Trends and Terminology

We'll wrap this chapter up by emphasizing once again that there is nothing inherently illegal or dishonest about providing supplemental information, which is often especially useful to external parties. But in the same breath, it's important to note that this type of information tends to be much more subjective in nature and is provided to sway or influence external-party analysis of a company, often not in conformity with GAAP and generally not audited by an external CPA firm.

WARNING

Red flags should be raised when you see terms like *EBITDA, adjusted GAAP, pro forma, non-GAAP, booked revenue* (not yet earned), and the like, especially when you notice a trend developing over a period of time (that is, year over year, a company is focusing on non-GAAP results as opposed to GAAP results).

WARNING

Further, when you see a company implementing changes to accounting policies, revisions to accounting estimates, and similar types of accounting events, make sure you pay close attention to the pertinent reasons; again, any trends that start to appear and repeat year after year should raise an eyebrow or two. If nothing else, it may indicate that the company's internal accounting and financial professional staff and team are struggling with getting a handle on critical financial transactions and information to report complete, accurate, reliable, and timely financial operating results (in its financial statements).

4

Leveraging Accounting in Managing a Business

Determine how to insightfully analyze profit with a well-thought-out P&L report.

Become familiar with the costs that managers work with day in and day out, and the problems associated with measuring costs.

Develop and utilize best-in-class forecasts, projections, and budgets to improve the financial performance of a business.

IN THIS CHAPTER

» Recognizing the profit-making function of business managers

» Scoping the field of managerial accounting

» Centering on profit centres

» Making internal P&L reports useful

» Analyzing profit for fun and more profit

Chapter **15**

Analyzing Profit

A s a business manager, executive, or owner (collectively referred to as *man-ager* through the remainder of this chapter), you get paid to make profit happen. That's what separates you from the employees at your business. Of course, you should be a motivator, innovator, consensus builder, lobbyist, and maybe sometimes a babysitter, too. But the hard-core purpose of your job is to make and improve profit. No matter how much your staff loves you (or do they love those doughnuts you bring in every Monday?), if you don't meet your profit goals, you're facing the unemployment line.

Competition in most industries is fierce, and you can never take profit performance for granted. Changes take place all the time — changes initiated by the business and changes from outside forces. Maybe a new superstore down the street is causing your profit to fall off, and you figure that you'll have a huge sale to draw customers, complete with splashy ads on social media and Dimbo the Clown in the store. Whoa, not so fast. First make sure that you can afford to cut prices and spend money on advertising and still turn a profit. Maybe price cuts and Dimbo's balloon creations will keep your cash register singing, but making sales does not guarantee that you make a profit. Profit is a two-sided challenge: Profit comes from making sales *and* controlling expenses.

This chapter focuses on the fundamental financial factors that drive profit — what you could call the *levers of profit*. Business managers need a sure-handed grip on these profit handles. One of the purposes of accounting is to provide this critical information to the managers, and to present the information in the most useful format for managers. Chapter 13 explains that externally reported income statements don't provide all the information that business managers need for sustainable profit performance. Managers need to thoroughly understand their external income statements, and they also need to look deep into the bowels of the business.

Helping Managers: The Fourth Pillar of Accounting

REMEMBER

As previous chapters explain, accounting serves critical functions in a business:

>> **Recordkeeping:** A business needs a dependable recordkeeping and bookkeeping system for operating in a smooth and efficient manner. Strong internal accounting controls are needed to minimize errors and fraud.

>> **Tax compliance:** A business must comply with a myriad of tax laws, and it depends on its chief accountant (controller) to make sure that all its tax returns are prepared on time and correctly.

>> **Financial reporting:** A business prepares financial statements that should conform to established accounting and financial reporting standards, which are reported on a regular basis to its creditors and external shareowners.

>> **Internal reporting and analysis:** Accounting should help managers in their decision making, controlling, and planning by providing the information they need in the most helpful format. This branch of accounting is generally called *managerial* or *management accounting*.

So the accountant has to wear four different hats. And don't forget that the accounting system of a business has to serve all four of these demands.

Branching out in the field of management accounting

This chapter pays particular attention to the internal reporting of profit to managers and providing essential information needed for plotting profit strategy and controlling profit performance. Chapter 16 examines the methods and problems of determining product costs (generally called *cost accounting*). Chapter 17 concentrates on financial planning, forecasting, projections, and budgeting.

REMEMBER

Designing and monitoring the accounting recordkeeping system, complying with complex federal and provincial laws, and preparing external financial reports put heavy demands on the time and attention of the accounting department of a business. Even so, managers' special needs for additional accounting information should not be given second-level priority or be done by default. The chief accountant (controller) has the responsibility of ensuring that the accounting information needs of managers are served with maximum usefulness. Ideally, a manager tells the accountant exactly what information they need and how to report the information. Managers should expect this from their accountants.

Following the organizational structure

In a small business, often only one manager (or in a number of cases, one owner) is in charge of profit. As businesses get larger, two or more managers have profit responsibility. The overarching rule of managerial accounting is to follow the organizational structure: to report relevant information for which each individual manager is responsible. (This principle is logically referred to as *responsibility accounting*.) If a manager is in charge of a product line, for instance, the accounting department should report the sales and expenses for that product line to the manager in charge. If a manager is in charge of building maintenance, all relevant costs should be reported to that manager.

REMEMBER

Generally speaking, a manager is responsible for one of two types of basic organizational segments:

>> **Profit centres:** These are separate, identifiable sources of sales revenue and connected expenses so that a measure of profit can be determined for each. A profit centre can be a particular product or a product line, a particular location or territory in which a wide range of products is sold, or a channel of distribution. Rarely is an entire business managed as one conglomerate profit centre, with no differentiation of its various sources of sales and profit.

>> **Cost centres:** Certain departments and other organizational units do not generate sales, but they have costs that can be identified to their operations. Examples are the accounting department, the headquarters staff of a business, the legal department, and the security department. The managers responsible for these organizational units need accounting reports that keep them informed about the costs of running their departments. The managers should keep their costs under control, of course, and they need informative accounting reports to do this.

TIP

The term *centre* is simply a convenient word that includes a variety of types of organizational segments, such as departments, divisions, branches, territories, and other monikers.

Centering on profit centres

In this chapter, we concentrate on profit centres. We don't mean to shun cost centres, but the type of accounting information needed by the managers of cost centres is relatively straightforward. They need a lot of detailed information, including comparisons with last period and with the budgeted targets for the current period. We don't mean to suggest that the design of cost centre reports is a trivial matter. Sorting out significant cost variances and highlighting these cost problems for management attention is important. But the spotlight of this chapter is on profit analysis techniques using accounting information for managers with profit responsibility.

TECHNICAL STUFF

Large businesses commonly create relatively autonomous units within the organization that, in addition to having responsibility for their profit and cost centres, also have broad authority and control over investing in assets and raising capital for their assets. These organization units are called, quite logically, investment centres. Basically, an *investment centre* is a mini business within the larger conglomerate company-wide setting. Discussing investment centres is beyond the scope of this chapter.

From a one-person sole proprietorship to a mammoth business organization such as Bombardier or BCE, one of the most important tasks of managerial accounting is to identify each source of profit within the business and to accumulate the sales revenue and the direct expenses for each of these sources of profit. Can you imagine an auto dealership, for example, not separating revenue and expenses between its new car sales and its service and parts departments?

REMEMBER

Even small businesses may have a relatively large number of different sources of profit. In contrast, even a large business may have just a few mainstream sources of profit. No sweeping rules exist for classifying sales revenue and costs for the purpose of segregating sources of profit — in other words, for defining the profit centres of a business. Every business has to sort this out on its own. The controller (chief accountant) can advise top management regarding how to organize the business into profit centres. But the main job of the controller is to identify the profit centres that have been (or should be) established by management and to make sure that the managers of these profit centres get the accounting information they need. Of course, managers should know how to use the information.

Internal Profit Reporting

External financial statements, including the profit report (income statement; see Chapter 6), comply with well-established rules and conventions, which we discuss in several places. In contrast, the format and content of internal accounting reports to managers is a wide-open field. If you could sneak a peek at the internal financial reports of several businesses (discussed in Chapter 13), we think you would be surprised at the diversity among the businesses. All businesses include sales revenue and expenses in their internal P&L (profit and loss) reports. Beyond this broad comment, it's difficult to generalize about the specific format and level of detail included in P&L reports, particularly regarding how operating expenses are reported.

Designing internal profit (P&L) reports

Profit performance reports prepared for a business's managers typically are called *P&L* (profit and loss) reports. These reports should be prepared as frequently as managers need them, usually monthly or quarterly — perhaps even weekly or daily in some businesses. A P&L report is prepared for the manager in charge of each profit centre; these confidential profit reports do not circulate outside the business. The P&L contains sensitive information that competitors would love to get hold of.

WARNING

Accountants are not in the habit of preparing brief, summary-level profit reports. Accountants tend to err on the side of providing a great deal of detailed data and information. Their mantra is to give managers more information, even if the information is not asked for. Our attitude is just the reverse. We're sure it's not news to you that managers are busy people, and they don't have spare time to waste, whether in reading long, rambling emails or in deciphering multi-page profit reports with too much detail. Our preference is that profit reports be compact for a quick read. If managers want more detail, they can request it as time permits. Ideally, the accountant should prepare a profit *main page* that would fit on one computer screen, although this may be a smidgeon too small as a practical matter. In any case, keep it brief.

Businesses that sell products deduct the cost of goods sold expense from sales revenue and then report *gross profit* (alternatively called *gross margin*) both in their externally reported income statements and in their internal P&L reports to managers. However, internal P&L reports have a lot more detail about sources of sales and the components of cost of goods sold expense. In this chapter, we use the example of a business that sells products. Businesses that sell products manufactured by other businesses generally fall into one of two types: *retailers* that sell products to final consumers and *wholesalers* (distributors) that sell to retailers. The following discussion applies to both.

TIP

One thing we've learned over the years is the need for short and to-the-point or quick-and-dirty profit models that managers can use for decision-making analysis and plotting profit strategy. By *short,* we mean on one page or even smaller than one full page — such as on one computer screen that the manager can interact with to test the critical factors that drive profit. For example, if sales price were decreased 5 percent to gain 10 percent more sales volume, what would happen to profit? Managers of profit centres need a tool to quickly answer such questions. Later in this chapter, we introduce just such a profit analysis template for managers (see "Presenting a profit analysis template").

Reporting operating expenses

Below the gross margin line in an internal P&L statement, reporting practices vary from company to company. No standard pattern exists. One question looms large: How should the operating expenses of a profit centre be presented in its P&L report? There's no authoritative answer to this question. One basic choice for reporting operating expenses is between the object of expenditure basis and the cost behaviour basis.

Reporting operating expenses on object of expenditure basis

By far the most common way to present operating expenses in a profit centre's P&L report is to list them according to the *object of expenditure basis.* This means that expenses are classified according to what is purchased (the object of the expenditure) — such as salaries and wages, commissions paid to salespersons, rent, depreciation, shipping costs, property taxes, advertising, insurance, utilities, office supplies, telephone costs, and so on. To do this, the operating expenses of the business have to be recorded in such a way that these costs can be traced to each of its various profit centres. For example, employee salaries of persons working in a particular profit centre are recorded as belonging to that profit centre.

REMEMBER

The object of expenditure basis for reporting operating costs to managers of profit centres is practical. And this information is useful for management control because, generally speaking, controlling costs focuses on the particular items being bought by the business. For example, a profit centre manager analyzes wages and salary expense to decide whether additional or fewer personnel are needed relative to current and forecast sales levels. A manager can examine the insurance expense relative to the types of assets being insured and their risks of losses.

WARNING

For cost control purposes, the object of expenditure basis works well. But there is a downside. This method for reporting operating costs to profit centre managers obscures the all-important factor in making profit: *margin.* Yes, internal P&L reports include *gross margin,* which is sales revenue minus the cost of goods sold.

But gross margin isn't the final amount of operating margin that managers need to know. This concept leads to the important distinction between the two types of operating expenses.

Separating operating expenses further on their behaviour basis

The first and usually largest *variable* expense of making sales is the cost of goods sold expense (for companies that sell products). In addition to cost of goods sold, an obvious variable expense, businesses have other expenses that depend either on the volume of sales (quantities sold) or the dollar amount of sales (sales revenue). And virtually all businesses have *fixed* expenses that are not sensitive to sales activity — at least, not in the short run. Therefore, it makes sense to take operating expenses classified according to object of expenditure and further classify each expense into either variable or fixed. There would be a variable or fixed tag on each expense.

TIP

The principal advantage of separating operating expenses between variable and fixed is that margin can be reported. *Margin* is the residual amount after all variable expenses of making sales are deducted from sales revenue. In other words, margin equals profit after all variable costs are deducted from sales revenue but before fixed costs are deducted from sales revenue. Margin is compared with total fixed costs for the period. This head-to-head comparison of margin against fixed costs is critical. We come back to this important point in the next section.

Although it's hard to know for sure — because internal profit reporting practices of businesses are not publicized or generally available — our experience is that the large majority of companies do not attempt to classify operating expenses as variable or fixed. If you gave us a dollar for every company you found that classifies its operating expenses on the object of expenditure basis and we gave you a dollar for every business that further separates between variable and fixed behaviour, we guarantee you that we would end up with many more dollars than you. Yet for making profit decisions, managers need to know the variable versus fixed nature of their operating expenses.

Looking at Strategic Profit Analysis

First, a word or two on expense analysis and control versus strategic analysis and planning. The well-worn expression in real estate is "location, location, location." In expense management, an equivalent expression is "detail, detail, detail." Controlling expenses is done at a detailed level. Another expression comes to mind here: "The devil is in the detail." In short, managers need a lot of detailed information to analyze expenses and to make decisions regarding these expenses — no surprise there.

We could go on and on about expense analysis and control. But instead, we shift attention here to the higher-level topic of making strategic decisions for profit maintenance and improvement. In particular, what can the accountant do to help the manager clearly understand and correctly analyze the factors that drive profit, which also helps the manager understand the interactions and tradeoffs among these factors? In our view, this key function of the accountant starts with a profit analysis template that the manager can use to think through and do the math.

Presenting a profit analysis template

Figure 15-1 presents a profit analysis template that has broad applicability for businesses that sell products. (Service businesses have to adapt the template and remove cost of goods sold expense.)

The example is for the same business introduced in Chapter 13. Figure 13-2 presents its income statement for the most recent year. The company's $34.939 million of total selling, general, and administrative (SG&A) expenses reported in Figure 13-1 are reclassified into three distinct types in Figure 15-1: revenue-driven, volume-driven, and fixed.

In Figure 15-1, we divide SG&A expenses according to how they behave relative to sales activity. So, four lines for expenses are above the profit line EBITDA, namely cost of goods sold (a variable expense), two variable operating expenses, and fixed operating expenses. The profit template stops at the operating earnings line, or earnings before interest and income tax (EBIT). Also, EBITDA is shown on a separate line. The business is treated as one conglomerate profit centre. Of course, the business could have its accounting staff prepare separate profit templates for each different profit centre of the business.

REMEMBER

The purpose of a strategic profit analysis template is to provide the manager with a different look at profit — one that's useful for thinking about how the business makes profit, for reaching profit decisions, and for planning based on forecasts of changes in the basic factors that drive the company's profit outcome. The template demands that SG&A expenses be separated into variable and fixed types. This is the one key difference between the standard income statement (Figure 13-2) and the strategic profit template (Figure 15-1). In our view, redesigning the profit report based on expense behaviour has high value to managers, but frankly, many businesses don't take the time to classify their expenses this way.

QW Example Tech., Inc. Income Statement for the Fiscal Year Ending 12/31/2024		
(all dollar amounts in thousands)	12/31/2024	% of Sales
Sales Revenue, Net	$71,064	100.0%
Costs of Goods Sold	$26,891	37.8%
Gross Profit (or Gross Margin)	$44,173	62.2%
Selling, General, & Administrative Expenses:		
Revenue-Driven Expenses	$10,660	15.0%
Volume-Driven Expenses	$8,528	12.0%
Operating Margin (aka Contribution Margin)	$24,985	35.2%
Fixed SG&A Expenses	$15,751	22.2%
Earnings Before Interest, Taxes, Depreciation, & Amortization Expense (EBITDA)	$9,234	13.0%
Depreciation & Amortization Expense	$1,739	2.4%
Operating Earnings Before Income Taxes & Interest	$7,495	10.5%

Confidential — Property of QW Example Tech., Inc.

FIGURE 15-1:
Strategic profit
analysis template.

© John Wiley & Sons, Inc.

Separating variable and fixed expenses

For managers to analyze a business's profit behaviour thoroughly, they need to know which expenses are *variable* and which are *fixed* — in other words, which expenses change according to the level of sales activity in a given period and which don't. The title of each expense account often gives a pretty good clue. For example, the cost of goods sold expense is variable because it depends on the number of units of product sold, and sales commissions are variable expenses as well. On the other hand, property taxes and fire and liability insurance premiums are fixed for a period of time. Managers should always have a good feel for how their operating expenses behave relative to sales activity.

Variable expenses

Virtually every business has *variable expenses*, which move up and down in tight proportion with changes in sales volume or sales revenue, like soldiers obeying orders barked out by their drill sergeant. Here are examples of common variable expenses:

>> The cost of goods sold expense, which is the cost of products sold to customers

>> Commissions paid to salespeople based on their sales

>> Franchise fees based on total sales for the period, which are paid to the franchisor

>> Digital advertising costs spent on social media (such as Instagram ads), which have a direct correlation to customer sales

>> Transportation costs of delivering products to customers via FedEx, UPS, and freight haulers (railroads and trucking companies)

>> Fees that a retailer pays when a customer uses a credit or debit card (in other words, merchant account fees)

REMEMBER

Cost of goods sold is usually (but not always) the largest variable expense of a business that sells products, as you'd suspect. Other variable expenses are the costs of making sales and running the business. The sizes of variable operating expenses, relative to sales revenue, vary from industry to industry. Delivery costs of Canadian Tire and Loblaw, for instance, are minimal because their customers take the products they buy with them. Other businesses deliver products to their customers' doorsteps, so that expense is obviously much higher (and dependent on which delivery service the company uses — Purolator or UPS versus Canada Post, for example).

Fixed expenses

Fixed operating expenses include many costs that a business is obligated to pay and cannot decrease over the short run without major surgery on the human resources and physical facilities of the business.

As an example of fixed expenses, consider the typical self-service car wash business — you know, the kind where you drive in, put some coins in a box, and use the water spray to clean your car. Almost all the operating costs of this business are fixed; rent on the land, depreciation of the structure and the equipment, and the annual insurance premium don't depend on the number of cars passing through the car wash. The main variable expenses are the water and the soap and perhaps the cost of electricity.

Fixed expenses are the costs of doing business that, for all practical purposes, are stuck at a certain amount over the short term. Fixed expenses do not react to changes in the sales level. Here are some more examples of fixed operating expenses:

>> Gas and electricity costs to heat, cool, and light the premises (although these will be influenced by seasonality factors)

>> Facility rent expense

>> Employees' salaries and benefits

>> Dues, subscriptions, and software licenses

>> Property taxes

>> Depreciation expense (which is not a cash expense but is fixed in nature)

>> Annual audit fee (if the business has its financial reports audited)

>> General liability, E&O (errors and omissions), employment practices, and officers' and directors' insurance premiums

WARNING

If you want to decrease fixed expenses significantly, you need to downsize the business (lay off workers, sell off property, and so on). When looking at the various ways for improving profit, significantly cutting down on fixed expenses is generally the last-resort option. Refer to the section "Know your options for improving profit" later in the chapter. A business should be careful not to overreact to a temporary downturn in sales by making drastic reductions in its fixed costs, which it may regret later if sales pick up again.

Stopping at operating earnings

In Figure 15-1, the profit template terminates at the *operating earnings* line; the template doesn't include interest expense or income tax expense. Interest expense and income tax expense are business-wide types of expenses, which are the responsibility of the financial executive(s) of the business. Generally, interest and income tax expenses aren't assigned to profit centres unless a profit centre is a rather large and autonomous organizational division of the business that has responsibility for its own assets, finances, and income tax. Other miscellaneous income and expenses are often driven at the company-wide level and tend to be excluded for the operating earnings line of a specific P&L centre.

REMEMBER

The measure of profit before interest and income tax is commonly called *operating earnings* or *operating profit*. It also goes by the name *earnings before interest and tax*, or EBIT. It is not and should not be called *net income*, because this term is reserved for the final bottom-line profit number of a business, after all expenses (including interest and income tax) are deducted from sales revenue.

Focusing on margin — the catalyst of profit

Figure 15-1 includes an important line of information: operating margin (sometimes referred to as *contribution margin*). *Operating margin* is operating profit before fixed expenses are deducted. Don't confuse this number with *gross margin*, which is profit after the cost of goods sold expense is subtracted from sales revenue but before any other expenses are deducted.

TIP

As a manager, your attention should be riveted on margin, and you should understand the reasons for changes in this key profit driver from period to period. A small change in unit margin can have a big effect on operating earnings. (See "Don't underestimate the effect of small changes in sales price" later in the chapter.)

DIFFERENT USES OF THE TERM *MARGIN*

Gross margin, also called *gross profit*, equals sales revenue minus the cost of goods sold expense. Gross margin doesn't reflect other variable operating expenses that are deducted from sales revenue. In contrast, the term *margin* refers to sales revenue less *all* variable expenses. Some people use the term *contribution margin* instead of just *margin* to stress that margin contributes toward the recovery of fixed expenses (and to profit after fixed expenses are covered); however, the word *contribution* isn't necessary.

As a general rule, businesses that sell products report gross margin in their external income statements (although some don't). However, they don't disclose their variable and fixed operating expenses. They report expenses according to an object of expenditure basis, such as "selling, administrative, and general expenses." The broad expense categories reported in external income statements include both variable and fixed cost components. Therefore, the operating margin of a business (sales revenue after all variable expenses but before fixed expenses) isn't reported in its external income statement. Managers carefully guard information about margins. They don't want competitors to know the margins of their business.

Further complicating the issue, unfortunately, is that journalists frequently use the term *margin* when referring to operating earnings. Inside the world of accounting, however, *margin* means profit after all variable expenses are deducted from sales revenue but before fixed expenses are deducted. So be careful when you see the term *margin:* It may refer to gross margin, to what accountants mean by *margin*, or to operating earnings (used in the press).

Using the template to explain profit

TIP

Suppose you're the CEO of the business whose profit template is shown in Figure 15-1. You should know how your business made its profit — beyond the obvious explanation that sales revenue is more than expenses. Your explanation should be expressed in terms of the dynamics of the business. As the CEO, you should be able to articulate the company's business model. In like manner, you should have at your fingertips an analytical model that explains how the company's profit factors blend together to yield profit.

So how did the business make profit? To be frank, there's no one universal way to answer the profit question. GAAP (generally accepted accounting principles) are no help here. Ask ten accountants, and we're sure you'll get ten different answers.

Our answer to the profit question pivots on the company's *break-even point*. In Figure 15-1, note that the company's fixed operating expenses (excluding depreciation) were $15.752 million for the year. Also, note that the company's margin was approximately 35.2 percent of sales revenue. In other words, variable expenses required 64.8 percent of sales revenue; only 35.2 percent was "left over" after deducting variable costs.

In Figure 15-1, depreciation expense is presented on the line below EBITDA. The amount of depreciation is a fixed expense for the year. To calculate the break-even point, the total of all fixed costs is needed. Therefore, fixed operating expenses above the EBITDA line and depreciation expense below the line are added to get total fixed expenses for the year. With this information, the company's break-even point is calculated as follows (refer to Figure 15-1 for data; all dollar amounts in the figure are in thousands):

$15.751 million fixed operating expenses + $1.739 million fixed depreciation and amortization expense = $17.491 million total fixed expenses (excluding interest expense)

$17.491 million total fixed expenses ÷ 35.2% margin on sales revenue = $49.690 million sales revenue break-even point

The company's sales revenue was $22.374 million higher than its break-even point for the year, which is good news, of course. Even more important, in just one more step you can determine operating profit for the year:

$21.374 million excess sales revenue over breakeven × 35.2% margin ratio = approximately $7.495 million EBIT for year (slight rounding difference)

After the break-even sales level is achieved, each additional dollar of sales revenue yields 35.2 cents of pure profit before tax because fixed expenses have been covered by the first $49.690 million of sales revenue. As soon as the company hurdles its break-even point, it's in its profit zone.

An irksome detail: The preceding break-even point calculation includes depreciation expense as a fixed expense for the period. The accountant records a fixed amount of depreciation expense for the period, so depreciation is logically included as a fixed expense. On the other hand, whether to include interest expense as a fixed expense is an open question. Most break-even calculations exclude it; only *operating* fixed expenses are included. Interest is a financial cost that depends on how much debt capital the business uses. In short, break-even analysis is usually based on the EBIT measure of profit — but not always.

TIP

Beyond explaining how the business made its profit for the year, the profit template is especially useful in asking what-if questions for exploring the profit impacts of changes in sales prices, sales volume, product costs, and operating costs. See the later section "Using the Profit Template for Decision-Making Analysis."

Taking a Closer Look at the Lines in the Profit Template

Profit centre managers depend heavily on the information in their P&L reports. Managers need to thoroughly understand these profit reports, so we want to spend some time going through each element of the profit template. Refer back to Figure 15-1 as needed.

Sales revenue

Sales revenue is the net amount of money received by the business from the sales of products, software, and services during the period. Note the word *net* here. The business in our example, like most, offers its customers many incentives to buy its products and to pay quickly for their purchases. The sales revenue amount takes into account deductions for rebates, allowances, sales promotions, prompt payment discounts, and any other incentives offered to customers that reduce the amount of revenue received by the business. (The manager can ask that these revenue offsets be included in the supplementary layer of schedules to the main page of the P&L report.)

As we're sure you know, the amount of sales revenue equals the number of units sold times the final, net sales prices. The number of units sold is called the *sales volume*. Sales volume should include only units that actually brought in revenue to the business. In general, businesses do a good job of keeping track of the sales volumes of their products (and services). These are closely monitored figures in, for example, the automobile and personal computer industries.

But here's a nagging problem: Some businesses sell a huge variety of products. No single product or product line brings in more than a small fraction of the total sales revenue. For instance, Home Hardware, a popular hardware store, carries more than 100,000 products according to their website. The business may keep count of customer traffic or the number of individual sales made over the year, but it probably doesn't track the quantities sold for each and every product it sells.

Cost of goods sold

Cost of goods sold is the cost of the products sold during the period. This expense should be net of discounts, rebates, and allowances the business receives from its vendors and suppliers. The cost of goods sold means different things for different types of businesses:

>> To determine product costs, manufacturers add three costs:

- The costs of raw materials
- Labour and direct burden costs
- Production overhead costs

  Accounting for the cost of manufactured products is a major function of *cost accounting,* which we discuss in Chapter 16.

>> For retailers and distributors, product cost basically is purchase cost. However, refer to Chapter 9, where we explain the differences between the FIFO, average cost, and specific identification methods for releasing inventory costs to the cost of goods sold expense. The profit centre manager should have no doubts about which cost of goods sold expense accounting method is being used. For that matter, the manager should be aware of any other costs that are included in total product cost (such as inbound freight and handling costs in some cases).

DEALING WITH INVENTORY SHRINKAGE

One common problem is how to report to managers the loss from *inventory shrinkage,* which refers to losses from shoplifting by customers, physical deterioration of products as they sit in inventory, employee theft of products, damage caused in the handling and storage of products, and so on. The amount of inventory shrinkage can be included in the cost of goods sold expense, or it may be included in volume-driven operating expenses. A manager definitely should know which other costs have been placed in the cost of goods sold expense, in addition to the product cost of units sold during the period.

Variable operating expenses

In the profit analysis template (Figure 15-1), variable operating expenses are divided into two types:

>> *Revenue-driven expenses* are those that depend on the dollar amount of sales revenue. This group of variable operating expenses includes commissions paid to salespersons based on the dollar amount of their sales, credit and debit card fees paid by retailers, franchise fees based on sales revenue, and any other cost that depends directly on the amount of sales revenue. In Figure 15-1, the company's revenue-driven variable expenses are 15.0 percent of sales revenue. If sales revenue increases $1 million, these expenses would increase $150,000.

>> *Volume-driven expenses* are driven by and depend primarily on the number of units sold or the total quantity of products sold during the period (as opposed to the dollar value of the sales). These expenses include delivery and transportation costs paid by the business, packaging costs, and any costs that depend primarily on the size and weight of the products sold. If sales volume increases 5 percent, these expenses would increase 5 percent.

Most businesses have both types of variable operating expenses. However, one or the other may be so minor that reporting it as a separate item wouldn't be useful. Only the dominant type of variable operating expense would be presented in the profit analysis template; the one expense would absorb the other type — which is good enough for government work, as they say.

Fixed expenses

REMEMBER

Managers may view fixed expenses as an albatross around the neck of the business. But in fact, these costs provide the infrastructure and support for making sales. The main characteristic of fixed operating costs is that they do not decline when sales during the period fall short of expectations. A business commits to many fixed operating costs for the coming period. For all practical purposes, these costs can't be decreased much over the short run. Examples of fixed costs are wages of employees on fixed salaries (from managers to company executives), property taxes, certain forms of insurance, depreciation and rent on the buildings and equipment used in making sales, and utility bills, professional fees for accountants and lawyers, and so on.

Certain fixed costs can be matched with a particular profit centre. For example, a business may advertise a specific product, and the fixed cost of the advertisement can be matched against revenue from sales of that product. A major product line may have its own employees on fixed salaries or its own delivery trucks on which depreciation is recorded. A business may purchase specific liability insurance covering a particular product it sells.

DEALING WITH A SHORTCOMING

The profit template in Figure 15-1 hinges on the separation of variable and fixed operating costs. The classification between variable and fixed operating expenses isn't needed for external financial statements and income tax returns. Operating expenses are reported by the nature of the expenditure in external financial reports and tax returns, so the accounting systems of many businesses don't tag operating expense accounts as fixed or variable. As a result, variable versus fixed information for operating expenses isn't readily available from the accounting system. What's a manager to do?

Well, here's a practical solution: As the profit centre manager, you can tell your accountant whether an operating expense is variable or fixed. Give your classification of the operating expenses in your profit centre to the accountant, and stress that you want this classification in the profit template for your profit centre. This may be extra work for your accountant, but the variable versus fixed classification of operating expense is of great value for your management decision-making, control, and planning.

In contrast, you can't directly couple company-wide fixed operating expenses to particular products, product lines, or other types of profit units in the organizational structure of a business. General administrative expenses (such as the CEO's annual salary and corporate legal expenses) are incurred on an entity-as-a-whole basis and can't be connected directly with any particular profit centre. A business may therefore allocate these fixed costs among its different profit centres. In our profit template example (Figure 15-1), the entire business is treated as one profit centre, so the allocation of total fixed operating expenses is not an issue.

Using the Profit Template for Decision-Making Analysis

The profit template (Figure 15-1) is useful for decision-making analysis. To demonstrate, suppose that you're under intense competitive pressure to lower the sales price of one product you sell. This product is one slice of the total activity reported in Figure 15-1. During the year, you sold 10,000 units of the product at $100 sales price, bringing in $1 million total sales revenue. The sales revenue from this product is a relatively significant part of your total sales revenue for the year. More importantly, how much margin does this product generate?

Suppose that the product's cost structure mimics the one shown in Figure 15-1 for the company as a whole. So the product's cost of goods sold is 37.8 percent of sales revenue, its revenue-driven expenses equal 15 percent of sales revenue, and its volume-driven expenses equal 12 percent of sales revenue. Thus, the product's expenses equal 64.8 percent of sales revenue, and its margin equals 35.2 percent of sales revenue. (See Figure 15-1 again.) On a per-unit basis, the margin is

$100 sales price – $37.80 cost of goods sold expense – $15 revenue-driven expenses – $12 volume-driven expenses = $35.20 margin per unit

Therefore, total margin from sales of the product is

$35.20 margin per unit × 10,000 units sales volume = $352,000 margin

Now suppose your competitors are undercutting your sales price, so you're thinking of cutting the sales price 10 percent next year, or $10 per unit. You predict that the price reduction will boost sales volume 25 percent and increase your market share. Seems like a good idea — or does it? You should run some numbers before making a final decision, just to be sure. Let's plug the new numbers into the formulas and see what happens if the sales price is dropped $10 and the business sells 12,500 units (an increase of 25 percent):

$90 sales price – $37.8 cost of goods sold expense – $13.50 revenue-driven expenses – $12 volume-driven expenses = $26.70 margin per unit

Therefore, total margin from sales of the product would be

$26.70 margin per unit × 12,500 units sales volume = $333,750 margin

The revenue-driven operating expense would drop $1.50 per unit with the $10 sales price decrease. Therefore, the new margin per unit would be $26.70 per unit. That's a 24 percent drop in margin per unit. A 25 percent gain in sales volume cannot make up for the 24 percent plunge in margin per unit. You'd need a much larger sales volume increase just to keep margin the same and even more sales to increase margin next year. You'd better think twice about dropping the sales price.

You may gain a larger market share, but your margin would drop from $352,000 to $333,750 on this product if you go ahead with the sales price cut. Is the larger market share worth this much sacrifice of margin? That's why you get paid the big bucks: to make decisions like this. As your controller, we can only help you do the analysis and calculate the effect on profit before you make a final decision.

REMEMBER
Another factor to consider is this: Fixed expenses (people, warehouse space, distribution channels, and so on) provide the *capacity* to make sales and carry on operations. A small increase in sales volume, such as selling 250 more units of the product in question, shouldn't push up the total fixed expenses of your profit centre (unless you're already bursting at the seams). On the other hand, a major

sales volume increase across the board would require additional capacity, and your fixed expenses would have to be increased.

This sales price reduction decision is just one example of the many decisions business managers have to deal with day in and day out. The profit analysis template is a useful — indeed, invaluable — analysis framework for many decisions facing business managers.

Tucking Away Some Valuable Lessons

The profit analysis template shown in Figure 15-1 offers managers several important lessons. As with most tools, the more you use it, the more you learn. In this section, we summarize some important lessons from the template.

Recognize the leverage effect caused by fixed operating expenses

Suppose sales volume had been 10 percent higher or lower in the year, holding other profit factors the same. Would profit have been correspondingly 10 percent higher or lower? The intuitive answer is yes, profit would have been 10 percent higher or lower. Wouldn't it? Not necessarily. *Margin* would have been 10 percent higher or lower because sales revenue would have been 10 percent higher or lower (assuming variable expenses remain at the same percent on sales revenue). A 10 percent change in margin in our example would be $2.499 million ($24.986 million margin from Figure 15-1 × 10 percent = $2.499 million change in margin, rounded). This is an awkward number, so let's round it off to an even $2.5 million. (Accountants actually round off some numbers.)

The $2.5 million change in margin would carry down to operating earnings *unless* fixed expenses would have been higher or lower at the different sales volume. The very nature of fixed expenses is that these costs do not change with relatively small changes in sales volume. In all likelihood, fixed expenses would have been pretty much the same at a 10 percent higher or lower sales level. Let's assume so.

Therefore, operating earnings would have been $2.5 million higher or lower. On the base profit of $7.495 million (see operating earnings in Figure 15-1), the $2.5 million swing in margin equals a 33 percent shift in profit. Thus, a 10 percent swing in sales volume causes a 33 percent swing in profit. This wider swing in profit is called the *operating leverage* effect. The idea is that a business makes better use of its fixed expenses when sales go up; its fixed expenses don't increase with the sales volume increase. Of course, the downside is that fixed expenses don't decrease when sales volume drops.

Don't underestimate the effect of small changes in sales price

What might seem to be a relatively small change in sales price can have a big effect on margin and the bottom line. The savvy manager knows to pay close attention to margin, which is the primary driver of profit. As an earlier example shows, cutting the product's sales price 10 percent would have caused a 24 percent plunge in margin per unit on sales of the product.

Most businesses don't take the time or effort to classify their operating expenses into fixed versus variable. The result is that their managers don't know margin — that is, they don't have a measure of profit after all variable costs are deducted from sales revenue but before fixed costs are deducted. Margin is a useful metric for managers, but if they don't get this information in their internal P&L reports, what can they do? Well, they can at least keep an eye on *gross margin*, which is sales revenue after cost of goods sold expense is deducted.

Using the same example as earlier, if the manager were to drop the sales price $10, or 10 percent (from $100 to $90), gross margin would also drop $10 (from $62.2 to $52.2 per unit). So, the gross margin per unit would decrease 16 percent, which is much more than the 10 percent sales price decrease. The 16 percent drop in gross margin gives the manager some idea of how much sales volume would have to increase to offset the sales price decrease. In fact, sales volume would have to increase to 11,916 units, which would be a roughly 20 percent increase over the 10,000 units sales volume to begin with:

> $622,000 present gross margin ÷ $52.2 gross margin per unit after sales price reduction = 11,916 units sales volume just to hold even

A 20 percent jump in sales volume may not be feasible, of course.

REMEMBER The moral of the story is to protect margin per unit above all else. Every dollar of margin per unit that's lost — due to decreased sales prices, increased product cost, or increases in other variable costs — has a tremendously negative effect on profit. Conversely, if you can increase the margin per unit without hurting sales volume, you reap large profit benefits.

Know your options for improving profit

TIP

Improving profit boils down to three critical factors, listed in order from the most effective to the least effective:

>> Increasing margin per unit

>> Increasing sales volume

>> Reducing fixed expenses

Say you want to improve your operating earnings (EBIT) 10 percent next year. See Figure 15-1 again for the most recent year. So how are you going to this? Here are your basic options:

>> Increase your margin 10 percent, from 35.2 percent of sales revenue to 38.72 percent. This would require some combination of improvements in sales prices, product costs, and variable expenses.

>> Sell 10 percent additional units at the present margin per unit.

>> Use a combination of these two strategies: Increase both the margin per unit and sales volume such that the combined effect is to improve total margin 10 percent.

>> Reduce fixed expenses substantially, enough to provide all the needed increase in total margin.

WARNING

The last alternative may not be realistic. Reducing direct fixed expenses by a large amount would probably reduce the company's capacity to make sales and carry out its operations. Perhaps the managers could do a little belt-tightening in the fixed expenses area, but in all likelihood, they would have to turn to the other alternatives for increasing profit.

The second approach is obvious — you just need to set a sales goal of increasing the number of products sold by 10 percent. (How you motivate the already over-worked sales staff to accomplish that sales volume goal is up to the CEO.) But how do you go about the first approach, increasing the margin from 35.2 percent to 38.72 percent? As we've said before, answering this question is why managers get paid the big bucks.

IN THIS CHAPTER

» **Measuring costs: The second-most important thing accountants do**

» **Recognizing the different needs for cost information**

» **Determining the right costs for different purposes**

» **Assembling the product cost of manufacturers**

» **Padding profit by producing too many products**

Chapter **16**

Accounting for Costs

Y ou could argue that measuring costs is the second most important thing accountants do, right after measuring profit. In fact, you need to measure costs to measure profit. But really, can measuring a cost be complicated? You just take numbers off a purchase invoice and call it a day, right? Not if your business manufactures the products you sell, that's for sure! In this chapter, we demonstrate that a cost, any cost, is not as obvious and clear-cut as you may think. Yet, obviously, costs are extremely important to businesses and other organizations.

Consider an example close to home: Suppose you just returned from the grocery store with several items in the bag. What's the cost of the box of detergent you bought? Should you include the Harmonized Sales Tax (HST)? Should you include the cost of gas you used driving to the store? Should you include some amount of depreciation expense on your car? Or suppose you returned some large water jugs for recycling while you were at the grocery store. You are returned the deposit you had paid earlier on the jugs when you purchased them full of water. Should you subtract this amount against the total cost of your purchases or should you subtract the amount directly against the cost of the water you bought? And is cost the before-tax cost? In other words, is your cost equal to the amount of income you had to earn before income tax so that you had enough after-tax income to buy the items? And what about the time you spent shopping? Your time could have been used for other endeavours. We could raise many other such questions, but you get the point.

These questions about the cost of your groceries are interesting (well, to us at least). But you don't have to come up with definite answers for such questions in managing your personal financial affairs. Individuals don't have to keep cost records of their personal expenditures. In contrast, businesses must carefully record all their costs correctly so that profit can be determined each period and so that managers have the information they need to make decisions and to make a profit.

Looking Down the Road to the Destination of Costs

All businesses that sell products must know their *product costs* — in other words, the costs of each and every item they sell. Companies that manufacture the products they sell — as opposed to distributors and retailers of products — have many problems in figuring out their product costs. Two examples of manufactured products are a new Cadillac just rolling off the assembly line at General Motors and a copy of our book, *Accounting For Canadians For Dummies*, 4th Edition hot off the printing presses.

Most production (manufacturing) processes are complex, so product cost accounting for manufacturers is complex; every step in the production process has to be tracked carefully from start to finish. Many manufacturing costs cannot be directly matched with particular products; these are called *indirect costs.* To arrive at the *full cost* of each product manufactured, accountants devise methods for allocating indirect production costs to specific products. Surprisingly, *generally accepted accounting principles* (GAAP) provide little authoritative guidance for measuring the manufacturing costs of products. Therefore, manufacturing businesses have more than a little leeway regarding how to determine their product costs. Even businesses in the same industry — Ford versus General Motors, for example — may use different product cost accounting methods.

Accountants determine many other costs, in addition to product costs:

>> The costs of departments, regional distribution centres, and virtually any identifiable organizational unit of the business

>> The cost of the retirement plan for the company's employees (with the help of actuaries)

>> The cost of marketing programs and advertising campaigns

>> The cost of restructuring the business or the cost of a major recall of products sold by the business, when necessary

A common refrain among accountants is "different costs for different purposes." True enough, but at its core, cost accounting serves two broad purposes: measuring profit and providing relevant information to managers for planning, control, and decision making.

WARNING

In our experience, people are inclined to take cost numbers for granted, as if they were handed down on stone tablets. The phrase *actual cost* often gets tossed around without a clear definition or with only a vague understanding. An actual cost depends entirely on the particular methods used to measure the cost. We can assure you that these cost measurement methods have more in common with the scores from judges in an ice-skating competition than the times clocked in a Formula One race. Many arbitrary choices are behind every cost number you see. There is no one-size-fits-all definition of *cost* and no one correct and best-in-all-circumstances method of measuring cost.

The conundrum is that, in spite of the inherent ambiguity in determining costs, we need exact amounts for costs. Managers should understand the choices an accountant has to make in measuring costs. Some cost accounting methods result in conservative profit numbers; other methods boost profit, at least in the short run. Chapter 9 discusses the choices among different accounting methods that produce financial statements with a conservative or liberal hue.

This chapter covers cost concepts and cost measurement methods that apply to all businesses, as well as basic product cost accounting of manufacturers. We discuss how a manufacturer could be fooling around with its production output to manipulate product cost for the purpose of artificially boosting its profit figure. (Service businesses encounter their own problems in allocating their operating costs for assessing the profitability of their separate sales revenue sources.)

Are Costs Really That Important?

Without good cost information, a business operates in the dark. Cost data is needed for the following purposes:

>> **Setting sales prices:** The common method for setting sales prices (known as *cost-plus* or *markup on cost*) starts with cost and then adds a certain percentage. If you don't know exactly how much a product costs, you can't be as

shrewd and competitive in your pricing as you need to be. Even if sales prices are dictated by other forces and not set by managers, managers need to compare sales prices against product costs and other costs that should be matched against each sales revenue source.

>> **Formulating a legal defence against charges of predatory pricing practices:** Many provinces have laws prohibiting businesses from selling below cost except in certain circumstances. And a business can be sued under federal or provincial law for charging artificially low prices intended to drive its competitors out of business. Be prepared to prove that your lower pricing is based on lower costs and not on some illegitimate purpose.

>> **Measuring gross profit:** Investors and managers judge business performance by the bottom-line profit figure. This profit figure depends on the *gross profit* figure you get when you subtract your cost of goods sold expense from your sales revenue. Gross profit (also called *gross margin*) is the first profit line in the income statement (see Figure 16-1 later in this chapter). If gross profit is wrong, bottom-line net income is wrong — no two ways about it. The cost of goods sold expense depends on having correct product costs (see later in this chapter "Assembling the Product Cost of Manufacturers").

>> **Valuing assets:** The balance sheet reports cost values for many (though not all) assets. To understand the balance sheet, you should understand the cost basis of its inventory and certain other assets. See Chapter 7 for more about assets and how asset values are reported in the balance sheet (also called the *statement of financial position*).

>> **Making optimal choices:** You often must choose one alternative over others in making business decisions. The best alternative depends heavily on cost factors, and you have to be careful to distinguish *relevant* costs from *irrelevant* costs, as we describe in the later section "Relevant versus irrelevant costs."

TIP

In most situations, the historic book value recorded for a fixed asset is an *irrelevant* cost. Say book value is $35,000 for a machine used in the manufacturing operations of the business. This is the amount of original cost that has not yet been charged to depreciation expense since it was acquired, and it may seem quite relevant. However, in deciding between keeping the old machine or replacing it with a newer, more efficient machine, the *salvage or residual value* of the old machine is the relevant amount, not the undepreciated cost balance of the asset.

By the way, the terms *residual* and *salvage value* are often used interchangeably, but they are slightly different in meaning. When the intention is to keep an asset until it is sold essentially for scrap, because it can't be used any further, you are supposed to use the term salvage value. On the other hand, if you are going to use an asset for part of its useful life and sell it to someone else who will use it for the same purpose but as a used asset, you are supposed to use the term residual value. We reveal our intentions by the terms we use.

Suppose the old machine has an estimated $20,000 residual value at this time; this is the relevant cost for the alternative of keeping it for use in the future — not the $35,000 book value that hasn't been depreciated yet. To keep using it, the business forgoes the $20,000 it could get by selling the asset, and this $20,000 is the relevant cost in this decision situation. Making decisions involves looking forward at the future cash flows of each alternative — not looking backward at historical-based cost values.

The amount paid for a piece of equipment is not always equal to the amount charged off to depreciation expense. That's because the business will be getting some of its investment back when it resells the used asset after it has finished using it for its purpose. The amount the business gets back depends on when it intends to resell the used asset. A business's intention for use will affect the amount of time the business has to depreciate the asset and the amount of cash flow it is expecting on the resale. Whether the business is expecting to get a residual or salvage value, that amount will be deducted from the original cost to come up with the total amount to be charged off as depreciation expense. Therefore, the amount of the residual or salvage value must be estimated when the business buys the asset and starts using it. That amount is taken into account when calculating depreciation and can be changed later if the business's intentions change.

ACCOUNTING VERSUS ECONOMIC COSTS

Accountants focus mainly on *actual costs* (though they disagree regarding how exactly to measure these costs). Actual costs are rooted in the actual, or historical, transactions and operations of a business. Accountants also determine *projected costs* for businesses that prepare forecasts (see Chapter 17), and they develop *standard costs* that serve as yardsticks to compare with the actual costs of a business.

Other concepts of cost are found in economic theory. You encounter a variety of economic cost terms when reading the *National Post* as well as in many business discussions and deliberations. Don't reveal your ignorance of the following cost terms:

- **Opportunity cost** is the amount of income (or other measurable benefit) given up when you follow a better course of action. For example, say that you quit your

(continued)

(continued)

$50,000 job, invest $200,000 you saved up, and started a new business. You earn $80,000 profit in your new business for the year. Suppose also that you would have earned 5 percent on the $200,000 (a total of $10,000) if you'd kept the money in whatever investment you took it from. So you gave up a $50,000 salary and $10,000 in investment income with your course of action; your opportunity cost is $60,000. Subtract that figure from what your actual course of action netted you — $80,000 — and you end up with a "real" economic profit of $20,000. Your income is $20,000 better by starting your new business, according to economic theory.

- **Marginal cost** is the *incremental,* out-of-pocket outlay required for taking a particular course of action. Generally speaking, it's the same thing as a *variable* cost (see "Fixed versus variable costs," later in this chapter). Marginal costs are important, but in actual practice, managers must recover fixed (committed) costs as well as marginal costs through sales revenue to remain in business. Marginal costs are most relevant for analyzing one-time ventures, which don't last over the long term.

- **Replacement cost** is the estimated amount it would take today to purchase an asset that the business already owns. The longer ago an asset was acquired, the more likely that its current replacement cost is higher than its original cost. Economists are of the opinion that current replacement costs are relevant in making rational economic decisions. For insuring assets against fire, theft, and natural catastrophes, the current replacement costs of the assets are clearly relevant. Other than for insurance, however, replacement costs are not on the front burners of decision making — except in situations in which one alternative being seriously considered actually involves replacing assets.

- **Imputed cost** is an ideal, or hypothetical, cost number that is used as a benchmark against which actual costs are compared. Two examples are *standard costs* and the *cost of capital.* Standard costs are set in advance for the manufacture of products during the coming period, and then actual costs are compared against standard costs to identify significant variances. The cost of capital is the weighted average of the interest rate on debt capital and a target rate of return that should be earned on equity capital. The *economic value added* (EVA) method compares a business's cost of capital against its actual return on capital, to determine whether the business did better or worse than the benchmark.

For the most part, these types of cost aren't reflected in financial reports. We've included them here to familiarize you with terms you're likely to see in the financial press and hear on financial talk shows. Business managers toss these terms around a lot.

Becoming More Familiar with Costs

This section explains important cost distinctions that managers should understand in making decisions and exercising control. Also, these cost distinctions help managers better appreciate the cost figures that accountants attach to products that are manufactured or purchased by the business.

Retailers (such as Wal-Mart and Costco) purchase products in a condition ready for sale to their customers — although some products have to be removed from shipping containers, and a retailer does a little work making the products presentable for sale and putting the products on display. Manufacturers don't have it so easy; their product costs have to be "manufactured" in the sense that the accountants have to accumulate various production costs and calculate the cost per unit for every product manufactured. We focus on the special cost concerns of manufacturers in the upcoming section "Assembling the Product Cost of Manufacturers."

REMEMBER

We cannot exaggerate the importance of correct product costs (for businesses that sell products, of course). The total cost of goods (products) sold is the first, and usually the largest, expense deducted from sales revenue in measuring profit. The bottom-line profit amount reported in a business's income statement depends heavily on whether its product costs have been measured properly during that period. Also, keep in mind that product cost is the value for the inventory asset reported in the balance sheet of a business. (For a balance sheet example, see Figure 7-2.)

Direct versus indirect costs

You might say that the starting point for any sort of cost analysis, and particularly for accounting for the product costs of manufacturers, is to clearly distinguish between *direct* and *indirect* costs. Direct costs are easy to match with a process or product, whereas indirect costs are more distant and have to be allocated to a process or product. Here are more details:

» **Direct costs** can be clearly attributed to one product or product line, one source of sales revenue, one organizational unit of the business, or one specific operation in a process. An example of a direct cost in the book publishing industry is the cost of the paper that a book is printed on; this cost can be squarely attached to one particular step or operation in the book production process.

» **Indirect costs** are far removed from and cannot be naturally attached to specific products, organizational units, or activities. A book publisher's telephone and Internet bills are costs of doing business but can't be tied down to just one step in the editorial and production process. The salary of the purchasing officer who selects the paper for all the books is another example of a cost that is indirect to the production of particular books.

WARNING

Each business must determine methods of allocating indirect costs to different products, sources of sales revenue, revenue and cost centres, and other organizational units. Most allocation methods are far from perfect and, in the final analysis, end up being arbitrary to one degree or another. Business managers should always keep an eye on the allocation methods used for indirect costs and take the cost figures produced by these methods with a grain of salt. If we were called in as expert witnesses in a court trial involving costs, the first thing we'd do is critically analyze the allocation methods used by the business for its indirect costs. If we were on the side of the defendant, we'd do our best to defend the allocation methods. If we were on the side of the plaintiff, we'd do our best to discredit the allocation methods — there are always grounds for criticism.

Following is a real-life example concerning the treatment of direct and indirect costs in a service business. A law firm that employs several lawyers typically practices in several specialty areas. Some of these specialties may include family law, civil litigation, and patent law. Each practicing lawyer refers to a bank of case law and reference material to ensure that the advice they give their clients is accurate and up to date. The reference material is in a common library that many lawyers use. The cost of maintaining the library is an indirect cost of providing the service to clients. On the other hand, if a lawyer pays a filing fee to register a document with the court on behalf of a client, this is a direct cost to that particular client.

Fixed versus variable costs

If your business sells 100 more units of a certain item, some of your costs increase accordingly, but others don't budge one bit. This distinction between variable and fixed costs is crucial:

>> **Variable costs:** Variable costs increase and decrease in proportion to changes in sales or production level. Variable costs generally remain the same per unit of product or per unit of activity. Manufacturing or selling additional units causes variable costs to increase in concert. Manufacturing or selling fewer units results in variable costs going down in concert.

>> **Fixed costs:** Fixed costs remain the same over a relatively broad range of sales volume or production output. Fixed costs are like a dead weight on the business. Its total fixed costs for the period are a hurdle it must overcome by selling enough units at high enough margins per unit to avoid a loss and move into the profit zone. (Chapter 15 explains the *break-even point*, which is the level of sales needed to generate enough margin to cover fixed costs for the period.)

The distinction between variable and fixed costs is at the heart of understanding, analyzing, and forecasting profit, which we explain in Chapter 17.

Relevant versus irrelevant costs

Not every cost is important to every decision a manager needs to make — hence the distinction between relevant and irrelevant costs:

>> **Relevant costs** are costs that should be considered and included in your analysis when deciding on a future course of action. Relevant costs are *future* costs — costs that you would incur or bring upon yourself depending on which course of action you take. For example, say that you want to increase the number of books that your business produces next year to increase your sales revenue, but the cost of paper has just shot up. Should you take the cost of paper into consideration? Absolutely — that cost will affect your bottom-line profit and may negate any increase in sales volume that you experience (unless you increase the sales price). The cost of paper is a relevant cost.

>> **Irrelevant (or sunk) costs** are costs that should be disregarded when deciding on a future course of action; if brought into the analysis, these costs could cause you to make the wrong decision. An irrelevant cost is a vestige of the past — that money is gone. For this reason, irrelevant costs are also called *sunk costs*. For example, suppose that your supervisor tells you to expect a slew of new hires next week. All your staff members use computers now, but you have a bunch of typewriters gathering dust in the supply room. Should you consider the cost paid for those typewriters in your decision to buy computers for all the new hires? Absolutely not — that cost should have been written off and is no match for the cost you'd pay in productivity (and morale) for new employees who are forced to use typewriters.

Generally speaking, most variable costs are relevant because they depend on which alternative is selected. Fixed costs are irrelevant, assuming that the decision at hand doesn't involve doing anything that would change these stationary costs. However, a decision alternative being considered might involve a change in fixed costs, such as moving out of the present building used by the business, downsizing the number of employees on fixed salaries, spending less on advertising (generally a fixed cost), and so on. Any cost, fixed or variable, that would be different for a particular course of action being analyzed is relevant for that alternative.

Furthermore, keep in mind that fixed costs can provide a useful gauge of a business's *capacity* — how much building space it has, how many machine-hours are available for use, how many hours of labour can be worked, and so on. Managers have to figure out the best way to utilize these capacities. For example, suppose your retail business pays an annual building rent of $200,000, which is a fixed cost (unless the rental contract with the landlord also has a rent escalation clause based on your sales revenue). The rent, which gives the business the legal right to occupy the building, provides 15,000 square feet of retail and storage space. You should figure out which sales mix of products will generate the highest total *margin* — equal to total sales revenue less total variable costs of making the sales, including the costs of the goods sold and all variable costs driven by sales revenue and sales volume.

Actual, projected, and standard costs

The actual costs a business incurs may differ (though we hope not too unfavourably) from its projected and standard costs:

» **Actual costs:** Actual costs are based on actual transactions and operations during the period just ended, or going back to earlier periods. Financial statement accounting is mainly (though not entirely) based on a business's actual transactions and operations; the basic approach to determining annual profit is to record the financial effects of actual transactions and allocate the historical costs to the periods benefited by the costs. But keep in mind that accountants can use more than one method for recording actual costs. Your actual cost may be a little (or a lot) different from my actual cost.

» **Projected costs:** These are future costs, for transactions and operations expected to take place over the coming period, based on forecasts and established goals. Fixed costs are projected differently from variable costs. For example, if sales volume is forecast to increase by 10 percent, variable costs will definitely increase accordingly, but fixed costs may or may not need to be increased to accommodate the volume increase. In Chapter 17, we explain the projection process and forecast financial statements.

» **Standard costs:** Standard costs are costs, primarily in the area of manufacturing, that are carefully engineered based on a detailed analysis of operations and forecast costs for each component or step in an operation. Developing standard costs for variable production costs is relatively straightforward because most are direct costs. In contrast, most fixed costs are indirect, and standard costs for fixed costs are necessarily based on more arbitrary methods (see "Direct versus indirect costs," earlier in this chapter). *Note:* Some variable costs are indirect and have to be allocated to specific products in order to come up with a full (total) standard cost of the product.

Product versus period costs

Some costs are linked to particular products, and others are not:

>> **Product costs** are attached directly or allocated to particular products. The cost is recorded in the inventory asset account and stays in that asset account until the product is sold, at which time the cost goes into the cost of goods sold expense account. (See Chapters 6 and 7 for more about these accounts; also, see Chapter 9 for alternative methods for selecting which product costs are first charged to the cost of goods sold expense.)

For example, the cost of a new Ford Explorer sitting on a car dealer's showroom floor is a product cost. The dealer keeps the cost in the inventory asset account until you buy the car, at which point the dealer charges the cost to the cost of goods sold expense.

>> **Period costs** are *not* attached to particular products. These costs do not spend time in the waiting room of inventory. Period costs are recorded as expenses immediately; unlike product costs, period costs don't pass through the inventory account first. Advertising costs, for example, are accounted for as period costs and are recorded immediately in an expense account. Also, research and development costs are treated as period costs (with some exceptions).

Separating product costs and period costs is particularly important for manufacturing businesses, as we explain in the next section.

Assembling the Product Cost of Manufacturers

Businesses that manufacture products have several cost problems to deal with that retailers and distributors don't have. We use the term *manufacture* in the broadest sense: Automobile makers assemble cars, beer companies brew beer, automobile gasoline companies refine oil, DuPont makes products through chemical synthesis, and so on. Retailers (also called *merchandisers*) and distributors, on the other hand, buy products in a condition ready for resale to the end consumer. For example, Levi Strauss manufactures clothing, and several retailers buy from Levi Strauss and sell the clothes to the public. This section describes costs unique to manufacturers.

Minding manufacturing costs

REMEMBER

Manufacturing costs consist of four basic types:

>> **Raw materials (also called *direct* materials)** are what a manufacturer buys from other companies to use in the production of its own products. For example, General Motors buys tires from Goodyear (or other tire manufacturers) that then become part of GM's cars.

>> **Direct labour** consists of those employees who work on the production line, the wages they are paid, and the burden associated with the wages (for example, payroll taxes, workers' compensation insurance, benefits provided to the employees such as paid time off or vacation days, and similar costs). As a reference point, it is not uncommon that for every $100 of wages paid to a production worker, another $30 of direct burden is incurred (for a direct burden ratio of 30 percent).

>> **Variable overhead** is indirect production costs that increase or decrease as the quantity produced increases or decreases. An example is the cost of electricity that runs the production equipment. Generally, you pay for the electricity for the whole plant, not machine by machine, so you can't attach this cost to one particular part of the process. When you increase or decrease the use of those machines, the electricity cost increases or decreases accordingly. (In contrast, the monthly utility bill for a company's office and sales space probably is fixed for all practical purposes.)

>> **Fixed overhead** is indirect production costs that do *not* increase or decrease as the quantity produced increases or decreases. These fixed costs remain the same over a fairly broad range of production output levels (see "Fixed versus variable costs," earlier in this chapter). Here are three significant examples of fixed manufacturing costs:

- Salaries for certain production employees who don't work directly on the production line, such as vice presidents, safety inspectors, security guards, accountants, and shipping and receiving workers

- Depreciation of production buildings, equipment, and other manufacturing fixed assets

- Occupancy costs, such as building insurance, property taxes, and heating and lighting charges

REMEMBER

Figure 16-1 presents a gross profit report for a business that manufactures just one product. To clearly drive home the concepts in this chapter, our fictitious business is a stand-alone manufacturing company as opposed to our sample technology company that we've used in other chapters. For now, limit your attention to the left side of the report, which lists sales volume, sales revenue, cost of goods sold expense, the four types of manufacturing costs (just discussed), and how total manufacturing costs end up either in cost of goods sold expense or in the increase to inventory. Manufacturing costs are shown both on the total basis for the year and per unit. First, we explain the numbers under the column headed "Base Output Case."

XYZ Fictional Mfg. Company, Inc.
Product Sales & Cost Analysis
for the Fiscal Year Ending
12/31/2024

Gross Profit Report for Year	Base Output Case		Excessive Output Case	
Sales Volume	Units	110,000	Units	110,000
	Per Unit	Totals	Per Unit	Totals
Sales Revenue	$1,400	$154,000,000	$1,400	$154,000,000
Costs of Goods Sold Expense	($760)	($83,600,000)	($690)	($75,900,000)
Gross Profit (aka Gross Margin)	$640	$70,400,000	$710	$78,100,000
Manufacturing Costs Summary for Year				
Production Capacity	150,000		150,000	
Actual Output	120,000		150,000	
Production Cost Components	Per Unit	Totals	Per Unit	Totals
Raw Material	$215	$25,800,000	$215	$32,250,000
Direct Labour & Burden	$125	$15,000,000	$125	$18,750,000
Variable Manufacturing Overhead Costs	$70	$8,400,000	$70	$10,500,000
Total Variable Manufacturing Costs	$410	$49,200,000	$410	$61,500,000
Fixed Manufacturing Overhead Costs	$350	$42,000,000	$280	$42,000,000
Total Manufacturing Costs	$760	$91,200,000	$690	$103,500,000
To Inventory Increase		($7,600,000)		($27,600,000)
To Costs of Goods Sold Expense		$83,600,000		$75,900,000

Confidential — Property of XYZ Fictional Mfg. Company, Inc.

FIGURE 16-1: Manufacturing costs example.

© John Wiley & Sons, Inc.

The $760 product cost equals manufacturing costs *per unit*. A business may manufacture 100 or 1,000 different products, or even more, and it must compile a summary of manufacturing costs and production output and determine the product cost of every product. To keep the example easy to follow (but still realistic), Figure 16-1 presents a one-product manufacturer. The multi-product manufacturer has additional accounting problems, but we can't provide that level of detail here. This example exposes the fundamental accounting problems and methods of all manufacturers.

Notice in particular that the company's cost of goods sold expense is based on the $760 product cost (or total manufacturing costs per unit). This product cost is determined from the company's manufacturing costs and production output for the period. Product cost includes both the variable costs of manufacture and a calculated amount based on total fixed manufacturing costs for the period divided by total production output for the period.

WARNING

The information in the manufacturing costs summary is highly confidential and for management eyes only. Competitors would love to know this information. A company may enjoy a significant cost advantage over its competitors and definitely does not want its cost data to get into their hands.

Classifying costs properly

Two vexing issues rear their ugly heads in determining product cost for a manufacturer:

>> **Drawing a bright line between manufacturing costs and nonmanufacturing operating costs:** The key difference here is that manufacturing costs are categorized as product costs, whereas nonmanufacturing operating costs are categorized as period costs (refer to "Product versus period costs," earlier in this chapter). In calculating product costs, you include only manufacturing costs. Remember that period costs are recorded right away as expenses. Here are some examples of each type of cost:

- Wages and associated direct payroll burden paid to production line workers are a clear-cut example of a manufacturing (that is, a product cost) component.

- Salaries paid to salespeople are a marketing cost and are not part of product cost; marketing costs are treated as period costs, which means they're recorded as an expense of the period.

- Depreciation on production equipment is a manufacturing cost, but depreciation on the warehouse in which products are stored after being manufactured is a period cost.

- Moving the raw materials and partially completed products through the production process is a manufacturing cost, but transporting the finished products from the warehouse to customers is a period cost.

The accumulation of direct and indirect production costs starts at the beginning of the manufacturing process and stops at the end of the production line. In other words, product cost stops at the end of the production line — every cost up to that point should be included as a manufacturing cost.

WARNING

If you misclassify some manufacturing costs as operating costs (nonmanufacturing expenses), your product cost calculation will be too low (see the following section, "Calculating product cost"). Also, the Canada Revenue Agency may come knocking at your door if it suspects that you deliberately (or even innocently) misclassified manufacturing costs as nonmanufacturing costs to minimize your taxable income.

REMEMBER

>> **Allocating indirect costs among different products:** Indirect manufacturing costs must be allocated among the products produced during the period. The full product cost includes both direct and indirect manufacturing costs. Creating a completely satisfactory allocation method is difficult; the process ends up being somewhat arbitrary, but it must be done to determine product cost. Managers should understand how indirect manufacturing costs are allocated among products (and, for that matter, how indirect nonmanufacturing costs are allocated among organizational units). Managers should also keep in mind that every allocation method is arbitrary and that a different allocation method may be just as convincing.

ALLOCATING INDIRECT COSTS IS NOT AS SIMPLE AS ABC

Accountants for manufacturers have developed many methods for allocating indirect overhead costs, most of which are based on a common denominator of production activity, such as direct labour hours or machine hours. A different method has received a lot of press: *activity-based costing* (ABC).

With the ABC method, you identify each supporting activity in the production process and collect costs into a separate pool for each identified activity. Then you develop a *measure* for each activity — for example, the measure for the engineering department may be hours, and the measure for the maintenance department may be square feet. You use the activity measures as *cost drivers* to allocate costs to products.

The idea is that the engineering department doesn't come cheap; when you include the cost of their computer hardware and software, as well as their salaries and benefits, the total cost per hour for those engineers could be $250 or more. The logic of the ABC cost-allocation method is that the engineering cost per hour should be allocated on the basis of the number of hours (the immediate cause, or driver of the cost) that each product requires. So, if Product A needs 200 hours of the engineering department's time and Product B is a simple product that needs only 20 hours of engineering, you allocate ten times as much of the engineering cost to Product A. In similar fashion, suppose the cost of the maintenance department is $20 per square foot per year. If Product C uses twice as much floor space as Product D, it would be charged with twice as much maintenance cost.

The ABC method has received much praise for being better than traditional allocation methods, especially for management decision-making. But keep in mind that this

(continued)

(continued)

method still requires rather arbitrary definitions of cost drivers, and having too many different cost drivers, each with its own pool of costs, is impractical.

Cost allocation always involves arbitrary methods. Managers should be aware of which methods are being used and should challenge a method if they think that it's misleading and should be replaced with a better (though still somewhat arbitrary) method. We don't mean to put too fine a point on this, but cost allocation essentially boils down to a "my arbitrary method is better than your arbitrary method" argument.

Calculating product cost

The basic calculation of product cost is as follows for the base output case in Figure 16-1:

$91,200,000 total manufacturing costs ÷ 120,000 units production output = $760 product cost per unit

WARNING

Looks pretty straightforward, doesn't it? Well, the equation itself may be simple, but the accuracy of the results depends directly on the accuracy of your manufacturing cost numbers. The business example we're using in this chapter manufactures just one product. Even so, a single manufacturing process can be fairly complex, with hundreds or thousands of steps and operations. In the real world, where businesses produce multiple products, your accounting systems must be very complex and extraordinarily detailed to keep accurate track of all direct and indirect (allocated) manufacturing costs.

In our example, the business manufactured 120,000 units and sold 110,000 units during the year, which is reasonable and not atypical, and its product cost per unit is $760. The 110,000 total units sold during the year is multiplied by the $760 product cost to compute the $83.6 million cost of goods sold expense, which is deducted against the company's revenue from selling 110,000 units during the year. The company's total manufacturing costs for the year were $91.2 million, which is $7.6 million more than the cost of goods sold expense. The remainder of the total annual manufacturing costs is recorded as an increase in the company's inventory asset account, to recognize that 10,000 units manufactured this year are awaiting sale in the future. In Figure 16-1, note that the $760 product cost per unit is applied both to the 110,000 units sold and to the 10,000 units added to inventory.

Note: The product cost per unit for our example business is determined for the entire year. In actual practice, manufacturers calculate their product costs monthly or quarterly. The computation process is the same, but the frequency of doing the computation varies from business to business. Product costs likely will vary each successive period the costs are determined. Because the product costs vary from period to period, the business must choose which cost of goods sold and inventory cost method to use. (If product cost happened to remain absolutely flat and constant period to period, the different methods would yield the same results.) Chapter 9 explains the alternative accounting methods for determining cost of goods sold expense and inventory cost value.

Examining fixed manufacturing costs and production capacity

Product cost consists of two distinct components: variable manufacturing costs and fixed manufacturing costs. In Figure 16-1, note that the company's variable manufacturing costs are $410 per unit and its fixed manufacturing costs are $350 per unit in the base output case. Now, what if the business had manufactured ten more units? Its total variable manufacturing costs would have been $4,100 higher. The actual number of units produced drives variable costs, so even one more unit would have caused the variable costs to increase. But the company's total fixed costs would have been the same if it had produced ten more units — or 10,000 more units, for that matter. Variable manufacturing costs are bought on a per-unit basis, as it were, whereas fixed manufacturing costs are bought in bulk for the whole period.

TIP

Fixed manufacturing costs are needed to provide *production capacity* — the people and physical resources needed to manufacture products — for the period. After the business has the production plant and people in place for the year, its fixed manufacturing costs cannot be easily scaled down. The business is stuck with these costs over the short run. It has to make the best use it can from its production capacity.

REMEMBER

Production capacity is a critical concept for business managers to stay focused on. You need to plan your production capacity well ahead of time because you need plenty of lead time to assemble the right people, equipment, land, and buildings. When you have the necessary production capacity in place, you want to make sure that you're making optimal use of that capacity. The fixed costs of production capacity remain the same even as production output increases or decreases, so you may as well make optimal use of the capacity provided by those fixed costs. For example, you're recording the same depreciation amount on your machinery regardless of how you actually use those machines, so you should be sure to optimize the use of those machines (within limits, of course — overworking the machines to the point where they break down won't do you much good).

The burden rate

The fixed-cost component of product cost is called the *burden rate*. In our manufacturing example, the burden rate is computed as follows for the base output case (see Figure 16-1 for the data):

$42,000,000 fixed manufacturing costs for period ÷ 120,000 units production output for period = $350 burden rate

Note that the burden rate depends on the number divided into the total fixed manufacturing costs for the period — that is, it depends on the production output for the period.

Now, here's an important twist on our example: Suppose the company had manufactured only 110,000 units during the period — equal exactly to the quantity sold during the year. Its variable manufacturing cost per unit would have been the same, or $410 per unit. But its burden rate would have been $381.82 per unit (computed by dividing the $42 million total fixed manufacturing costs by the 110,000 units production output). Each unit sold, therefore, would have cost $31.82 more than in the Figure 16-1 example simply because the company produced fewer units. The company would have fewer units of output over which to spread its fixed manufacturing costs. The burden rate is $381.82 at the 110,000 output level but only $350 at the 120,000 output level, or $31.82 lower.

If only 110,000 units were produced, the company's product cost would have been $791.82 ($410 variable costs plus the $381.82 burden rate). The company's cost of goods sold, therefore, would have been $3.5 million higher for the year ($31.82 higher product cost × 110,000 units sold). This rather significant increase in its cost of goods sold expense is caused by the company's producing fewer units, even though it produced all the units that it needed for sales during the year. The same total amount of fixed manufacturing costs is spread over fewer units of production output.

Idle capacity

The production capacity of the business example in Figure 16-1 is 150,000 units for the year. However, this business produced only 120,000 units during the year, which is 30,000 units fewer than it could have. In other words, it operated at 80 percent of production capacity, which results in 20 percent *idle capacity*:

This rate of idle capacity isn't unusual — the average manufacturing plant normally operates at 80 to 85 percent of its production capacity.

The effects of increasing inventory

Look back at the numbers shown in Figure 16-1 for the base output case: The company's cost of goods sold benefited from the fact that the company produced 10,000 more units than it sold during the year. These 10,000 units absorbed $3.5 million of its total fixed manufacturing costs for the year, and until the units are sold, this $3.5 million stays in the inventory asset account (along with the variable manufacturing costs, of course). It's entirely possible that the higher production level was justified — to have more units on hand for sales growth next year. But production output can get out of hand, as we discuss in the next section, "Puffing Profit by Excessive Production."

Managers (and investors as well) should understand the inventory increase effects caused by manufacturing more units than are sold during the year. In the example shown in Figure 16-1, the cost of goods sold expense escaped $3.5 million of fixed manufacturing costs because the company produced 10,000 more units than it sold during the year, thus pushing down the burden rate. The company's cost of goods sold expense would have been $3.5 million higher if it had produced just the number of units it sold during the year. The lower output level would have increased cost of goods sold expense and would have caused a $3.5 million drop in gross margin.

THE ACTUAL COSTS/ACTUAL OUTPUT METHOD — AND WHEN NOT TO USE IT

The product cost calculation for the business example shown in Figure 16-1 is based on the *actual cost/actual output method*, in which you take your actual costs — which may have been higher or lower than the projected costs for the year — and divide by the actual output for the year.

The actual costs/actual output method is appropriate in most situations. However, this method is not appropriate and would have to be modified in two extreme situations:

- **Manufacturing costs are grossly excessive or wasteful due to inefficient production operations:** For example, suppose that the business represented in Figure 16-1 had to throw away $1.2 million of raw materials during the year. The $1.2 million should be removed from the calculation of the raw material cost per unit. Instead, you treat it as a period cost — meaning that you record it immediately into expense. Then the cost of goods sold expense would be based on $750 per

(continued)

(continued)

unit instead of $760, which lowers this expense by $1.1 million (based on the 110,000 units sold). But you still have to record the $1.2 million expense for wasted raw materials, so EBIT would be $100,000 lower.

- **Production output is significantly less than normal capacity utilization:** Suppose that the Figure 16-1 business produced only 75,000 units during the year but still sold 110,000 units because it was working off a large inventory carryover from the year before. Then its production output would be 50 percent instead of 80 percent of capacity. In a sense, the business wasted half of its production capacity, and you can argue that half of its fixed manufacturing costs should be charged directly to expense on the income statement and not included in the calculation of product cost.

Puffing Profit by Excessive Production

WARNING

Whenever production output is higher than sales volume, be on guard. Excessive production can puff up the profit figure. How? Until a product is sold, the product cost goes in the inventory asset account rather than in the cost of goods sold expense account, meaning that the product cost is counted as a *positive* number (an asset) rather than a *negative* number (an expense). Fixed manufacturing overhead cost is included in product cost, which means that this cost component goes into inventory and is held there until the products are sold later. In short, when you overproduce, more of your total of fixed manufacturing costs for the period is moved to the inventory asset account and less is moved into cost of goods sold expense for the year.

You need to judge whether an inventory increase is justified. Be aware that an unjustified increase may be evidence of profit manipulation or just good old-fashioned management bungling. Either way, the day of reckoning will come when the products are sold and the cost of inventory becomes cost of goods sold expense or the excess inventory becomes obsolete and can't be sold.

Shifting fixed manufacturing costs to the future

The business represented in Figure 16-1 manufactured 10,000 more units than it sold during the year — see the base output case in the left columns. This isn't unusual. In many situations, a manufacturer produces more units than are sold in the period. It's hard to match production output exactly to sales for the period — unless the business produces the exact number of units ordered by its customers.

Anyway, the situation in Figure 16-1 in the base output case isn't unusual and wouldn't raise any eyebrows (well, unless the company already had a large inventory of products at the start of the year and didn't need any more).

With variable manufacturing costs at $410 per unit, the business expended $4.1 million more in variable manufacturing costs than it would have if it had produced only the 110,000 units needed for its sales volume. In other words, if the business had produced 10,000 fewer units, its variable manufacturing costs would have been $4.1 million less — that's the nature of variable costs. In contrast, if the company had manufactured 10,000 fewer units, its *fixed* manufacturing costs wouldn't have been any less — that's the nature of fixed costs.

Of its $42 million total fixed manufacturing costs for the year, only $38.5 million ended up in the cost of goods sold expense for the year ($350 burden rate × 110,000 units sold). The other $3.5 million ended up in the inventory asset account ($350 burden rate × 10,000 units inventory increase). The $3.5 million of fixed manufacturing costs that are absorbed by inventory is shifted to the future. This amount won't be expensed (charged to cost of goods sold expense) until the products are sold sometime in the future.

REMEMBER

Shifting part of the fixed manufacturing cost for the year to the future may seem to be accounting sleight of hand. It has been argued that the entire amount of fixed manufacturing costs should be expensed in the year that these costs are recorded. (Only variable manufacturing costs would be included in product cost for units going into the increase in inventory.) Established accounting standards require that *full* product cost (variable plus fixed manufacturing costs) be used for recording an increase in inventory. This is referred to as *absorption accounting* because fixed manufacturing costs are absorbed, or included in product cost.

In the example shown under the base output case in Figure 16-1, the 10,000-unit increase of inventory includes $3,500,000 of the company's total fixed manufacturing costs for the year:

$350 burden rate × 10,000 units inventory increase = $3,500,000 fixed manufacturing costs included in inventory increase

Are you comfortable with this effect? The $3,500,000 escapes being charged to cost of goods expense for the time being. It sits in inventory until the products are sold in a later period. This results from using the full cost (absorption) accounting method for fixed manufacturing overhead costs. Now, it may occur to you that an unscrupulous manager could take advantage of this effect to manipulate gross profit for the period.

Let us be very clear here: We're not suggesting any hanky-panky in the example shown in Figure 16-1. Producing 10,000 more units than sales volume during the year looks — on the face of it — to be reasonable and not out of the ordinary. Yet at the same time, it's naïve to ignore that the business did help its pretax profit to the amount of $3.5 million by producing 10,000 more units than it sold. If the business had produced only 110,000 units, equal to its sales volume for the year, all its fixed manufacturing costs for the year would have gone into cost of goods sold expense. The expense would have been $3.5 million higher, and operating earnings would have been that much lower.

Cranking up production output

Now let's consider a more suspicious example. Suppose that the business manufactured 150,000 units during the year and increased its inventory by 40,000 units. It may be a legitimate move if the business is anticipating a big jump in sales next year. On the other hand, an inventory increase of 40,000 units in a year in which only 110,000 units were sold may be the result of a serious overproduction mistake, and the larger inventory may not be needed next year.

Figure 16-1 also shows what happens to production costs and — more importantly — what happens to the profit at the higher production output level. See the columns under the *excessive output case* in Figure 16-1. The additional 30,000 units (over and above the 120,000 units manufactured by the business in the base output case) cost $410 per unit of variable manufacturing costs. (The precise cost may be a little higher than $410 per unit because as you start crowding production capacity, some variable costs per unit may increase a little.) The business would need $12.3 million more for the additional 30,000 units of production output:

$410 variable manufacturing cost per unit × 30,000 additional units produced = $12,300,000 additional variable manufacturing costs invested in inventory

Again, the company's fixed manufacturing costs would not have increased, given the nature of fixed costs. Fixed costs stay put until capacity is hit. Sales volume, in this scenario, also remains the same.

But check out the business's gross margin: $78.1 million, compared with $70.4 million in the base output case — a $7.7 million higher amount, even though sales volume and sales prices remain the same. Whoa! What's going on here? How can cost of goods sold expense be less? The business sells 110,000 units in both scenarios. And variable manufacturing costs are $410 per unit in both cases.

The culprit is the burden-rate component of product cost. In the base output case, total fixed manufacturing costs are spread over 120,000 units of output, giving a $350 burden rate per unit. In the excessive output case, total fixed manufacturing costs are spread over 150,000 units of output, giving a much lower $280 burden rate, or $70 per unit less. The $70 lower burden rate multiplied by the 110,000 units sold results in a $7.7 million lower cost of goods sold expense for the period, a higher pretax profit of the same amount, and a much-improved bottom-line net income.

Being careful when production output is out of kilter with sales volume

WARNING

In the highly suspect example shown in the excessive output case, the business produced 150,000 units (full capacity). As a result, its inventory asset includes an additional $7.7 million of the company's fixed manufacturing costs for the year as compared with the base output case (see Figure 16-1 again). Its cost of goods sold expense for the year escaped this cost (for the time being). But get this: Its inventory increased 40,000 units, which is quite a large increase compared with the annual sales of 110,000 during the year just ended. Who was responsible for the decision to go full blast and produce up to production capacity? Do the managers really expect sales to jump up enough next year to justify the much larger inventory level? If they prove to be right, they'll look brilliant. But if the output level was a mistake and sales don't go up next year, they'll have you-know-what to pay next year, even though profit looks good this year. An experienced business manager knows to be on guard when inventory takes such a big jump.

REMEMBER

The cost of goods sold expense of a manufacturer, and thus its operating profit, is sensitive to a difference between its sales volume and production output during the year. Manufacturing businesses don't generally discuss or explain in their external financial reports to creditors and owners why production output differs from sales volume for the year. Financial report readers are pretty much on their own in interpreting the reasons for and the effects of underproducing or overproducing products relative to actual sales volume for the year. All we can tell you is to keep alert and keep in mind the profit impact caused by a major disparity between a manufacturer's production output and sale levels for the year. Managers should understand this point very well. We hope they wouldn't use this tactic to artificially boost profit for the period.

Chapter **17**

Preparing Forecasts, Projections, and Budgets

L et's start this chapter with an extremely important statement: In today's rapidly changing and evolving economy, all businesses, no matter the size, shape, legal structure, or industry of operation, need to develop business plans. Period! While this statement may appear to be very logical and represent common sense, you would be absolutely amazed at how often businesses simply operate by "the seat of their pants" without a well-developed and structured business plan.

The planning process for most businesses is very broad and includes numerous elements ranging from assessing current market conditions to understanding the macroeconomic environment to evaluating personnel resources to preparing budgets, forecasts, and/or projections. This chapter focuses on one of the most critical elements of the planning process — preparing a financial forecast.

REMEMBER

For the balance of this chapter, the term *forecasts* will be used for consistency purposes, but it should be noted that businesses often utilize other terms including *budgets* or *budgeting*, *projections*, and *proformas* (which basically all mean the same thing). We prefer to use the term *forecasts* because it is broader in scope and helps drive home the all-important concept that business financial forecasting needs to be complete, accurate, reliable, and timely.

Focusing on Key Forecasting Concepts

REMEMBER

Before we delve too deeply into the forecasting process, we want to call out three key concepts to keep in mind:

>> **Forecasts *are not* based on the concept of "How much can we spend in our division this year?"** Rather, forecasts are more comprehensive in nature and are designed to capture all relevant and critical financial data, including revenue levels, costs of sales, operating expenses, employment requirements, fixed asset expenditures, capital requirements, and the like. All too often, forecasts are associated with expense levels and management, which represent just one element of the entire forecasts.

>> **The forecasting process does not represent a chicken-and-egg riddle.** From a financial perspective, the preparation of forecasts represents the end result of the entire planning process. Hence, you must first accumulate the necessary data and information on which to build a forecasting model prior to producing projected financial information (for an entire company or a specific division). There is no point in preparing a forecast that does not capture the real economic structure and viability of an entire entity or operating division.

>> **Preparing complete financial information within the financial forecasts is very important indeed.** Too often, companies prepare financial forecasts focused on just the income statement and downplay the importance of the balance sheet and statement of cash flows. The importance of preparing complete financial forecasts is on full display in this chapter, because we include forecasts for both the balance sheet and statement of cash flows. (Head to Part 2 of this book for details on these statements.)

The bottom line with forecasting (and the entire planning process) is that, without having clearly identified business financial and performance objectives, the business is operating blind. Put simply, it is like flying a plane without having a destination. The need for having clearly identified benchmarks and a road map to reach the benchmarks is essential for every business, regardless of size, shape, or form. Often, the most important question comes down to this: "How are we doing against the plan?"

REMEMBER

Looking at it from a different perspective, a business can't open its doors each day without having a pretty good idea of what to expect. And it can't close its doors at the end of the day not knowing what happened. Recall the Scouts' motto: "Be prepared." A business should follow that dictum: It should plan and be prepared for its future, and it should control its actual performance to reach its financial goals.

Of course, business managers do not have the option of waiting for results to be reported to them on a "look back" basis and then wing it from there (which is something we strongly advise against!). Or they can look ahead and carefully plan for sales revenue, expenses, cash flows, and financial position to chart the course of the business into the future. Forecasting is a tool of financial planning and control. The business entity's accountants and financial team pull the company's planning details all together and prepare financial forecasts including the financial statement, against which actual performance is compared.

Putting Forecasting in Its Place

Getting into the topic of forecasting puts us in the larger field of management — in particular, management planning and control. This is not a book on management. Goodness knows, enough books on management theory and practices have already been published. In this section, we simply offer a few words regarding how forecasting fits into the broader field of management.

Planning reasons for forecasting

REMEMBER

In previous editions of this book, we made the following statement: "Budgeting is optional for most businesses; the business is not required to do any budgeting."

Although this is true, our view has definitely changed because of just how competitive and fast-paced today's business world has become. As previously stated, it's essential that all businesses, organizations, governments, and so on develop well-thought-out business plans that include complete financial forecasts. To emphasize just how important preparing business plans and financial forecasts are, here are four scenarios:

>> **The business birth:** In the start-up phase of a new business, preparing forecasts is usually indispensable for raising capital and getting the venture off the ground. You simply cannot approach any type of capital source, whether looking to raise equity or secure a loan, without having a well-developed business plan and financial forecast available. Trust us when we say you will be shown the door you entered extremely quickly if you attempt to raise capital without a forecast.

» **The business pivot:** The COVID-19 pandemic taught us the importance of how quickly businesses must adapt to rapidly changing operating conditions. While COVID-19 may be an extreme situation, businesses operating in vastly different industries can often have their operating models upended by any number of events, including government intervention (for example, sanctions placed on foreign suppliers), technological innovation (that makes your products obsolete), and changing sales channel (online/e-commerce shopping, anyone?) . . . just to name a few. When these events hit, businesses must quickly update their plans and revise their financial forecasts to figure out how to survive and how to prosper moving forward.

» **The business exit:** Most businesses, in one form or another, will eventually cease to exist after operating for years. In some cases, businesses simply fail as the owners decide to terminate operations or the business is no longer economically viable. In most cases, however, the goal is to build a business and eventually sell it to another party and realize a very handsome "exit." To maximize third-party interest in acquiring a business, it must have a well-developed business plan, including current and relevant financial forecasts. There is simply no way a business owner can approach a potential acquirer and achieve the correct valuation without having this vital information.

» **Business operations management:** Forecasting, in the broader management context, is an essential technique for keeping the business on course toward achieving its goals. One purpose of forecasting is to force managers to create a definite and detailed financial plan for the coming period. To construct a forecast, managers have to establish explicit financial objectives for the coming year and identify exactly what has to be done to accomplish these financial objectives. Financial forecasts and their supporting schedules provide clear destination points — the financial flight plan for a business.

REMEMBER

The process of putting together a forecast directs attention to the specific things that managers must do to achieve their profit objectives and optimize assets and capital. Basically, forecasts push managers to answer the question "How are you going to get there from here?"

TIP

Forecasting can also yield other important planning-related benefits:

» **Forecasting prompts a business to articulate its vision, strategy, and goals.** A business needs a clearly stated strategy guided by an overarching vision, and it should have definite and explicit goals. It isn't enough for business managers to have strategies and goals only in their heads. Developing financial forecasts forces managers to be explicit and definite about the objectives of the business as well as to formulate realistic plans for achieving the business objectives.

>> **Forecasting imposes discipline and deadlines on the planning process.** Forecasting pushes managers to set aside time to prepare a detailed plan that serves as a road map for the business. Good planning results in a concrete course of action that specifies how a company plans to achieve its financial objectives.

Control reasons for forecasting

REMEMBER

Many people have the mistaken notion that the purpose of forecasting is to rein in managers and employees, who otherwise would spend money like drunken sailors on shore leave. But forecasting shouldn't put the business's managers in a financial straitjacket. Tying the hands of managers isn't the purpose of forecasting. That said, it's true that forecasts serve a management control function. *Management control*, first and foremost, means achieving the financial goals and objectives of the business, which requires comparing actual performance against some sort of benchmarks and holding individual managers responsible for keeping the business on schedule in reaching its financial objectives.

By using forecast targets as benchmarks against which actual performance is compared, managers can closely monitor progress toward (or deviations from) the forecast goals and timetable. You use a forecast plan like a navigation chart to keep your business on course. Significant variations from the forecast raise red flags, in which case you can determine that performance is off-course or that the forecast needs to be revised because of unexpected developments.

TIP

For management control, a forecast profit report is divided into months or quarters for the coming year. The forecast balance sheet and cash flow statement should also be put on a monthly or quarterly basis. The business shouldn't wait too long to compare forecast sales revenue and expenses against actual performance (or to compare actual cash flows and asset levels against the forecast). Managers need to take prompt action when problems arise, such as a divergence between forecast expenses and actual expenses. In fact, in today's on demand tech-enabled global economy, sales revenue is now not just monitored on a weekly or even daily basis but by the hour or even by the minute.

At a macro level, profit is the main thing to pay attention to, but accounts receivable, trade accounts payable, inventory levels, other liabilities, and capital expenditures can also quickly get out of control (become too high relative to actual sales revenue and cost of goods sold expense), causing cash flow problems. (Chapter 8 explains how increases in accounts receivable and inventory are negative factors on cash flow.) A business can't afford to ignore its balance sheet and cash flow numbers until the end of the year.

Exploring Forecasting

REMEMBER

The financial statements included in the financial reports of a business are prepared *after the fact*; they're based on transactions that have already taken place. (We explain business financial statements in Chapters 6, 7, and 8.) Forecast financial statements, on the other hand, are prepared *before the fact* and reflect future transactions that are expected to take place based on the business's financial plan. Detailed financial statement forecasts are not shared outside the business; they're strictly for internal management use. However, summarized financial statement forecasts are often distributed to critical external third parties such as investors or lending sources (a bank, for example). These parties have just as much vested interest in making sure the company has a well-developed business plan and stays on course as the internal management team.

The board of directors of a corporation focuses its attention on the *macro-level forecast* for the whole business: the forecast income statement, balance sheet, and cash flow statement for the business for the coming year. The chief executive officer (CEO) of the business focuses on the macro-level forecast as well, but the CEO must also look at how each manager in the organization is doing on their part of this forecast. As you move down the organization chart of a business, managers have narrower responsibilities — say, for the business's northeastern territory or for one major product line. A macro-level forecast consists of different segments that follow the business's organizational structure. In other words, the forecast is put together from many pieces, one for each separate organizational unit of the business. For example, the manager of one of the company's far-flung warehouses has a separate forecast for expenses and inventory levels for their bailiwick.

Initial forecasting for a new business

For businesses or professionals that have already prepared prior-year forecasts, this section may not be all that relevant. For first timers preparing a forecast for a new business, you want to become familiar with three acronyms: BOTE, WAG, and SWAG. These stand for *back of the envelope*, *wild-ass guess*, and *scientific wild-ass guess*. You may notice a little humour when referring to these acronyms, but we are being quite serious:

1. The forecasting process needs to start somewhere and often resides with executive management team members discussing a business idea or opportunity, jotting down some thoughts and basic numbers on the back of a napkin or envelope.

2. This may then evolve into a wild-ass guess where an actual (albeit quite simple) preliminary forecast is prepared using a standard technology tool such as Microsoft Excel.

3. Then, as additional information is obtained and incorporated into the forecast model, it transforms into a scientific wild-ass guess (where key data points and assumptions can be documented and defended).

You would be amazed at how many businesses and forecasts get started with such a simple initial step, but you would be equally amazed at how quickly the forecast model evolves into a very sophisticated management tool.

Initial forecasting for an existing business

REMEMBER

To start an initial forecast for an existing business, you need a solid understanding of your company's historical financial information and operating results. This history may stretch back three months, one year, five years, or longer, but the key concept is that having sound internal financial information represents an excellent place to start. However, remember that while the financial operating history of a company may provide a foundation on which to prepare a forecast, it by no means is an accurate or guaranteed predictor of future operating results. If the economic environment of a business has changed, benchmarking off other similar businesses represents an effective means to build a reliable forecast.

Gathering reliable data

The availability of quality market, operational, and accounting/financial data represents the basis of the forecast. A good deal of this data often comes from internal sources. For example, when a sales region is preparing a forecast for the upcoming year, the sales manager may survey the direct sales representatives on what they feel their customers will demand in terms of products and services in the coming year. With this information, you can determine sales volumes, personnel levels, wage rates, commission plans, and so on.

While internal information is of value, it represents only half the battle because external information and data is just as critical to accumulate. Having access to quality and reliable external third-party information is essential to the overall business planning process and the production of reliable forecasts. Market forces and trends may be occurring that can impact your business over the next 24 months (that may not be reflected in the previous year's operating results).

Involving key team members

The forecasting process represents a critical function in most companies' accounting and financial department and rightfully so, as these are the people who understand the numbers the best. Although the financial and accounting types produce the final budget, they rely on data that comes from numerous parties such as marketing, manufacturing, and sales.

Ensuring consistency and completeness

TIP

The financial forecasts prepared should be both complete and consistent to maximize their value:

>> When we say *complete,* we mean that all relevant financial information should be presented in the forecasts to ensure that the target audience has the proper output and data on which to base economic decisions.

>> By *consistent,* we mean that the financial forecasts are prepared in a like format to the periodic financial information provided to the target audience (including all critical financial data points, key performance indicators or KPIs, and so on). There is no benefit to preparing financial forecasts in a format that is different to the periodic internal financial information produced and delivered to the management team (you can imagine the confusion that would ensue). Financial forecast models should be designed to be in sync with critical reporting and utilize the same format for ease of understanding and decision making.

Considering timing and presentation

The annual budgeting process is a thing of the past. While an annual forecast can be produced just prior to the beginning of a new fiscal year to start the process, management should be prepared, on at least a quarterly basis and for more fluid, high-paced businesses, monthly, to revise and update forecasts as business conditions change.

Presentation-wise, generally the nearer the term covered by the forecasts the more detailed the information and frequency of reporting periods being prepared. If you're preparing a forecast for the coming fiscal year, the monthly financial information should be provided, but if you're looking out three to five years, providing quarterly financial information should suffice (for years three through five).

Projections as financial models

REMEMBER

Business managers should make detailed analyses to determine how to improve the financial performance and condition of their business. The status quo is usually not good enough; business managers are paid to improve things — not to simply rest on their past accomplishments. For this reason, managers should develop good economic models of profit, cash flow, and financial position for their business. *Models* are blueprints or schematics of how things work. A financial model is like a road map that clearly marks the pathways to profit, cash flow, and financial condition.

TIP

Don't be intimidated by the term model. Simply put, a model consists of variables and how they interact. A variable is a critical factor that, in conjunction with other factors, determines results. A model is analytical, but not all models are mathematical. In fact, the financial models in this book are not mathematical — but you do have to look at each factor of the model and how it interacts with one or more other factors. Chapter 15 presents a profit model for managers which, at its core, is a model. It includes the critical variables that drive profit: sales volume, sales price, product cost, and so on. A good profit model provides the framework for understanding and analyzing profit performance and also serves as the platform and the point of departure for mapping out profit strategies for the coming period.

Likewise, business managers need a model, or blueprint, in planning cash flow from operating activities. (We explain this source of cash flow in Chapter 8.) Managers should forecast the amount of cash they'll generate during the coming year from making profit. They need a reliable estimate of this source of cash flow to plan for other sources of cash flow they'll need during the coming year — to provide the money for replacing and expanding the long-term operating (fixed) assets of the business and to make cash distributions from profit to owners. Managers need a map that provides a clear trail of how the sales and expenses of the business drive its assets and liabilities, which in turn drive the cash flow from operating activities.

Generally, a business should seriously consider preparing all three forecast financial statements based on the appropriate model for each:

» **Forecast income statement (profit report):** A profit analysis model, such as the one shown in Figure 15-1, highlights the critical variables that drive profit. Remember that this profit template separates *variable* and *fixed* expenses and focuses on *sales volume, margin per unit,* and other factors that determine profit performance. These are the key factors that must be improved to enhance profit performance in the coming period. The highly condensed basic profit model provides a useful frame of reference for preparing the much more detailed, comprehensive profit forecast.

» **Forecast balance sheet:** The key connections and ratios between sales revenue and expenses and their corresponding assets and liabilities are the elements in the model for the forecast balance sheet. These vital connections are explained throughout Chapters 7 and 8. The forecasted changes in operating assets and liabilities provide the information needed for forecasting cash flows during the coming year.

>> **Forecast statement of cash flows:** The forecast changes during the coming year in the assets and liabilities used in making profit (conducting operating activities) determine forecast *cash flow from operating activities* for the coming year (see Chapter 8). In contrast, the cash flows of *investing* and *financing* activities depend on the managers' strategic decisions regarding capital expenditures that will be made during the coming year, how much new capital will be raised from debt and from owners' sources of capital, and the business's policy regarding cash distributions from profit.

REMEMBER

In short, forecasting requires good working models of profit, financial condition (assets and liabilities), and cash flow. Forecasting provides a strong incentive for business managers to develop financial models that help them make strategic decisions, do better planning, and exercise effective control.

Increasing the Power of Your Forecasts

We start this section noting that the list of concepts, strategies, and tools overviewed here is not meant to be all-inclusive; rather these topics have been selected to assist with helping make financial forecasts even more useful and powerful. To avoid overkill, we have limited our discussion to summarizing four very helpful planning and forecasting tools.

Using the SWOT

SWOT stands for strengths, weaknesses, opportunities, and threats; it's a business management assessment tool designed to assist the company's management team with preparing a qualitative assessment of the business, helping to keep all parties focused on key issues. The SWOT analysis is often incorporated into a company's planning function but can also be extremely helpful with preparing financial forecasts.

A SWOT analysis is usually broken down into a matrix of four segments. Two of the segments are geared toward positive attributes (strengths and opportunities), and two are geared toward negative attributes (weaknesses and threats). In addition, the analysis differentiates between internal company source attributes and external, or outside of the company, source attributes.

Checking top down or bottom up

Two forecasting strategies are used by most businesses, *top down* versus *bottom up*:

>> *Top-down* forecasting is exactly how it sounds (that is, the top line for a company, which is sales), as it starts with projecting critical sales revenue data, including sales unit volumes (by all significant product lines or SKUs), pricing by product, any potential sales discounts, seasonality in sales, customer contact to sales timing relationships, and similar data. After this information is incorporated into the forecast model, the balance of the forecast model, including cost of sales, direct operating expenses, business overhead expenses, and other expenses or income (for the income statement), as well as all critical balance sheet assumptions, are incorporated by utilizing relationships or correlations rather than inputting hard data and information.

   For example, using a top-down forecasting model, the number of sales representatives required, and any commissions earned would be determined based on X number of product sales at Y price. A relationship for the business might be established that states for every 250,000 units of products sold, one senior sales rep is required and would earn a commission of 5 percent on the sales.

>> *Bottom-up* forecasting is different because, although certain key correlations or relationships may be incorporated into the forecast model, this approach tends to be much more detailed and includes a large number of hard or firm data points and assumptions being built into the forecast model. For example, in a top-down approach, an expense estimate of $1,000 per month per sales rep may be input to capture all travel, lodging, meals, and entertainment-related (TLM&E) costs. In other words, estimated sales revenue drives the number of sales reps, which drives the monthly TLM&E expense. In a bottom-up approach, an estimate of each type of expense is prepared on a line-by-line basis that then rolls up into a subtotal. Further, sales revenue may be driven by how many sales reps are working or employed; if 10 sales reps are working any given month and, on average, each sales rep should be able to generate $250,000 of sales, total sales for the month would be forecast at $2.5 million.

TIP

Companies often use a hybrid of these two approaches; most financial forecast models utilize some type of correlation and relationship assumptions as well as incorporate hard data for various overhead or fixed costs:

>> The bottom-up approach tends to be better suited for well-established, predictable business models that have a large amount of historical data and operational stability. It also tends to be detailed and static but definitely has use/value within the right business framework, such as when detailed or specific management reporting is required for cost analysis of a bill of material or expense control is a high priority (to track all expenses at a line-item level).

>> The top-down approach is better suited for newer businesses or companies operating in rapidly changing environments where you need to understand important financial results quickly under different or "what if" operating scenarios (see the next section). Top-down forecasting approaches focus on understanding financial correlations and relationships at a macro level to help the management team in evaluating multiple operating scenarios with potentially vastly different outcomes.

To be quite honest, most properly structured top-down forecasting models end up relying on a select few key business drivers or assumptions that really are "make or break" for the company in terms of producing profitable results. Senior-level management members are usually so well versed in understanding their businesses that, when as few as a half dozen assumptions and data inputs that drive sales are known, the senior management team members can usually accurately and quickly calculate what the net profit or loss will be. This is why top-down forecasting models are utilized more frequently at the strategic business planning level, whereas bottom-up forecasting models are utilized actively at the business tactical and implementation level. Under either approach, the goal is to make it easy for team members to participate in the forecasting process and utilize the financial information to assist with improving operating results.

Exploring "what if"?

One concept strongly associated with the top-down forecasting approach (see the previous section) is the *what-if* analysis. It should be obvious that the purpose of the what-if analysis is just like it sounds — that is, what will the results or impact be if this situation or set of events occurs? For example, if a company has to implement a significant product price reduction to match the competition, a what-if analysis will help it quickly calculate and decipher the potential impact on its operating results and associated cash flows.

TIP

The reason the what-if analysis is easier to use with a top-down forecast approach is that the goal of this analysis tool is to focus on the macro-level impact (to a business) from a potential material change in key business operating metrics. Thus, by being able to change 6 to 12 key variables or forecast assumptions, a management team can quickly assess the impact on the business (which is one of the key strengths of the top-down forecasting approach). This is not to say that what-if analyses cannot be generated using a bottom-up forecasting approach, but when focusing on macro-level company operating results, starting at the top with sales revenue and watching the waterfall impact on overall operations is a particularly useful and powerful analysis for senior management.

TIP

What-if analyses are extremely helpful when preparing multiple versions of the financial forecasts, which most companies do (or should do). It is common practice for companies to produce high, medium, and low versions of the financial forecasts to assist with business planning and evaluate different operating scenarios. Having this information available well in advance allows a business to build different plans to ensure that financial performance targets are achieved. For example, if sales revenue is trending down, management can develop a plan that identifies expenses to cut and by how much and when. Conversely, if the company is having a strong year, this may dictate that additional capital may be needed to support the unanticipated growth (again, allowing management to identify when, what, and how much is needed).

As you see in Figures 17-1, 17-2, and 17-3 later in this chapter, the forecast operating results from our high, medium, and low scenarios are vastly different and indicate that management needs to have proactive plans in place to address potential underperformance issues. By the way, another version of the forecast model that companies have incorporated into their planning process is the *Arm* (which stands for Armageddon) version — when all hell breaks loose. Companies generally keep a tight lid on this version because whether you are dealing with internal or external parties, nobody wants to entice unwarranted panic.

Rolling forecasts

REMEMBER

Finally, we close this section by discussing the value and benefits of employing *rolling forecasts* (such as 12 months, 18 months, or longer). The purpose of utilizing rolling forecasts is to always have at least one year's (and preferably longer) visibility on your business's operating performance at any point in time. For example, if a business uses a standard fiscal year end (FYE) of 12/31/24, a 12-month rolling forecast model updated at, let us say, the third quarter ending 9/30/24 would provide visibility for the 12-month period of 10/1/24 through 9/30/25. After each month, the forecast model is "rolled" forward as part of the company's ongoing planning process to provide executive management with the proper business management visibility.

Companies often utilize rolling forecasts to assist with managing their business interests as summarized in the following two examples:

>> **Recast operating results:** In our example, a company could combine the actual operating results for the nine months of operations ending 9/30/24 with the updated three months of forecast operating results for the period of 10/1/24 through 12/31/24 to produce recast operating results for the FYE 12/31/24. We use the term *recast* in the context of combining actual operating results with updated forecast operating results to produce revised or recast operating results for a specific time period. Companies often need to provide

both internal and external parties with updated outlooks on a periodic basis and utilize recast operating results to achieve this objective.

>> **Operational pivots:** Companies that experience an unexpected shock to their operations can use rolling forecasts to reset operating targets and objectives for internal management planning purposes. For example, employee commission or bonus plans can be adjusted (based on a revised 12-month outlook) to reflect a new operating norm that was not anticipated. This allows the company to proactively manage difficult environments as well as effectively communicate with the employee base.

Seeing a Financial Forecast in Action

So far in this chapter, we have covered the topic of forecasts from a conceptual perspective; now we offer examples of financial forecasts for our fictious company. Each figure presents high, medium, and low case forecasts, with Figure 17-1 presenting the income statement, Figure 17-2 presenting the balance sheet, and Figure 17-3 presenting the statement of cash flows. We call out a couple of key issues in each figure to help you understand the importance of preparing multiple forecast versions.

REMEMBER

We could highlight additional issues and findings with the financial information presented in the forecast versions, but these are the points:

>> Having complete financial forecasts, including the income statement, balance sheet, and statement of cash flows, is critical for management planning purposes.

>> The power and importance of utilizing the what-if forecasting tool (covered earlier in this chapter) is on full display.

>> Even in a forecast, the all-important concept of realizing that accounting (and finance) is more of an art than a science holds true.

The income statement

Figure 17-1 presents the income statement for our sample company, for which we have elected to provide additional financial information. You see that more detail has been provided with KPIs, sales revenue, costs of goods sold, and selling, general, and administrative expense. The reason for this is two-fold. First, we want to emphasize the fact that internal company forecasts should provide far more detail and information to develop a proper business plan. Second is that certain performance issues we call out in the low forecast version refer back to this level of detail.

(all dollar amounts in thousands, except KPIs)	High — FYE 12/31/2025	% of Net Rev.	Medium — FYE 12/31/2025	% of Net Rev.	Low — FYE 12/31/2025	% of Net Rev.
QW Example Tech., Inc. **Income Statement Forecast** Forecasts — High, Medium, & Low for the Fiscal Year Ending 12/31/2025						
Key Performance Indicators:						
Revenue Per Full-Time Employee	$626,333		$551,000		$439,000	
Product Sales, Avg. Order Value (Net)	$19,800		$19,800		$12,467	
Macro Level Analysis:						
Year-Over-Year Sales Growth	32.20%		16.30%		−7.34%	
Gross Margin	66.72%		62.34%		57.71%	
Operating Income Margin	17.95%		12.01%		2.01%	
Debt Service Coverage Ratio	10.41		6.42		1.48	
Sales Revenue:						
Software Platform & SAAS Sales	$79,100	84%	$67,800	82%	$56,500	86%
Product Sales	$16,500	18%	$16,500	20%	$11,000	17%
Other Sales, Discounts, & Allowances	($1,650)	−2%	($1,650)	−2%	($1,650)	−3%
Net Sales Revenue	$93,950	100%	$82,650	100%	$65,850	100%
Costs of Goods Sold:						
Direct Product Costs	$9,240	10%	$9,488	11%	$6,600	10%
Wages & Burden	$21,026	22%	$20,637	25%	$20,248	31%
Direct Overhead	$750	1%	$750	1%	$750	1%
Other Costs of Goods Sold	$250	0%	$250	0%	$250	0%
Total Costs of Goods Sold	$31,266	33%	$31,124	38%	$27,848	42%
Gross Profit	$62,684	67%	$51,526	62%	$38,003	58%
Gross Margin	66.72%		62.34%		57.71%	
Selling, General, & Administrative Expenses:						
Advertising, Promotional, & Selling	$12,701	14%	$10,958	13%	$8,965	14%
Personnel Wages, Burden, & Compensation	$6,107	7%	$5,992	7%	$5,597	9%
Corporate & Facility Operating Expenses	$10,950	12%	$10,350	13%	$9,750	15%
Research, Development, & Design & Other Expenses	$14,703	16%	$12,997	16%	$11,096	17%
Depreciation & Amortization Expense	$1,362	1%	$1,301	2%	$1,270	2%
Total Operating Expenses	$45,823	49%	$41,597	50%	$36,678	56%
Operating Income (EBIT)	$16,860	18%	$9,928	12%	$1,325	2%
Operating Margin (EBIT Margin)	17.95%		12.01%		2.01%	
Other Expenses (Income):						
Other Expenses, Income, & Discontinued Ops.	$500	1%	$500	1%	$500	1%
Interest Expense	$263	0%	$263	0%	$263	0%
Total Other Expenses (Income)	$763	1%	$763	1%	$763	1%
Net Income Before Taxes	$16,098	17%	$9,166	11%	$562	1%
Income Tax Expense (Benefit)	$5,634	6%	$3,208	4%	$197	0%
Net Income After Taxes	$10,463	11%	$5,958	7%	$365	1%

Confidential — Property of QW Example Tech., Inc.

© John Wiley & Sons, Inc.

FIGURE 17-1: Forecast income statement: high, medium, and low.

QW Example Tech., Inc.			
Balance Sheet Forecast			
Forecasts — High, Medium, & Low			
12/31/2025			

(all amounts in thousands)	High — FYE 12/31/2025	Medium — FYE 12/31/2025	Low — FYE 12/31/2025
Assets			
Current Assets:			
Cash & Equivalents	$19,940	$15,935	$10,015
Accounts Receivable, Net	$11,744	$10,331	$9,054
Inventory, LC&NRV	$1,540	$1,779	$2,200
Prepaid Expenses	$322	$283	$226
Total Current Assets	$33,546	$28,329	$21,496
Long-Term Operating & Other Assets:			
Property, Plant, & Equipment	$9,537	$9,104	$8,887
Accumulated Depreciation	($5,682)	($5,621)	($5,590)
Net Property, Plant, & Equipment	$3,855	$3,483	$3,297
Other Assets:			
Intangible Assets, Net	$500	$500	$500
Goodwill	$100	$100	$100
Total Long-Term Operating & Other Assets	$4,455	$4,083	$3,897
Total Assets	$38,001	$32,412	$25,393
Liabilities			
Current Liabilities:			
Accounts Payable	$2,936	$2,583	$2,037
Accrued Liabilities	$543	$533	$517
Current Portion of Debt	$1,000	$1,000	$1,000
Income Taxes Payable	$1,409	$802	$49
Other Current Liabilities	$791	$678	$565
Total Current Liabilities	$6,678	$5,595	$4,168
Long-Term Liabilities:			
Notes Payable & Other Long-Term Debt	$5,000	$5,000	$5,000
Other Long-Term Liabilities	$300	$300	$300
Total Long-Term Liabilities	$5,300	$5,300	$5,300
Total Liabilities	$11,978	$10,895	$9,468
Shareholders' Equity			
Share Capital — Common	$5,000	$5,000	$5,000
Share Capital — Preferred	$5,000	$5,000	$5,000
Dividends	($400)	($400)	($400)
Retained Earnings	$5,959	$5,959	$5,959
Current Earnings	$10,463	$5,958	$365
Total Shareholders' Equity	$26,022	$21,517	$15,924
Total Liabilities & Shareholders' Equity	$38,001	$32,412	$25,393

Confidential — Property of QW Example Tech., Inc.

© John Wiley & Sons, Inc.

FIGURE 17-2:
Forecast balance sheet: high, medium, and low.

Confidential — Property of QW Example Tech., Inc.

QW Example Tech., Inc.
Statement of Cash Flow Forecast
Forecasts — High, Medium, & Low
for the Fiscal Year Ending
12/31/2025

(all dollar amounts in thousands)	High — FYE 12/31/2025	Medium — FYE 12/31/2025	Low — FYE 12/31/2025
Net Profit	$10,463	$5,958	$365
Operating Activities, Cash Provided (Used):			
Depreciation & Amortization	$1,362	$1,301	$1,270
Decrease (Increase) in Accounts Receivable	($2,861)	($1,448)	($171)
Decrease (Increase) in Inventory	$193	($46)	($467)
Decrease (Increase) in Prepaid Expenses	$3	$42	$99
Increase (Decrease) in Accounts Payable	$1,007	$654	$108
Increase (Decrease) in Accrued Liabilities & Other	($287)	($297)	($313)
Increase (Decrease) in Other Current Liabilities	$996	$276	($590)
Net Cash Flow from Operating Activities	$10,876	$6,438	$301
Investing Activities, Cash Provided (Used):			
Increase in Property, Plant, & Equipment and Intangibles Assets	($867)	($434)	($217)
Net Cash Flow from Investing Activities	($867)	($434)	($217)
Financing Activities, Cash Provided (Used):			
Dividends or Distributions Paid	($400)	($400)	($400)
Repayments of Debt	($1,000)	($1,000)	($1,000)
Other Financing Activities	$50	$50	$50
Net Cash Flow from Financing Activities	($1,350)	($1,350)	($1,350)
Net Increase (Decrease) in Cash & Equivalents	$8,659	$4,654	($1,266)
Beginning Cash & Equivalents Balance	$11,281	$11,281	$11,281
Ending Cash & Equivalents Balance	$19,940	$15,935	$10,015

FIGURE 17-3:
Forecast
statement of
cash flows: high,
medium, and low.

© John Wiley & Sons, Inc.

Overall, the operating results in the high and medium versions of the forecast model appear reasonable. Solid sales growth, strong profitability, and key financial ratios, including the debt service coverage ratio (see Chapter 12), are more than adequate. Turning our attention to the low version, significant concerns start to emerge. On top of the company performing poorly with negative year-over-year (YOY) sales growth and basically operating at a breakeven level, two important ratios need further attention.

First, the company's operating income margin is just 2.01 percent, which basically indicates the company would be operating at a breakeven level. Clearly, this is not desirable and also indicates that the company has no margin for error if it finds itself operating at this level. We should also note that a number of lenders have what are called *minimum profitability covenants* that state the company must generate a profit in order to not be considered in default of the loan agreement. As you can see in the low case scenario, the company would be in trouble with this type of covenant. The same goes for the debt service coverage ratio, which comes in at 1.48 to 1.00; if the debt facility has a covenant that requires this ratio be 1.5 or above (not at all unreasonable for lenders), again the company may be in technical default.

Obviously, the company is not in default of these covenants today and does not expect to be in default, because even under the medium case forecast, the company has more than enough breathing room. But for management purposes, having a clear understanding of the operating performance level at which the company does begin to operate under financial stress is extremely helpful, so that if the business does head south, the executive management team can plan for and implement necessary adjustments (for example, expense reductions) to avoid a rather messy situation with the lender.

The balance sheet

We now turn our attention to the balance sheet presented in Figure 17-2. Here again we provide high, medium, and low forecast scenarios for evaluation and draw your attention to a couple of items.

First, you notice that the ending inventory balance in the low version is actually higher than the high version. This may make sense on the surface, because FYE 2025 product sales in the low version are forecast to reach only $11 million versus $16.5 million in the high version (lower sales equals more inventory on hand and a higher value). However, it may also mean that the company's inventory is rapidly becoming obsolete and is becoming harder to sell, raising an all-important question as to whether the inventory is actually worth $2.2 million or whether management should write off a portion of the inventory as worthless (which means the company would have to incur an additional expense and most likely push it from profitability under the low version to a loss — ouch!).

Second, you may ask why the company would pay a dividend when at best it is operating at a breakeven level. Basically, what it comes down to is that when the company raised preferred equity, this tranche of equity comes with an implied promise of an annual dividend of 8 percent. This is the capital raise understanding between preferred shareholders and the company — shareholders invest in preferred shares (and give up voting ability) but are "promised" an annual dividend. Hence, the company is usually required to pay the dividend if it can, to satisfy the demands of its preferred shareholders.

The statement of cash flows

Finally, we reach the statement of cash flows as presented in Figure 17-3, which also sheds additional valuable information in the low version of the forecast model.

Reviewing the statement of cash flows in more detail, you notice that the low version of the forecast model produces approximately $301,000 of positive cash flow from operations, compared to required financing payments of $1.4 million, which is comprised of preferred equity dividend payments of $400,000 and debt repayments of $1 million. The good news is that the company has enough cash resources and liquidity to cover this shortfall derived from the guaranteed payments, given its relatively large cash balance forecast to be approximately $10.015 million as of the end of 2025 (see Figure 17-2). But looking closer, this really could become a problem over the long run because in effect the company is using short-term working capital to repay long-term financial commitments (an imbalance that should be avoided). The low version also shows that the purchase of property, plant, and equipment is much lower. This can spell trouble in future years as the company is likely to neglect replacing needed assets. This could hurt future productivity and profits.

Revisiting the Value of Forecasts

Chapters 6 through 8 of this book introduce you to the three primary financial statements and the purpose and importance of each one. Each is a relatively long chapter, as is this chapter on financial forecasting, because all cover a large amount of material. Our goal is not to bury you with too much information, but rather to help you understand just how important complete, accurate, reliable, and timely financial information really is, including forecasts and how top management teams utilize the accounting and finance departments as a competitive weapon (especially with forecasts).

REMEMBER

With this said, we want to rehash some valuable gems and secrets related to financial forecasting that successful business owners, managers, and investors use every day:

>> **Graduate:** Bottom-up forecast models are valuable tools for businesses, but to move up in the executive management hierarchy, you need to graduate and become comfortable using top-down forecasts (both types are covered earlier in this chapter). Top executives usually have such a solid understanding of the economic structure of their business that they can simply change a select number of critical operating assumptions and almost immediate know

what the end result will be (for example, a change to top-line sales revenue leads to a bottom-line result). To be an effective executive-level manager, you need to efficiently understand the macro-level impact on your business from economic changing conditions. That is, you "can't see the forest for the trees."

» **The P&L focus:** Too many businesses focus only on the profit and loss (P&L) when preparing forecasts. It should be clear from this chapter (and this entire book) just how important the balance sheet and cash flow statement are, especially as they relate to cash flow and third-party capital source management. More than a few companies have failed because they fixated on their P&L performance while neglecting their balance sheet and cash flow statement. Best-in-class forecasts always should include projections for all three financial statements.

» **External/internal:** Internal financial forecasts include significant amounts of detail and confidential information that should not be distributed to external parties. Not only is the level of detail on a line-item basis excessive, but the high and low versions of the forecast model should not be distributed externally (because these are for internal management use). Again, what a business distributes to external parties is vastly different to what's needed for internal consumption.

» **Tone it down:** Most companies produce forecasts that derive financial data from multiple internal operating divisions (for example, a company may have a dozen operating divisions that they consolidate to prepare a company-wide forecast). What tends to happen during the consolidation process is that everyone is a bit too optimistic, so when the combined results are produced, the operating results look great (see the high version in Figures 17-1 through 17-3). In reality, somewhere along the line, certain divisions are going to stumble and not perform as well, so although it is fine to set internal expectations relatively high, finalizing a company-wide forecast should be toned down to be more realistic (for distribution to external parties, the company's board of directors, and so on). Nothing is worse than overpromising and underdelivering — and then having to explain yourself.

REMEMBER

One final thought to keep in mind is that at the base or heart of preparing, understanding, and utilizing financial forecasts is the all-important concept of accounting. That is, if you don't have a basic understanding of accounting, even attempting to prepare and understand a forecast will be next to impossible. This is not a chicken-and-egg question; to master financial forecasts, you must understand basic accounting concepts.

5
The Part of Tens

Check out ten tips to help managers get the most bang for their buck out of the business's accounting system. Think of these ten topics as a compact accounting tool kit for managers.

Discover ten tips for investors regarding what to keep in mind and what to look for when reading a financial report. These tips help you gain the maximum amount of information in the minimum amount of time.

IN THIS CHAPTER

» Getting a grip on profit analytics

» Taking charge of your business's accounting policies

» Using sensible forecasting techniques

» Getting the accounting information you need

» Being a pro as you talk about your financial statements

Chapter **18**

Ten Tips for Managers

We have put together the top ten concepts discussed in this book. If you're reading this chapter first, these short statements will guide you to the chapters that contain the discussions that will be most interesting to you and the most useful to your business.

Financially speaking, business managers have four essential jobs:

» Securing adequate capital from debt and equity sources

» Earning adequate profit on that capital

» Expediting cash flow from that profit

» Controlling the solvency of the business

How can accounting help make you a better business manager? That's the bottom-line question, and the bottom line is the best place to start. Accounting provides the financial information you need for making good profit decisions — and it stops you from plunging ahead with gut-level decisions that feel right but don't hold water after due-diligence analysis. Accounting also provides cash flow and financial position information you need. You have to understand and know how to interpret accounting information to do all these wonderful things.

Reach Breakeven and Then Rake in Profit

Almost every business has *fixed expenses*. These are operating costs that are locked in for the year and remain the same whether annual sales are at 100 percent or below half your capacity. Fixed expenses are a dead weight on a business. To make profit, you have to get over your fixed costs hurdle. How do you do this? Obviously, you have to make sales. Each sale brings in a certain amount of *margin*, which equals the revenue minus the variable expenses of the sale. (If your sales don't generate an adequate margin, you're in trouble.)

Suppose you sell a product for $100. Your purchase (or manufacturing) cost is $60, which accountants call the *cost of goods sold expense.* Your variable costs of selling the item add up to $15, including sales commission and delivery cost. Thus, your margin on the sale is $25: $100 sales price — $60 product cost — $15 variable costs = $25 margin. Margin is before interest and income tax expenses and before fixed expenses for the period are considered.

Your annual fixed operating costs total $2.5 million. These costs provide the space, facilities, and people that are necessary to make sales and earn profit. Of course, the risk is that your sales will not be enough to overcome your fixed costs. This leads to the next step, which is to determine your break-even point. *Breakeven* refers to the sales revenue you need just to recoup your fixed operating costs. If you earn 25 percent average margin on sales, to break even you need $10 million in annual sales: $10 million × 25 percent margin = $2.5 million margin. At this sales level, margin equals fixed costs and your profit is zero (you break even). Not very exciting so far, is it? But from here on it gets much more interesting.

REMEMBER

Until sales reach $10 million, you're in the loss zone. After you cross over the break-even point, you enter the profit zone. Each additional $1 million of sales over breakeven yields $250,000 profit. Suppose your annual sales revenue is $4 million in excess of your breakeven point. Your profit (earnings before interest and income tax) is $1 million: $4 million sales over breakeven × 25 percent margin = $1 million profit. The main lesson is that after you cross over the break-even threshold, your margin goes entirely toward profit.

TIP

Your regular profit and loss (P&L) reports might not separate fixed and variable operating expenses — in fact, we would bet that this is your situation. What to do? We suggest sorting operating expenses into fixed and variable groups based on the titles of the expense accounts in your P&L. You'll probably have to make some estimates, but this isn't rocket science. In any case, you should understand the leverage effect on operating profit caused when you exceed your break-even sales level.

Set Sales Prices Right

In real estate, the three most important profit factors are location, location, and location. In the business of selling products and services, the three most important factors are margin, margin, and margin. Of course, a business manager should control expenses. But the secret to making profit is both making sales *and* earning an adequate margin on sales revenue. (Remember, margin equals sales price less all variable costs of the sale.) Chapter 15 explains that internal P&L reports to managers should separate variable and fixed costs so the manager can focus on margin.

In the example in the preceding section, your sales prices earn 25 percent margin on sales. In other words, $100 of sales revenue generates $25 margin (after deducting the cost of product sold and variable costs of making the sale). Therefore, $16 million in sales revenue generates $4 million margin. The $4 million margin covers your $2.5 million in fixed costs and provides $1.5 million of profit (before interest and income tax).

An alternative scenario illustrates the importance of setting sales prices high enough to earn an adequate margin. Instead of the sales prices in the previous example, suppose you had set sales prices 5 percent lower. Therefore, your margin would be $5 lower per $100 of sales. Instead of 25 percent margin on sales, you would earn only 20 percent margin on sales. How badly would the lower margin ratio hurt profit?

On $16 million annual sales, your margin would be $3.2 million ($16 million sales × 20 percent margin ratio = $3.2 million margin). Deducting $2.5 million fixed costs for the year leaves only $700,000 profit. Compared with your $1.5 million profit at the 25 percent margin ratio, the $700,000 profit at the lower sales prices is less than half. The point of this story is that a 5 percent lower sales price causes 53 percent lower profit!

Don't Confuse Profit and Cash Flow

To find out whether you made a profit or had a loss for the year, you look at the bottom line in your P&L report. But you must understand that the bottom line does *not* tell you cash flow from your profit-making activities. Profit does not equal cash flow. Don't ever assume that making profit increases cash the same amount.

Cash flow can be considerably higher than bottom-line profit, or considerably lower. Cash flow can be negative even when you earn a profit, and cash flow can be positive even when you have a loss. If we know the profit number, we may not have a clue about the cash flow number because cash flow depends on additional factors.

TIP

If you're a busy manager, our advice is to boil down your cash flow analysis to three main factors that cause cash flow to be higher or lower than net income for the period:

>> Depreciation (plus amortization) expense is not a cash outlay in the period it is recorded, so add this amount to bottom-line net income.

>> Group the three current assets: accounts receivable, inventory, and prepaid expenses. If the total change in these three assets is an increase, deduct the amount from bottom-line net income. If it's a decrease, add the amount.

>> Group the current operating liabilities: accounts payable, accrued expenses payable, and income tax payable. If the total change in these three assets is an increase, add the amount to bottom-line net income. If it's a decrease, deduct the amount.

After doing this jig a few times, the process will become more or less automatic. Furthermore, you should become more aware of and pay closer attention to the drivers of cash flow from bottom-line profit (net income). You'll also be better able to explain cash flow to your banker and investors in the business.

Call the Shots on Accounting Policies

You may have heard the adage that war is too important to be left to the generals. Well, accounting is too important to be left to the accountants alone — especially when choosing which accounting methods to use. We're oversimplifying, but measuring profit and putting values on assets and liabilities boils down to choosing between conservative accounting methods and more liberal (or aggressive) methods. Conservative methods record profit later rather than sooner; liberal methods record profit sooner rather than later. It's a "pay me now or pay me later" choice. (Chapter 9 gives you the details on different accounting methods.)

TIP

We encourage you to get involved in setting your company's accounting policies. Business managers should take charge of accounting decisions just like they take charge of marketing and other key activities of the business. Some business managers defer to their accountants in choosing accounting methods for measuring sales revenue and expenses. Don't! You should get involved in making these decisions. The best accounting method is the one that best fits the operating methods and strategies of your business. As the manager, you know the business's operations and strategies better than your accountant. Finally, keep in mind that a default accounting method does not exist; someone has to choose every method.

REMEMBER

Remember that the accounting depreciation method you choose won't affect the amount your business pays in taxes. Your chosen method has no tax consequences, so don't let that factor motivate your accounting depreciation strategy. We discuss capital cost allowance (CCA), the tax equivalent of depreciation, in Chapter 9.

WARNING

Many businesses choose conservative accounting methods to defer paying their income tax. Keep in mind that higher expense deductions in early years cause lower deductions in later years. Also, conservative, income tax-driven accounting methods make the inventory and fixed assets in your balance sheet look anemic. Recording higher cost of goods sold expense takes more out of inventory and recording higher depreciation expense causes the book value of your fixed assets to be lower. Nevertheless, you may decide that postponing the payment of income taxes is worth it, in order to keep your hands on the cash as long as possible.

Prepare Accurate Forecasts and Projections

When you hear the word "forecasts" or "projections," you may immediately imagine a planning system involving many people, detailed forecasting, negotiating over goals and objectives, and page after page of detailed accounting statements that commit everyone to certain performance goals and use benchmarks for the coming period. In reality, all kinds of projection methods and approaches exist. You don't have to budget like BCE or a large business organization. You can do one-person limited-purpose projections. Even developing small-scale projections or simple forecast models can pay handsome dividends.

REMEMBER

We explain in Chapter 17 the reasons for developing flexible and adaptable forecast — first for understanding the profit dynamics and financial structure of your business, and second for planning for changes in the coming period. Forecasting forces you to focus on the factors for improving profit and cash flow. It's always a good idea to look ahead to the coming year; if nothing else, at least plug the numbers in your profit report for sales volume, sales prices, product costs, and other expenses, and see how your projected profit looks for the coming year. It may not look too good; in which case you need to plan how you'll do better.

The P&L forecast, in turn, lays the foundation for changes in your assets and liabilities that are driven by sales revenue and expenses. Your profit forecast should dovetail with your assets and liabilities forecast and with your cash flow forecast. This information is very helpful in planning for the coming year — focusing in particular on how much cash flow from profit will be realized and how much capital expenditures will be required. Next, you can figure out how much additional capital you have to raise and how much cash distribution from profit you'll be able make.

Demand the Accounting Information You Want

Experienced business managers spend a good deal of time dealing with problems, because things don't always go according to plan. Murphy's Law (if something can go wrong, it will, and usually at the worst possible time) is all too true. To solve a problem, you first have to know that you have one. Managers need to get on top of problems as soon as possible. A well-designed accounting system should set off alarms about any problems that are developing, so you can nip them in the bud.

You can identify the handful of critical factors that you need to keep a close eye on. Insist that your internal accounting reports highlight these factors. Only you, the business manager, can identify the most important numbers that you must closely watch to know how things are going. Your accountant can't read your mind. If your regular accounting reports do not include the exact types of information you need, sit down with your accountant and spell out in detail what you want to know. Don't take no for an answer. Don't let your accountant argue that the computer doesn't keep track of this information. Computers can be programmed to spit out any type of information you want.

TIP

These accounting information variables should *always* be on your radar:

>> Sales levels, volumes and prices

>> Margins (gross, operating, and bottom line)

>> Variable expenses

>> Fixed expenses

>> Internal cash flow

>> Overdue accounts receivable

>> Slow-moving inventory items

Experience is the best teacher. Over time, you discover which financial factors are the most important to highlight in your internal accounting reports. The trick is to make sure that your accountant provides this information.

Tap into Your CPA's Expertise

As you know, a CPA performs an audit of your financial report. And the CPA will probably assist in preparing your corporate income tax returns. In doing the audit, your CPA may find serious problems with your accounting methods and call these to your attention. Also, the CPA auditor will point out any serious deficiencies in your internal controls (see the next section). And it goes without saying that your CPA can give you valuable income tax advice and guide you through the labyrinth of federal and provincial income tax laws and regulations.

Also consider taking advantage of other services a CPA has to offer. A CPA can help you select, implement, and update a computer-based accounting system best suited for your business and can give expert advice on many accounting issues such as cost allocation methods. A CPA can do a critical analysis of the internal accounting reports to managers in your business and suggest improvements in these reports. A CPA has experience with a wide range of businesses and can recommend best practices for your business. If necessary, the CPA can serve as an expert witness on your behalf in lawsuits. A CPA may also be accredited in the areas of business valuation, financial advising and forensic methods.

WARNING

You have to be careful that the consulting services provided by your CPA do not conflict with the CPA's independence required for auditing your financial report. If any possible perception of conflict exists, you should use one CPA for auditing your financial report and another CPA for consulting services. Does the CPA have experience in providing the expert services? You might ask for names of clients that the CPA has provided these services to and check out whether these businesses were satisfied.

Critically Review Your Controls over Employee Dishonesty and Fraud

Every business faces threats from dishonesty and fraud — from within and from without. Your knee-jerk reaction may be that this sort of stuff couldn't possibly be going on under your nose in your own business.

WARNING

Without you knowing about it, your purchasing manager may be accepting kick-backs or other "gratuities." Your long-time bookkeeper may be embezzling. One of your suppliers may be short-counting you on deliveries. We're not suggesting that you should invest as much time and money in preventing fraud and cheating against your business as do Las Vegas casinos. But every now and then you should take a hard look at whether your fraud controls are adequate.

Preventing fraud starts with establishing and enforcing good internal controls, which we discuss in Chapter 3. In the course of auditing your financial report, the CPA evaluates your internal controls. The auditor will report to you any serious deficiencies. Even with good internal controls and having regular audits, you should consider calling in an expert to assess your vulnerability to fraud and to determine whether evidence exists of any fraud going on.

Lend a Hand in Preparing Your Financial Reports

Many business managers look at preparing the business's annual financial report like they look at its annual income tax return — it's a task best left to the accountant. This is a mistake. You should take an active part in preparing the annual financial report. (We discuss getting the financial report ready for release in Chapter 10.) You should carefully think of what to say in the letter to shareholders that accompanies the financial statements. You should help craft the notes to the financial statements. The annual report is a good opportunity to tell a compelling story about the business.

The owner/manager, president or chief executive of the business has the ultimate responsibility for the financial report. Of course, your financial report should not be fraudulent and deliberately misleading; if it is, you can, and probably will, be sued. But beyond that, lenders and investors appreciate a frank and honest discussion provided in the annual report showing how the business did, including its problems as well as its successes.

TIP

In our view, the gold standard for annual reports is set by Warren Buffett, the CEO of Berkshire Hathaway. He lays it on the line; if he has a bad year, he makes no excuses. Buffett is appropriately modest if he has a good year. Every annual report of Berkshire Hathaway summarizes the nature of the business and how it makes profit. If you knew nothing about this business, you could learn what you need to know from its annual report. (Go to www.berkshirehathaway.com to get the company's latest annual report.)

Speak about Your Financial Statements as a Pro

On many occasions, a business manager has to discuss their financial statements with others and come across as very knowledgeable and very persuasive in what they say. Not understanding your own financial statements does not inspire confidence. Sometimes, including the following, your financial statements are the centre of attention and you're expected to talk about them convincingly:

>> **Securing for a loan:** The loan officer may ask specific questions about your accounting policies and methods as well as items in your financial statements.

>> **Talking with individuals or other businesses that may be interested in buying your business:** They may have questions about the recorded values of your assets and liabilities.

>> **Dealing with the press:** Large corporations are used to talking with the media, but even smaller businesses are profiled in local news stories.

>> **Dealing with unions or other employee groups in setting wages and benefit packages:** They may think that your profits are very high and that you can afford to increase wages and benefits.

>> **Explaining the profit-sharing plan to your employees:** They may take a close interest in how profit is determined.

>> **Putting a value on an ownership interest for divorce property settlement purposes:** These values are based on the business's financial statements (and other factors).

>> **Reporting financial statement data to national trade associations or Statistics Canada:** Statistics Canada has the legal right to gather business information from you. Trade associations also collect financial information from their members. Make sure that you're reporting the financial information consistently and using the same definitions as Statistics Canada and the industry.

>> **Presenting the annual financial report before the annual meeting of owners:** The shareholders may ask penetrating questions and expect you to be very familiar with the financial statements.

IN THIS CHAPTER

» Judging profit performance

» Spotting unusual gains and losses

» Comparing cash flow with profit

» Looking for signs of financial distress

» Recognizing the limits of financial reports

Chapter **19**

Ten Tips for Reading a Financial Report

eading a business's financial report is like shucking an oyster: You have to know what you're doing and work to get at the meat. You need a good reason to pry into a financial report. The main reason to become informed about the financial performance and condition of a business is *because you have a stake in the business.* The business's financial success or failure makes a difference to you.

Shareholders have a major stake in a business, of course. The lenders of a business also have a stake, which can be substantial. But there are often others who have a financial stake in a business.

In this chapter, we offer practical tips to help investors, lenders, or anyone who has a financial stake in a business glean important insights from its financial reports. These tips also help anyone else with an interest in the financial reports of a business.

TIP

In Chapter 12, we explain the basic ratios that investors and lenders use for judging the profit performance and financial position of a business. We don't repeat that discussion in this chapter, so our first tip is to read or reread that chapter. The following tips assume you know the ratios.

Get in the Right Frame of Mind

So often we hear non-accountants say that they don't read financial reports because they are not "numbers" people. You don't have to be a math wizard or rocket scientist to extract the essential points from a financial report. We know that you can find the bottom line in the income statement and compare this profit number with other relevant numbers in the financial statements. You can read the amount of cash in the balance sheet. If the business has a zero or near-zero cash balance, you know that this is a serious — perhaps fatal — problem.

REMEMBER

Therefore, our first bit of advice is to get in the right frame of mind. Don't let a financial report bamboozle you. Locate the income statement, find bottom-line profit (or loss!), and get going. You can do it — especially when you have a book like this one to help you along.

Decide What to Read

Suppose you own shares in a public corporation and want to keep informed about its performance. You could depend on articles and news items in the *Financial Post* that summarize the latest financial reports of the company and go to websites such as Google Finance. Generally, these brief articles capture the most important points. If you own an investment portfolio of many different shares, reading news articles that summarize the financial reports of the companies is not a bad approach. But suppose you want more financial information than you can get in news articles.

The annual financial reports of public companies contain lots of information: a letter from the chief executive, a highlights section, trend charts, financial statements, extensive notes to the financial statements, historical summaries, and a lot of propaganda. (We discuss the variety of information in financial reports in Chapter 10.) And you get photos of the top brass and directors, of course. In contrast, the financial reports of most private companies are significantly smaller; they contain financial statements with notes, and not much more.

So, how much of the report do you actually read? You could read just the highlights section, which might do in a pinch. However, we think you should read the chief executive's letter to shareholders as well. Ideally, the letter summarizes in an even-handed and appropriately modest manner the main developments during the year. Be warned, however, that these letters from the top dog often are self-congratulatory and typically transfer blame for poor performance to factors beyond management's control. Read these letters, but take them with a grain of salt.

TIP

Many public businesses send shareholders a *condensed summary version* in place of their much longer and more detailed annual financial reports. This is legal, as long as the business mentions that you can get its "real" financial report by asking for a hard copy or by going to its website. The idea, of course, is to give shareowners an annual financial report that they can read and digest more quickly and easily. Condensed financial summaries are also more cost effective.

The scaled-down, simplified, and shortened versions of annual financial reports are adequate for average share investors. They are not adequate for serious investors and professional investment managers. These investors and money managers should read the business's full-fledged financial report.

Improve Your Accounting Savvy

Financial statements — the income statement, balance sheet, and statement of cash flows — are the hard core of a financial report. To make sense of financial statements, you need at least a rudimentary understanding of financial statement accounting.

TIP

You don't have to be a CPA, but the accountants who prepare financial statements presume that you are familiar with accounting terminology and financial reporting practices. If you're an accounting illiterate, the financial statements probably look like a Sudoku puzzle. There's no way around this demand on financial report readers. After all, accounting is the language of business. The solution? Read and apply the information in this book. And when you're finished, consider reading another book or two about reading financial reports and analyzing financial statements. If you need a suggestion, check out another of Tage's books, *How to Read a Financial Report*, 9th Edition (John Wiley & Sons, Inc., 2020).

Judge Profit Performance

A business earns profit by making sales and by keeping expenses less than sales revenue, so the best place to start in analyzing profit performance is not the bottom line but the top line: *sales revenue.* Here are some items to focus on:

> **>>** **How does sales revenue in the most recent year compare with the previous year's revenue?** Higher sales should lead to higher profit, unless a company's expenses increase at a higher rate than its sales revenue. If sales revenue is relatively flat from year to year, the business must focus on

expense control to help profit, but a business can cut expenses only so far. The real key for improving profit is improving sales. Therefore, stock analysts put first importance on tracking sales revenue year to year.

>> **What is the business's gross profit ratio?** Even a small slippage in its gross profit ratio (which equals gross profit divided by sales revenue) can have disastrous consequences on the company's bottom line. Stock analysts would like to know the margin of a business, which equals sales revenue minus all variable costs of sales (product cost and other variable costs of making sales). But external income statements do not reveal margin; businesses hold back this information from the outside world (or they don't keep track of variable versus fixed expenses).

TIP

>> **Based on information from a company's most recent income statement, how do gross margin and the company's bottom line (net income, or net earnings) compare with its top line (sales revenue)?** It's a good idea to calculate the gross margin ratio and the profit ratio for the most recent period and compare these two ratios with last period's ratios. If you take the time to compare these two ratios for a variety of businesses, you may be surprised at the variation from industry to industry. By the way, few businesses provide profit ratios on the face of their income statements — which is curious, because they know that readers of their income statements are interested in their profit ratios.

REMEMBER

One last point: Put a company's profit performance in the context of general economic conditions. A down economy puts downward pressure on a company's profit performance, and you should allow for this in your analysis (although this is easier said than done). In an up economy, a company should do better, of course, because a rising tide lifts all boats.

Test Earnings per Share (EPS) Against Change in the Bottom Line

REMEMBER

As you know, public companies report net income in their income statements. Below this total profit number for the period, public companies also report earnings per share (EPS), which is the amount of bottom-line profit for each share. Figure 6-1 shows an example. Strictly speaking, therefore, the bottom line of a public company is its EPS. Private companies don't have to report EPS, but the EPS for a private business is fairly easy to calculate: Divide its bottom-line net income by the number of ownership shares held by the equity investors in the company.

The market value of shares of a public company is strongly correlated to its EPS although many other factors influence market value. Individual investors obviously focus on EPS, which they know is a key driver of the market value of their investment in the business. The higher the EPS, the higher the market value tends to be for a public company.

Now, you would naturally think that if net income increases, say, 10 percent over last year, then EPS would increase 10 percent. Not so fast. EPS may change more or less than 10 percent:

>> **Less than 10 percent:** The business may have issued additional shares during the year, or it may have issued additional management stock options that get counted in the number of shares used to calculate diluted EPS. The profit pie may have been cut up into a larger number of smaller pieces. How do you like that?

>> **More than the 10 percent:** The business may have bought back some of its own shares, which decreases the number of shares used in calculating EPS. This could be a deliberate strategy for increasing EPS by a higher percent than the percent increase in net income.

TIP

Compare the percent increase/decrease in total bottom-line profit over last year with the corresponding percent increase/decrease in EPS. Why? Because the percent changes in EPS and profit can diverge. For a public company, use its diluted EPS if it's reported. Otherwise, use its basic EPS. (We explain these two critical profit ratios in Chapter 12.)

WARNING

EPS doesn't necessarily move in perfect sync with the profit performance of a business. A deviation in the change in EPS compared with the change in profit can hamper or boost market value or book value per share. Check the percent change in profit against the percent change in EPS, but be warned: You have to do this on your own because neither public nor private companies volunteer this comparison. Most likely, they don't want to call attention to any disparity between the change in profit versus the change in EPS.

Tackle Unusual Gains and Losses

Many income statements start out normally: sales revenue less the expenses of making sales and operating the business. But then a layer of unusual gains and losses happens on the way down to the final profit line. (We discuss unusual gains and losses in Chapters 6 and 14.) For example, a business may shut down and abandon one of its manufacturing plants and record a huge loss due to asset write-downs and severance compensation for laid-off employees. A business may suffer a large loss from an uninsured flood. Or a business may lose a major lawsuit and have to pay millions in damages. What's a financial statement reader to do when a business reports such gains and losses?

No easy answer to this question exists. You could blithely assume that these things happen to a business only once in a blue moon and should not disrupt the business's capability to make profit on a sustainable basis. We call this the *earthquake mentality* approach: When an earthquake happens, there's a lot of damage, but most years have no tremors and go along normally. Unusual gains and losses are supposed to be for events that are outside the business's main operating activities. The classification of unusual gains and losses on the income statement is reserved for infrequent or one-time gains and losses. In practice, however, many businesses report gains and losses on a regular and recurring basis — like having an earthquake every year or so.

WARNING

Unusual losses are a particular problem because large amounts are moved out of the mainstream expenses of the business and treated as nonrecurring losses in its income statement, which means these amounts do not pass through the regular expense accounts of the business. Profit from operations is reported at higher amounts than it would be if the unusual losses were treated as regular operating expenses. Investment managers complain in public about the special treatment of unusual gains and losses in financial reports. But in private, they seem to prefer that businesses have the latitude to maximize their reported earnings from operations by passing off some expenses as unusual, infrequent losses when, in fact, these gains and losses occur more frequently than you would expect. Check out Chapter 14 to better acquaint yourself with how businesses "massage" the numbers.

Check Cash Flow from Profit

The objective of a business is not simply to make profit, but to generate cash flow from making profit as quickly as possible. Cash flow from making profit is the most important stream of cash inflow to a business. A business could sell off some assets to generate cash, and it can borrow money or get shareholders to put more money in the business. But cash flow from making profit is the spigot that should always be turned on. A business needs this cash flow to make cash distributions from profit to shareholders, to maintain liquidity, and to supplement other sources of capital to grow the business.

REMEMBER

The income statement does not — we repeat, does *not* — report the cash inflows of sales and the cash outflows of expenses. Therefore, the bottom line of the income statement is not a cash flow number. The net cash flow from the business's profit-making activities (its sales and expenses) is reported in the statement of cash flows. When you look there, you will undoubtedly discover that the *cash flow from operating activities* (the official term for cash flow from profit-making activities) is higher or lower than the bottom-line profit number in the income statement. We explain the reasons for the difference in Chapter 8.

Businesses seldom offer any narrative or footnote explanation of the difference between profit and cash flow. What you see in the statement of cash flows is all you get — no more. You're pretty much on your own to interpret the difference. No general benchmarks or ratios exist for testing cash flow against profit. We couldn't possibly suggest that cash flow should normally be 120 percent of bottom-line profit, or some other ratio. One rough rule does apply: Growth penalizes cash flow — or, more accurately, growth sucks up and consumes cash because the business has to expand its assets to support the higher level of sales.

WARNING

Cash flow from operating activities can be a low percentage of profit (or even negative). This situation should prompt questions about the company's *quality of earnings,* which refers to the credibility and soundness of its profit accounting methods. In many cases, cash flow is low because accounts receivable from sales haven't been collected and because the business made large increases in its inventories. The surges in these assets raise questions about whether all the receivables will be collected and whether the entire inventory will be sold at regular prices. Only time will tell. Generally speaking, you should be more cautious and treat the net income that the business reports with some skepticism.

Look for Signs of Financial Distress

A business can build up a good sales volume and have very good profit margins, but if the company can't pay its bills on time, its profit opportunities could go down the drain. *Solvency* refers to the prospects of a business being able to meet all of its debt and other liability payment obligations on time. Solvency analysis looks for signs of financial distress that could cause serious disruptions in the business's profit-making operations. Even if a business has a few billion bucks in the bank, you should ask: "How does its solvency look? Is there any doubt that it can pay its bills on time?"

Frankly, detailed solvency analysis of a business is best left to the pros. The credit industry has become sophisticated in analyzing solvency. For example, bankruptcy prediction models have been developed that have proven useful. We don't think the average financial report reader should spend the time to calculate solvency ratios. For one thing, many businesses massage their accounting numbers to make their liquidity and solvency appear to be better than they are at the balance sheet date.

Although many accountants and investment analysts would view our advice here as heresy, we suggest that you just take a quick glance at the company's balance sheet. How do its total liabilities stack up against its cash, current assets, and total assets? Obviously, total liabilities should not be more than total assets. Duh! And obviously, if a company's cash balance is close to zero, things are bad. Beyond these basic rules, things are a lot more complex. Many businesses carry a debt load you wouldn't believe, and some get into trouble even though they have hefty cash balances.

TIP

The continued solvency of a business depends mainly on management's ability to convince creditors to continue extending credit and renewing loans. The credibility of management is the main factor, not ratios. Creditors understand that a business can get into a temporary bind and fall behind on paying its liabilities. As a general rule, creditors are slow to pull the plug on a business. Shutting off new credit may be the worst thing lenders and other creditors could do. Doing so may put the business in a tailspin, and its creditors may end up collecting little. Usually, forcing a business into receivership or bankruptcy is not in creditors' best interests — doing so is a last resort.

Recognize the Possibility of Restatement and Fraud

A few years ago in the United States, the CEO of one of the Big Four global public accounting firms testified on the state of auditing and financial reporting. He said that one out of every ten financial reports issued by public companies is revised and restated at a later time. If that's true, a 10 percent chance exists that the financial statements you're reading are not entirely correct and could be seriously misleading. An earlier study of financial restatements arrived at a much lower estimate. We're sure future studies will show variation in the rate of restatements. You'd think that the incidence of companies having to redo their financial reports would be extremely rare, but you see financial restatements with alarming regularity. You may recall that Nortel Networks Corporation restated its financial statement three times — and for the same fiscal year!

REMEMBER

When a business restates its original financial report and issues a new version, it does not make restitution for any losses that investors suffered by relying on the originally reported financial statements. In fact, few companies even say they're sorry when they put out revised financial statements. Generally, the language explaining financial restatements is legalistic and exculpatory. "We didn't do anything wrong" seems to be the underlying theme. This attitude is hard to swallow.

All too often the reason for the restatement is that someone later discovered that the original financial statements were based on fraudulent accounting. Auditors don't have a good track record for discovering financial reporting fraud. What it comes down to is this: Investors take the risk that the information in financial statements they use in making decisions is subject to revision at a later time. We suppose you could go to the trouble of searching for a business that has never had to restate its financial statements, but there's always a first time for fraud.

Remember the Limits of Financial Reports

Investing involves a lot more than reading financial reports. Financial reports are an important source of information, but investors also should stay informed about general economic trends and developments, political events, business takeovers, executive changes, technological changes, and much more. Undoubtedly, the information demands required for investing have helped fuel the enormous popularity of mutual funds; investors offload the need to keep informed to the investment managers of the mutual fund. Many advertisements of financial institutions stress this point — that you have better things to do with your time.

REMEMBER

When you read financial statements, keep in mind that these accounting reports are somewhat tentative and conditional. Accountants make many estimates and predictions in recording sales revenue and gains, and expenses and losses. Some soft numbers are mixed in with hard numbers in financial statements. In short, financial statements are iffy to some extent. You can't get around this limitation of accounting. Having said that, let us emphasize that financial reports serve an indispensable function in any developed economy. We really couldn't get along without financial reports, despite their limits and problems. People wouldn't know which way to turn in a financial information vacuum. Even though the financial air is polluted, we need the oxygen of financial reports to breathe.

Index

public companies
  accounting standards for, 46–47
  annual financial report/annual report of, 109, 193, 199–201, 208–209, 217–218
  compared to private companies, 208–209
  comparing private and public business financial reports, 217–218
  pressure on, 204–205
  reports from, 208–209
  trend among to undercut income statements, 187
publicly owned corporation, 91
purchasing and inventory, as responsibility of accounting department, 16

Q

quality of earnings, 367
quarter end (QA), 230
quarter to date (QTD), 230
quarterly summaries of profit performance and share prices, 192
quick ratio, 133–134, 237

R

rainmakers, 98
ratios
  about, 247
  acid-test ratio, 237
  analyzing financial statements with, 227–247
  asset turnover ratio, 264
  current ratio, 236
  debt service coverage ratio, 246
  debt-to-equity ratio, 238–239
  debt-to-tangible net equity, 239–240
  earnings per share (EPS), 106, 216, 243–244, 364–365
  importance of, 228
  net working capital, 235–236
  price/earnings (P/E) ratio, 216, 245
  quick ratio, 237

return on assets (ROA) ratio, 243
return on equity (ROE) ratio, 39, 242–243
return on sales (RPS), 240–241
raw materials, 316
RCMP, 132
real-time reconciliations, 80
receivable, accounts, 115–116, 138–139, 155–156, 174–175, 257–258
reconciliations, real-time, 80
recordkeeping, 14, 284
Registered Retirement Savings Plan (RRSP), 215
relevant costs, 308, 313–314
replacement costs, 182, 310
report format, of balance sheet, 34
reporting, 63. *See also* financial reporting/financial report
residual value (of assets), 183, 184, 308–309
responsibility accounting, 285
restatement, 368–369
retailers, 287, 315
retained earnings, 88, 114, 122–123, 144, 162, 169, 263
return on assets (ROA) ratio, 243
return on equity (ROE), 39, 242–243
return on sales, as measure of profit performance, 39
return on sales (RPS) ratio, 240–241
revenue
  deferred, 115–116
  deferred revenue, 112
  effects of on assets and liabilities, 112–113
  fundamental nature of, 112
  management discretion in timing of, 206–207
  as part of profit-making transactions, 17
  pinpointing assets and liabilities used to record, 115–120
  recording of, 112–113
  sales, 30
  sales revenue, 28, 109, 138–139, 174–175, 268–269, 296–297, 363–364
  scanning of, 185–187

revenue-driven expenses, 298
roll over, 146
rolling forecasts, 341–342
RRSP (Registered Retirement Savings Plan), 215
rules-based approach, of FASB, 45

S

safeguarding assets (SGA), 72
salary rosters, 52
sales
  cash flow characteristics of, 267
  inventory, 116
  making of, 115–116
sales price, 302, 307–308, 353
sales revenue, 28, 30, 109, 138–139, 174–175, 268–269, 296–297, 363–364
sales revenue recognition, 275–276
sales skimming, 68
sales volume, 296, 327
salvage value (of assets), 183, 184, 308–309
Sampath, Vijay (author)
  Forensic Accounting For Dummies, 204
samples
  balance sheet, 128, 232, 255
  financial statements, 230–234
  forecast balance sheet, 344
  forecast income statement, 343
  forecast statement of cash flows, 345
  income statement, 231
  income statement for business that sells products, 105
  income statement for business that sells services, 107–108
  manufacturing costs example, 317
  statement of cash flows, 233
  statement of cash flows using direct method, 152
  statement of cash flows using indirect method, 154
  statement of changes in shareholders' equity, 169
  strategic profit analysis template, 291

About the Authors

Cécile Laurin is a retired professor of accounting at Algonquin College of Applied Arts and Technology in Ottawa. She also taught part-time at the University of Ottawa. Her career began in public accounting, performing audits with the firm now known as KPMG. She then became the chief financial officer of three engineering firms, and the international law firm Gowling Lafleur Henderson LLP, now Gowling WLG. She obtained a Bachelor of Administration and a Bachelor of Commerce (Honours) from the University of Ottawa, and is a member of Chartered Professional Accountants of Ontario and Chartered Professional Accountants of Canada. She is the coauthor of *Bookkeeping for Canadians For Dummies* and has written several learning tools for professors and students in accounting. Cécile has also developed several distance-learning courses offered previously through Algonquin College.

Tage C. Tracy (pronounced "Tog"/Scandinavian descent) has for 30 years operated a financial consulting firm focused on offering CFO/executive-level support and planning services to private companies on a fractional basis. These services include providing guidance and support with raising debt and equity capital, completing complex financial analysis, supporting risk management assessments, guiding accounting system designs and structuring, proactively managing merger and acquisition activities, and being an integral part of the strategic business planning management functions. Tage is also an active author and has been the lead or coauthor (with his late father, John A. Tracy) for several books, including: *Business Financial Information Secrets*; *Accounting For Dummies*, 7th Edition; *How to Read a Financial Report*, 9th Edition; *How to Read a Financial Report, Comprehensive Version*; *Cash Flow For Dummies*; *Small Business Financial Management Kit For Dummies*; and *Accounting Workbook For Dummies*, 2nd Edition. Tage can be reached on his website http://financemakescents.com or directly at tagetracy@cox.net.

Dedication

For my son, Marc, and my daughter, Marie.

— Cécile Laurin

For my dad, John A. Tracy, aka The Old Pro, who passed away in 2022.

— Tage C. Tracy

Authors' Acknowledgments

I would like to thank: my editor, Dan Mersey; my reviewer, Maria Bélanger; executive editor Lindsay Berg; and the team at Wiley for making the process of updating the fourth edition enjoyable and low-stress. I learned a lot through this experience.

— Cécile Laurin

We're deeply grateful to everyone at Wiley who, for over 25 years, have helped produce successive editions of *Accounting For Dummies*. Wiley's professionalism, courtesy, dedication, and good humor have always been much appreciated. It has been a pleasure working with everyone at Wiley and our problem here is that there are too many people to thank individually. So we mention only the first person who contacted my late father, John A. Tracy, about doing this book: Kathleen Welton, to whom we owe a huge thank you. The others know how deeply grateful we are for their invaluable help in making our books so successful.

— Tage C. Tracy

Publisher's Acknowledgments

Acquisitions Editor: Lindsay Berg

Development Editor: Dan Mersey

Technical Editor: Maria Bélanger

Managing Editor: Ajith Kumar

Production Editor: Pradesh Kumar

Cover Image: © fizkes/Getty Images